The Politics of
GARBAGE

PITT SERIES IN POLICY
AND INSTITUTIONAL STUDIES

Bert A. Rockman, *Editor*

The Politics of

GARBAGE

A COMMUNITY
PERSPECTIVE
ON SOLID WASTE
POLICY MAKING

Larry S. Luton

UNIVERSITY OF PITTSBURGH PRESS

Published by the University of Pittsburgh Press, Pittsburgh, Pa. 15260
Copyright © 1996, University of Pittsburgh Press
All rights reserved
Manufactured in the United States of America
Printed on acid-free paper
10 9 8 7 6 5 4 3 2 1

Library of Congress Cataloging-in-Publication Data

Luton, Larry S., 1949–
    The politics of garbage : a community perspective on solid waste
policy making / Larry S. Luton.
        p.   cm. — (Pitt series in policy and institutional studies)
    Includes index.
    ISBN 0-8229-3946-0 (cloth : acid-free paper).
    ISBN 0-8229-5605-5 (pbk. : acid-free paper)
    1. Refuse and refuse disposal — Government policy — Washington
(State) — Spokane.   2. Spokane (Wash.) — Politics and government.
3. Incinerators — Washington (State) — Spokane.   4. Refuse and refuse
disposal — Government policy — United States — Case studies.
5. Metropolitan government — United States — Case studies.   I. Title.
II. Series.
    HD4484.W2L88   1996
    363.72'88 — dc20   96-10050
                                                                CIP

A CIP catalogue record for this book is available from the British Library.

The cartoon on p. 8 is reprinted with the kind permission of Milt Priggee; figure 3.1, from
Spokane and the Inland Empire, edited by David H. Stratton, is reprinted with the permission of
Washington State University Press.

. . . garbage has to be the poem of our time because
garbage is spiritual, believable enough

to get our attention, getting in the way, piling
up, stinking, turning brooks brownish and

creamy white: what else deflects us from the
errors of our illusionary ways, not a temptation

to trashlessness, that is too far off, and,
anyway, unimaginable, unrealistic . . .

From A. R. Ammons, "Garbage: A Poem"

CONTENTS

ACKNOWLEDGMENTS

A person cannot reasonably attempt to write a book like this without the assistance of a number of people. Some of those are people you have never met, but whose work has been crucial to your project. Others are professionals with whom you consulted as you attempted to understand and to explicate what your research had revealed. Still others are family, friends, and colleagues without whose support and understanding you would never have been able to find the time and energy to attempt the project.

To all those whom I do not know personally, but whose work I used in order to write this book, I thank you sincerely. Without your help, I would not have been able to see over this hurdle, much less surmount it.

To my professional contacts and colleagues, I thank you for your time, patience, and assistance. In this regard, some people merit specific mention: Terry Novak, Phil Williams, Jack Geraghty, Bob Dellwo, Glen Yake, Pete Dennison, Curt Messex, Jim Malm, Mike Hibbler, Eric Skelton, Karen Dorn Steele, George Durrie, and Steve Blewett. Your willingness to give of your time and knowledge was crucial to my completion of this book. To my colleagues in the Graduate Program in Public Administration at Eastern Washington University (Ann, Terry, Doug, and Bob), thank you for letting me evade my normal responsibilities as a faculty member for one year so that I might attempt this project. To my students, your feedback in the early stages when I was developing my ideas and working on how to present the materials in this book was of immeasurable assistance.

To my family and friends, your caring, support, and sharing were welcome islands upon which I rested from my diving and swimming in the unknown waters involved in researching and writing this book. Most of you have little idea how much you helped me during this endeavor. My wife, I think, has some understanding of how she helped; and, to you, Susan, I offer an especially warm thanks for putting up with the enhanced intensity of my weirdnesses during the fourteen months when I devoted myself exclusively to researching and writing this book.

I also want to thank the various editors and reviewers at the University of Pittsburgh Press. Cynthia Miller helped to revive this project when it appeared to have been captured by a black hole. Jane Flanders and Kathy McLaughlin kept me going through the dreary process of finalizing the text. Bert Rockman provided encouraging support and helpful advice. Finally, to those who provided me with blind peer reviews, I sincerely appreciate your time and effort in taking my work seriously and providing valuable feedback that helped me improve the manuscript.

Even with the help of all these people, I am sure that this book will contain errors, omissions, and offenses of various sorts. I take full responsibility for them.

The Politics of
GARBAGE

Introduction

O nce a kind of "orphan utility," solid waste management has become one of the largest economic, ecological, and intellectual challenges faced in the United States today. Not so long ago, public utilities that picked up and removed garbage from our curbs and dumpsters were not given much attention. People were more concerned about electric, gas, phone, and water utilities, perhaps because those utilities delivered a product or service into the home rather than taking something away. People noticed when there was some problem in these delivery systems because their service was interrupted and they could not go merrily about their daily activities. An interruption in the delivery of the garbage service, though, merely meant the cans sat on the curb longer than planned. Only when the "garbage men" went on strike and a delay in pickup meant that the garbage became an unsightly and smelly mess did people think much about their solid waste management system. Only when people like Martin Luther King Jr. came to town to support the garbage workers' strike did people think of garbage as related to politics.

Recently, however, this has begun to change. As part of our increasing environmental awareness, greater attention has been given to both the green (wilderness, endangered species, etc.) and the brown (air, water, and land pollution) aspects of our interaction with the environment. People are not only more concerned about old growth forests, Pacific yew trees, northern spotted owls, salmon, bald eagles, peregrine falcons, whooping cranes, red cockaded woodpeckers, marbled murrelets, California condors, grizzly bears, gray wolves, and whales; they are also more attentive to the quality of the air they breathe, the water they drink, and the ground upon which they live. In 1990 clean air and clean water were two of the five most important characteristics cited by *Money* magazine readers

1

as criteria they would use in selecting a place to live.[1] Stories such as Love Canal and the Islip garbage barge have become mythic in their impact on our collective psyche.

Coinciding with this rise in environmental awareness has been a rebirth in citizen activism. In the late 1970s a rediscovery of the initiative process was invigorated by California's Proposition 13. Grass-roots movements began to turn more and more to activist tactics to direct and control government. As a second stage of that movement, the less-government-is-better people, led by Ronald Reagan, began a withdrawal of the federal government from direct control of policy making in America. Faced with serious resource shortages and shrinking public support, the federal government delegated much policy implementation to state and local governments. While the federal government continued to set guidelines and to insist upon determining the general directions of national policy, the garnering of implementation resources was increasingly left to the lower levels of government and to the private and nonprofit sectors.

In addition, the overburdened and aging infrastructure upon which late twentieth-century America depends will soon require a dramatic infusion of new resources for maintenance and updating. From electronic highways to sewers, public facilities need a great deal of attention. Increased environmental awareness, increased demands on local governments, a newly invigorated citizen activism, and a decaying and overburdened infrastructure have set the stage for a dramatic change in our awareness of and attention to solid waste policy making.

Despite the fact that solid waste management is a national problem, at this time a study of solid waste policy making needs to focus on the local government level. That is where the above-mentioned factors come to life, and where we will determine much about how we are going to manage our solid waste streams. Still, the question remains: Why a book about Spokane, Washington? It is true that many people in Spokane would like the rest of the world to know more about their city than that former Speaker of the House Tom Foley was their congressman. They are tired of people thinking that Spokane is somewhere next to Seattle, which is actually 276 miles to the west. They are tired of people asking them, "Doesn't it rain a lot there?" when their annual rainfall is about the same as that of Los Angeles. They are also tired of people mispronouncing the name of their city: it's Spo-can, not Spo-cane. But this book is not so much about Spokane as it is about solid waste policy making. Spokane is a convenient place for me to gather my central examples of the dynamics involved in the formulation and implementation of solid waste management policy, because it is where I live. Although the specifics of the story vary, the political dynamics of solid waste policy making in Spokane have been experienced all over this country—in places like San Diego, Austin, Chicago, Minneapolis, Knoxville, Boston, New York City, and Pinellas County, Florida. Nationally it is a story that includes Islip's garbage barge and Waste Management Incorporated's giant state-of-the-art landfill in Arlington, Oregon.

In Spokane it is a story that revolves around a decision to make a waste-to-energy facility the centerpiece of the next generation in solid waste management. It's probably a story most Americans would not expect to find in Spokane. Located in an arid region of low population density and relatively vast tracts of less-than-prime farmland, Spokane could be expected to have an easy time deciding what to do with its solid waste. But that was not the case, and the fact that it was not easy here has ominous implications for those in more densely populated and environmentally less flexible areas of this country.

In a sense, Spokane plays the same role in this book that New Haven, Connecticut, played in Robert Dahl's *Who Governs?* Few people outside of New Haven were particularly interested in who governed New Haven, but Dahl's analysis and insight made that city a vehicle for improving our understanding of the dynamics of local politics. Although I do not claim to have the insight and analytical skills of Robert Dahl, *Who Governs?* does in some ways model what I would like to accomplish with this book. I hope the comparison does not offend or embarrass Dahl.

Like *Who Governs?*, this book is a case study. Like all case studies, its objective claims to generalization are rather weak. It is through the shared experiences of those in cities that have faced the difficulties in making solid waste management policy decisions that the Spokane story may claim relevance to a national audience. Those who read this book will judge whether the forces and players fundamental to the Spokane story sound familiar to them. I think they will, or I wouldn't have bothered to write this book. But this book is not simply a story; it is a case study. Its organization is informed by the use of systems theory to explain how the plethora of factors involved in solid waste policy making are related to each other. I think those who have experienced the politics of solid waste policy making will find the story familiar and the analysis illuminating; those who have not yet faced the difficulties described herein will be better prepared for them after having read the book.

As a book about solid waste policy making, it may also be understood in a

larger sense as a book about policy making generally. The systems approach
to analyzing a case is one I teach to students in Eastern Washington University's Graduate Program in Public Administration. They have applied it to a
wide range of policy formulation scenarios, from the local to the international level. It is an extremely adaptable approach that may be used to
examine many kinds of public policy making.

This book is not an exposé of solid waste policy making. Its general
design was first conceived as a way of teaching students in a Master of Public
Administration program how to understand the social and political context
within which public administrators work. It does not engage in a direct
critique of that context; neither is it intended to prescribe a solution to the
solid waste problem facing the United States at the close of the twentieth
century. Its purpose is to examine how a very complex combination of
cultural, social institutional, political, organizational, ecological, historical,
and relational dynamics affected the adoption and implementation of solid
waste policies in one metropolitan area of the United States. From that
examination, we hope to gain some insight into the system of intergovernmental public policy making in the United States. If we do, then we should
also be better prepared to work within that system to improve the fit between what we want to do and the policies we adopt.

In the first chapter I tell a brief version of Spokane's solid waste policy-
making story. It focuses on the events surrounding Spokane's decision to
build a solid waste management system that depended heavily on a waste-to-
energy facility, and provides a background for better understanding the
analysis that comes in later chapters.

In the second chapter I review the wide variety of theories about public
policy making found in social science literature. Each theory provides insight into specific aspects of the complex dynamics involved in policy development, but none of them alone provides a complete explanation of
those dynamics. I review the major theories' strengths and weaknesses and
provide a rationale for the theoretical foundation I have chosen — political
systems theory applied to a case study.

Political culture is the subject of the third chapter. I begin exploring the
systems model by focusing on political culture, because it is both so easily
taken for granted and so enveloping. One cannot adequately understand
the dynamics involved in the formulation of a public policy without some
recognition of the impact of the values and history of the participants. The
import of the later chapters for the larger picture is also more easily compre-
hended within the context of political culture.

Chapter 4 explores the history and the institutions of the local political system. The history and structure of local government in Spokane affected the decisions made. The structure of relations among the local political institutions and the leadership styles of various key players influenced the content of the decisions. Traces of the Progressive and Populist movements are evident in Spokane's solid waste policy making — both in the forms of government found there and in the specific arrangements adopted for dealing with solid waste.

Chapter 5 begins with an overview of the formal structure and changing dynamics of federal and state government relations. Then it delves into the operational impacts of those structures and dynamics on local officials' efforts to formulate and implement solid waste policy. While federal government's direct action in setting solid waste policy has been formally reduced, it has continued to exert much influence over state and local policy making.

The various ways in which businesses, business interests, and business values influenced solid waste policy making are examined in chapter 6. Government agencies often contract with businesses to do some of the work required for making or implementing public policy. In a mixed economy such as that found in the United States, economic and business interests are frequently presumed to have a powerful impact on public policy making. This chapter examines that influence, but it also explores the ways businesses impact policy through their roles in the implementation phase.

Chapter 7 explores the nature and effect of various forms of citizen participation in this case study of solid waste policy making. Citizens participate in public policy making in many different ways and with varying degrees of impact. Most citizens might be said to "participate" through their quiet acquiescence to the results of the process. Many citizens participate only through their suffrage. Others participate by belonging to interest groups, but only a part of that number are actively involved in the groups. Still others participate by volunteering to sit on boards, committees, and commissions established by government initiatives. Among the actively involved, the time and energy spent varies according to the items on the public agenda and how far those items have progressed through the policy-making process. In public facility siting decisions such as the one in Spokane, NIMBYs (not in my backyard) often become active only when the process has reached the phase of specific siting decisions.

No examination of public policy making in the late twentieth century would be complete without giving serious attention to the impact of the media. The role of the media in public policy making is a complex and controversial subject. Many people who work in the media espouse a belief in the myth of objectivity. Some argue that the media must be sympathetic to government officials in order to maintain access to information that they can then share with the public. Others, however, argue that the media represent a "fourth estate" in our republic and that they have a democratic obligation to play an antagonistic role in their relations with the government. Chapter 8 examines the complex role of the media by detailing the discernible impacts of the media on solid waste policy making in Spokane.

The final chapter reexamines the utility of the political systems analysis of the Spokane case study and its implications for the study of solid waste policy making — and for U.S. public policy making in general. I argue that the structure provided by a political systems model, combined with attention to the influence of political culture and a detailed examination of the dynamics of a specific case study, provides a powerful vehicle for improving understanding of public policy making in a complex modern democracy.

Though the model is elegant in its simplicity, the picture it presents is not necessarily an aesthetic pleasure. It has been said that no one who eats sausage should see how it is made. It has also been said that if you think that watching how sausage is made is disgusting, then you do not want to see how legislation is made. The making of solid waste policy is even less hygienic than the making of solid waste legislation. To some the resulting mess in our landfills is a fitting tribute to both the dynamic processes and the substantive results. To others the awesome technologies that have been applied to the solid waste problem represent the marvels human intelligence and ingenuity may accomplish when they are directed to dealing with a very earthy human problem. Whichever view better describes your own, I invite you to explore with me the impacts on a local community of a marvelously complex, ever changing, yet uniquely American system for solid waste policy making.

The Spokane
Story

This chapter provides the reader with an introduction to the major events of the controversy surrounding Spokane's decision to build a new solid waste management system that had at its center a waste-to-energy facility. This chronological sketch should facilitate a quicker grasp of the analysis that follows in later chapters. The controversy around the waste-to-energy facility arose within a larger and quite complex context—a context that included the history of solid waste management in the United States, the fairly recent entrance of the federal and state governments as major players in solid waste management policy making, and the contemporary policy making milieu in the United States. Subsequent chapters will bring in this larger context, but here we focus on a recent period in Spokane's solid waste policy making that may sound familiar to many American readers.

The waste-to-energy facility was a divisive political issue for the Spokane area. In 1989, while the rest of the country was experiencing issueless campaigns that consisted primarily of personal attacks, Spokane was deciding its city elections based largely on the candidates' positions on the waste-to-energy facility. Although general public interest in solid waste and the intensity of waste-related disputes have cooled down considerably since the election, controversy continues around various aspects of Spokane's new solid waste management system.

THE MOVE AWAY FROM DUMPS AND
TRADITIONAL LANDFILLS

For most of the twentieth century the residents of the greater Spokane area handled their garbage like the rest of the people in the United States—they sent it to "the dump." For example, the

Moran Prairie township dumpsite southeast of the city (see fig. 1.2) began operation in 1905, was acquired in 1960 by the city of Spokane, was transformed into the "Southside landfill" in the late 1960s, and was closed down in 1987. Although there have been at least two dozen different public disposal areas in use at various times during the twentieth century, at the beginning of the 1990s the vast majority of the Spokane area's garbage was being disposed of in four landfills: two owned by the county (Mica and Colbert), one by the city (Northside), and one privately operated (Marshall).

Also, as in some other places in the United States, during the first half of the twentieth century Spokane's solid waste system included the use of "crematories"—garbage incinerators. Spokane's first was authorized in 1903, and a second was added later. These crematories and the traditional landfills were the heart of Spokane's solid waste disposal system for five decades. During much of this era many people delivered their garbage to the dump themselves. It was 1949, nearly halfway through the century, before the city of Spokane passed its first "Universal Garbage Collection Ordinance," requiring every resident in the city to participate in the now familiar curbside garbage collection. To this day there is no universal collection ordinance in Spokane County.

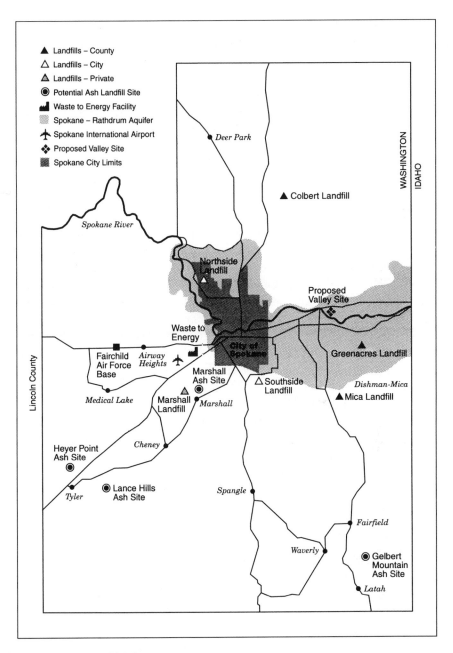

Legend:
- ▲ Landfills – County
- △ Landfills – City
- △ Landfills – Private
- ◉ Potential Ash Landfill Site
- 🏭 Waste to Energy Facility
- ▨ Spokane – Rathdrum Aquifer
- ✈ Spokane International Airport
- ❖ Proposed Valley Site
- ▨ Spokane City Limits

WASHINGTON

IDAHO

Deer Park

▲ Colbert Landfill

Spokane River

Northside Landfill

Proposed Valley Site

Waste to Energy

Lincoln County

Fairchild Air Force Base

Airway Heights ✈

City of Spokane

❖

Greenacres Landfill

Marshall Ash Site ◉

△ Southside Landfill

Dishman-Mica

Medical Lake

Marshall Landfill △

Marshall

▲ Mica Landfill

Cheney ●

Heyer Point Ash Site ◉

Spangle ●

● *Tyler*

◉ Lance Hills Ash Site

Fairfield ●

Waverly ●

◉ Gelbert Mountain Ash Site

● *Latah*

Figure 1.2   Map of Spokane

The 1960s saw a gradual transition from dumps to sanitary landfills. In dumps the garbage was often reduced in volume by open burning. Sanitary landfills did not burn the garbage, but covered it with dirt on a daily basis. It is interesting to note that when the Northside site was converted from an "open burn" dump to a sanitary landfill, local citizens were quite anxious about this new solid waste management technology. To help convince them that conversion to a sanitary landfill operation was an improvement, in the spring of 1961 the local chapter of the League of Women Voters (LOWV) sponsored a "picnic at the landfill."[1] As will be seen later, this was not the last time the local chapter facilitated acceptance of a new solid waste management technology.

The 1970s were also an important decade in Spokane's management of solid waste. In 1971 a solid waste management study by the city recommended: (1) continued use of landfills, (2) a feasibility study for a waste-to-energy facility that would utilize municipal waste and timber waste, and (3) a joint landfill operation by the city and the county. That study contained the main elements of what would in the 1990s become the area's new solid waste management system—a waste-to-energy facility and an interlocal agreement between the city and the county. The waste-to-energy idea did not get much support in the 1970s. In 1971 and 1972 grant proposals for feasibility studies were turned down by the Environmental Protection Agency. The city of Spokane's first flirtation with the waste-to-energy concept occurred in 1971, when as a member of the Inland Empire Waste Conservation Association (a nonprofit association including industry and government members) it participated in submitting to the Environmental Protection Agency (EPA) a proposal for funding preliminary research into the feasibility of a regional waste-to-energy plant intended to burn household waste and wood waste from the forest products industry. In 1978 a funding proposal for a marketing and economics feasibility study of a regional waste-to-energy system was rejected by the U.S. Department of Energy.

Also in 1978, the EPA designated the Spokane-Rathdrum aquifer a "sole source" aquifer under the Federal Safe Drinking Water Act. The aquifer covers approximately 350 square miles and is the source of water for more than 300,000 people. At least as early as 1966 the city of Spokane had recognized the aquifer as the "community's greatest natural resource."[2] In 1979 the Spokane County Engineering Department produced a water quality management plan recommending "no further degradation" as the basic goal.[3] Among the plan's recommendations were specific ways of controlling pollution from solid waste disposal. So, following the sole source designation, protection of the aquifer became a critical factor in solid waste management planning decisions. 1978 also ushered Spokane into the era of citizen lawsuits when a group of residents living near the Northside landfill organized as Residents Against Garbage Encroachment (RAGE) and filed a suit contesting the city's plans to enlarge the operational size of the landfill. Although the city's plans did not involve enlarging the legal boundaries of the landfill, many residents who had moved into the area saw the operational boundaries as the real boundaries. These residents saw expanded operations at the site as a serious threat to them and their property values. This experience with RAGE foreshadowed the citizen opposition that was to become a crucial element in the controversy surrounding the proposed waste-to-energy facility in the late 1980s.

As the 1970s ended, the relation between solid waste disposal techniques and groundwater quality drew official attention in two reports by the Spokane County Engineer's Office.[4] The second of these, the Water Quality Management Plan, recommended prohibiting new landfill sites over the Spokane-Rathdrum aquifer. By the end of 1980, studies had confirmed that the county's Colbert landfill was posing a serious threat to neighboring wells. Though Colbert was not over the Spokane-Rathdrum aquifer, the importance of the aquifer and the public's reaction to the Colbert situation prompted a quick response by the city when in 1982 their tests found contaminants seeping into the groundwater at the Northside landfill (which was over the aquifer): the city provided water lines to the residents near the Northside landfill within two months. These two groundwater pollution threats (both Colbert and Northside were placed on the Superfund list), legal problems involving the Southside, Northside, and Colbert landfills, and the limited capacity of the landfills in operation confirmed on a visceral level that the city and the county had a common problem that would require a cooperative effort. Recognition of the seriousness of this situation led city and county officials to put protection of the aquifer among their top priorities when they began to develop concepts for the next generation of solid waste management techniques. Although Spokane saw its aquifer as a special environmental concern, and incineration of solid waste as one way of reducing dependence upon landfills, the inclination to move away from dependence upon sanitary landfills and toward utilization of waste-to-energy facilities was a national trend.[5]

The Move Toward Waste-to-Energy

The 1980s initially appeared to usher in an era of creative cooperation among local government jurisdictions and publicly regulated utilities. In 1981 the city and county again submitted an application for a $150,000 matching grant to fund a marketing and economics study of a waste-to-energy incineration system designed by Washington Water Power (WWP), a privately owned and publicly regulated utility company. To meet the matching requirement, WWP contributed $100,000 and the city and county each contributed $25,000. On February 22, 1982, the city council approved hiring Morrison-Knudsen (M-K) to do a study examining alternatives for a waste-to-energy project's "siting, design, ownership, financing and licensing."[6] In 1983, after the M-K study identified a Spokane Valley site near the Kaiser Aluminum and Chemical plant in Trentwood (east of Spokane city limits; see fig. 1.2) as the most desirable location for a waste-to-energy facility — one that would produce both steam and electricity — the city council authorized application to the Washington State Department of Ecology (WDOE) for Referendum 39 funds to help pay for its construction. (In 1980 Washington State voters approved Referendum 39, which authorized $450 million in state general obligation bonds to support design, acquisition, construction, and improvement of public waste disposal facilities.)[7]

In 1984 both the city and the county adopted a solid waste master plan that included construction of a waste-to-energy plant.[8] The importance of the selection of a waste-to-energy plant as the cornerstone of the next generation of solid waste management (and perhaps the expected difficulty in implementing it) was implicitly recognized when in 1985 the city and county jointly created the Solid Waste Disposal Project (SWDP), a project policy committee, a citizens' advisory committee, and a technical advisory committee. The SWDP's mission was to construct and begin operating a new solid waste disposal system for the area.

Although a firm commitment had not yet been made, the inclination of local government officials toward a waste-to-energy system was well established prior to the creation of SWDP. In January 1985 city and county officials toured waste-to-energy facilities in three Florida cities. (City Solid Waste Management Office staff had previously toured waste-to-energy facilities in Saugus, Massachusetts; Nashville, Tennessee; Hampton, Virginia; and Pinellas County, Florida.) In February Henningson Durham & Richardson (HDR) was hired to do an Environmental Impact Statement (EIS) and "other services as needed." HDR first did a siting analysis, which when completed in April recommended that a Spokane Airport Business Park site and a site in the Spokane Valley continue to be considered for a waste-to-energy plant. In May the county adopted Flow Control Ordinance #85–0395, requiring that all solid waste generated in the county be delivered to the waste-to-energy facility when it became operational.

In 1986 another key step was taken in the development of Spokane's next generation of solid waste management technology: SWDP proceeded to identify a specific site for the facility. The Spokane Valley site near the Trentwood Kaiser plant was favored at first, for two reasons: (1) the potential sale of steam energy to Kaiser, and (2) the potential use of the incinerator by Kootenai County (Idaho). But arrangements with Kaiser were not successfully completed.[9] The official explanation revolved around Kaiser's lack of confidence in the plant's reliability as a source of steam power,[10] but it is quite possible that Kaiser officials changed their minds when it became clear that having the waste-to-energy plant as a neighbor would bring more air pollution monitoring to the area. Kaiser was also initiating moves toward greater energy independence, purchasing natural gas wells in Wyoming and leasing pipeline space so that they could end their reliance on Washington Water Power (WWP) as a supplier. Whatever the reason for their change of heart, when Kaiser's interest in purchasing steam energy from a nearby waste-to-energy plant waned, attention shifted to a site near the Spokane International Airport. (The original airport site identified in the EIS process was later dropped in favor of a site slightly farther south. It was said that the new site would reduce operational conflicts between the facility and the airport.)

In November 1986, WDOE approved a Referendum 39 grant of $60 million to assist Spokane in financing the construction of a waste-to-energy plant. This grant may have been the critical element in keeping the waste-to-energy facility alive when citizen opposition reached its peak in 1989. Certainly its impact in reducing the direct cost to the ratepayers in Spokane weakened opponents' arguments regarding the cost of the facility.

THE RISE OF CITIZEN OPPOSITION

While the city's approval of a contract with Wheelabrator Spokane to construct the waste-to-energy facility was significant, the most important political development of 1987 was the rise in citizen opposition to the facility. In the late summer and autumn of that year opponents put together a petition for the right to vote on large capital projects such as the waste-to-energy facility. A group calling themselves Citizens for Clean Air sponsored Proposition 4, arguing "That the city charter of the City of Spokane [should] be amended to provide that a vote of the people be required for capital expenditures . . . requiring indebtedness of the taxpayers and property owners for capital projects, including the proposed mass burn plant for refuse disposal (Waste to Energy Plant)."[11] As the November 3 vote approached, it became clear that Proposition 4 had strong support.

The main item on the agenda of the November 2 city council meeting was approval of the Wheelabrator contract. Because Spokane city council meetings included a public comment period, and because the length of that period was not specified, council members listened to citizen opinions on the proposed contract (mostly in opposition) until well past midnight before voting to approve the contract. Consequently, Proposition 4 passed with 70 percent support on the same day the city approved the contract. Many citizens saw the council's action as a direct affront to the will of the people. Compounding that affront, the council later decided to file suit, claiming that Proposition 4 did not apply to the waste-to-energy project. The trial court found for the city, so Citizens for Clean Air sought and received direct review by the Washington State Supreme Court. In a 5–4 decision, the court held that the proposition did not apply to the waste-to-energy project; the majority opinion agreed with the city that the project would "not create indebtedness for the taxpayers [because] repayment of the City's obligations will not come from general taxes, but rather from specific sources such as revenues of the solid waste disposal system."[12] Though the city eventually prevailed in that suit, it could not have selected a day for approving the contract or a way of evading the intent of the voters that would contribute more momentum to the cause of the opposition. Throughout the controversy, the one issue upon which a clear majority of the citizens agreed with the active citizen opponents of the facility was that they should have an opportunity to vote on it.

Having failed in their attempt to force a vote on the project itself, the opposition began to look for other ways to stop the project. One approach they identified was to use environmental legal appeals to delay construction until an opportunity arose to elect new city council members who might oppose the project. By focusing attention on the incinerator issue, the opposition might then make the council races an indirect vote on the project.

When the site for the waste-to-energy plant was changed to an airport site that had not been considered in the EIS, opponents of the facility requested a supplemental EIS. The request was refused. When the city filed suit claiming that Proposition 4 did not apply to the waste-to-energy project, Citizens for Clean Air incorporated in order to take part in the legal confrontation. They later appealed Spokane County Air Pollution Control Authority (SCAPCA), WDOE, and EPA decisions to grant the project air pollution permits. They also filed suit to invalidate the city's contract with Wheelabrator when they discovered that Wheelabrator was not properly registered with the state.[13]

A second way to stop the project was to change the state's plans to provide Referendum 39 funds for construction of the facility. Opponents wrote, called, and visited legislators and WDOE officials in hopes of finding some way to rescind the grant before the funds were actually appropriated and disbursed. In the state legislature, opponents found allies in Rep. Art Sprenkle, a Democrat from Snohomish, and Sen. Jim West, a Republican from Spokane. Testifying against appropriation of the funds for the grant WDOE had promised Spokane, Sprenkle called the incinerator Spokane's Vietnam: "The Vietnam analogy that I have stated with respect to Spokane is appropriate. They [the city] have invested a huge amount of financial and intellectual capital. We are now at the end of the war, and we're seeing that it [the incinerator] is the wrong approach to the problem."[14] WDOE reauthorized the grant in December 1988, but subject to the following new conditions: (1) establishment of a curbside recycling program by January 30, 1991; (2) attempts to renegotiate the "put or pay" clause of the contract with Wheelabrator; (3) attempts to market the incinerator to other cities and counties; (4) completion of a human health and environmental toxic substances monitoring study; (5) establishment of an ongoing hazardous waste collection program; (6) development of a means of separating heavy metal sources such as batteries from the waste stream; and (7) identification and implementation of special procedures for handling the ash. These new conditions were a response to the awkward position WDOE found itself in as a result of the "unprecedented controversy over a grant amendment request."[15] While opponents found some sympathy in both forums, they were unable to persuade either the legislature or WDOE to reverse itself and take away the promised funds.

Another development in 1988 that opened fronts for the facility's opponents was the search for an ash landfill site. After examining more than 200 potential sites, SWDP announced in July the results of a study that identified three sites as being the most promising: Lance Hills, Marshall, and Gelbert Mountain.[16] All the sites under consideration were within Spokane County because city and county officials insisted that they needed jurisdiction over the landfill to assure that the waste was handled properly. The announcement of these three sites led to the formation of three new citizen groups that were vigorously opposed to at least some aspect of the waste-to-energy facility. Around each site, neighbors who had never before met each other began to work together to spread the word and organize their communities to oppose selection of the site near their homes. Starting as NIMBYs (not in my backyard), leaders of the groups opposed to ash landfills in their neighborhood were quickly convinced by the established opposition that stopping the entire waste-to-energy project was the most certain way to keep an ash landfill from being constructed in their backyards. Activists from Citizens for Clean Air shared their views on the waste-to-energy project and cautioned the ash landfill opponents not to miss any opportunity to express their opposition. Citizen opposition to the project received a real boost from the additional numbers and energies contributed by these groups. With the addition of the ash landfill opponents, instead of 50 or 60 opponents appearing at public hearings and city council sessions there were 200 or more.

In spite of the increasing opposition, in January 1989 the city council and county commission in joint session approved a $105 million bond sale to fund the waste-to-energy project. The vote also authorized City Manager Terry Novak to issue Wheelabrator a "conditional notice to proceed" with construction. Novak acted quickly in order to avoid further delay costs — the contract allowed inflation and penalty assessments that amounted to thousands of dollars per day and millions in additional total cost. He could not, however, issue a straightforward "notice to proceed" as stipulated in the contract, because opponents' appeals had delayed a required air pollution permit. Obviously, opponents of the project questioned the legality of Novak's action.

Meanwhile, the environmental legal challenges, in addition to delaying permit acquisitions, began to have a substantive effect as well. The Washington State Pollution Control Hearings Board (PCHB) issued a ruling limiting nitrogen oxide (NOx) emissions to 428 tons per year and requiring a one-year study prior to placing a limit on dioxin emissions. Shortly thereafter, the regional office of the EPA recommended that the air pollution permit request be sent back to WDOE so that it might analyze the advisability of reducing NOx emission limits and including recycling among the best available control technologies (BACT). At one point in the process, EPA was considering a NOx limit of 251 tons per year. When the permit was appealed to PCHB, the NOx limit was set at a 40 percent reduction from uncontrolled emission levels, and a temporary dioxin limit of 4.5 nanograms per cubic meter was set, with a permanent limit to be set at the end of two years.[17] Sulfur dioxide limits were set at 146 tons per year, an 80 percent reduction from uncontrolled emission levels. When the plant had difficulty meeting hourly limits, SCAPCA and WDOE allowed SWDP to be held to an 85 percent reduction standard using daily limits.[18] Though the emission limits were not as low as opponents had hoped, their challenges had resulted in stricter emission controls than would have resulted without their input.

Opponents of the facility also began to engage in dramatic protest actions designed to attract media attention. One such action involved members of three opposition groups: Citizens for Clean Air, the Lance Hills Coalition for a Clean Environment, and Spokane Area Watchdogs.[19] After notifying the media of their plans, protesters dressed in black clothes and surgical masks and delivered dead fish and bags of ash to city hall. They said the purpose of their "dead carp award" was to tell city officials that the idea of the waste-to-energy plant stinks.

Opponents demonstrated with signs and songs outside city hall prior to one of the weekly city council meetings (which had become the focal point for anti–waste-to-energy presentations).[20] In the meeting itself, during the period for testimony on a proposal to study another potential ash landfill site (Heyer Point), one opponent attempted to sing her testimony and was led away by police. Another was not allowed to testify until he took off a banner bearing anti–waste-to-energy slogans. Rattled by the actions of the protesters and by the audience's obvious support of those actions, the council called a recess while they discussed whether to move the meeting elsewhere. They decided to resume the meeting in the same location, but had police stationed in the chambers to quell any further disturbances.

At that meeting, the council voted 6–1 to fund a study of the new potential ash landfill site. One of the sites originally listed among the top three had been purchased by a neighboring farmer, and so was taken out of consideration. SWDP then proposed to add an area at Heyer Point to the list of sites under full consideration in the EIS process for siting an ash landfill. This site was a bit north of one of the previously identified sites; therefore, while it added to the membership of an already formed opposition group, it did not significantly increase the number of energetically opposed people.

Incinerator opponents, however, continued to raise their visibility through actions guaranteed to get media coverage. They submitted a petition to the elections office requesting the recall of all the council members except Sheri Barnard — the only member who opposed the waste-to-energy project. They went to the legislature to testify against funding the $60 million grant. They appealed a county ruling that Boeing did not have to complete an environmental impact statement (EIS) prior to constructing a new $20 million plant west of Spokane.[21] None of these actions resulted in their realizing their putative substantive goal, but all of them increased incinerator opponents' visibility in the community.

THE ELECTION AND ITS AFTERMATH

A major goal of the opposition, however, was drawing near. City elections in 1989 were to include races for mayor and for three council seats. If opposition forces could win all of those positions, they would have a majority on the council and would be able to stop the waste-to-energy project. Even before the campaigns officially began, it was clear that the opposition would mount a serious effort to win those offices.[22]

In the campaigning prior to the primary election in September 1989, the main issue distinguishing candidates from one another was their stance on the waste-to-energy project. Opponents were more pleased by this than proponents, but proponents were able to use such actions as the challenge to the Boeing plant as evidence that opponents were antigrowth as well as anti-incinerator. If they could convince voters that opponents of the project were not part of the mainstream, then they might be able to overcome the anti–waste-to-energy sentiment. One council member running for reelection, recognizing the appeal of the anti-incinerator position, continued his support for the project, but criticized his colleagues on the council for refusing to put it to a vote. He compared the polarization of the community over the incinerator to a cancer in the local body politic.[23]

In addition to the battle of the candidates, the primary election was enlivened by a "battle of the white papers." In June, "Risking Spokane," a paper sponsored by an opponent of the incinerator, was distributed to approximately 25,000 households in Spokane.[24] The report, written by Larry Shook, then editor of *Washington Magazine,* presented four arguments against the waste-to-energy project: (1) the decision-making process was seriously flawed; (2) the economic risks of the project were unacceptable; (3) the environmental impact would be unacceptable; and (4) better alternatives were available. The most serious flaw identified in the decision-making process was the failure to explore alternatives. The economic risk was described as entailing a "staggering debt" for local government. The report said that the city would be forced to pay whatever costs the incinerator's operation might demand, even at the cost of failing to meet other basic service needs. The environmental impact was described as the emission of dangerous poisons such as lead, arsenic, mercury, acid gases, dioxins, and furans. This was compounded by the "catch-22 of incineration" — the more effective an incinerator is at trapping those emissions before they leave the stacks, the higher their concentration in the ash residue. Finally, the report said that the "new waste management industry" was developing alternatives to mass burn incinerators that could "separate the waste, recycle what can be recycled, burn what is safe to burn, compact and bury what shouldn't be burned . . . produce methanol gas . . . and compost remaining waste."[25]

The second white paper, "Waste-to-Energy Works," was written by Jim Correll, an engineer working for the local CH2M Hill office (a firm involved in managing landfill cleanup projects in the area) and chair of a group supportive of the waste-to-energy project. It was an explicit attempt to counter the impact of "Risking Spokane." The paper began by explaining why a new solid waste management system was needed, and then proceeded to pose and answer questions about the system, the alternatives, its cost, and the decision-making process. A new system was needed, it said, because the old landfills had been found to be environmentally unsound and were being closed and cleaned up, and would require monitoring for many years. The new system, it was pointed out, included waste reduction, recycling, the waste-to-energy process, and landfilling of ash and nonburnables. In defending the safety of the waste-to-energy process, the report cited literature to the effect that "living down wind [of a waste-to-energy plant] can be compared to smoking 1.4 unfiltered cigarettes during a lifetime or living in Boston or New York City for two days." It also said that all current similar facilities were meeting all current environmental standards. Correll argued that alternatives had been considered, but decision makers had insisted on building the new system around a proven technology. Recycling was considered a necessary part of any new system, but it was not an alternative since the best that could be hoped for was recycling of about 50 percent of the waste stream. Correll admitted that the cost of the new system would be high; but alternative systems would have similar costs, and the waste-to-energy facility would account for only about 25 percent of the total cost of the new system. Finally, Correll argued that citizens had had ample opportunity to be heard in the decision-making process, but that "decisions should be based on the realities and practicalities of the problem, not on the basis of political or emotional rhetoric."[26]

Both authors recognized the role their white papers might play in the up-coming elections, and any doubt about whether or how the solid waste man-agement issue would affect the upcoming elections disappeared after the primary election. The general election campaign was going to be a proxy referendum on the waste-to-energy facility—just as the incinerator's oppo-nents had wanted. The two remaining candidates for mayor were Sheri Bar-nard, who had gained much attention as the only city council member who opposed the facility; and Rob Higgins, one of the council's staunch support-ers of waste-to-energy. The three council positions to be filled in the election were also sought by candidates who differed on the waste-to-energy project. One race pitted an incumbent who regularly voted in support of the facility against an opponent who ran her campaign on a single issue—her opposi-tion to the project. In a second race, a candidate who supported the project and had much business district support was running against a former chair of Citizens for Clean Air, the original group organized to oppose the waste-to-energy facility. The candidates for the third seat differed less clearly on the project, but they failed to divert voters' attention to other issues.

Much to the chagrin of the incinerator's opponents, the election gave an indisputable, but hardly enthusiastic, "go ahead" to the project. The only candidate opposed to the project who won in the general election was Sheri Barnard. She had never wavered in her opposition to the project, but she had not welcomed identification with the anti-incinerator slate and had taken pains to distance herself from them and to assure audiences that she would be an effective mayor even if she should have to preside over the construction of the facility. However, the election of "pro-incinerator" can-didates did not signal clear support for the facility. A study released about one week before the election estimated the sunk costs in the project at between $55 and $70 million.[27] Voters may have been reluctant to throw away that much money by killing the project.

THE NEW GENERATION OF LANDFILLS

The landfilling aspect of Spokane's new solid waste system also gener-ated opposition, as neighbors to the potential ash landfill sites organized to prevent the intrusion on their lives such a facility would bring. Nine days after the election a public hearing was held on the draft EIS for an ash landfill. At that hearing two new forces appeared in the decision-making dynamic. Waste Management Incorporated (WMI) appeared in a new role

— hoping to secure the contract for disposal of the ash. WMI wanted to haul the ash to their "state-of-the-art" landfill in Gilliam County, Oregon. Also appearing at the hearing were Lincoln County commissioners. They were opposed to Spokane County's apparent selection of the Heyer Point site because of concerns about the potential impact of an ash landfill in the Crab Creek watershed on Lincoln County, and on the aquifer upon which much of that county's population depended.

Based on environmental and economic considerations, in January 1990 SWDP staff recommended Heyer Point as the in-county option for an ash landfill, but under pressure from opponents they also contracted for an economic analysis, which indicated that a long-haul option might be competitive and deserved further examination.[28] This led SWDP to prepare an RFP (Request for Proposals) for long-haul alternatives to the in-county option. Rabanco, Washington State's largest garbage company, and Washington Waste Systems of Redmond, a subsidiary of WMI, were the top two competitors for the contract. Their competition was unusually hostile and went well beyond the delivery of bids. Washington Waste Systems, for example, contended that Rabanco's low bid was simply unrealistic and that Rabanco would not be able to deliver on it.[29] On June 1 SWDP recommended Rabanco for the long-haul contract — if that option were chosen — and on June 25 the city council and county commission, in separate meetings, voted to accept the Rabanco long-haul bid, which meant sending Spokane's ash about 210 miles away to a landfill in Klickitat County. They also voted to purchase the Heyer Point site as a backup to the long-haul contract.[30]

But that was not the end of the ash landfill subplot. Some residents of Klickitat County were not happy that Spokane planned to dump its ash in their area. In July, in response to a suit filed by the Yakama Indians and Klickitat County Citizens vs. Imported Waste, a superior court judge ruled that the Rabanco landfill that was to be the depository of Spokane's ash had not been properly planned and required further study, including a full EIS process. At that point the Rabanco landfill was already 80 percent completed. In September the same judge, responding to a different action filed by the same groups, ordered Rabanco to stop construction on the landfill until Klickitat County officials had complied with state environmental guidelines. In response to these rulings, Spokane extended to January 1991 its deadline for completing contract negotiations with Rabanco. In June 1991 the lawsuit holding up operations at the landfill was dismissed.[31] SWDP has used Rabanco's ash landfill since it opened.

RECYCLING, COMPOSTING, AND OTHER ASPECTS OF THE NEW SOLID WASTE MANAGEMENT SYSTEM

In addition to these landfill issues, the SWDP had to attend to other aspects of the new solid waste management system they had created for the Spokane area. While its primary feature was the incinerator, the system also included waste reduction, recycling, and composting.

In June 1987 Resource Conservation Consultants produced a recycling study for the project office. The study was designed to provide "estimates of the potential impact of specific waste reduction and recycling programs that could be provided for area citizens and businesses," to help the city and county attain the goal of 31 percent recycling. It recommended that the city design a recycling strategy that (1) did not harm the existing recycling system; (2) targeted wastes such as glass containers, corrugated cardboard, newspapers, printing, writing, and computing papers, and tin and aluminum cans; (3) employed only proven technologies; and (4) cost less to operate than the projected cost of waste disposal. The main difficulty the study foresaw was public resistance. In a survey of registered voters in Spokane County, the study found that "fewer than half thought recycling practices should be mandatory, only one-third were willing to transport materials to a recycling site, and only one-quarter of the respondents supported paying a fee to have recyclables collected from their home."[32]

In November 1988, SWDP's Project Liaison Board (PLB) voted against recommending a curbside recycling program for the city, preferring a program built around a "partnership of government, private recyclers, schools, nonprofit service organizations, churches, community centers and citizens groups."[33] The program included posters, commercials, and public service announcements. Large red, white, and blue bins were placed in shopping centers and schoolgrounds, and school children were targeted by a recycling promotion program. The promotion program included a robot named R3U2, whose message to the children was that "you, too" should reduce, reuse, and recycle (hence the R3). When it realized this program would not meet WDOE's expectations, the city dropped it and adopted a curbside recycling program.

The city of Spokane began its curbside recycling program in the autumn of 1990[34] by distributing blue box-like containers residents were to place on the curb next to their garbage cans. Residents were initially allowed to place clear and colored glass, tin and aluminum cans, code 1 plastic bottles, used batteries (sealed in a plastic bag and set on top of the other recyclables), and

employees as a result. The Lions Club, which had depended on money they raised by selling donated newspapers, complained about the lower prices for recycled newspaper that resulted from the increased supply, and about the decline in donations resulting from the city's curbside service.

The new composting program also had its problems. When SWDP selected for its composting facility a 43-acre site across the highway from the old Colbert landfill and the North County Solid Waste Transfer Station, it found the same kind of neighborhood resistance it had faced in siting other facilities. Neighbors were worried about its impact on the rural nature of the area, about its odor, and about a decline in their property values. The city eventually bought two of the houses near the site; they also paid moving expenses for the families and costs related to the purchase of the properties.[40]

But that was not the only difficulty SWDP faced in beginning a large-scale composting program. At first, even though the operation of the plant was contracted out, the county commissioners were not sure this was a proper government activity. They wanted to let competing private businesses provide composting services for the area. The city and county settled their differences by means of a compromise that eliminated free dumping for commercial landscapers at the government-supported composting facility, thus enabling private composting businesses to compete effectively with the government-supported operation. To further complicate matters, the zoning adjuster ruled against the proposed site for the composting facility, citing potential noise and odor as incompatible with the area. SWDP appealed that decision to the County Board of Adjustment and won. The neighbors, however, continued to make complaints to SCAPCA about the odors coming from the facility, and in July 1994, as a result of city council action, SWDP temporarily discontinued delivery of compost materials to the facility. Materials that were intended to be diverted from the incinerator were instead being sent to it.[41] In the fall delivery of materials was resumed, but by June 1995 the odor from the facility caused the city council to notify its operators, O. M. Scott, that they had 30 days to correct the problem. Failure would be considered a breach of contract. Dancing between pressure from the plant's neighbors and concerns about being sued for breach of contract, the council spent the summer of 1995 trying either to find a way out of the contract with Scott or to solve the problem. They pressured SCAPCA to find the plant in violation of air pollution regulations, which SCAPCA did three times during the spring and summer. But that was not sufficient cause for canceling the contract. Fed up with the continuing complaints, the council first voted 4–2 to try to cancel the contract, but three weeks later, afraid of losing a suit for contract violation, they reversed and voted 4–3 to purchase new equipment they hoped would reduce the odors in the neighborhood sufficiently.[42]

Another difficulty in implementing the new system involved siting a transfer station at which ash hauled away from the incinerator in trucks could be transferred to railroad cars and shipped to the landfill in Klickitat County. Some residents and the mayor of Airway Heights, a small town just west of Spokane, expressed "major concern" about a proposal to locate the transfer station within 800 feet of the town's two municipal wells. Rejecting assurances from Rabanco that the facility would be harmless, the mayor said, "If something is toxic, how are we going to know? . . . We don't have the expertise to monitor something like this."[43]

The delays caused by this transfer station squabble and the Klickitat landfill lawsuit were later blamed for another problem that arose for the new solid waste system:[44] Wheelabrator threatened to fine the city and county $110,000 — between $7,000 and $10,000 for each day the incinerator was ready to operate but SWDP was not ready to use it. SWDP could not begin operations without WDOE's approval of the ash management plan. WDOE could not approve the ash management plan until the thirty-day public comment period was closed, and SWDP had not been able to initiate the public comment period until the Klickitat lawsuits and the transfer station problem were resolved.

This prospect was especially unsettling to local government officials, as it would have been the second time Wheelabrator collected fines from SWDP because of delays in obtaining permits. In 1989 a delay in receiving permits needed before construction could begin had cost SWDP $1.2 million.[45] A county commissioner and a city council member were so upset by the threat of additional fines that they urged starting up the incinerator without WDOE approval. SWDP's director suggested to WDOE that they give him "interim" approval. But neither action was taken, Wheelabrator never used its authority to fine, and the incinerator began operation on September 6, 1991.[46] It was "the first built by Wheelabrator west of the Mississippi and the first of its kind in Washington [State]."[47]

While the timing of the incinerator's ignition set off a few sparks, SWDP realized substantial economic benefits by starting operation of the waste-to-energy facility three months ahead of schedule.[48] The facility had a contract to sell electricity generated through the burning of garbage to Puget Sound Power and Light. The earlier start-up was estimated to add over $3 million to the value of that contract.

Once it had begun operating, tests were run to see that the incinerator was working properly. The contract with Wheelabrator called for a "continuous seven-day, 24-hour-a-day test," but because of fog at the airport the test was shut down twice.[49] (The plant is required to shut down when there is fog at the airport because its operation might exacerbate the fog problem.) Citizens for Clean Air complained to WDOE that the tests needed to be run again, but those tests would have cost $250,000 to repeat and the opinion of the director of SWDP was that the plant performed better than expected under more challenging conditions — the shutdowns made passing the tests more difficult. WDOE did not require new tests.

Within the first year of operation, SWDP proposed to increase the revenue generated by the incinerator by contracting with medical waste haulers to burn their loads for about $300 per ton.[50] The standard fee for municipal waste at the incinerator at that time was about $65 per ton. Although the Project Liaison Board told SWDP to seek a contract to burn about 13 tons of medical waste per month, the proposal was effectively vetoed by Wheelabrator, who said they did not want their employees handling large quantities of medical waste.

Five months after the medical waste contract proposal was made public, officials were considering burning tires in the incinerator. SWDP saw the proposal as a positive way of dealing with the 8 million old tires piled in three places in the county and the 350,000 tires discarded in Spokane County each year. Opponents expressed concern about the toxic substances that would be added to the plant's air pollution. Initially the council was not ready to approve the plan, and when the proposal came back to the city council the director of the Spokane County Air Pollution Control Authority (SCAPCA) said the request would be treated as a substantial change in the facility's operating permit and so would subject the incinerator to the more stringent air toxics regulations the state had enacted since the incinerator received its permits. In July 1993 the city council voted 4–3 to approve burning tires in the incinerator, but after the November 1993 election installed several new members on the council, that decision was reversed.[51]

Shortly after the proposal to burn tires was floated, an article on the front page of the Sunday paper announced that the incinerator had already reached its burning capacity and costs were running higher than expected.[52] Because of increasing costs the rate stabilization fund was, the article said, "rapidly dwindling." The director of the city's garbage service, it went on, predicted a significant increase in city collection fees by 1995. To add insult to injury, the article also noted that it would be less expensive to ship the raw garbage to the Rabanco landfill in Klickitat County than it was to incinerate it and send the ash to that landfill. The director of SWDP blamed the higher than expected costs on a number of unforeseen expenses related to the incinerator's operation, including extra costs for ash disposal, pollution controls, and transfer stations. He also noted that the costs of closing, capping, and maintaining the old landfills added to the cost of solid waste management in Spokane County.

The same paper carried a related article explaining that if the incinerator should be required to meet new or additional pollution control standards, the costs would be borne by SWDP, not Wheelabrator.[53] The contract required SWDP to pay for any pollution control equipment needed to meet new standards. The example mentioned in the article was the possibility that the Clinton administration might require carbon injection systems to capture more mercury. The article also raised the threat of changes in the method of handling incinerator ash. Oddly, it did not mention the potential impact of a decision to burn tires, even though that possibility was under active consideration by the city council. As mentioned earlier, any decision to burn tires would subject the incinerator to new, more stringent pollution control standards passed by the state after the incinerator received its operating permit.

Shortly thereafter, an editorial in the paper introduced four options the community faced in dealing with the fact that the incinerator was already at capacity: "(1) Enlarge the plant, at considerable cost; (2) Build a landfill within the county for overflow trash, on a site purchased and studied for landfill purposes; (3) Ship overflow trash to the Rabanco landfill in Klickitat County; (4) Increase recycling."[54] Noting that only 60 percent of the area's households participated in curbside recycling, the editorial recommended increasing the recycling rate in order to avoid the additional expenses involved in the other three options.

Four months later, and only 20 months into the incinerator's 20-year contract, it was announced that there were times when the incinerator could not burn all the solid waste in the system's stream. Raw garbage was being sent to the Klickitat landfill. While that landfill was charging $40 per ton to accept the ash, it charged $39.80 per ton for the raw garbage. At this point officials were blaming the excess on seasonal variations (spring and summer being the heavier load periods), but one month later when the excess of garbage showed no signs of abating, the plant manager said, "We are still getting 1,000 tons a week more than last year, and nobody can figure out why." Officials continued to hope that the excess was seasonal, but, as journalist Karen Dorn Steele pointed out, population projections had underestimated the growth of Spokane County: "In 1989, the state Office of Financial Management said the county wouldn't reach 365,000 people until the year 2000. In fact the county had 350,000 residents in 1992 and probably will exceed 380,000 when new estimates for 1993 are out next month."[55]

Ironically, opponents of the incinerator had argued that the scale of the plant was too large. The "put or pay" clause in the contract with Wheelabrator meant that SWDP would be legally bound to send an adequate supply of garbage through the incinerator; consequently, they claimed, the facility would discourage recycling. At this point it seemed that significant increases in recycling and composting were the system's best hope for evading a charge that it was inadequate to the task of managing Spokane's solid waste stream. In June 1994 it was reported at a Project Liaison Board meeting that the 1993 excess appeared to have been an anomaly. Though no one really knew what caused the anomaly, possible causes included (1) unusual weather, causing a lot of material to be delivered to the facility in a short period of time, and (2) input of stockpiled trash.[56]

Despite the seasonal overabundance of garbage for the incinerator, SWDP regularly contracted to burn various forms of industrial waste. The incentive for accepting such items as magnetic tapes from Boeing, ink sludge from Cowles Publishing Company, and carbon dust from Kaiser Aluminum and Chemical Corporation appears to have been revenues.[57] The practice was generally unpublicized until a question arose as to the wisdom and legality of burning plastic jugs that had at one time contained chemicals. The local paper editorialized against the practice and inquired further into it. The director of SCAPCA objected to SWDP burning the jugs without permission from his agency, and the state Department of Labor and Industries investigated a worker's complaint that burning the jugs gave him a headache. The director of SWDP would probably have been fined by SCAPCA, but the SCAPCA Board refused to authorize it. They did, however, decide to reconsider their policies regarding such decisions, and SWDP's Policy Liaison Board decided to hold a public workshop on the issue.[58] So, operational details continued to raise policy problems.

But the main problem facing the incinerator at the operational stage was financing the new system. Each time increased tipping fees were announced, the plant was subjected to attacks regarding the financial impact of the area's dependence on it. When a fee increase from $75 to $85 per ton was announced for 1994, Mayor Barnard said that it underlined how serious a mistake it had been to build the plant.[59] Any new approach to solid waste management would have increased costs, but official underestimations of the rate of increase did not make accepting the new costs any easier. Plans had predicted that rates of $75 per ton would not occur until 1998.

To make matters worse, in May 1994 the United States Supreme Court handed down two decisions that undermined key assumptions on which SWDP had based its projected revenues and expenditures. When the Court ruled that under current federal law ash from municipal incinerators that do not burn only household waste must (if it contains toxic materials) be managed as hazardous waste, Spokane's new solid waste management system faced a serious threat of increased costs.[60] It was estimated that diverting Spokane's ash to a hazardous waste landfill would increase disposal costs from $40 per ton to between $90 and $100 per ton. Two weeks later the court exacerbated Spokane's financing problem by ruling that flow control ordinances like the one passed by Spokane County to insure an adequate supply of garbage for the incinerator violated the Interstate Commerce Clause of the U.S. Constitution.[61] Despite the implications these rulings seemed to carry, Spokane officials were reluctant to predict that the rulings would seriously damage the financial health of their waste-to-energy–centered solid waste management system. SWDP Director Phil Williams presented a list of options for responding to the ash ruling, ranging from swallowing the increased cost of sending all of the ash to a hazardous waste landfill to separating the more toxic fly ash from the greater volume of bottom ash for special treatment.[62] As a temporary measure, SWDP purchased from Wheelabrator equipment for treating the ash with phosphoric acid so that it would pass the hazardousness test. Two months later, Williams presented to his Project Liaison Board a proposal to make permanent alterations to the plant that would incorporate Wheelabrator's WES-Phix process.[63] Acceptance of the proposal, he said, would entail $372,000 in one-time capital expenditures. He estimated the additional annual operating cost at $401,000. In January 1995 EPA announced new ash testing regulations that were expected to make it easier for ash to pass the toxicity test.[64] In relation to the flow control decision, an attorney who had advised local officials regarding the sale of $105 million in bonds to pay for the system estimated that it would take two years for someone to challenge Spokane's flow control ordinance in court.[65] In June 1995 it was reported that the U.S. Senate had passed a bill designed to overrule Supreme Court decisions prohibiting states and local governments from regulating the flow of solid waste in interstate commerce; quick House action was anticipated.[66] Nonetheless, there was little doubt that the two rulings had at least temporarily shaken the financial foundation on which Spokane had built its waste-to-energy facility and related aspects of its new solid waste management system.

PROBLEMS WITH TRADITIONAL LANDFILLS CONTINUE

At the same time the new solid waste management system was getting underway, the city and county were still having to deal with problems resulting from the days of sanitary landfill use. Efforts to keep the landfills from polluting their surrounding environment were going to require much time, patience, and money. As one WDOE official put it, "We are having to spend a lot of money fixing mistakes from the past."[67] One city-owned and three county-owned landfills were placed on the Superfund cleanup list because of the threat they posed to the environment. The privately owned Marshall landfill also had to be properly closed down.

The shutdown of the city's Southside landfill was completed prior to the inception of the new solid waste system (in 1988). The city's Northside landfill was placed on the Superfund list in 1985 because of evidence of groundwater contamination from dry-cleaning solvents that had been dumped in the landfill for years. Part of the area continued to be used for dumping nonburnables such as construction debris, but its old landfill portion was capped with plastic to prevent water from leaching through and polluting the aquifer.[68] A water collection system was placed on top of the cap to redirect rainwater to an infiltration basin. Underneath the cap a gas-extraction system was installed to pull methane gas (formed as the garbage decomposes) to stacks where it could be burned. Also underneath was a groundwater extraction system to pump water from the aquifer, collecting water with traces of the dry-cleaning solvents and directing it to the wastewater treatment plant. Closing down the old landfill portion of the Northside landfill was expected to cost about $27 million.[69]

Spokane County had to see that the Colbert, Mica, and Greenacres landfills were properly closed. The Colbert landfill, sometimes credited with first attracting the attention of the city and county to the seriousness of the landfill threat to the aquifer, was placed on the Superfund list and in 1986 was closed to the public. The plan for treating its pollution potential included a process of extracting water from the landfill, treating it, then pumping it into the Little Spokane River.[70] Closed to the public in 1992, the Mica landfill was caught one year later in a disagreement between the county and WDOE that resulted in the county ordering the engineering firm designing a cover to stop work.[71] Greenacres was closed to the public in

1972 and placed on the Superfund list in 1983. Here, too, WDOE and the county differed on which measures were needed to protect the surrounding environment from pollutants. WDOE wanted a cap placed over the landfill; the county preferred to extract and treat the pollutants. Ten years after Greenacres was placed on the Superfund list, WDOE agreed to continue monitoring the site through 1996 to see whether the rate of pollutants emitted from the site slowed appreciably. If not, WDOE would insist on having the site capped. In March 1994, however, WDOE sent the county an ultimatum requiring the county to agree to cap the site by 1999; otherwise WDOE would require it to be capped by 1997. Risking fines up to $25,000 per day, the county refused to meet the ultimatum.[72]

Another problem involved the future of the Marshall landfill, the only privately operated landfill in Spokane County. Since the county flow control ordinance requiring that solid waste in the county be delivered to the new solid waste management system would put them out of business, the owners of Marshall landfill were not pleased with it. As of this writing they had not gone to court to challenge that ordinance under the May 1994 Supreme Court ruling, and as noted earlier other events may obviate the need for such a suit. Prior to that ruling they had, however, tried several ways of remaining open. First they suggested that they be allowed to build a new modern, lined landfill and accept solid waste from outside the county. That plus contracts to accept construction debris and compost materials, they said, would help them fund the major cleanup they expected to have to undertake when the old landfill was put on the Superfund list. Superfund listing was expected because there was evidence of groundwater contamination from the landfill. But on December 7, 1991, the Spokane County Health District denied an appeal to allow the Marshall landfill to remain open. They cited the risk of groundwater contamination as the reason for denying the appeal. The Marshall landfill was unlined, and therefore no longer met state guidelines. There also appeared to be grounds for concern regarding whether the operators were preparing adequately for eventual closure — they only had $550,856 in their closure account.[73]

In April 1993, a county zoning panel unanimously rejected the Marshall landfill's proposed plans for continued operation. Their plan at this juncture was to build a new state-of-the-art landfill to accept solid waste from outside the county for 40 years, to mine sand and gravel, and to operate a compost facility. When they appealed the decision to the county commissioners, the owners were told that they could not open a new landfill or extend their mining operation, but they could operate a composting facility.[74]

Displeased with the progress Marshall landfill was making on capping their old landfill, in 1993 WDOE took charge of seeing that the landfill was properly closed, which meant that taxpayer funds were likely to supplement those that could be collected from private businesses responsible for the potential pollutants in the landfill.[75] WDOE began by naming Marshall Landfill Incorporated as a potentially liable party. That caused the landfill owners to begin a search for other potentially liable parties with whom they might share the costs of cleanup. Their first list included Fairchild Airforce Base and some of the major companies in the area — including Kaiser Aluminum and Chemical Corporation and United Paint & Coatings. The owners also claimed to have proof that Spokane County was a potentially liable party.

Conclusion

In the late 1980s and early 1990s, Spokane moved from a solid waste system dependent on local sanitary landfills to one built around a waste-to-energy incinerator and a large regional landfill more than 200 miles away. That change did not come easily. It took 15 years to advance from the initial grant proposal to the first grant authorization to support the expense of a waste-to-energy facility. The next hurdle was a critical mass of active citizens opposed to the facility and to other locally unpopular land uses related to the new system. This opposition used various appeals processes to delay final approval of the incinerator, and attempted through the electoral process to alter the composition of the city council; but in the end these efforts failed. The remaining problems have derived from various aspects of the new system's implementation — resistance to change, increased costs, operational problems, changes in state and national policies, and continuing problems in dealing with pollution threats from the old landfill system.

In a very real sense this story has no ending. As long as the people of Spokane continue to generate solid waste, they will continue to adjust their solid waste management policies. In this as in many policy-making arenas, there is no final solution — only a continuing series of policy resolutions and attempts to implement them.

Public Policy
Theory

Social science literature contains a wide variety of theories for understanding how communities and societies formulate their public policies. Each theory provides insight into specific aspects of the complex dynamics involved in policy development, but none of them provides a perfect and complete explanation of those dynamics. Since no theory can be identified as the perfect theory, and because I rely on a theoretical foundation for my description of policy formulation, I think it is necessary both to review the major theories' strengths and weaknesses and to provide a rationale for the theoretical foundation I have chosen.

This chapter is designed to provide that review and rationale, and to demonstrate the utility of a creative and qualitative use of systems theory for describing and explaining a specific case study in public policy formulation — solid waste management policy in Spokane. My selection of systems theory as a vehicle for analysis is not meant to imply that it is the best theoretical base. Each theory provides an important avenue for better understanding the policy-making process. Systems theory provides a flexible framework for incorporating aspects of each theory's analytics, a framework that connects them in a multifaceted web of relations.

Each of the types of theory covered in this chapter is used to some extent in later chapters as I focus on a particular aspect of policy formulation as exemplified in the case of Spokane. Process theory is used most directly to examine the local political institutions in chapter 4, and in a less direct manner in examining federal and state policies in chapter 5. The types of political institutions found in a community, their structures and processes and their relations to each other have a significant impact on policy formulation. Federal and state institutions and processes, and the policies they adopt establish an influential context within which local politi-

cal institutions make decisions. Pluralist theory informs the examination in chapter 6 of citizen participation. Active citizens take it as a given that in order to influence public policy making they must organize into interest groups. Pluralist assumptions undergird most of the ways they attempt to sway public policy toward their preferred directions. Both elite and pluralist theories inform the analyses in chapter 7 on business influence and chapter 8 on media influence. If business's impacts on public policy formulation can be understood in pluralist terms, we must recognize that business interests have a special (elite?) place in interest group competition. The resources they bring to bear and the ways they operate seem better explained by the more sophisticated forms of elite and pluralist theory—structuralist and issue network theory.

Public Policy Theories

In 1971 David Ricci described five types of public policy theory: process, group, reputational elitism, positional elitism, and pluralism. At that time Ricci's work was a valuable overview and synthesis of the state of public policy theory, but our understanding of policy making has evolved over the years. In the more than twenty years since Ricci's work a number of other typologies have been proposed. Dye delineated seven models of policy making: institutionalism, group theory, elite theory, rationalism, incrementalism, game theory, and systems theory. Anderson delineated three types of decision-making theory (rational, incremental, and mixed scanning—after Charles Lindblom and Amitai Etzioni; cf. note 10 below), and four approaches to studying policy making (systems, group, elite, and institutional theory). Bosso's typology included pluralists, subgovernments, and issue networks (or presence politics).[1]

Despite the accumulation of additional policy theories and attempts to categorize those theories, the field has continued to suffer from an undertow caused by the continuation of what Ricci described as the pluralist-antipluralist impasse.[2] The lasting value of Ricci's typology was that it did not succumb to the temptation to take sides in the pluralist-antipluralist debate. Ricci simply described the theories and how they illuminated different aspects of policy making. Though he bemoaned the scholarly impasse public policy theory was in, and made some suggestions for future work, he did not reach an inclusive synthesis. Instead, he suggested that we lay "aside theoretical disputation and [concentrate] all our analytical energies on understanding and coping with" the many problems facing America. He suggested that we extricate ourselves from this impasse by examining "specific issues where the country clearly suffers great social, economic, and political problems."[3]

The work Ricci left undone, the evolution of policy making, and the evolution of our understanding of policy making since his work all demand an updated typology. Like Ricci's, the updated typology should not take sides in the pluralist-elitist debate; rather, it should include those sides within a more congenial perspective. I think the foundation for such a perspective was laid by David Easton's work on political systems theory (which was begun prior to Ricci's work). I also think that my work, building upon that foundation, operates in a manner Ricci would appreciate. As he suggested, it includes attention to process and a focus on the important problems facing the nation. The attention to process is provided by the dynamic interplay among and within the elements of the system. The focus on an important problem is provided by the case study of solid waste policy making.

The value of this inclusive perspective has not been realized previously because policy theorists, in addition to succumbing to this ideological distraction, have retreated into trivial methodological issues raised by the dominant behavioral school of political and social studies. It is beyond the scope of this work to provide an adequate review of the methodological dispute in political studies. Suffice it to say that while I appreciate the insights into politics and policy contributed by behavioralists, I believe a thorough appreciation of politics includes understanding that derives from sources other than the scientific method.

This book depends on case study methodology, one of many methods that supplement behavioral approaches. As a form of qualitative research,[4] case studies are grounded in the phenomena being studied. As a form of interpretive research, case studies provide a better understanding of what people say and do in social situations. Seeking to understand meaning(s) in a set of dynamics, the researcher enters into the situation and asks the participants "what it means to them, what they are doing, and why they are doing it."[5]

The major weakness of the case study approach is that it is difficult to generalize a case study's conclusions. Often there is no way of assuring the representativeness of the case; as Yin says, case studies "are generalizable to theoretical propositions and not to populations or universes."[6] Further, generalization may be impossible if the case study is told in narrative format with nothing more than a story line to organize it. As Heclo points out, under those conditions a case study may only "represent confused realism in search of an analytical framework."[7] In this book the case study is told in a brief narrative format in chapter 1, but chapters 3 through 8 are organized in the analytical format described later in this chapter. Still, my claim is better understood as one of transferability than of generalizability.[8] When I discuss this case with others interested in solid waste policy making (or, in some cases, in environmental or public works policy making), they tell me whether it sounds similar to phenomena they have studied or been involved in. They decide whether it transfers meaningfully into their context. And often they tell me it does.

A New Typology

As I mentioned earlier, my typology is based on Ricci's, but has been modified to take into account the evolution of public policy theorizing and understanding since his book. My first modification of Ricci's work is to treat group theory and pluralism together and to combine the two elitism theories. This should be relatively uncontroversial, since Ricci himself referred to those combinations as the pluralists and antipluralists.[9] Further, there are additional theories that require attention: subgovernment theory, structuralist theory, issue networks theory, public choice theory, and systems theory, to name a few. Although individual applications of each theory would show significant variations within them, this is not the place to examine all their possible permutations. The purpose of this review is to describe the types generally in order to introduce their major features, strengths, and weaknesses. Then I will present an introductory description of a general systems model derived from the work of David Easton and an argument supporting its utility in examining a specific case study by incorporating theoretical insights from a variety of perspectives. Finally, I will offer a brief initial application of my systems theory model to a case study of solid waste policy making in Spokane.

Process Theory

Process theory might be divided into two subtypes — institutional and abstract. Institutional process theory is one of the most basic theories for understanding how public policy is formulated. Its focus is on the role of government institutions and the manner in which their formal and legal aspects affect the creation of public policy. It explains policy by reference to such institutions as the executive, legislative, and judicial branches of government, the separation of powers, checks and balances, and federalism.

Less macroscopic versions of institutional theory focus on the internal processes of the institutions. For example, in explaining energy policy an institutionalist might describe how a particular energy bill became law — what the formal steps were and how assignment to particular committees or subcommittees for review might affect the substance and/or prospects of the bill.

The primary benefit of institutionalist theory is that an understanding of the government institutions involved in formulating it is a valuable beginning point for any approach to public policy. A good understanding of the formal structural and legal arrangements helps one to see how those arrangements affect the potentials for policy, but it is often insufficient as an explanation of why a particular policy took the shape it did. To use a game metaphor, knowing the rules of chess — which pieces can move in what manner — is a beginning point for understanding how to play chess, but it is not sufficient for a very sophisticated understanding of the plays made in a match between two masters of the game.

One of the weaknesses of institutional process theory is that its explanation of policy development within a particular context is difficult to apply to another set of institutions. We need to go beyond the processes evident within or among specific given institutions to a conception that can be applied to policy formulation in different settings involving a wide variety of institutions. Abstract process theory has answered that need. A contemporary example of abstract process theory is found in the conceptual framework of James E. Anderson's *Public Policy-Making*. Abstract process theory provides a way to compare public policy making among different institutional and cultural settings.

Versions of abstract process theory that focus on a more microcosmic level of policy making (i.e., decision making) include rationalism and incrementalism.[10] Rationalism describes decision making as involving a complete understanding of the problem, a thorough review of the options, and a decision based on a rational evaluation of those options. Incrementalism describes decision making as involving minor adjustments of the status quo that arise from the application of rational thinking limited by the human capacity for rational thinking, time and cost constraints, and the need for compromise, bargaining, and adjustments among a diverse set of participants.

Although abstract process theories address the generalizability weakness of institutional process theory, they do little to deal with another significant weakness of process theory: most process theorists recognize that policy development does not follow a single, consistent, linear map, but their theoretical model strongly implies such a linear path.[11] Moreover, because the steps in the process are rarely followed in a straightforward fashion, applying the models to specific policy-making cases can be frustrating and confusing.

In addition to these theoretical weaknesses, process theories do not adequately address what some believe to be the most pressing political question for public policy theory: Is this democracy? They fail in two ways. First, as Ricci points out, if they address the question they beg it—they simply label the processes they observe as democratic.[12] Second, in limiting their criteria for democracy to process issues they most often fail to address the substantive dimension of democracy.

Elitist Theory

Elitist theory constituted a significant rebuttal to process theory, challenging it in two ways. First, it challenged whether the processes examined by process theory were significantly related to policy making. Second, in arguing that policy making was not accomplished in the open processes of representative democracy, it asserted that policy making in the United States was not democratic.

Elitist theory can be subdivided into three types: reputational, positional (also known as instrumental), and structural. The first two are based on how the elites are identified. Floyd Hunter's reputational approach identified the powerful elites influencing policy making in a community by asking people whom they thought of as powerful.[13] Because he believed that "to have power requires access to major institutions," C. Wright Mills's positional approach identified elites by their position in important social institutions.[14] Despite the methodological differences, both of these elitist theories focus on identifying a "ruling elite" not directly involved in public political processes, but "pulling the strings" of those who are directly involved. According to these theories the real power resides within a narrow concentration of people, the uppermost social stratum.

Finding some method for identifying the members of the elite is an important aspect of these elite theories because they hold that the elite are by definition not publicly active, and therefore not readily visible as public policy influencers. Most often their influence has to be inferred from the visible evidence of policy formulation; for example, it might be inferred from the adoption of a policy change that the elites preferred that particular change (or at least did not oppose it). Because the elites do not engage in

public discussion and debate about the pros and cons of policies, the benefits they perceive as deriving from a policy must also be a matter of speculation. The logic of inference and speculation can become rather circular:
"they" must have supported (or not opposed) this policy because it was
passed; since it passed, it must result in some benefit to them; and their
continued status as the elite is evidence that "they" continue to benefit from
public policy in general, which must mean that "they" generally support the
policies adopted.

Beyond this circular logic, which makes elitist theories virtually impossible to prove (or disprove), there are a few other problems with these
theories of public policy formulation. First, they effectively dismiss political
activity as meaningless. Deutsch expressed the elite theorists' position by
arguing that the question "Who governs?" is irrelevant; the relevant question is "Who benefits?" Political activity provides only indirect evidence of
the real and important policy-making activities.[15] Political actors are seen as
mere puppets of the elite; but the "puppets" are often egotistical, ambitious, aggressive, and dynamic people who would be unlikely to accept such
an arrangement passively and compliantly. Second, simply because someone has (or is reputed to have) access to resources does not necessarily
mean that s/he will use them for political purposes. The main thesis of
Bellah et al. is that people in American society have become too little ori-
ented toward public, community, and political concerns.[16] If they are correct the "elite" are quite likely to be focused upon acquiring their material
goods and going to vacation resorts when they are not working for material
rewards, leaving public policy to the few citizen activists and professional
politicians remaining in the community.

Finally, the Hunter and Mills elitist theories both depend on a stable set
of elite relations. Mills admits that the three sectors of his elite structure
(economic, political, and military) do have a "tension" among them. It is
difficult to imagine a loosely knit group of powerful, aggressive, ambitious
individuals who would not have serious and contentious differences. But for
traditional elite theorists it is clear that "somebody has got to run the
show,"[17] and because it is not us, it must be them.

A more recent version of elite theory includes political activists among
the policy-making elite. It is a different kind of elite theory, pointing as it
does to a different elite. Bosso calls this theory the subgovernment or "presence politics" approach. Within it he includes those who describe policy as
being formulated within "iron triangles" or policy issue networks. This approach qualifies as an elite theory because it describes policy making as an

activity in which only a select group may participate. Those who participate in presence politics are, by definition, regularly present in forums where policy is being discussed. Their participation hinges upon "deep and expert knowledge of an issue." That means that only a small percentage of the populace belongs to the "presence politics" club. Presence politics is by nature exclusive; "subgovernments seek to privatize conflict." Expansion of the pool of policy-making participants beyond the members of the subgovernment is the point at which "subgovernment explodes into pluralist policy making."[18]

There are other reasons why subgovernment politics should be classified as an elitist theory. The first is that among those who do participate policy making is more often accomplished through mutual accommodation than through competition. In pluralist theory (as will be explained shortly) competition among interest groups is the key dynamic among participants. Second, most often the general public is not aware of the subgovernment's policy-making activity. Because subgovernment policy making is done among a limited set of participants, and competition might lead one group of participants to bring in other participants to improve their odds, the practice of mutual accommodation facilitates relative secrecy. Secrecy is more characteristic of elite theories than of pluralist theories.

Probably the most sophisticated evolution of elite theory is structuralist theory. Instead of arguing that the elite operate government through their puppets, by personally connecting with and dominating state officials, structuralism argues "that the government is constrained to serve the interests of large corporations by the economic, ideological, and political underpinnings of capitalism (by the 'structure' of American society), regardless of the intentions of government officials or the machinations of business leaders." Government relies on corporate cooperation to go about its function in society, and corporations rely on government to maintain sufficient stability for them to go about their business. Moreover, both government and corporate leaders possess a common ideology, "one that assumes that people are naturally selfish and that decentralization of power is the best solution to the problems produced by this unfortunate psychological reality."[19] That ideology functions as another structural force keeping potential policy choices within safe parameters.

Structuralist theory retains the main theme of elite theory — that policy making in the United States is essentially at the service of the elite — but it also incorporates the most compelling arguments of the process and pluralist theories. Using the insights of institutional process theory, structuralists describe the ways in which government institutions are linked to private institutions. Using the insights of pluralist theory, structuralists describe the ways in which those linkages help government institutions to serve the corporate elite's interests. With the advent of structuralist theory, elite theory has evolved beyond its simple conspiratorial depiction of a ruling class engaged in remote control of the institutions of government. In their disputation with pluralists, structuralists have adapted some of pluralism's insights to fit a more sophisticated depiction of policy making in late-twentieth-century America.

Group Theory and Pluralist Theory

Both group theory and pluralist theory explain public policy by focusing on the manner in which interest groups drive its formulation and substance. Competition among interest groups to influence the structure, content, and timing of policy results in some kind of compromise, accommodation, or victorious coalition. Pluralism has become the dominant theoretical perspective in political writing in the United States; it comes in many varieties. I will, however, limit this review to an explanation of the fundamental aspects of pluralist theory. Pluralism is defined by Ladd as a "concept referring to a society as composed of diverse interests and groups which compete to achieve their social and political objectives and share in the exercise of political power." Truman defines the term *interest group* as "a shared-attitude group that makes certain claims upon other groups in the society."[20]

The difference between David Truman's group theory and Robert Dahl's pluralism[21] is essentially one of historical context. Truman's early work, which preceded the elite theories of Hunter and Mills, attempted to add a degree of sophistication to process theory by gathering empirical data "to demonstrate that the political process in America is dominated by the behavior and attitudes of groups."[22] When Truman analyzed the significance of his work twenty years later, he too equated the general theoretical perspectives of his group theory with those of the pluralists. And as Truman notes, a school of political philosophers known as the pluralists preceded his and Dahl's work and reached their apex of influence in the first quarter of the twentieth century. Truman says of them: "They were so bent upon discrediting prevailing conceptions of the state that they frequently overlooked the central significance of their point of view."[23]

Dahl was working in direct contention with the supporters of elitist theory. He said that the argument between elitists and pluralists regarding power distribution in a community revolves around the question of whether the elite "dominate the decisions of public governments; if so, how, where, and why? If not, what groups or strata do have the most influence over the decisions of public governments, how, where, why, etc.?"[24]

In contrast to elite theorists, pluralist theorists describe government as playing a very important role in policy making — it is the referee. "Government provides the arena for conflict resolution within which social forces lock horns; government supplies the procedures for conflict resolution, sets the rules of the game, but takes no sides in the ensuing fight. Government is neutral."[25] Its activity is aimed at ensuring that all "active and legitimate groups" can be heard in the policy discourse on any given topic.[26]

This is not to say that pluralists are Pollyannic about the role of government. Truman recognized that the "characteristics of government" at any given time are the product of the gradual evolution of its relations to interest groups, potential groups, and the rules of the game. He also considered "the notion of the administrator as a neutralized public servant" an illusion, and said that the groups with which administrators identify (or from which they have been recruited) will make a difference in how they perceive disputes between conflicting groups.[27] Neither are they unmindful of the differences among interest groups with respect to their influence on policy making. Like the elite theorists, pluralists recognize the superior organization and influence of business interests. It is the fluidity of participation that they think prevents the establishment of a power elite. Dahl, however, preferred the term *polyarchy* to signify this type of system, which is not dominated by an elite, falls short of pure democracy because it has elite leaders, but has democratic elements.[28]

In addition to the constantly changing cast of characters that results from the many avenues through which interests may participate in policy making, pluralist theory identifies three basic forces that keep public policy making a democratic process. The first is portrayed as some kind of "potential" power. Truman used the term *potential group* to denote one that can either form or renew its activism given the proper incentive. He argued that a potential group would become an actual one if the government failed in its role of assuring fair play.[29] Dahl used the term *slack power* to refer to power available to the ordinarily passive citizens, power they can use if given sufficient incentive. These concepts are crucial to the pluralist theories' explanation of how apparently uninvolved and apathetic masses can nonetheless indirectly set significant parameters around potentially self-serving abuses of the policy-making processes in which elites or organized groups might otherwise engage. The potential power of inactive groups and of the general public are threats that keep public policy within a democratically acceptable range, that keep the more actively influential elites or interest groups from simply raiding the public resources for their own selfish purposes.

The second force that, according to pluralism, maintains the democratic nature of policy making is the legitimizing recognition of some generally acceptable format for democratic decision making. Truman argued that groups recognized certain "rules of the game," and Dahl argued that they adhered to a kind of "democratic creed." Truman offered a tentative list of those rules:

> Acceptance of the rule of law over a resort either to violence or to arbitrary official action, the guarantees of the Bill of Rights, effective modes of mass participation both in the institutions of government itself and in the organized groups in the society broadly, and a measure of equality of access to the fruits of the social enterprise.[30]

Adherence to the rules, Truman noted, is stronger among the politically active than among the general public. In both theories, the procedures and values attached to a general notion of democracy are portrayed as forming the foundation for the actions of the more politically involved citizens, and it is those people who make public policy.

The third force that gives pluralistic policy making a claim to democratic status is the "invisible hand" in the dynamic of the marketplace of ideas. With each group speaking on behalf of its interests, the theory says that the competition among the groups will lead to a resolution that approximates the public interest. This may be expressed in a simple mathematical formula:

$$f(g1 + g2 + g3 + \ldots gn) = G$$

meaning that the common good (G) is achieved as a function (f) of the combined activities of each group seeking its own self-interest (g). It is important to note here that in pluralistic theory there is no need (or allowance) for groups or persons explicitly pursuing their vision of the common good.

Pluralism, of course, also has its problems, and they may be divided into two types: theoretical and political. By theoretical problems I mean those adversely affecting a theory's ability to describe adequately public policy-making dynamics. Included among these problems are the theories' potential for understating the importance of elites and for overestimating the power of quiescent groups or the general public. Political participation tends to increase with socioeconomic status and education, so we need to "stop talking about interests as if they were free and equal."[31] In addition, the pluralist position that government acts as a neutral referee is dubious. "Government takes sides through its structures, its rules and laws, and through a systematic consensus about what does or does not legitimately fall within its purview."[32] As Salisbury points out, the relationship between interests and government institutions is dynamic and protean. As interests gain or lose clout, the institutions through which they seek to wield their influence change in structure and mission.[33] When the relationships become so intertwined that they may be described as codependent, they are better described by subgovernment theory. Even when they are not that cozy, the players are not evenly matched and they do not play on an even (or stable) field.

Further, when pluralist theories attempt to describe the nature of intergroup relations, they tend to reduce them to a kind of economic exchange dynamic,[34] thereby overemphasizing economic rationality at the expense of interpersonal, psychological, political, and moral aspects. The problems with this facet of pluralism can perhaps best be seen by looking at a policy theory that has evolved from pluralism and has been the basis for an elaboration of the rational economic aspect of the pluralist argument. Public choice theory is "the application of economics to political science," and adopts a modified Pareto optimality framework to explain policy formulation.[35] Though public choice theory can also be understood as a variant of rational choice theory, I see it as a variant of pluralism. Like pluralism, public choice theory rejects elitist theory "because genuine consensus under constitutional rules does not imply a class basis for social change. . . . In this approach public policy is not something legislated by or for powerful lobbies or the wealthy capitalists."[36]

Pluralism takes the interest group as its basic unit of analysis; public choice theory, however, takes as its basic unit the rational, self-interested individual (although it also applies its rational economic model to group behavior).[37] Given a specific set of assumptions, public choice theory describes individual behavior as seeking to maximize utility.[38] Proceeding from an assumption that the actors are economically rational, public choice theorists have difficulty allowing that people (individually and collectively) do not always act in ways that redound to their material benefit. But as important as economic interests may be, people's sense of right and wrong, their view of the common good, and their interest in expressing their views are also part of their decision making.[39]

The political problems of pluralist theories result from pluralists' defense of the existence of true democracy (as distinct from pure democracy) by explaining how group or pluralist dynamics are democratic in nature and effect. This has given their descriptions an ideological tint that detracts from their contribution to political studies. A general theme running through these problems is democratic equality: in a democracy each person and each group should have the same potential for affecting public policy. But even if it were fair to assume that all political interests could and would be represented and defended through group activities, interest groups would still differ in size and resources, so their impact on policy deliberations would also likely be different. Truman, in fact, describes the "constantly changing pattern of relationships involving through the years continual shifts in relative influence" as "the most significant feature of group politics."[40] Dahl also admits that inequalities of power exist, but, he argues, they are dispersed rather than cumulative.[41] For him, this means that no group can gather sufficient power to dominate all policy making, because of the power held by other groups. But interest groups also differ significantly in their zones of interest; therefore, they do not necessarily check each other's power through their individual political activities.[42] There may be no effective group to counterbalance the influence of those who advocate a particular policy. Traditional pluralist theories do not assure democratic equality; they tend either to assume it or to assert that since the inequalities are not cumulative, they pose no threat to democracy.

Just as structuralist theory represents a sophisticated version of elitist theory, issue network theory represents a sophisticated kind of pluralist theory. As a counterargument to the theory of subgovernments, Heclo in 1978 introduced under the term *issue networks* a conception of interest group dynamics that is more complex than traditional pluralism. Arguing that the notions of iron triangles and subgovernments were "disastrously incomplete," he critiqued them for describing the participants in policy making as largely autonomous.[43]

Participation in issue networks is open, and no one is in charge. Intellectual and emotional commitment outstrip economic interest as motivation for action. Members of issue networks do not become involved in issues because of the way they affect their interests; they become interested in policies because of the way those policies affect their issues. Sharing a way of understanding policies, they are a shared-knowledge group, but they may not coalesce into a shared-action group, much less a shared-belief group. Instead of policy being formed by the machinations of a stable set of elites

(or, for that matter, by competition among a stable set of interest groups),
discussion of policy issues takes place in the "kaleidoscopic interaction of
changing issue networks."[44]

Because issue networks are depicted as open and fluid, it is fair to categorize policy theories based on them as pluralist. But Heclo says this new
dynamic augments subgovernment politics rather than replacing it. This
makes issue network theory a more sophisticated kind of pluralism. Instead
of competing with elite theory, it subsumes it. It accepts elitist theory's
concern that only a small portion of the public becomes involved in policy
making, but it identifies those who do participate as the more knowledgeable and/or the more interested, not the economic elite. In response to this
challenge to democratic governance, Heclo offers a traditional pluralist line
in explaining how the rest of the public depend upon "the ability of government institutions to act on their behalf."[45]

Like elite theory, pluralist theory has become more sophisticated in its
depiction of policy making. From Dahl's adoption of the concept of polyarchy to Heclo's issue networks, there is an admission that the American
democracy comprises significant impurities—impurities that validate some
of the objections elite theory raised against pluralist theory. Still, pluralist
theory continues to emphasize that the glass is half full.

Systems Theory

Political systems theory has the potential to incorporate insights from all
of the theories discussed above. One way of understanding systems theory is
to see it as an abstract process theory that successfully addresses the problem of linearity. Because the processes in systems theory circle back through
the system, they do not imply a misleading "it begins here and ends there"
linearity. Political systems theory includes attention to the institutions and
processes of government, describing those processes as part of a cyclical
dynamic within an abstraction called a political system. As will be demonstrated later, political systems theory also includes the impacts of elites and
groups among the multitude of environmental factors affecting the system.
In addition, both pluralists and elitists recognize the significance of the
political system,[46] but neither group takes the concept seriously enough to
develop it the way systems theorists do.

In 1955, similar developments in such diverse fields as physics, biology,
the study of biological populations, econometrics, cybernetics, information
theory, and operations research led Ludwig von Bertalanffy to propose a
general system theory, designed to offer a chance to identify the "universal

principles applying to systems in general."[47] Since his work establishes a foundation for more easily understanding Easton's political systems theory, it merits a brief review.

The first principle of general systems theory Bertalanffy discusses is the difference between open and closed systems. Closed systems are assumed to be isolated from their environments, and thus not influenced by them. Open systems, on the other hand, maintain themselves through continuous inflow and outflow between themselves and their environments. Through feedback they are able to engage in purposive behavior, to learn from changes in information, to adapt accordingly, and to progress toward an identified goal. Open systems also provide a basis for explaining cyclical fluctuations, and—in a principle that sounds a lot like pluralism—the explanation of fluctuations relates the stability of a system to the number of competing organizations: the more competing organizations, the greater the stability of the system.[48]

David Easton defines the political system as all those activities and institutions involved in the formulation and execution of social policies that are binding upon society—the authoritative allocations of values. "A policy is authoritative when the people to whom it is intended to apply or who are affected by it consider that they must or ought to obey it."[49] Easton also presents a graphic depiction of that system. His model is an example of an open system, depicting the inflow and outflow of exchanges between the political system and its environment.[50] Easton's model divides environmental influences on the system into intra- and extrasocietal categories. These environmental factors are described as affecting the "political system" (Easton's version of institutions) by either placing demands on or providing support for the system.

Political systems theory, like the other theories of public policy making, has its problems. One problem is that it depicts a set of interrelationships in a way that appears to freeze them into a particular configuration. As I will explain shortly, the system should depict a relatively stable complex of relationships, but it need not imply that those relationships are static. There remains much potential for fluctuation within the system without necessitating a change in its basic structure.

Another problem derives from the generality and inclusiveness of systems theory. On the one hand its level of abstraction means that it can incorporate other theoretical perspectives; on the other, its incorporation of other theories means that to some degree it incorporates their problems as well as their insights. Utilized to best advantage, however, it ameliorates their problems by recasting them and, in the case of political systems theory, by balancing its use of the elite and pluralist perspectives. Still, the inclusiveness of political systems theory can be seen as both a strength and a weakness. While the abstract categories it uses to generalize across systems enable it to explain actions after they have taken place, they also make problematic the use of systems theory to predict future events in any given political system. The predictions of the "limits to growth" model, for example, derived significantly from the assumptions built into it. If one assumes that a system has limited carrying capacities, and that the demand on those capacities is going to continue to grow, then no matter what policy adjustments are made some carrying capacity is eventually going to be overtaxed.[51]

The interrelatedness of all of the elements of the system and its environment can account for the many ways in which public policy can be influenced, but it does not help us to assess which of those elements will have greater influence in a specific instance. In order to understand the impact of elements of the system, one must examine it rigorously and in detail; that is why when I use it I apply it to a specific case study.

THE SPOKANE SOLID WASTE POLICY SYSTEM MODEL

By combining the abstractness of political systems theory with the concreteness of a particular case study, we can gain some appreciation for the usefulness of a specific application of a systems model as well as for the general import of the dynamics of the case study. The system depicts a general set of relationships involved in policy making. The case study demonstrates the particular ways those relationships manifest themselves in and influence policy making in a given arena, and the degree and significance of fluctuations within the system's structure. Combining a systems model with a case study also addresses one of the major problems systems theory has faced—its rather static presentation of the relationships among the elements. While the systems model represents the basic structure of the relationships, the case study brings in the changes in those relations that take place over time. By applying an adaptation of Easton's systems model, I will begin to demonstrate how the abstractness of a systems model, combined with the particulars of the Spokane solid waste policy system, provides a powerful heuristic tool for better understanding solid waste policy making.

Figure 2.1 shows my general model of a local solid waste policy system. While it is based on Easton's system model, it differs from his in some significant ways. First, it describes a local rather than a national political system. Changes in the model that result from the local focus include the transformation of the intra- and extrasocietal environments into intra- and extracommunity environments, and the political system into the local political system. It also changes what is depicted within the "system" and what is included in the "environment." These changes are not significant departures from Easton's theoretical framework, because his understanding of the political system included recognition of it as a subsystem of the more inclusive social system and of the interrelatedness of it all. According to Easton, "All systems are constructs of the mind," and the tests of a system construct are whether it coheres and whether it assists understanding.[52] For him the political system is a reasonable delimitation of the focus of political

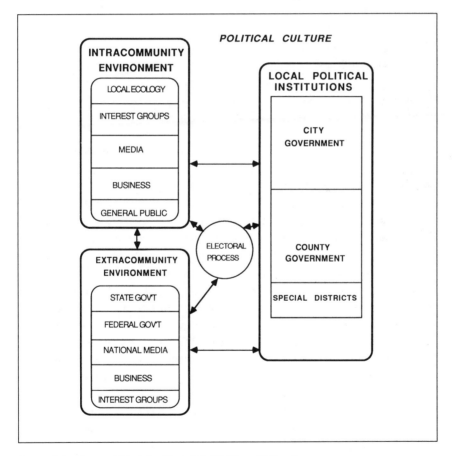

Figure 2.1   General Model of Local Solid Waste Policy System

science. Since one of the contributions of my study is the examination of policy making from a local perspective, it is reasonable to alter the model to reflect that. Easton might call the system in my model a "parapolitical system" because it is a subsystem of a societal political system.[53]

Second, my model does not explicitly differentiate the flows (i.e., interactions) between the environment and the system according to Easton's concepts of demand, support, input, and output. I could have used those terms, or differentiated them in more concrete terms, but because the kinds of flows are too numerous to delineate in a simple model such as this, and because some inputs may be received as demands by some portions of the political system and as support by others, the model does not attempt to reflect all the variations the abstract concept of flows may comprise. Instead, it simplifies the flows by incorporating within a single graphic feature a variety of kinds of interactions, including studies, press communications, official papers, and personal contacts.

Third, neither my general model nor its application in the Spokane model (fig. 2.2) leaves the political system as some kind of black box containing unnamed authorities who make binding allocations of values. The application of the general model to the specific case helps to explain the reasons behind this difference. It is easier to follow the complex web of interactions in the case study when these details are included in the model. For example, the Spokane model contains explicit recognition of specific institutional elements of special importance in Spokane solid waste policy making. The local government institutions of greatest importance are the city and county governments and the Solid Waste Disposal Project office (SWDP). The city government is a council-manager type with a weak mayor. The county government is a commission form with many elected officials, the most important in solid waste policy making being the three commissioners; there is also an appointed county administrator. SWDP is depicted as within and between the city and county government institutions because it is the creation of an interlocal agreement between the two more traditional institutions. Within SWDP are two other key institutions: the Solid Waste Advisory Committee (SWAC) and the Technical Advisory Committee (TAC). Both SWAC and TAC were citizen advisory committees. Adjacent to SWDP are a couple of policy organs that served as vehicles for coordinating with the city council, county commission, and the smaller cities within the county — the Project Policy Committee (PPC) and the Project Liaison Board (PLB). Other local institutions that are of importance to this case study include the Spokane County Health District, the Spokane County Air Pollution Control Authority, and the Spokane International Airport Authority. The roles the local political institutions played in this case study will be detailed in chapter 4.

Also given special attention within the Spokane model are a few characteristics suggested by Robert Waste's city ecology model.[54] The age and growth process factors suggest that an elected body such as a city council tends to have a life cycle similar to that described by Anthony Downs for bureaus.[55] In the earlier stages of its life cycle a city council may be dominated by aggressive advocates of change, but once those advocates have either obtained most of their goals or tired of the frustrations involved in making the attempt, the council tends to become dominated by "conservers" who strive simply to maintain the basic set of city services and are not

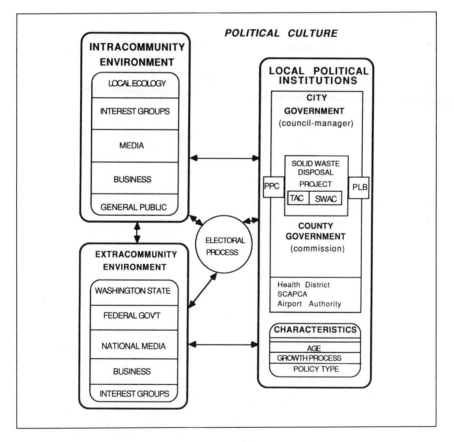

Figure 2.2   Spokane's Solid Waste Policy Model

interested in moving in new directions. When the city management staff has been in office much longer than most of the city council members and has become indispensable to the agenda of the dominant conservers, the elected officials are likely to become quite dependent on them. An attempt by a new set of aggressive change agents to win elected office is often perceived as a threat by both the dominant council members and the management staff. In Spokane, which changed to a city manager form of government in 1960 and had had the same city manager for 12 years, the 1989 elections represented such a threat. Members of the "anti-incinerator slate" were often described as incapable of working with the continuing members of the council, and many expected that a victory by that slate would result in the ouster of the city manager because of his role in promoting the waste-to-energy project.

Waste further suggests that the type of policy being considered may be a significant factor within the local political system. Among the policy types he discusses is Paul Schulman's distinction between large-scale and smaller scale policies.[56] A major distinguishing feature of large-scale policies is their "go–no go" nature, which results from the requirement to commit to large outlays of resources over a significant span of time. This feature can pose a threat to traditional democratic policy making, which often includes more flexibility both in the original decision and over the life span of a program. Public facility projects such as waste-to-energy facilities seem to fit Schulman's description. In Spokane's solid waste policy making there were three "go–no go" decisions.[57] The first came at the end of a round-table discussion by the core government officials after their tours of other waste-to-energy facilities; the second was the creation of the liaison board and the SWDP through an interlocal agreement; and the third came in the midst of citizen opposition at a point when the contract with Wheelabrator had to be renegotiated. At this last decision point, government officials did a head count of the opposition appearing at the city council meeting that night and decided that the opposition had not grown sufficiently to cause them to reverse their direction.

Spokane's waste-to-energy facility was budgeted at more than $600 million over a thirty-year life span. Not only was that a relatively long-term commitment for the city; it was also a rather large financial outlay for a city with an annual budget in the neighborhood of $125 million. One aspect of the threat to democratic decision making and accountability is the fact that so few contractors were capable of delivering such a project that the city found itself in a weak negotiating position — weaker even than in other relatively large public facility projects. For example, a new coliseum for Spokane was estimated to cost $38 million, and numerous contractors bid on the project.

Let us consider one more instance of the impact of policy type. Ripley and Franklin distinguish four types of domestic policy: distributive, competitive regulatory, protective regulatory, and redistributive.[58] In the scope of policy making covered in this case study, those distinctions are applicable to portions of the policy making, but not to the overall dynamics. Examples of distributive policy in this case study included the technical and financial incentives EPA used to urge states to adhere to federal standards, and the $60 million grant WDOE provided to assist Spokane in financing the waste-to-energy facility. Competitive regulatory policy was exemplified by Washington State's Utilities and Transportation Commission's regulation of solid waste collection and hauling companies. The air and water pollution regulations governing solid waste management were protective regulatory policies. Flow control ordinances, since their purpose was to assure that payments for local solid waste collection and hauling accrued to the benefit of the governmentally sanctioned solid waste management system rather than to competing private operations, might be considered a kind of redistributive policy. But solid waste policy in general does not fit within the parameters of any one policy type.

A fourth way in which both my general model and the Spokane model differ from Easton's is that I identify different aspects of the intra- and extra-environments than did Easton. Both of my models bring into focus many of the ways in which the local community affects (or attempts to affect) policy. The intracommunity environment includes the local ecology, interest groups, media, businesses, and the general public. Some of the inputs from this part of the environment were active and some were passive. For example, once the importance to the local community of the Spokane-Rathdrum aquifer was recognized and a threat to that aquifer by past solid waste management practices was identified, the influence of that ecological factor on solid waste policy making derived from the generally accepted assumption that no new policy could be allowed to increase that threat. This ecological factor (though it had a defender in the Aquifer Protection Program within the county engineering department) did not, then, require active and aggressive assertion in the political system. As a consequence, no one ever effectively questioned whether an in-county ash landfill would have to be sited outside the aquifer protection zone. That was a given with which all of the policy options had to cope.

My model also depicts interactions between the intra- and extra-environments, while Easton's does not. This is one point on which I believe my model clearly improves upon his. I do not think Easton would argue that there is no interaction between, for example, the social systems of his intra-societal environment and the international social systems of his extrasocietal environment. In this connection both my models give special attention to the electoral process as one type of interaction between the local political system and its environments. In this case study the significance of the 1989 elections dictated that the electoral process be given special attention; inclusion in my general model may be read as an optimistic note regarding the significance of elections in American public policy making.

The ways in which all the elements in the system interrelate with each other is quite varied and complex. Personal contacts are found among the intra- and extracommunity environments and the local political system. They range from conversations between interest group members and SWDP staff to interviews conducted by journalists with proponents or opponents of the facility, and include informal relations among individual consultants, businesspersons, journalists, citizen activists, and public officials. Specific examples of personal contacts would include the father-son relationship between city council member Bob Dellwo and Dennis Dellwo, who served as attorney for WMX for a while, as well as personal attacks by opponents of the incinerator on county commissioner Pat Mummey.[59]

There were also many public hearings and workshops conducted in relation to this project. Most, but not all, of the hearings were conducted by government officials. Interest groups such as the Lance Hill Coalition held many meetings at which the public was welcome, and some to which the public was expressly invited. The local chapter of the League of Women Voters organized their own meetings, inviting speakers to discuss the project with the general public. The League also contracted with SWDP to facilitate the public workshops the latter conducted in connection with many facets of the project. Since county commission meetings did not include an open public comment session and city council meetings did, each time the agenda of the council meetings included an item related to the project, the open public comment session became an avenue for complaints about the project.

Studies, official papers, and press communications were commonly used by the local governments to communicate with their local community. Although the studies did not generally attain a wide readership, they were carefully read by the most active citizen participants. Often citizen activists made an issue out of the availability of the studies, complaining about the number of copies made available, the absence of clear procedures for obtaining copies, and the amount of time it took for them to gain access to a copy. Official papers, such as contracts and letters pertaining to contracts or grants, were even less widely distributed, but were also obtainable by persistent citizens. Most citizens obtained their knowledge of the results of the studies and the conditions of grants and contracts through press coverage. The media were also used by government officials to present to the public information they considered important — including notices of public meetings and workshops as well as interpretations of their studies and favorable opinions concerning the project.

Flows of interaction between the local political system and the extra-community environment can also be generally described as public hearings/workshops, personal contacts, studies, press communications, official papers, and lobbying. The nature, frequency, and direction of those flows are, however, somewhat different. Although state and federal officials might attend local government hearings or workshops, they are more likely to conduct hearings and workshops that local government officials will be required (or well advised) to attend. For example, when WDOE held workshops for local SWAC members, local elected officials and local government staff members also attended. Similarly, although state and federal officials read the official papers of and studies done by or for local officials, they were probably overseeing compliance with their guidelines; but when local officials read federal or state studies and official papers, they were probably taking instructions limiting their options.

The term *lobbying* covers a wide variety of ways in which people attempt to communicate with and influence government officials. Spokane local government officials have expressed a preference for personal, face-to-face conversations, phone calls, and letters from individuals; they do not find mass produced letters terribly impressive. Spokane citizen activists, on the other hand, have found direct lobbying to be among the least effective methods they might use to influence policy.[60]

Lobbying activities flow in both directions between the extracommunity environment and the local political system. When the Washington State legislature was considering whether to rescind their appropriation of $60 million for WDOE's grant to support the Spokane waste-to-energy facility, SWDP, city, and county officials engaged in various efforts to prevent such an action. They had someone in Olympia working on this issue every week during that legislative session. Similar efforts were made by the same parties to keep WDOE from changing its decision to provide the grant. WDOE seemed interested in seeing what else they might do with the $60 million. From the other direction, both private sector and interest group representatives from the extracommunity environment participated in efforts to influence those in the local political system. Spokespersons for waste management companies and for environmental groups from elsewhere in the state and the country wrote letters and made visits as part of an effort to affect local decisions, especially when they were seen as potentially setting precedents for the state and/or the nation.

Interaction between the intracommunity and extracommunity environments also flows in both directions and takes many forms. For example, appeals of local decisions by local interest groups often went to the state or federal courts — or to the administrative agencies (EPA, WDOE) authorized to override local decisions. Also, local interest groups' attempts to stop the waste-to-energy facility through action at the state level precipitated the lobbying of the legislature and WDOE by local officials mentioned above. In addition, networking among local interest groups around the nation is assisted by national interest groups with parallel agendas and contributes to the likelihood of national groups lobbying local decision makers. Similarly, there are corporate connections among local, state, and national companies engaged in various aspects of public facility and solid waste management planning, consulting, and contracting.

A fifth way my models differ from Easton's is the inclusion of political culture. I doubt that Easton would deny the significance of political culture, but it is not clear where it might fit into his model. It is also true that explicit treatment of political culture in Easton's model would have made the boundary between political system and environment less distinct — a development Easton would not have welcomed. Because political culture affects a political system in so many different ways, my models acknowledge its impact by depicting it as enveloping the system. As will be explained in the next chapter, Spokane's political culture is best understood as a subculture of the political culture of the state of Washington, the American West, and the United States. Since political cultures change only gradually, the local policy options that can be considered seriously are those that will be accepted as legitimate within the local culture. In Spokane this meant that those wishing to commit very large sums of money to the waste-to-energy option had to find a way to do it without depending too heavily on the local public's willingness to pay for it. It also meant that those opposed to the waste-to-energy option faced a difficult, but not impossible, task in convincing locals that they had to become involved in the political struggle to derail the waste-to-energy project. In contrast to the San Diego experience,[61] even though opponents in Spokane were able to polarize the community on the waste-to-energy issue, they were unable to generate enough dissatisfaction to elect a majority on the city council and stop the project.

Unlike Easton's, the system in my models includes all of the elements in the models — even the environments. In Easton's model the political system is distinct from the environment; in my models the local political institutions are in a position parallel to Easton's political system. This is a sensitive point for systems analysis. It brings to the fore the difficulty of establishing boundaries in systems. One of the most basic ideas in systems analysis is that everything is related to everything else. In order to depict those relations, we must identify elements of the system as distinct entities, thus implying that they are separate from each other. As Easton explains, boundaries in systems "are products of analytic selection,"[62] but the relationships are more vital aspects of the understanding the analysis is intended to communicate.

The final, and perhaps most fundamental difference between my use of systems theory and Easton's is that I do not use systems theory to examine how the system copes with the stresses it is subjected to by the environment, while Easton does.[63] Though the ability of a system to adapt, and therefore to survive, is a traditional feature of systems theory, my concern is directed toward how the system responds to a policy problem. I want to know whether and how the system's responses serve the communities it affects, not whether the system is able to survive the stresses arising from the problem's appearance on the political agenda.

Even careful readers of Easton might be surprised by my claim that he might approve of the use I make of his systems model. After all, his development of the political systems approach and the model were key parts of his program for improving "the reliability of political knowledge and understanding"[64] through behavioral rigor in empirical political science research. I find that qualitative empiricism contributes significantly to our understanding of policy making, and my use of the model is mainly qualitative or postbehavioral. In the 1950s Easton was a leading figure in the behavioral movement within political science; but by the 1970s his perspective had evolved to include a recognition of the need to apply what professional students of political phenomena had learned to the pressing problems of the day.[65] Easton recognized that political science had not achieved a general theory, and that his systems theory was a conceptual structure, a theoretical framework for analysis, not a broadly integrated statement about the relationship of variables. Though political systems analysis might appear "forbiddingly remote from reality," he saw it as providing "some simple imagery to help us understand the scope of our interests in most inclusive terms" and as facilitating "research about practical social issues."[66]

CONCLUSION

Bosso may be correct in his assessment: "Perhaps no single image of policy making can convey the rich complexity of policy roles and lines of influence evident in this political system."[67] But a systems model offers a good approximation. Within it one can include insights gained through attention to political and social processes. One can examine the influence of elites, whether they are seen as members of a ruling class, as members of a policy network, or as beneficiaries of the structure of government-business relations. The impact of interest group competition and accommodation can also be included, as can the influence of general cultural patterns and specific cultural changes. A policy systems model is an attempt to depict the relationships among, within, and between all these factors that affect the formulation of public policy.

The specific nature of these interrelations and their impacts, as well as the specifics of the other major elements delineated in the model, are the heart of the politics of solid waste policy making. This chapter has begun to demonstrate the utility of a systems model in providing a framework for the introduction of important aspects of the dynamic relationships involved in this policy-making arena. In combination with chapter 1, it provides an overview of solid waste policy making from a local perspective. The heart of the story remains to be told in the following chapters.

Political Culture

The political cultures of American states ought to be a major
focus of study, in terms of systematic analysis, in terms of inhibi-
tions or restrictions on the scope and substance of policy issues,
and in terms of policy processes and applications.

— *Samuel Patterson*

The political culture of a community is a difficult aspect of the
policy system to describe with any degree of certitude. Unlike businesses, media, citizen participants, and the federal,
state, and local governments, there is no readily identifiable subset
of the people or institutions in the community on which to focus in
examining political culture.

Still, an examination of how the local political culture affects
public policy making is important because "a sensitivity to the perspective that [political culture] provides on political life adds depth
and richness to our appreciation of political events."[1] The role of
big businesses like Waste Management in solid waste policy making
in Spokane, for example, cannot be adequately understood without
an appreciation of Spokane's and Washington State's history of
populist distrust of large, nonregional corporations. Similarly, the
Spokane area's particular mix of dependence on and mistrust of
the federal government is better understood as one variant of a
historically strong aspect of the political culture of the American
West.

A final introductory example of the significance of political
culture in the Spokane solid waste policy-making story may be taken
from the chapter on citizen participation. The populist political
tradition left Washington State's constitution with two features promoting direct democracy: the referendum and the initiative. Both
features played key roles in solid waste policy making in Spokane.
The initiative provided the foundation for Spokane's Proposition 4,
through which active citizens sought to stop the waste-to-energy
facility. The referendum provided the means by which Washington

59

State's Department of Ecology was authorized to grant Spokane $60 million toward the cost of the waste-to-energy facility.

Because it is both so easily taken for granted and so enveloping, political culture is the first thing we should consider in our exploration of the systems model introduced in the previous chapter. Subsequent chapters' explanations of the roles of local political institutions, federal and state policies, citizen participation, businesses, and the media all need to be understood within the context of the political culture in which their roles are played out.

THE MEANING OF POLITICAL CULTURE

The concept of political culture has been part of political studies since the ancient Greeks and Hebrews.[2] Many great Western political theorists included in their work some notion that might be fairly labeled political culture, but it was Gabriel Almond who introduced the contemporary version of the concept in 1956.[3] Since then many attempts have been made to define political culture. Most have focused on a community or society's relatively stable pattern of beliefs and attitudes toward political aspects of their world. Such a pattern delimits its adherents' views of and actions involving political affairs. The literature on political culture, of course, includes numerous disputes about the meaning of the term. Behavioralists object that it should refer not to a classificatory scheme, but to a method of analyzing the basic beliefs of a given group.[4] Here, however, we will use the concept in a way that honors its definition as a classificatory scheme.

Lucian Pye defines political culture as "the set of attitudes, beliefs, and sentiments which give order and meaning to a political process and which provide the underlying assumptions and rules that govern behavior in the political system." Similarly, Almond and Verba define political culture as "the specifically political orientations — attitudes toward the political system and its various parts, and attitudes toward the role of the self in the system."[5] In their definition, the term *orientation* included (1) knowledge of and beliefs about the political system, (2) feelings about the political system, and (3) value-based judgments — involving information and feelings — about elements of the political system. Lane adds a dynamic element to the definition.[6] She thinks the concept of political culture should connect values to attitudes, attitudes to behavior, behavior to choices, choices to policies and institutions, and policies and institutions to social changes — which would then affect values and start the cycle again.

Recognizing that it affords two levels for analysis, Rosenbaum offers two

definitions of political culture.[7] His first definition focuses on the individual: "It entails all the important ways in which a person is subjectively ori-
ented toward the essential elements in his political system." It includes how
a person "feels, and thinks about the symbols, institutions, and rules that
constitute the fundamental political order" and how that person responds
to them. Rosenbaum's second definition focuses on the collective, systems
level, and says that political culture entails how the masses evaluate their
political institutions and officials. My focus here is on the collective, systems
level, but the reader should keep in mind that the collective level includes
the individual. As Stegner puts it, "culture is a pyramid to which each of us
brings a stone."[8]

The concept of political culture was first used in cross-national comparative studies, but it did not take long for someone to point out that national
cultures were not homogeneous.[9] The political culture of Spokane is but
one manifestation of the American political culture. It is not identical to
those found in other cities or regions of America, but it has developed in
much the same way and includes aspects shared by other cities and regions.
It may therefore be useful to begin our consideration of the political culture
involved in this case study by examining the more common national roots,
then gradually narrowing our scope to the regional and subregional roots.

Elazar's Three American Cultures

Daniel Elazar describes three kinds of American political culture — individualistic, moralistic, and traditionalistic — and sketches their application
to sections and regions of the country.[10] At first glance, these three cultures
may appear separate and distinct, but the American political culture is actually composed of admixtures of the three.

Elazar says the individualistic political culture was the foundational political culture of the United States. It envisions society as a marketplace in
which government is best limited to activities that encourage private initiative — or at least do not interfere unnecessarily with it. Politics does not hold
a special place in this culture. It is just one of several ways one might strive to
serve oneself and one's friends. In the individualistic political culture, politics is simply part of the economic system. Participants are neither held in
particularly high esteem nor expected to meet unusual moral standards.
Politics is expected to be as dirty as any other business, and amateurs are well
advised to stay out of the way. As to the government bureaucracy, if it has a
merit system, that system is expected to respond efficiently to the demands

of the politicians, not to resist political influence. In the United States, the vehicle most often used to further individualistic politics is the political party. The party is the means for coordinating a complex "system of mutual obligations rooted in personal relationships."[11] Advancement in such a system is better achieved by attending to those personal relationships than by proposing solutions to public policy problems or espousing a vision of good government. In short, individualistic politics is patronage politics.

The moralistic political culture sees society as a commonwealth. It judges government by its service to the public welfare. Politics is considered an ennobling activity, in which persons gain stature by striving to advance the public interest. The community's willingness to intervene in the private sphere on behalf of the common good tempers the pursuit of individual self-interest. That intervention may be undertaken through governmental or nongovernmental instruments, but government action is seen as a positive way to promote the general welfare. Because loyalty to the local community takes precedence, interventions by local government are more readily accepted than interventions by state or national government. According to Elazar, though, political leaders at both state and local levels in a moralistic political culture are more likely than those in an individualistic one to risk initiating new government programs or projects that address a need not yet recognized by most of the community (but see Miller's more recent study, in which individualistic political cultures had higher local activism and moralistic political cultures had higher state activism).[12]

In the moralistic political culture, politics is the community's means for grappling with public policy issues, so every citizen is encouraged to participate. Unlike individualistic political culture, the moralistic political culture expects those who engage in politics to accept more demanding moral obligations than those who pursue their private interests in the commercial marketplace. People are not to profit personally from public service. Corruption in government is not tolerated. The moralistic political culture expects a merit system to be conscientiously politically neutral. Further, political officials are expected to place their commitment to the community ahead of any obligations they may have because of personal ties. Political party affiliations, like personal ties, are not ultimately important. Nonpartisan systems are likely to develop, but if there are political parties, loyalty to them is not paramount. Shifts from one party to another may be justified based on political beliefs.

In the traditionalistic political culture, political parties are once again not very important. But, as in the individualistic political culture, politics is very personal. Political parties are used as a convenient way to organize the recruitment of people for public office, but it is not unusual for a one-party system to suffice. The traditionalistic political culture is paternalistic and elitist. Because it sees the existing hierarchy as part of the natural order, it expects the political system to help maintain that hierarchy. Any political competition is among factional alignments based on social and family ties. As long as they help to secure the existing order, politics and government in the traditionalistic culture are accepted as having a positive role in the community: " 'Good government' . . . involves the maintenance and encouragement of traditional patterns."[13] Political leaders may help to adjust the social order to changing conditions, but their role is more likely to be maintaining or conserving than initiating. Although the traditionalistic culture is distinctly hierarchical, it is antibureaucratic. Bureaucracy's dependence on impersonal rules applied impartially runs counter to the "fine web of informal interpersonal relationships"[14] that form the basis of this culture's hierarchy. Where bureaucracy is introduced, it is expected to administer programs and policies established by the elite.

Elazar says these three political cultures exist in the United States in various blends, not in any pure form. Each of the three cultures began in a roughly defined geographic region along the east coast of the United States. As people from those regions moved across the continent, the three cultures blended to create multiple manifestations of the American political culture. Over time, regions or sections of the country began to evolve their own distinctive (but ever dynamic) political cultures. Consequently, we must go beyond the national political culture to understand the political activity of a particular area.

POLITICAL CULTURE OF THE AMERICAN WEST

Before discussing the political culture of the American West, I should define the region. For some people, the West is more a state of mind than an identifiable portion of the United States.[15] A computer search for books and articles on the American West is likely to find as much in art and literature as in the social sciences. To be useful in the context of this chapter, however, the concept must have fairly clear geographical boundaries. Stegner, arguing that the West is defined by aridity, said:

> The West that we are talking about comprises a dry core of eight
> public-lands states — Arizona, Colorado, Idaho, Montana, Nevada,

New Mexico, Utah, and Wyoming—plus two marginal areas. The first of these is the western part of the Dakotas, Nebraska, Kansas, Oklahoma, and Texas, authentically dry but with only minimal public lands. The second is the West Coast—Washington, Oregon, and California—with extensive arid lands but with well-watered coastal strips and also with many rivers.[16]

This definition has considerable merit, is widely accepted, and is sufficiently specific for this chapter's purposes. Spokane is thus part of a "marginal" state, but much of the state's marginality is a function of the "well-watered coastal strip." Stegner would have no difficulty seeing the eastern side of Washington State and Spokane as part of the West.

A distinctive regional political culture has evolved in the American West. That culture lies within the parameters of the American political culture as described by Elazar, but it has its own special aura and flavor.[17] Francis and Thomas state that "while some of the characteristics of western politics may not be unique to the region, the way in which they manifest themselves in the West is usually distinctive," and have identified eleven factors that influenced the development of the West.[18] In the remainder of this section, I will consider only those that clearly manifested themselves in the Spokane case study.

In Elazar's mapping of the political cultures of the states and substate regions, the West did not appear to be a coherent mixture of his three cultures; rather, it included many different mixtures of the three cultures, as well as some pockets of relatively pure versions of each. Still, as Bartlett points out, "It has often made sense to talk about the West as a region, implying some common interests, common values, common orientations, common beliefs, common assumptions."[19] He identifies as commonalities a strong emphasis on individualism, a belief in local control over resource decisions, a resentment of economic control by outsiders (real or imagined), an emphasis on economic growth, and a confidence in the ability of technology to modify and control the environment. Ironically, his description also includes assumptions that government will intervene extensively in the economy and federal aid will be there to assist in modifying and controlling the environment. Bernard DeVoto is credited with describing the western culture's bimodal attitude toward government as "Get out and give us more money."[20]

Ever since the West became a part of the United States, the federal government has been the chief landlord in the region. To a significant extent this is a legacy of the time when all of the western territory was federal land; but the federal government still owns 29 percent or more of the land in eleven of the western states, over 50 percent of four of them, and 85.4 percent of Nevada[21] The resulting relationship between the federal government and the locals is fraught with uncomfortable dependencies and periodic outbursts of hostility—the Sagebrush Rebellion and the Wise Use Movement being two of the more recent examples.

In the arid West, perhaps the greatest impact of the federal government has been in water projects. "Every major river of the West [has come], to a greater or lesser extent under the control of the dam builders and water pumpers."[22] It is now becoming more apparent at what costs the water has been gained. The Ogallala aquifer, the world's largest underground reservoir of fresh water, is being used faster than it is being replenished. In the Northwest, salmon runs have been disastrously depleted, largely due to dams.

The West has historically had a boom-and-bust economy (symbolized by the image of the ghost town). Because the economy has operated so much on speculative opportunity, it has been described as a "hit-and-run economy."[23] Despite the personal anguish felt by those who failed in their attempts to make an independent living or who found themselves bound to an industry that no longer required their services, the economy as a whole has moved on down the road. In the nineteenth and early twentieth centuries, easterners and foreigners often provided the private capital that supported economic development in the West.[24] Frederick Jackson Turner thought a central dynamic of the development of the frontier was the tension between the western pioneers and the controllers of capital in the East.[25] "The distance from one coast to the other established a kind of leverage by which costs, profits, and risks all tended to be much greater . . . and the time that news and goods took to move made for extreme shortages and surpluses."[26] In addition, the cost and speed of transportation fluctuated radically.

As the twentieth century progressed, the West's subservience to the East reduced. Decreasing reliance on extractive industries and increased economic activity in service, tourist, and high-tech industries made the West more often a leader in national economic trends. Still, competition in and dependence on the international economy continue to make the West vulnerable to external economic decisions and actions.

The federal government financed much of the western economy in the late nineteenth century when it offered free land first to the railroads and then to homesteaders in order to encourage the westward expansion. It has also been the chief financier of the West's twentieth-century economy.[27] In the twentieth century, the main vehicles for federal subsidization of the western economy have included defense expenditures, the aerospace industry, water projects, and crop subsidies.

Another factor often credited with influencing the special flavor of western culture is the physical environment. This view is not necessarily founded on a belief in geographic or environmental determinism; it merely recognizes that the physical features of the environment in which a culture develops affect its characteristics. In addition to the aridity Stegner cited as defining the region, a main feature of the West's physical environment is vast spaces. William Least Heat Moon says, "The true West differs from the East in one great, pervasive influential and awesome way: space. The vast openness changes the roads, towns, houses, farms, crops, machinery, politics, economics, and naturally, ways of thinking."[28] The large tracts of public domain in the West were influential in creating a national government that was no longer dependent on the states to empower it, but was itself the creator of states.

The most obvious demographic factor in the history of the West involves the engagement of Elazar's cultural streams with the cultures of hundreds of tribes of American Indians. White settlers not only took over western lands on which Indians lived; they also moved tribes from east of the Mississippi River onto reservations in western territories. Another cultural engagement that began as white settlers moved westward involved the Hispanic population of the land annexed as the American Southwest. "Anglos who flooded the area pushed their predecessors aside until most of these Spanish-named Americans retained little of their former sociocultural status."[29] The coming of the railroad in the second half of the nineteenth century set the stage for the evolution of the West into a multicultural region by making it easier for European, Mexican, Asian, Indochinese, Pacific Islander, and African American immigrants and laborers to spread throughout the region. Twentieth-century developments in transportation —superhighways and a large airline industry—have helped to enhance dramatically the multiculturalism of the region. "It was not simply different races that converged on this frontier, but different ways of life."[30] However, in relation to Spokane's solid waste policy making the most significant factor of the West's twentieth-century demographic history has been its rapid and continuing urbanization. Around 1900, only about 25 percent of the region's population was in urban areas, but now more western people live in urban areas than is true of any other region of the country—80.4 percent in 1980, compared to a national average of 73.7 percent.[31]

Perhaps no aspect of the American West has had a greater impact upon its political culture than the frontier ethos. Turner argued that the frontier was the crucial element in giving a distinct character not only to the American West, but to American values and character in general.[32] He credited the frontier with giving birth to our versions of democracy, individualism, and nationalism. According to Turner, the return on the frontier to primitive ways of life produced a "democracy born of free land, strong in selfishness and individualism, intolerant of administrative experience and education, and pressing individual liberty beyond its proper bounds."[33]

The political culture of the West has also been shaped by its populist and Progressive traditions. The populist movement may have been more significant in the long term to western United States history as a precursor to Progressivism, but populist candidates did obtain significant victories in western states in the late nineteenth century. Agrarian dissatisfaction with the high capital investment it took to be successful and the declining market prices for farm produce were behind such populist proposals as the free coinage of silver (to increase the volume of currency in circulation and improve the value of farms and farm produce). The unrest that fueled populist victories in the West, however, was somewhat different from that in the East. There was greater concern in the West about protection from both foreign and immigrant competition and monopolies than about the problems of farm production. Given the distances involved in getting goods to market, unfair railroad rate policies were a particular concern to western farmers.[34]

In addition, Progressivism has been more entrenched, and at times more extreme, in the West than in the rest of the nation. Its popularity has been fed by the regional distaste for eastern and foreign capitalists, who have historically controlled much of the private property in the region. Westerners have also found attractive the Progressive Movement's faith in the ability of the authority of government and the ballot box to control the greed of large private corporations, and to help establish the infrastructure (e.g., water projects and public utilities) necessary for exploitation of the region's natural resources. Progressives' belief in the authority of the state also set the stage for creation of our systems of national parks and national forests.

According to Link and McCormick, "Perhaps the most distinctive aspect of western Progressivism was its passion for the more democratic, anti-institutional political reforms, such as the initiative, the referendum, and the recall, and a form of the direct primary which allowed voters to cross party lines."[35] Two other Progressive hallmarks — prohibition and women's suffrage — also found a welcoming niche in the West. One year before passage of the Eighteenth (prohibition) and Nineteenth Amendments (female suffrage), all the western states except California had gone "dry," and all but four had given women the vote.[36]

The constitutions of the western states, of course, reflected these same leanings. In one of the more dramatic examples of western exceptionalism, Arizona proposed a state constitution that allowed voter recall of judges. When President Taft voiced his strong objections to such a provision, they removed it — but they later readopted the recall provision after the territory gained admission as a state.[37]

In the twentieth century, the West has been less different and more a part of the trends of the rest of the nation. Before the United States' entry into World War I, the West was passionately isolationist and pacifist. Once their country was in the war, the region was intolerant of those who did not support it. When prohibition was part of the moral cause of Progressivism, the people of the West supported it. When it appeared that enforcement of prohibition was a threat to civil liberties, they supported repeal of prohibition. When Franklin Roosevelt's New Deal was seen as the way out of the Great Depression, he got the votes of the western states. As the pendulum swung to the right after World War II, the West followed, participating fully in the McCarthy red scare. When the pendulum swung back to the left in the late 1950s, the West elected more Democrats, but showed a regional loyalty to Richard Nixon in his loss to John Kennedy in 1960. It also "joined fully in the fray"[38] in the politics of activism and confrontation of the 1960s and early 1970s. In the conservative and Republican resurgence of the mid-1970s and 1980s, the West led the way.

The West has also been a full partner in the national trend toward an increasing role in politics for women and minorities. Key elected positions throughout the West — including mayoralties, state legislative positions, governorships, and seats in the United States House and Senate — have been won by women, African Americans, Hispanic Americans, and Japanese Americans.

The liberal politics of the West had its foundation in Progressivism, but as the end of the twentieth century approached, Progressivism's key bases of liberal support (labor unions and family farmers) had decreased in numbers and in political clout. The middle-class urban support for more conservative Progressive policies such as making government more businesslike began to hold greater sway. Much of the change resulted from migration into the region. "The new westerners . . . tended to be middle or upper class, suburban, non-union if not antiunion, and comfortably conservative in outlook."[39]

Still, the Progressive values of direct democracy and government regulation and support of private economic activities (especially on public lands) remain important elements of the political culture of the West. Federal landlordship continues, as does dependence on federal regulation and subsidization of the economy. The external power of eastern capital, however, has been replaced by (1) the power of urban numbers in the ballot box and in representative institutions, and (2) the power of corporate interests in all corners of the economy — from agribusiness to high-tech enterprises to energy producers to service providers.

A final aspect that must be covered in any attempt to describe the regional identity of the West is subregionalism. Subregions in the West are sufficiently important to justify considering it not a unified region but a set of American Wests, "each distinct from its neighbors as well as from some of the dominant national patterns."[40] This is not the place to examine that argument. In the next section on Spokane's political culture, however, I will place it in the context of the subregion to which it belongs.

SPOKANE'S POLITICAL CULTURE

Spokane's political culture is largely a function of its geography and its history. As the largest city between Minneapolis–St. Paul and Seattle, the city of Spokane is the main part of an urban area surrounded by vast reaches of sparsely populated agricultural, forested, and public lands that have supported mining, agriculture, stock-growing, orcharding, and lumbering. As the one place in the region where one might (1) obtain bank financing, (2) find a major medical center, (3) go in order to get somewhere else, and (4) get one's news,[41] Spokane is the urban center of a subregion that has been called the Inland Empire, the Great Columbia Basin, and the Inland Northwest. That region has been defined as "a vast area extending from southeastern British Columbia on the north to northeastern Oregon in the south, and from the Cascade Range in the west to the Rocky Mountains on the east"[42] (see fig. 3.1). This inland region is so salient to area residents that many proposals have been made, before and after Washington State was formed, to create a state approximating its boundaries.

Geographically and historically linked to the Inland Northwest, Spokane is certainly part of the American West. With an average of 16.7 inches of liquid precipitation per year,[43] it meets Stegner's primary defining char-

acteristic of aridity. Spokane and the Inland Northwest also lie within the
geographic boundaries of Stegner's definition of the American West. Finally, the Inland Northwest also meets William Least Heat Moon's main
criterion: space. Outside the urban-suburban area around Spokane (containing a population of about 400,000), almost all of the Inland Northwest
has a population density of less than 25 persons per square mile.[44] Adding to
the sense of space is Spokane's isolation. As described by Timothy Egan, it is
"isolated from the rest of the world by a fence of mountains . . . and the
trench of Hells Canyon . . . where the Snake River cut the deepest gorge on
the continent."[45]

Figure 3.1 Map of the Inland Northwest

Spokane's history is a particular subset of the history of the American West. The first human inhabitants of the region probably were descendants of people who came over the Bering land bridge during the last Ice Age. The Spokan tribe (from which the city took its name) was one of several Salish-speaking tribes that inhabited the area when white fur traders from Canada established the Spokane House in 1810 as the first white settlement in what is now Washington State.

Spurred by the call of manifest destiny and seeking to escape economic depression in the East, whites came across the Oregon Trail in search of a better life. They did not settle in the land that eventually became the city of Spokane until the early 1870s. In 1880 Spokane had become a village of about 350, by 1910 its population was recorded as 104,402, and the 1990 census gave the city's population as 176,196.[46]

As with most of the rest of the West, Spokane was first settled by people looking for a better life and lured west by (1) promotional pamphlets that told of cheap land and promised farming and ranching success — "the best poor man's country in the world"; (2) dreams of mining their way to fortune — in the 1880s gold and silver were discovered east of Spokane in the Coeur d'Alene Mining District, the world's richest silver mining area; and/or (3) the ease of railroad transportation. The Northern Pacific Railway came to Spokane in 1881, and by 1893 it had been joined by the Union Pacific, the Great Northern, and a number of smaller lines. With the rails came lumbermen seeking to harvest the virgin stands, and the merchants, lawyers, and speculators seeking to harvest wealth in the frontier towns.[47]

The people who moved to the Inland Northwest were initially attracted to Spokane because of the Spokane River. Water is an especially valuable resource in an arid climate, and the waterfalls in Spokane were also an important source of energy for urban development. The river and its falls were so instrumental to white settlement in the area that the city was first chartered in 1881 as Spokane Falls, changing its name to Spokane in 1891.[48]

Although its population still reflects a heavily western European heritage, people of many national and ethnic origins have settled in the Inland Northwest. Among the other national or ethnic groups represented in the area are Germans, Russians, Italians, Jews, Poles, Chinese, Japanese, Koreans, African Americans, Africans, Hispanics, Middle Easterners, Vietnamese, Laotians, Hmong, and, of course, American Indians. Although these minority cultures do not share the same perspective on the history of the region, their reasons for settling in the area have often been similar to those of the dominant culture — "refuge from political, ethnic, and religious op-

pression, the promise of individual, political, legal and economic opportunity," equality, education, and creation of a community for the preservation of key aspects of their "homeland" cultures.[49]

Inland Northwest Indians have also sought to preserve their cultures, but
their perspectives on the movement of whites and other immigrants into the
region present quite another story. Tribes native to the region include:
Spokane, Coeur d'Alene, Kalispell, and Palouse. Although the Palouse Indians have a distinct history and culture, key aspects of their story are not too
different from many other American Indians' stories. As the largest collection of tribes that lived just south of present-day Spokane, their perspective
may fairly represent the perspective of American Indians in the Inland
Northwest. According to Trafzer, "The Palouse would argue that [the era of
white settlement] was not an era of glory, growth, and development, but a
time of depression, despair and death." Whites forced treaties on the Palouse and separated tribe members from each other. They were assigned to
different reservations, some as far away as "Indian Territory" in present-day
Oklahoma. Some Palouse chose to homestead off the reservations as neighbors of the whites, but many Palouse saw the way the whites divided the land
as a violation of the earth and the spirits. To this day, some Palouse still
gather each year at Sacajawea State Park on the Snake River in southeastern
Washington to strengthen old bonds and form new ones among their
people. "They feast on salmon, roots, and berries, and talk about the 'old
days.' The people sing and pray for an end to the earth as it is."[50]

Elazar's three-culture model ignored the impact of American Indian
cultures (or of any non-European culture) on the variations in American
political cultures. In this he reflected accurately the perspective of many
whites in the American West generally and in Spokane in particular. Because Spokane is about 93 percent Caucasian, it is easy for most whites to
remain unaware of the nondominant cultures in the area. More significantly, they often deny that racism exists in Spokane, pointing to such supporting evidence as the election in 1982 of African American Jim Chase as
mayor, and ignoring the presence of John Birchers, Aryans, and other white
supremacists.[51] Though the pattern of ethnic and racial settlement in Spokane is not as territorial as in much of the West, there are still areas where
members of certain nondominant cultures are more likely to be found.

Elazar placed Spokane's political culture (i.e., the dominant culture he
considered) more into his moralistic and individualistic categories. In his
explanation of the "geology" of the United States' political cultures, the
foundational strata of Spokane's political culture are based on streams of

migration that began in the northeastern and Middle Atlantic states. The moralistic strata derive from "the Puritans of New England and their Yankee descendants." As they migrated across the northern part of the country, the Yankees were joined and their moralism was reinforced by Scandinavians and other northern Europeans. As they pressed westward, the "Yankees settled the Willamette Valley of Oregon and eastern Washington."[52]

The individualistic strata have their origins with people from non-Puritan England and the interior Germanic states of Europe. This very diverse group "established the basic patterns of American pluralism"[53] and the search for an idealized vision of individualism and the pursuit of happiness. As their search took them west, they began to settle with people from the moralist and traditionalist streams — the moralist stream being generally on the northern side and the traditionalist stream on the southern side.

According to Elazar, in eastern Washington and northern Idaho the settlers of the first frontier brought with them moralist and individualist cultural tendencies. Later, more mixing of the three cultures resulted from north-south flows of migration that avoided the difficulties of crossing the mountains of the West. As the industrial revolution transformed urban life, more people settled in the cities, seeing them as the land of opportunity. Postindustrial technological developments then diffused the settlement pattern around the cities and led to the suburbanization of the population. Despite the admixtures of political culture these and other migrational patterns caused, the first settlers created a base, and later settlers — having chosen to settle among established communities — were more influenced by than influences on the cultural base they found.

Using Elazar's analytical format to gain some insight into the political aspects of Spokane's dominant culture, we begin by noting that in Spokane the public sector is viewed both as a marketplace (individualistic) and as a commonwealth (moralistic). It is expected to both respond efficiently to demands and take positive action to improve the community. The general policy direction in solid waste management exemplifies this mixture of the two cultures. The decision to lead the community into a new generation of solid waste management, rather than waiting for a policy direction to come from the citizens is typical of the moralist political culture. The decision to work with the private sector in order to build and operate an efficient and effective solid waste management system fits more comfortably within the individualist political culture.

The specific issue most illustrative of the community's view of the role of the public sector was the dispute over how to design a composting program.

The dispute took place after the citizens had begun to express their views on solid waste matters, and directly involved the question of the proper role of government.

SWDP proposed to establish a government-supported composting program because it saw the development of a composting program as a positive action that would improve the community. It would reduce the amount of garbage sent to the waste-to-energy facility by as much as 17 percent, increase the recycled waste in the county from the 1990 level of 28 percent to as much as 41 percent, allow residents to dispose of yard waste at about half the cost of dumping it, and help to minimize future increases in the cost of managing solid waste.[54]

SWDP invited bids on a contract to provide composting services in the county, and awarded the contract to O. M. Scott & Sons. Another company, Ecocycle Inc., which lost in the competition for the contract, appealed SWDP's decision to the city council and the county commissioners. The County Flow Control Ordinance required that all wastes be delivered into the SWDP-controlled solid waste management system, and SWDP felt that allowing Ecocycle into the system would undercut the contract with O. M. Scott. They argued that it might also increase the cost to the city and county of managing solid waste.[55]

The county commissioners initially voted 2–1 to reject the proposal to award a single contract to O. M. Scott. They questioned whether it was proper for government to own a composting facility and preferred to let the private sector provide composting services to the community.[56] After one commissioner retired and a new one was elected, the commission agreed to support an amended contract, one that left room for Ecocycle to obtain materials for composting from commercial landscapers.[57]

The agreement on how to manage composting operations in Spokane County demonstrates how a local political culture may show evidence of influence by more than one of Elazar's three political cultures. It was within the parameters of an individualistic political culture in its acceptance of the importance of private concerns and in its belief that government interference in private affairs needs to be limited. It also honored the moralistic political culture in its acceptance of the role of government in pursuing the public interest, in allowing government to intervene in the private sphere for the well-being of the community.

In Spokane, government is expected to promote economic development (a characteristic of the individualistic political culture), but it is also expected to be a vehicle for social and economic regulation (moralistic). In deciding to build a waste-to-energy facility, the city and county believed they were doing what was necessary to make the Spokane area attractive to developers.[58] Both governments are periodically accused of encouraging development at the expense of zoning guidelines and affected neighborhoods. In a 1993 example the city council approved a new zoning code that many neighborhood activists considered too friendly to developers. Neighborhood activists conducted a campaign that recalled the populist movement, and the support they gained for a referendum to rescind the code was sufficient to cause the council to rescind the code and agree to redraft it. In the November 1993 city elections, the victorious mayoral candidate and two of the three winning council candidates presented themselves as very sympathetic to neighborhoods' concerns. When the revised code is presented, it is expected to reflect better the concerns of the neighborhoods.[59]

Although some people in Spokane would like it to refrain from initiating programs or projects without a clear public demand, as further evidence of its moralistic political culture leanings local government has occasionally acted not only without public pressure, but in spite of perceived public indifference or potential public resistance when it believed the initiative to be in the public interest. For example, when the city council feared public resistance and was unwilling to request public support for a bonding issue, city management found internal funding mechanisms to renovate a former Montgomery Ward building for a new city hall.

The Spokane public's attitude toward the public bureaucracy provides evidence of both individualistic and moralistic political cultures. The public are ambivalent toward the bureaucracy because they expect it to bring political neutrality to the running of government, but they also think it restricts efficiency and meddles in political matters. City council members have insisted openly that the "staff" really run things. In local elections candidates frequently attack the bureaucracy's efficiency record. The county commissioners who opposed the original composting contract with O. M. Scott did so in part because they thought public management of composting would be less efficient than private competition. The manner in which they argued their position also seemed to identify Ecocycle as their favored client — as expected in an individualistic political culture.

Showing signs of a moralistic political culture, in the twentieth century Spokane's local government structure has reflected the goals of the Progressive Era, which sought professional management of government and nonpartisan leadership for government. As the result of a local Progressive uprising, in 1911 the city instituted a commission form of government.[60]

The commission had five members, each of whom served as the executive head of an administrative unit. A mayor was selected from the commission by a vote of the commissioners. The mayor lacked a veto over commission actions. Another local Progressive uprising led to adoption of a council-manager form of government in 1960. The council consists of six members and a mayor elected in at-large, nonpartisan elections. The mayor lacks a veto in this structure as well. Both the city and county now have merit systems. The county also has an administrator who serves as an intermediary between the commission members and department heads.

The role of political parties in Spokane fits the moralistic political culture. Political parties are not particularly strong, since the city elections are formally nonpartisan, but they do provide an organizing foundation for the coalitions involved in city elections. The local patterns of competition are as much among coalitions and over issues as between parties. In the partisan county elections it is not unusual for public officials to support candidates from other parties. Recently, during his second term, a county commissioner switched from the Democratic to the Republican Party.

As in most of the United States, the majority of citizens in the Spokane area have refrained from becoming involved in politics and government unless they felt compelled by a personal stake in some issue. Generally they have preferred to leave politics and governance to someone else. Often that reluctance to become involved has been related to a belief that one has to be among the "power elite" to have any chance of affecting such matters.

The belief in a local power elite has a sound historical foundation. Three men are credited with starting the city. When they were ruined by the 1893 depression, it did not take long for a new set of powerful men "who could afford to buy land after the panic"[61] to rise as the city leaders. One of them was named Cowles. Armed with an inheritance, he bought land and two of the city's newspapers, which he turned into the *Spokesman-Review* in 1894. As publisher of that newspaper, he was a powerful figure in the intellectual and political life of Spokane.

The members of the elite group to which Cowles belonged were classic examples of Progressivism:

> They shared a conviction that they could control their economic
> and physical environment and, to a lesser degree, their social and
> natural environment. They believed they could make Spokane the
> kind of city they chose. Their public lives demonstrated their certi-
> tude that they shaped the city, and the Spokane they wanted was

prosperous and pleasant — the right kind of people, selected merchants and factories, quiet, green neighborhoods, and an unobtrusive municipal government with low taxes, adequate services, and no monkey business. If their progress toward this consensus ideal sometimes seemed heavy-handed and self-seeking (as it occasionally was), their outlook was benevolent, and . . . they achieved much of what they intended.[62]

Almost a century later there was still a small group of local business leaders who were believed to make the major decisions on community issues.[63] They included the publisher of the local newspapers (still a man named Cowles), the CEO of a major utility, a former bank chair, a current bank chair, the president of the chamber of commerce, and some entrepreneurs. It was believed that these people worked behind the scenes, using their considerable resources to control major decisions — even if those decisions were formally made by local government. More direct vehicles for their agendas included Spokane Unlimited, a private, nonprofit downtown planning and development organization that was instrumental in bringing Expo '74 to Spokane; and Momentum, a local economic development movement that during the 1989 election campaign helped to overcome opposition to the waste-to-energy facility by financing a study detailing the costs of a decision to stop the project in midstream.

Such a set of elites continues to represent a Progressive element in the mix of local politics, but there also remains an element of populism. As Plummer notes, "Although the Spokane municipality gives the impression of being an overgrown small town, it is truly an urban center in which civic participation is high and levels of community dissatisfaction continuously rise and fall."[64] Opposition to the waste-to-energy facility and to the related proposal for an in-county ash landfill had a strong populist tinge. Many individuals involved lived in the more rural areas of Spokane County and felt that the interests of the city were being pursued at their expense. Because the waste-to-energy facility was to be built and operated by the largest waste management company in the world, Waste Management, Inc., the populist refrain against the power of large corporations was also heard. When citizens used the local referendum procedure to try to stop the city from making the capital commitments necessary to build the waste-to-energy facility, they exercised an option made possible because of Washington State's populist past in a way that would have made the late nineteenth-century populists proud. The anti-incinerator slate in the 1989 city election and the pro-neighborhood candidates in the 1993 election also had roots in the populist movement.

Residents of the area describe it as a conservative, western, blue-collar community, but it was not always a conservative town. When in 1889 a fire destroyed the heart of downtown, the city rebuilt in elaborate style, with the help of Dutch financing.[65] Perhaps Spokane became conservative as a result of its extended stagnant period in the twentieth century: "From 1929 until the mid-1980s, the city was essentially frozen." In the first three decades, Protestant Republicans who discouraged disruption of the existing political order ran the city.[66] Outsiders were not welcomed, and from 1910 to 1990 the city population increased only about 70,000. "Spokane's experience forced a drastic and what for many must have been a painful change in outlook. Its spokesmen began to stress the virtues of a stable, quiet, comfortable community, and conservatism in the best sense — a city of homes, and a fine place to bring up a family."[67] Whether Spokane is conservative "in the best sense" is, however, a matter of perspective. Neal Peirce in 1972 described it as insular, ingrown, and dominated by reactionary business groups. But Jack Olsen, in a book that was seldom flattering to Spokane, wrote: "The town is the perfect size: big enough to offer cosmopolitan amenities, small enough to sustain neighborliness and pride."[68]

Though it has a good record of supporting basic infrastructure needs (streets, parks, libraries, schools, etc.), Spokane remains rather conservative in its attitude toward change; proposals for something new have to overcome considerable inertia. In recent history the community has not supported proposals for a badly needed new airport and city hall. Proposals for a new arena to replace the old coliseum (the "Boone Street Barn") were initially rejected, but were later modified and gained voter support. If Progressive proposals are to be funded, local leaders have often found it necessary to go beyond appeals to the citizenry. For example, when Spokane was proposed as host of a World's Fair in 1974 a vote to underwrite the effort with general obligation bonds failed (58 percent voted in favor, but 60 percent was required), so funding had to be found elsewhere. The city council passed a business and occupation tax and issued councilmanic bonds. Downtown businesses created a Local Improvement District to finance some infrastructure improvements. And Senators Magnusen and Jackson and Congressman Foley were able to secure federal assistance.

Spokane is western both in its geographic location and in its culture. The urban hub of the Inland Northwest, its western culture partakes of the parochial loyalties common to the American Midwest and the rugged individualism associated with the Far West. Many area residents moved to the region to take advantage of the large tracts of relatively inexpensive land, which allow them to pursue a lifestyle that includes much independence and privacy.

Like the West in general, the Inland Northwest's belief in its rugged individualism depends on a refusal to recognize the role of the federal government in making its lifestyle possible. Federal aid encouraged the railroads and the airports and built the interstate highway system; they in turn make it possible to send goods to market and to receive goods and services from elsewhere. If not for the damming of the Columbia River and the irrigation the Columbia Basin Project has made possible, a significant portion of the Inland Northwest's agriculture would not exist.[69] In the 1930s Spokane acted as if the Grand Coulee Dam was a project built for it. Its newspapers and Chamber of Commerce pointed to Grand Coulee with pride and explained how it would bring growth and wealth to the region. By 1959 the amount of irrigated acreage in eastern Washington had tripled, and the productivity of the acreage has since improved significantly.[70]

Advances in Inland Northwest agriculture have also been aided by other federal actions. The Morrill Land Grant College Act of 1862 — which led to the establishment of Washington State University and the University of Idaho — and experiment stations authorized by the Hatch Agricultural Experimental Station Act of 1887 made possible improvements in knowledge and technique. Roosevelt's New Deal included a series of laws that aided agriculture. Public Law 480 (1954) was important in opening foreign markets. And of course, federal crop subsidies have also been important.

Other federal impacts on the local economy include: Fairchild Air Force Base (the largest employer in Spokane County) and the Bonneville Power Administration. Kaiser Aluminum is the fourth largest employer in Spokane County.[71] Aluminum production began as a local industry because of the World War II demand for aluminum to make airplanes and the availability of cheap electricity — made possible by the damming of the Columbia and the Bonneville Power Administration.[72] "Before 1939 there were no aluminum plants west of the Mississippi; . . . by the end of the war the region was producing 42 percent of America's aluminum, a ratio that has persisted into the 1990s."[73] One also might credit the recent addition of a small Boeing plant to federal contracts — and to the political clout of Congressman Tom Foley, who at the time represented the Spokane area and was Speaker of the House.

Although it is currently in a period of transition where services such as tourism are becoming more important, the Spokane area economy has historically depended on manufacturing and extraction — logging, mining, farming, etc. This continues to affect the region's view of itself as a blue-collar area where pickup trucks are considered more representative of the population than computers. (Three of the top ten industrial firms in the area are computer related.)[74]

Until very recently, living has been relatively inexpensive in the area. In 1990 the average home sold for around $65,000 — more than $30,000 less than the national average — but a recent growth spurt and an influx of Californians moved the 1993 price a bit over the national average. With a 1990 mean total family income of about $22,000 more than 60 percent of the population had family incomes under $30,000 and less than 10 percent over $50,000.[75]

Higher education has been fairly accessible in Spokane. There are two private four-year colleges, two public two-year colleges, one public university that offers bachelor's and master's degrees, and another that has a small branch campus operation downtown. About 40 percent of the adult population have attended college, and about one-fifth have obtained a bachelor's degree. If Spokane were a state, it would rank fourteenth in percentage of population over 25 years of age who have had at least four years of college.[76]

As Lane suggests,[77] political culture is dynamic. The links among values, policies, and institutions mean that a change in any of them affects them all. The history of Spokane's values is written into the history of its institutions, and the history of its institutions has affected its policies. Since changes in policy preferences may portend shifts in political culture, it is important to examine carefully trends in public opinion. Before concluding this chapter, I want to take a brief look at public opinion surveys that were designed to gauge public support in Spokane for the move from landfills to waste-to-energy in solid waste management.

SPOKANE PUBLIC OPINION ON WASTE-TO-ENERGY

In one sense, public opinion is too volatile to be considered as part of the political culture; but as Rosenbaum pointed out in his second definition of political culture, how the masses evaluate their political institutions and officials is definitely part of political culture.[78] Relations between public officials and citizens are also part of the political culture. One indicator of the nature of those relations is the degree of congruence between public opinion and public policy.

The public officials promoting the solid waste disposal project did not take citizen support for granted. In order to verify that the waste-to-energy facility they favored would be acceptable to the citizens, in the summer of 1985 the city commissioned a survey of over 1,500 residents.[79] According to that survey, 55 percent favored incineration over the other well-known alternative, sanitary landfills. Based on this show of support, the city felt it could continue to pursue the waste-to-energy approach.

Nonetheless, the question of citizen support was not definitively answered by the results of that survey, nor by the results of the other surveys conducted between 1985 and 1990. Until 1989, surveys consistently showed a strong majority favoring the waste-to-energy facility. In March 1986 a survey commissioned by the city showed 71 percent favored an incinerator over a sanitary landfill.[80] In May 1987 another city-sponsored survey found 70 percent favoring a waste-to-energy facility.[81] A March 1988 survey conducted by KXLY news radio found 62.7 percent favoring the proposed facility.

But by April 1989 a Market Trends survey showed the support had dwindled significantly. Only a plurality remained in favor — 45 percent supported the waste-to-energy project and 38 percent opposed it. Perhaps even more important for the issue of citizen support, 86 percent in that poll said they wanted an opportunity to vote on the project — an opportunity they would never directly obtain.[82] In October 1989 another Market Trends poll found that 46 percent opposed the waste-to-energy project and 39 percent supported it.[83] This still was not the definitive statement on the public's willingness to support the project — that came in the November 1989 city election — and though the supporters of the project won that election, it was clear that citizen support for the project had gone from substantial to marginal in a period of 4–5 years.

How the city happened to suffer such a loss of support for the waste-to-energy facility is a common story in solid waste management policy development in the United States. At the national level the resurgence of waste incineration technology experienced in the 1980s peaked in the year Spokane's facility began operating. There were 171 plants operating in 1991, but by 1993 the number had dropped to 162.[84] The story involves the birth of citizen groups that often begin simply as NIMBYs (not in my back yard). It involves government officials ill-prepared for a change in public temperament, and a political structure that allows changes in public temperament to affect public policy making and makes it easier to veto policies than to establish them. It involves consultants and corporate spokespersons who believe their perspective is the most rational and should be the driving force in policy formulation. It also involves a media industry that uses and is used by the various active participants in public policy formulation.

The story of how the Solid Waste Disposal Project fended off all challenges and began operation in September 1991 shared these factors. In addition, it involved government officials who had to climb a steep learning curve and figure out how much they needed to bend to the political winds — and how they could best keep from being swept off their feet by those winds. It involved a political structure that promoted stability and depended on private consultants and experts to design, construct, and operate technologically complex facilities. It involved the ways businesses used their political and economic power to promote their interests. And it involved citizens who had limited resources, limited time, and limited energy to devote to any single public policy issue — most of whom ultimately depended on their government officials to make decisions that promoted the public interest.

Summary and Conclusions

In Elazar's terms, the history of Spokane's political culture has been mainly a function of competition between the moralistic and individualistic cultures. When the excesses of individualistic machine politics became untenable, the community moved more toward moralistic values and institutions. There has also been an occasional hint of traditionalism, perhaps at its strongest in the first three decades of the twentieth century when the entire country was experiencing a rise in fundamentalism. But the pluralist and Progressive traditions continue to influence the local political culture toward individualistic and moralistic characteristics.

From a short-term perspective, the polarization of the people of Spokane over the Solid Waste Disposal Project appeared to be an unusual circumstance in the political culture of the area. In the second half of the twentieth century, the Spokane political culture has avoided open conflict. Elections have most often been civilized competitions among candidates with little to distinguish them from each other except the names of people and groups who supported them. In 1988 an election to a position on the county commission, one of the most powerful elected positions in the local community, was won by a candidate whose major campaign strategy consisted of standing along the more heavily traveled streets at peak traffic times and waving at the passing drivers.

The impact of the Solid Waste Disposal Project on local politics seemed significant at the time, especially to those involved in it. Whether the change was a temporary jolt or a more permanent transformation in the political culture remains an open question. It could be that the activism that surrounded the project, buttressed by the recent resurgence of populism in the national political culture, is a harbinger of a climatic change in the local political culture; or it may pass.

On the other hand, it was not totally out of character for Spokanites to vote against the waste-to-energy facility when the item on the ballot was an initiative to give them a vote on capital projects. Populism has deep roots in Spokane politics. Those unfamiliar with Spokane's populist past may have been surprised when many area residents became involved in debating the locational, operational, and environmental issues around the project. Considering the past, however, one might expect an occasional eruption of activism to protect a way of life (especially an agricultural or rural way of life) from the political and economic machinations of a large corporation from back east.

As will be demonstrated throughout the following chapters, other features of the political culture of the American West also had their impacts. A common feature among political cultures of the West is a resentment of economic control by outsiders. But that was not the only way Spokane showed itself a part of the West. Rapid urbanization in the twentieth century gave rise to the need for better solid waste management. The frontier belief in individualism was a part of Spokane's beginnings and remains a part of the self-image of many Spokanites. The two were bound to clash. County residents resented the threatened imposition on their lifestyles of the in-county ash landfill solution to the urban problem of solid waste management. Moreover, a belief in the need to retain local control over resource decisions undergirded the decision by city and county officials to maintain ownership of the waste-to-energy facility even though they chose to contract out its construction and operation to Wheelabrator. That same belief was the foundation for their preference for an in-county ash landfill. A confidence in technology and a firm belief in the need for economic growth were important components of their decision to place a waste-to-energy facility at the center of their solid waste management plans. The way the $60 million state grant supported local officials' dependence on the waste-to-energy facility reflected the way government aid has assisted in using technology to modify and control the environment of the American West. The federal government's historic role as imposer and crucial supporter continued as the Environmental Protection Agency adopted guidelines for solid waste management that became virtually compulsory when technical and financial assistance were made contingent on them. The environment of the West also had its impacts. The construction of mega-landfills in eastern Washington and Oregon was predicated on the region's vast tracts of dry, less-than-prime agricultural land. In Spokane, the aridity of the region underscored the importance of protecting the Spokane-Rathdrum aquifer from potential degradation by solid waste management facilities. The list could continue, but evidence of the role of political culture suffuses the remaining chapters of the book.

Local Political
Institutions

Historically, solid waste management has moved from being the responsibility of individuals or families to being a responsibility primarily of the local community. In the United States for most of the twentieth century, municipal governments have held the ultimate responsibility for solid waste collection and disposal. Not until the latter third of the century did state and federal governments show much interest in solid waste policy making. Even then the pattern has been for state and federal governments to set guidelines and parameters for local policy makers, with the locals retaining direct responsibility for policy making and implementation.

This chapter begins with a sketch of the Progressive municipal reform movement, which coincided with and influenced local government's assumption of responsibility for managing solid waste. The sketch establishes the themes of Progressivism that facilitated the rise of solid waste managment professionals as part of the move to reduce partisan corruption arising from cronyism in municipal employment. Next I briefly describe the history of municipal solid waste management in the United States, showing how industrialization, urbanization, science, and technology combined to pave the way for Progressive politics to reform American solid waste management and how solid waste management professionals contributed to the rise and to the successes and failures of the Progressives. The national history review closes by describing the forces that began to take control of solid waste management away from local governments. I then explain how the history of Spokane's local government was affected by national historic and political culture dynamics, and describe how the shape and flavor of Spokane's local government structures influenced its approach to the task of solid waste management. Underlying this analysis is a perspective artic-

ulated by Wildavsky—the political institutions that people construct are shaped in conformity with their political culture.[1]

PROGRESSIVE MUNICIPAL REFORM

Traditionally, the dates of the Progressive Era are set around 1900–1915, but when it comes to Progressive urban reform, this range needs to be expanded. Holli suggests expanding the range to 1893–1920; Green says that the Progressive "reliance on the solons of big business" lasted until the stock market crash of 1929.[2] As we will see, a case could be made that the Progressive impact on urban reform lasted much longer than that. Certainly many United States cities have structured their local political institutions around Progressive assumptions, policies, and principles.

In 1888 James Bryce's *American Commonwealth* described the set of urban problems the Progressives would later attempt to address. Included in the list of problems were: (1) incompetent and/or corrupt officials who wasted or put to personal use taxpayer money, (2) the use by partisan politicians of patronage spoils appointments to fill municipal positions, (3) the undermining of local control by state legislatures' intervention in municipal affairs, and (4) defects in local government structure.

When the 1893 depression caused people to consider urban reform seriously, their list of urban ills and prescriptions for their resolution echoed Bryce. Citizens and taxpayers' associations demanded that municipal governments cut waste and costs, and reduce taxes. Local politicians and urban government professionals responded to the crisis by calling for municipal reform. Reform organizations proliferated: the National Municipal League, the League of American Municipalities, the American Society for Municipal Improvements, the American League for Civic Improvement, and the New York Municipal Research Bureau.

Three of the more common elements in reformers' prescriptions for the urban problem were: (1) increasing the involvement of business and business principles in urban governance, (2) decreasing the impact of partisan politics on urban administration, and (3) advocating an increased role for public administration in promoting the general welfare (provided the first two prescriptions were carried out). Specific structural reforms included citywide (instead of ward-based) elections, nonpartisan local elections, and commission or council-manager structures for local governments.

Reformers were able to fuse arguments regarding the immorality of local government with arguments regarding its potential effectiveness by emphasizing the doctrine of efficiency. In 1894 Theodore Roosevelt told the First National Conference for Good City Government: "There are two gospels I always want to preach to reformers. . . . The First is the gospel of morality; the next is the gospel of efficiency."[3] But as the reformers' arguments evolved, calls for morality became subsumed under calls for efficiency. "It was not the lack of virtue or a lack of honesty but a lack of efficiency and a lack of competence that wasted scarce municipal resources."[4] Consequently, the prescription entailed increasing the number and power of technicians in local government.

Aiding the rise of professional and technical expertise in municipal administration was the Progressive theme that business principles should be applied to public administration — even at the expense of American political principles. Infusion of business principles into municipal government took three paths. The commission form of government emulated a business corporation's board of directors as it abandoned the American political principle of separation of powers. The strong mayor form emulated the corporation's use of a chief executive officer, but it also compromised separation of powers by placing legislative and executive authority in the hands of a single official chosen in a citywide election. The city manager form of government promoted managerial expertise but compromised the political value of responsiveness by concentrating administrative authority in a single official appointed by the elected members of the council or commission.

Whichever path it took, one of the more significant impacts of the municipal reform movement was to alter the status of professionals and technically skilled persons in local governance. Though the Progressives also took credit for innovations that enhanced the role of direct democracy mechanisms (the initiative, referendum, and recall), within the structure of representative government power was concentrated in fewer hands, and more often in the hands of persons of elevated occupational and class status. "Experts in business, in government, and in the professions measured, studied, analyzed, and manipulated ever wider realms of human life, and devices which they used to control such affairs constituted the most fundamental and far-reaching innovations in decision-making in modern America."[5]

Still, according to Banovetz, "professional local government administration" did not really take hold in the United States until after World War II:

Council-manager government became the most common form of government in the nation in medium-sized and large cities; strong mayor-council governments began to incorporate professional chief administrative officer positions; and county government began adopting county administrator forms. Special districts, municipal leagues, councils of governments, and associations of local government officials also relied with increasing frequency on professional administrators to function as their CAOs.[6]

Two areas of local government directly affected by the Progressive reforms and the accompanying increase in professional municipal administration were public health and public works administration. Public health professionals and sanitarians (and, later, civil engineers) both participated in and benefited from Progressive municipal reforms.

History of Municipal Solid Waste Management

Today most urban residents in the United States take for granted that some garbage collection and disposal service will be available, but that has not always been the case. According to Mumford, "For thousands of years city dwellers put up with defective, often quite vile, sanitary arrangements, wallowing in rubbish and filth."[7] The population density was so low and people were so insensitive to garbage that they simply tossed it on their floors, in the streets, or wherever seemed convenient.

The Industrial Revolution generated the most wide-ranging change in solid waste management history has yet seen. As large numbers of people crowded into industrial cities, the volumes of garbage could no longer be ignored. The awful noises of industrial life were accompanied by foul air, filthy streets, and stinking water. When an 1842 report by the English Poor Law Commission concluded that disease was somehow caused by unsanitary environmental conditions, the stage was set for government response to the conditions generated by industrialism and urbanization.

While Europe was passing public health laws, America was still in a preindustrial condition; it remained a highly decentralized society. "The first federal census of 1790 showed that city dwellers represented only 5.1% of the population, and only two cities exceeded 25,000."[8] People had not yet begun to overwhelm the continent's natural resources. There seemed to be plenty of land and water to absorb the poor sanitation habits of European Americans.

Late Nineteenth Century

When the Industrial Revolution hit America, the New World experienced some of the same problems that faced the Old World. "Between 1840 and 1920 — the period of the first major wave of [U.S.] industrialization — the urban population grew from 1,845,000 to over 54 million, that is, from 10.8 percent of the population to a little more than 51 percent."[9] As industrial cities multiplied in the United States, problems such as crowded living conditions, polluted air and water, amplified noise, and increased volumes of garbage developed. American cities responded to these problems, but their responses were often insufficient. New Orleans had a problem with typhoid and Memphis with yellow fever. Near the turn of the century New York City's Sanitary District A included about 300,000 people — 986.4 people per acre. "A 1905 study indicated that fourteen American cities averaged 860 pounds of mixed rubbish per capita per year, while in eight English cities the amount was 450 pounds per capita, and in seventy-seven German cities, 319 pounds."[10]

As the nineteenth century closed, a new attitude toward garbage was beginning to take hold in the United States. Public health professionals and sanitarians played a major role in the new thinking about solid waste. In 1887 the American Public Health Association appointed a Committee on Garbage Disposal. Professional and popular periodicals began to address the garbage problem. *Harper's Weekly* posed the question: "What shall be done with the garbage? This is one of the great problems in the administration of modern cities."[11]

When Americans began to understand the seriousness of their sanitation problem, the first casualty was faith in individual responsibility. It became clear that refuse collection and disposal was a community problem that required a community response.

At the same time, the prevailing scientific theory of disease (the miasmic, or filth theory) pushed American cities toward organized efforts to reduce the garbage problem. "According to the theory, gases emanating from putrefying matter or sewers were the cause of contagious diseases, and city cleanliness, proper drainage and sewerage, and adequate ventilation of buildings would suffice in arresting them."[12] (By the turn of the century, the germ theory of disease began to be preferred over the filth theory, but the change in city sanitation habits had by then become normalized.)

The first community efforts were driven by an "out of sight, out of mind" philosophy. Their main goal was to move the garbage away from the people. The most common disposal methods included dumping the refuse on open land or in water, or putting it to some utilitarian purpose such as fertilizer for farms, farm animal feed, road surfacing, or landfill. "Whatever the method of disposal, few precautions were taken to ensure that it was sanitary."[13] Moreover, as the volume of garbage increased, the limited number of people wanting to put it to some purpose meant that more was dumped.

Since urbanites had come to expect their cities to be somewhat sanitary, a major question facing communities was who would be ultimately responsible for collection and disposal of the refuse. The two options were: (1) to establish a government-owned and run service, or (2) to contract for the service with private companies. According to the 1880 census, 24 percent of all cities ran their own garbage service, 19 percent contracted for the service, 30 percent left the responsibility to private enterprise, and 25 percent had some combination of approaches.[14]

Recognizing that the traditional methods of disposal were inadequate to the task, authorities began to look for other options. They found that in Europe burning had become a favored method of waste disposal. The first systematic approach to burning refuse at the municipal level (in an incinerator they called a *destructor*) was conducted in 1874 at Nottingham, England. The first United States incinerators were built in the late 1880s. Another method found in Europe was the Vienna or Merz process. It extracted oils and other by-products by compressing municipal waste. In the United States this method became known as the reduction process and was adopted by cities seeking to recover some of the cost of solid waste management by selling the by-products.

Around the turn of the century, the Progressive Movement's faith in public administration guided by business principles inclined cities to establish public sanitation or refuse departments. Embodying that faith and leading the battle was George E. Waring, Jr., the "father of modern refuse management."[15] Having spent his earlier years in the military, in agriculture, and in engineering, Waring was the street-cleaning commissioner of New York City from 1895 to 1898. He first entered the sanitation profession when, as an engineer, he designed and constructed municipal sewer systems. When the Progressive leaders of the civic reform movement in New York City were able to defeat Tammany Hall and elect William Strong as mayor, Strong appointed other Progressive leaders such as Theodore Roosevelt (police commissioner) and Waring to bring the affairs of the city under the guidance of business principles.

"From his first day on the job as street-cleaning commissioner, Waring . . . recognized that his immediate task was to gain control of a department which had been little more than a source of patronage for Tammany Hall."[16] At first he tried to work with the people already in the street-cleaning department, but eventually he reorganized the department and appointed young men with military backgrounds or engineering degrees to supervisory positions. He also changed the lower echelons of the department, organizing them into a military-style unit (his "White Wings") with white uniforms to wear, morning roll calls to answer, and an elaborate set of written rules to follow. This change in image enjoyed a positive response from the public and gave the street cleaners a new pride in their positions.

But Waring did not stop there. He increased salaries, instituted an eight-hour day, and established a formal grievance procedure. To insure that the streets were kept clean, he organized a systematic sweeping program using his army of White Wings — 1,450 workers swept 433 miles of paved streets. To improve the collection of household and commercial waste, he designed a "primary separation" program, which required households and businesses to keep organic waste, rubbish, and ashes in separate bins for more efficient collection. Despite resistance from the public, the program was fairly successful and made recycling and reusing the waste much easier. As part of his attempt to improve the reusability of the waste, he "established the first rubbish-sorting plant in the United States."[17]

When Tammany Hall retook New York City in the 1898 election, Waring's reform efforts came to an end. But he had had his impact as part of the Progressive Movement's alteration of the way municipal government was run. Although a bit primitive and autocratic, his department was organized to perform more efficiently and effectively, and was designed to improve the public welfare through enlightened management. He saw his crusade to clean up the city as going beyond sanitizing the streets and into improving the physical and social environment of the city. Such an improvement, he and the other Progressives believed, would result in a healthier local body politic.

Early Twentieth Century

A 1906 issue of *Charities and the Commons* called sanitary engineering "a new social profession."[18] Heirs of Waring and the other pioneering sanitation professionals connected to the Progressive Movement, twentieth-century sanitary engineers were among the experts reformist politicians needed to improve the administration of municipal affairs.

First, however, municipal sanitation had to adapt to a change in the science upon which it had been established. The filth theory of disease was being replaced by the germ theory, and that meant the public health foundation for sanitation was undercut. This resulted in sanitation no longer being exclusively under the control of health departments. Because sanitation was a task that required administrative and technical expertise, cities turned to engineers to run their sanitation programs. According to Schultz and McShane, "Labeling themselves neutral experts, engineers professed to work above the din of local politics."[19] Sanitary engineers, attaching their future to cries for nonpartisan municipal management, rode the Progressive wave of urban reform into public service in local government. They were eager to accept the challenge. A 1908 *Engineering News* editorial opined:

> Besides bad politics and general inefficiency in municipal administration, the chief hindrance to putting refuse collection and disposal on a satisfactory basis is the failure of the public and of nontechnical officials to recognize that the most difficult of the problems involved are engineering in character and will never be satisfactorily solved until they are entrusted to engineers.[20]

Some engineers were even ready to tackle the problems of "bad politics and inefficiency in municipal administration." Taking on the title "public engineers," they saw themselves as community leaders and civic educators.

With regard to whether municipalities should control refuse management or allow private enterprise to provide the service, as good Progressives, sanitary engineers were strongly behind municipal control. Hering and Greeley simply declared, "The collection of public refuse is a public utility."[21] Municipalities, of course, were not of one mind on the responsibility question, but the trend in the early twentieth century was toward municipal control. "By World War I at least 50 percent of American cities had some form of municipal collection system, as compared with only 24 percent in 1880."[22]

Sanitary engineers also helped municipalities improve their techniques of refuse disposal. They strongly opposed such nineteenth-century approaches as dumping on open land or in water, open burning, and using untreated wastes as landfill. Still, they did not agree on any single method as the "one best way" to manage refuse. Each municipality needed to design its own approach — keeping in mind the types and quantities of wastes, the local transportation infrastructure, the physical characteristics of the city, and social, political, and organizational factors. Still, some methods of disposal were no longer acceptable. Dumping waste into water was almost universally condemned—too much floated back to the shores, it was too costly, and downstream cities began to file lawsuits. By order of the United States Supreme Court, as of July 1, 1934, all ocean dumping of municipal waste (but not industrial or commercial waste) was to stop.[23] Though it remained the most common approach to disposal, dumping on land also began to be criticized. The dumps were breeding places for rats, cockroaches, and other pests. Light materials such as paper would blow out of the dump into neighboring properties. There were also periodic fires, with their accompanying smoke and odor.

Two other forms of land dumping—filling and burial—continued to attract sanitary engineers. Fills were used to build up levies and to fill in shorelines. Experiments in plowing waste into farmlands also received serious attention.[24] The two engineering approaches to refuse disposal discussed most, however, were incineration and reduction. In 1916, the American Society for Municipal Improvement's (later the American Society of Municipal Engineers) Committee on Refuse Disposal and Street Cleaning recommended the reduction process for large cities, where economies of scale came into play. Incineration, they said, appeared better suited to smaller cities.[25] It was considered sanitary, efficient, and economical.

But American experience with incinerators around the turn of the century was not encouraging. "Of the 180 furnaces erected between 1885 and 1908, 102 had been abandoned or dismantled by 1909."[26] Sanitary engineers became frustrated with faulty designs, improper operation, and poor quality equipment sold by unscrupulous companies. While they had reduced partisanship in municipal engineering departments, the Progressives could not thoroughly insulate solid waste management from partisan cronyism. "Contracts were obtained by personal and political favor, by influential pull, by manipulation and graft, with little regard to the interests of the city or town."[27] On the other hand, the problems with incineration itself could be addressed by the engineers—if they were allowed to do their jobs without amateur political interference. By the end of the twentieth century's first decade engineers claimed they had created a new generation of incinerators, and by the 1930s more than 600 cities had built incineration plants.[28]

The reduction process was not so able to weather the criticism aimed at it. In 1905 Cleveland became the first U.S. city to own a reduction plant. The profitability of that plant encouraged other midwestern cities to build their own plants, but the process never gained wide acceptance. In 1914, only 22 of the 45 reduction plants in the United States were in operation. Though the technology had originally come from Europe, the process was not in general use there either. American advocates of the process believed that our affluence made our refuse more likely to contain valuable recoverable elements. But even at its best reduction could only handle 30 percent of the waste stream — the organic garbage. After World War I, few reduction plants remained in operation.[29]

The process did, however, help sustain interest in utilization of wastes and recycling. The same economic logic that supported the reduction process supported a belief in other waste utilization approaches. "Turning waste into wealth"[30] became a popular American theme. Older reutilization ideas — such as using waste as fertilizer, landfill, and road building material — gained new life. Before a series of swine epidemics ruined its profitability, up to 40 percent of U.S. cities fed garbage to swine in "piggeries."[31] Used paper and rags were recycled to produce more paper. "In 1916 the United States produced more than 15,000 tons of paper a day, using 5,000 tons of old paper in the process."[32] Waste was also turned into energy. A Texas man patented "oakcoal," fuel bricks made from refuse. Scientists in England developed "coalesine," a fuel briquette made from refuse. Incinerators were used to generate steam power and electricity.

But the waste-to-wealth promise did not quite match up to economic and environmental practice. America was rich in resources and the marketplace found seemingly less expensive alternatives for almost all the reutilization schemes. With the advent of the sanitary landfill, disposal of garbage appeared to be less expensive than reutilization. Though the preferred method of disposal was little more than an aesthetically enhanced dump, by the end of the 1930s every U.S. city with a population of 100,000 or more offered or contracted for garbage services.[33] By midcentury the country was living comfortably on its environmental credit account, unaware of the balloon payments looming on the horizon.

Mid-Twentieth Century

"In the years between 1945 and 1978, municipal budgets for trash collection (and other forms of sanitation) increased by 765 percent."[34] (During the same period municipal expenditures for education rose about the same percentage, for crime and law enforcement 527 percent, and for fire protection 365 percent.) That increase was only the beginning of a sharp upward curve in the price Americans would pay for solid waste management. When the bill for cleaning up and maintaining the dumps and landfills of the past started to come due, that increase looked like a gentle slope.

In the 1950s, engineers and municipal officials thought the garbage problem was under control. The task was seen basically as one of disposing the garbage, and landfilling had become the primary disposal method. It seemed all that was needed was to expand the size and/or number of landfills.

Sanitary landfills were seen as the state-of-the-art approach to land-filling. The first sanitary landfills in the United States were built in the 1930s. By the mid-1940s approximately 100 municipalities were using the approach. But the definition of "sanitary landfill" was not very precise, and some of them "were similar to the open dumping that remained by far the most prevalent method of land disposal well into the 1970s." (In 1972 14,000 communities were still using traditional land dumps.)[35] Still, as an approach to disposal, sanitary landfilling was simply a better supervised and maintained modification of primitive landfill approaches.

In the 1960s it began to be apparent that the garbage problem had not been solved. The volume of municipal waste generated was overtaking dis-posal capacity. "In 1920 per capita production of waste was about 2.75 pounds per day; in 1970, about 5 pounds per day; and in 1980, about 8 pounds per day."[36] The federal Bureau of Solid Waste Management said that the volume of waste generated was causing a "refuse disposal problem that far outstrips the waste handling resources and facilities of virtually every community in the nation."[37] In 1968 the *Wall Street Journal* ran an article on how desperate cities were seeking new methods of dealing with the growing solid waste problem.[38]

The problem was not only the volume of the waste, but its composition. In the early twentieth century horse manure and ashes from wood and coal were significant portions of municipal waste, but by the 1970s paper and plastic were the fastest growing components. According to the EPA, in 1970 paper was 33.1 percent of all municipal solid waste and plastics were 2.7 percent; by 2000 those figures were expected to be 41.0 percent and 9.8 percent, respectively.[39]

Problems with sanitary landfills also became apparent. First, landfill sites were no longer easily obtained. Second, the potential future use of areas that had been sanitary landfills did not appear as promising as had once been thought. As the materials in them settled and decomposed, the land-fills were not sufficiently stable to be used as residential or commercial construction sites. Third, as surface water worked its way through the buried waste it leached compounds that polluted groundwater, and sometimes emissions of methane and other gases caused health and safety problems.

Solid waste, therefore, became seen as part of a much larger problem — environmental pollution. As with air and water pollution, "land pollution" did not respect political boundaries. The problems resulting from it went beyond the capabilities and jurisdictions of local governments. As a consequence, "interlocal agreements began replacing more traditional collection and disposal arrangements."[40]

As solid waste management overwhelmed local governments, the issue of control reemerged. In the 1965 Solid Waste Disposal Act (amended in 1970 and retitled the Resource Recovery Act) Congress brought the federal government into solid waste policy making. Saying that "while the collection and disposal of solid wastes should continue to be primarily the function of State, regional, and local agencies, the problems of waste disposal . . . have become a matter national in scope,"[41] the act allowed federal involvement in research and development of new solid waste technologies. By the late 1980s federal environmental guidelines and standards strictly limited the options available to local governments.

In addition, large private firms began identifying solid waste management as an area sure to hold profit potential in the not-too-distant future. Large waste hauling firms took over smaller ones. New or reconfigured firms appeared and offered disposal options such as waste-to-energy and mega-landfills. Through contracts and public-private partnerships, municipal control over solid waste management gradually and steadily eroded.

This was the beginning of a new era in solid waste management. No longer were local governments left to their own devices in dealing with the garbage problem. Now it was seen as a national problem, beyond the capacities of the local governments, and too rich a vein for private enterprise to leave to government at any level.

Later chapters will address the dynamics of intergovernmental approaches to solid waste management and of the increasing role of solid waste management–related businesses. Now it is time to examine how its history and structures affected Spokane's solid waste policy making.

Spokane's Local Political Institutions

The most significant local political institutions in the Spokane Solid Waste Policy System are the city of Spokane, Spokane County, and three special districts — the Spokane County Health District, the Spokane County Air Pollution Control Authority (SCAPCA), and the Spokane International Airport Authority (see fig. 4.1). The city has a council-manager form of

government and in the area of solid waste management includes two units
— the Solid Waste Management Department, which is responsible for collection, and the Solid Waste Disposal Project Office, which was created
through an interlocal agreement with Spokane County. Spokane County
has a commission form of government. Its Engineering Department was the
only subdivision involved in solid waste–related policy making in this case
study, but the commissioners were thoroughly involved, both as commissioners and as members of boards overseeing other political institutions
involved in solid waste policy making and management. The Health District
was the special district formally charged with overseeing solid waste management in the county. SCAPCA became involved because of air pollution
problems resulting from solid waste management in the county. The Air-

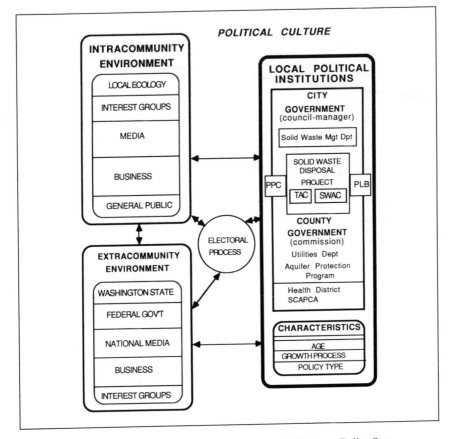

Figure 4.1 Local Political Institutions in Spokane's Solid Waste Policy System

port Authority became involved because the waste-to-energy facility was located near the airport and threatened to exacerbate the fog problem there.

The Progressive Movement's urban reforms and the history of municipal sanitation have left their mark on Spokane's solid waste policy making. The Progressive Movement's preferred municipal government structures—first the commission form, then the council-manager form—have both had their day in the city of Spokane. Despite the fact that it has the same basic structure as when Washington was admitted as a state, Spokane county government has also been affected by Progressive reforms. Over the years it has gradually recognized a need for more professional and technically trained personnel, including a county administrator. Special districts are also derivative of the Progressive Movement's push for more expert, less political management of public affairs.

Spokane's solid waste policy history is a microcosm of the nation's. As people began to crowd into the town, it began to perceive a need for sanitation, and it depended initially on a health professional to lead the way. Throughout the twentieth century, it has followed the mainstream in adopting technical solutions to solid waste management problems—a land dump, an incinerator, sanitary landfilling, a new state-of-the-art incinerator, a plastic-lined mega-landfill. As is common throughout the country, the main local government structures in Washington State are counties, municipalities, and special districts. According to the Washington State Local Governance Study Commission, the major components of the state's local governance tradition are an insistence on local control, and an evolving relationship between municipalities, counties, and special districts.[42]

This certainly fits the Spokane experience. I will begin this section with the history of the city of Spokane's government structure and solid waste policy making. Then I will focus on Spokane County, special districts related to solid waste management, and interlocal agreements related to solid waste management.

The City of Spokane

Throughout its history, the city of Spokane has recognized the need for professional management of solid waste. Originally chartered in 1881 as the city of Spokane Falls, it incorporated into its city charter as early as 1883 explicit provisions regarding the management of solid waste. Under that charter the city had a mayor-council form of government, and a health officer (who had to be a physician) was appointed by the city council to oversee solid waste management; the chief of police was to carry out the health officer's orders. The charter also said that "offal, garbage, night soil or refuse" were not to be deposited within the city or within one mile of the city, except in the "regularly established city garbage grounds."[43]

In its history, the city of Spokane has had all three forms of municipal government specifically provided for in the current Washington State Constitution: mayor-council, commission, and council-manager. When the city was incorporated as the City of Spokane in 1891, it kept the mayor-council form of government. With regard to solid waste management, the 1891 charter prohibited refuse in the streets and fouling of the river. Like the 1883 charter, it authorized the city to hire a physician as health officer, and named the chief of police as the "sanitary policeman."[44] In addition, the municipal code provided for a board of health that could, with the permission of the city council, appoint sanitary inspectors. The code also regulated garbage collection, requiring licenses for collectors and limiting the hours during which collection could take place.[45]

By 1903, the city also regulated the burning of rubbish and the prices "scavengers" could charge. In that same year the city adopted an ordinance authorizing the board of public works "to build, construct and erect in the City of Spokane a Decarie incinerating furnace for the consumption and destruction of all garbage."[46] The public works department was authorized to spend $3,500 to construct a building to house the incinerator and, after a 30-day demonstration that it performed as promised, to pay the Decarie Company $6,000 for the incinerator. Records show that a couple of years later Spokane began using a dumpsite in Moran Prairie, south of the city limits.

It is fair to say, then, that around the turn of the century Spokane was in the mainstream of U.S. municipal solid waste history as described above. The leading experts in solid waste management were health officers and engineers. Garbage collection was provided by private contractors, but was beginning to be regulated by the municipality. The major disposal techniques included land dumping and incineration.

Influenced by the Progressive Movement and seeking a form of government that did not concentrate power in the hands of a single individual,[47] in 1911 Spokane adopted a commission form of government. There were five commissioners, all elected to four-year terms in citywide elections. As was typical in commission governments, the commissioners had both legislative and executive duties. As members of the commission, they performed a legislative function; as heads of various departments (Public Utilities, Public Works, Public Affairs, Public Finance, and Public Safety), they functioned as the city's executives.[48]

By 1915, the commission had decided against private enterprise involvement in solid waste management. Finding that the private sector had collected wastes in a manner detrimental to the public health, the commission created a "crematory department" and authorized it to "collect and dispose of all manure, garbage, offal, refuse, rubbish, dead animals, or any vegetable or animal matter detrimental to health under the sanitary ordinances." They also authorized public works to purchase an additional 80-ton crematory. In 1925, they allowed the private sector back into the collection business, but only under the regulatory guidance and inspection of the city health officer.[49]

During the 1930s Spokane's experience was thoroughly enmeshed with that of the state and nation. The Great Depression brought a common experience to all of the nation's communities. Depression-reduced tax revenues made Spokane and other municipalities reluctant to expand the area for which they provided services. In Washington State this fostered the growth of special districts, new interlocal cooperative arrangements, and increased local dependence on state and federal assistance.[50] With regard to solid waste management, like the rest of the nation, Spokane depended on land dumping of its solid waste; the Northside dump site was opened in 1931.

Arthur R. Meehan's years as mayor (1945–1955) constituted a significant period for local solid waste management under the commission form of government. In addition to serving as mayor for ten years, Meehan was commissioner of Public Works for sixteen years. He was also a professional municipal administrator, serving as street superintendent before being elected commissioner of Public Works in 1942. He was elected president of the Association of Washington Cities in 1947. Aided by post–World War II population growth, Meehan's administration was classically Progressive in tone and accomplishments. He has been credited with making many improvements at low cost. He helped the city acquire a minor league baseball team, a coliseum, a stadium, and new libraries. His administration also improved the city's traffic system by adding bridges, widening streets, and providing snow removal services. During his tenure as mayor the voters also approved a sewage disposal construction bond, an auditorium, and a charter amendment allowing primary elections.[51] In 1949, under Meehan's leadership, the city passed its first universal garbage collection ordinance.

Meanwhile, the state decided in 1943 to allow its largest municipalities to adopt the council-manager form of government.[52] This set the stage for the next period's disruption and change. The period between 1955 and 1960 was one of significant discord in Spokane politics. Two different mayors were chosen in that short time. In the 1958 election three incumbent commissioners were defeated. Finally, in March 1960, the same year the city began converting its Northside dump site into a sanitary landfill, Spokane voters adopted a charter amendment that led to a council-manager form of government, which form the city has retained to this day.

The campaign for the charter amendment was just what one would expect in Progressive reforms. A group called the Mayor–Council-Manager Committee, headed by a local businessman, began a petition campaign in 1959. The campaign was supported by W. T. Cowles (owner and publisher of the *Spokesman-Review*), the Spokane Municipal League, and the League of Women Voters. Included in the arguments for change were allegations of waste, fraud, corruption, and inefficiency. Opponents countered that the proposed reform was undemocratic because the manager would not be directly responsible to the electorate. There were also attempts to depict the battle line as drawn along class lines, with Republicans, businessmen, and the social elite favoring the council-manager plan and organized labor, some public employees, and the working class opposing it. Council-manager proponents won a significant victory in the election of candidates to fill positions in the new form of government. They promoted a banker for mayor, and a slate of candidates known as the "Citizens Six" for the council positions. Despite a backlash against their well-financed campaign, the banker, Neal R. Fosseen, won a close election for mayor and four of the "Six" council candidates also won.[53]

In the council-manager form of government, the city council — six members plus the mayor, all elected to four-year terms in citywide elections — performs the legislative function. Elections are nonpartisan and are held in odd years to avoid coinciding with state and national elections. Every two years, three council members' terms expire. The mayor in the council-manager form of government is a "weak mayor" with no executive function and no veto power over council actions — only a vote that counts the same as other council members'. Any leadership role a mayor might have in the city council is a function of the regard council members have for the person in the position; the position itself is mostly ceremonial and has no special authority. Six mayors served in the years between 1960 and 1993, including the city's first African-American mayor and the first and second female mayors.

Under the council-manager form of government, the chief administrative officer is the city manager. The city manager is appointed, and may be removed at any time, by a majority vote of the council. With the council's approval (explicit or tacit) the city manager has general administrative authority in the city. The city manager may appoint or remove administrative personnel, but must work within the civil service system and with various unions in personnel decisions.

From 1960 to 1993, the city of Spokane had four city managers. Though adoption of the council-manager form of government usually implies that a city desires a more professional municipal administration, in what may be an expression of the western inclination toward local control Spokane has most often selected managers with roots in the area. The first city manager was Henry Nabers, a man from Abilene, Texas, whose management style was insufficiently businesslike for the reform council. He was forced to resign in 1963.

The position was next filled by F. Sylvin Fulwiler, a Spokane native who had begun his municipal service career in Washington State and had most recently been city manager in Chula Vista, California. While his tenure was rather tumultuous, he retained the position for twelve years before he "retired under pressure."[54] In 1965 advocates of a strong mayor form of government placed a proposed charter amendment on the ballot; it was narrowly defeated. In 1967 a number of proposed charter amendments were placed on the ballot, but they were all defeated handily.

As they overcame their opposition, the council and manager also worked to deliver promised reforms for those who had supported them and the council-manager form of government. Responding to a deteriorating downtown, Fulwiler and the council began trying to revitalize the area. The primary vehicle for that revitalization was development of a downtown site for a World's Fair in 1974. During Fulwiler's tenure, street paving was improved and sewage treatment upgraded. In 1971 his public works director was involved in Spokane's first waste-to-energy proposal. His administration also completed the conversion of the Northside dump site into a sanitary landfill.

When Fulwiler retired in 1975, Glen Yake stepped in as interim city manager while the council sought a replacement. A city government insider, Yake had already put in more than 20 years of service (including a stint as the director of public utilities and public works) when Fulwiler appointed him assistant city manager. Yake is often given credit for pioneering the idea of a waste-to-energy plant in Spokane. He had been involved in the 1971 bid by the Inland Empire Waste Conservation Association for an EPA grant for a preliminary feasibility study, and in a 1972 resubmission of that proposal (both unsuccessful). In the summer of 1978 the city submitted another application for a grant to fund a marketing and economics study for a waste-to-energy facility. That proposed project was also a cooperative venture — this time involving the city, the local electric utility (Washington Water Power), and the regional forest industry, and would have burned wood waste and municipal garbage.[55] After serving as interim city manager, Yake was appointed manager of engineering by Spokane's third city manager. In 1985 he also was appointed interim project coordinator for the newly created Solid Waste Disposal Project (SWDP) while the city and county conducted a nationwide search for a permanent coordinator. He retired in April 1985, having served the city of Spokane for 35 years.

Terry Novak was the third city manager. Unlike Fulwiler and Yake, he did not have roots in Spokane. Holding a doctorate in political science with an emphasis in public administration, he was recruited in 1978 from the position of city manager of Columbia, Missouri, and had served as city manager in Hopkins, Minnesota, and as assistant city manager in Anchorage, Alaska. An energetic and enthusiastic person who appears most satisfied when he is making things happen, Novak held the position in Spokane for thirteen years, retiring in 1991. Like Fulwiler, he served during tumultuous times, and though he says he never felt it, he appears to have retired under pressure. Controversies during his tenure included purchasing and renovating a former Montgomery Ward building for a new city hall, selection of a new police chief from outside the system, obtaining voter approval and sufficient financing for a new multipurpose arena to replace the old coliseum, and of course, the waste-to-energy facility — a project he has described as "the largest local public works project in the history of the Inland Northwest."[56] Because of his leadership in promoting SWDP, his job was in jeopardy in the 1989 elections, but with the exception of the mayor, the victorious candidates were not among his vociferous critics.

With Novak as city manager the city entered a new era in solid waste management. In 1980, refuse department head Dennis Hein applied to WDOE for a Referendum 39 grant to assist in funding a waste-to-energy facility. In 1984 the city adopted a waste management plan that included a waste-to-energy incinerator. In 1985 the city entered into an interlocal agreement with the county and established SWDP. A contract with Wheelabrator to construct a waste-to-energy facility was approved in 1987. The city council authorized the sale of bonds to finance the waste-to-energy facility, and Novak gave Wheelabrator "notice to proceed" in 1989. He retired about two months before the waste-to-energy facility began operating.

The fourth city manager was Roger Crum; he had master's degrees in Systems Engineering Management, Environmental Systems, and Marketing and Finance, and had served the previous eleven years as Novak's deputy city manager. Like Yake, Crum served as interim city manager in 1991 while the council sought a permanent replacement for his predecessor. Unlike Novak, he is a soft-spoken person and has not generated much controversy, but he has had to weather some. Most of it might be described as a function of the general taxpayer resistance movement across the country. The controversies revolved around city administrator salary levels, the amount and cost of professional travel taken by city staff and elected officials, the cost of providing city-owned vehicles to staff, and the cost and proper use of cellular phones. In addition, Crum's tenure included the continuing controversies involved in getting the new solid waste disposal system in operation. Problems like where to site the ash transfer station, whether to contract for incineration of medical waste, whether to burn tires, what role local government should play in encouraging composting, where to site the government-supported composting operation, how much the city should pay for building the composting facility, whether the city should close down the compost facility because of the stench with which it smothered its neighbors, and whether the city's solid waste department and the SWDP ought to be merged. Overall, however, the project remained rather smoothly on track under his leadership.

SWDP was designed as a cooperative project of the city and county, but the city was the "lead agency," which meant that it had final legal responsibility in running the project. As will be explained later, the actual balance of power and responsibility varied over time, partly in response to pressures from active citizens in the county and partly due to the commissioners' desire for a more equal partnership. Because the city was the lead agency and because its meeting format included time for citizen comments, city council meetings became the major public forum in which policy options were discussed. Formal policy decisions involving the project were made in one of two ways: (1) by the council in its regular meeting with concurrence by the commission in its regular meeting (to become effective, any policy had to be approved by both bodies), or (2) by the council and commission in special joint session. In the workshops and other public meetings directly pertaining to the environmental impact statement process, both city council members and county commissioners participated on a periodic basis.

The workshops themselves were run by SWDP with the assistance of the local chapter of the League of Women Voters. After the startup decisions had been made and the project moved into its operational phase, the normal pattern was for SWDP staff to take the initiative on relatively minor decisions (subject to review by the Policy Liaison Board), and for the council and commission to decide major issues. Sometimes the distinction was not clear to all involved parties. For example, the executive director of SWDP thought he should be able to decide whether the waste-to-energy facility could accept a contract to burn plastic jugs that had contained pesticides. When that decision became a public controversy, the council members and commissioners became involved.

Throughout its history the city of Spokane's solid waste policy making has reflected a combination of elected official authority and professional expertise. As solid waste issues became more complex and the tendency of environmental problems to ignore political boundaries became more manifest, the city began to cooperate with the county and other local political institutions.

Spokane County

Legally, local governments are created by the state, so the basic laws governing them are found in the state constitution, state legislation, and sometimes, home rule charters. The Supreme Court of Washington State has several times agreed that "a county has no inherent powers of its own — only those granted to it by the state legislature or the constitution."[57] Among the limited powers specifically granted by the state constitution to county governments is the power to make and enforce sanitary regulations that do not conflict with state laws.[58]

In practice, however, counties in Washington State have considerable authority. Some of the counties in Washington State existed prior to the territory's admission as a state in 1889. The original Spokane County was one of three counties formed east of the Cascade Mountains in 1859.[59] By the time its present boundaries were established in 1883, the original Spokane County had been divided into twenty-three counties: five in Idaho, six in Montana, and twelve in Washington.[60] Counties were the local unit of government through which the territorial government acted.[61] So, while county government serves primarily as an administrative arm of the state, its tradition also includes an awareness of the authority it held before the state existed.

Another traditional role of counties has been that of general services provider to county residents who do not live within municipalities. Increasingly, that role has included functions and powers typical of municipalities. For example, the state legislature authorized counties in 1943 to operate solid waste disposal sites, in 1959 to engage in land use planning, and in 1965 to issue revenue bonds for general purposes.[62] Since the late 1960s that trend has continued, with the state legislature enacting "statutes that authorize—and often direct—counties to take the lead" in specific areas, including solid waste management systems.[63]

Since Washington was admitted to statehood, the powers of counties have been significantly increased. A 1948 amendment to the state constitution gave counties the option of adopting a home rule charter. A 1972 amendment to the state constitution allowed combined city-county government.[64]

Though it employed its first county administrator in the late 1970s, and in 1995 voters were considering whether to adopt a new charter, the formal structure of Spokane County's government has not changed since Washington became a state. It is governed by a three-person board of county commissioners. After winning a primary election in one of three districts, each commissioner is elected to a four-year term in a partisan, countywide general election. In one election year two commissioner seats are at issue; two years later the other seat is up for election. The commissioners decide which of them is to serve as chair of the commission, usually for a one-year term.

The commissioners have legislative, executive, and judicial functions. They pass ordinances, supervise other county officials, and (as the board of equalization) adjudicate complaints. There are a number of other elected county officials (e.g., assessor, coroner, sheriff, prosecuting attorney, and district and superior court judges); the commissioners' primary duties are to levy taxes and to adopt a balanced budget for the entire county government. Appointed administrative department heads report to the commissioners through the county administrator, an appointed professional public administrator. Within the utilities department is a solid waste section, which prior to the creation of SWDP was responsible (acting under the authority of the commissioners) for all aspects of solid waste management in the unincorporated areas of the county.[65]

As early as 1921 Spokane County had health regulations that dealt with some aspects of solid waste management. One such ordinance still in the county code provides:

No garbage, pomace, offal, dead animals, decaying matter or organic waste substance of any kind shall be thrown or deposited in any ravine, ditch or gutter; on any street or highway; into any waters of the State or be permitted to remain exposed upon the surface of the ground.

Another requires the burial or incineration of the carcass of a dead animal within twenty-four hours after its death, and a third regulates the construction and operation of piggeries. In 1948 the county adopted an ordinance prohibiting the dumping of trash on county property, and in 1963 that ordinance was amended to prohibit throwing trash on public or private property.[66]

In 1971 the county prepared its first solid waste management plan. As required by the Washington State Solid Waste Management-Reduction and Recycling Act, that plan was updated in the 1973 Multi-Jurisdictional Solid Waste Management Planning Study.[67]

In the early 1980s, the county utilities department worked cooperatively with the city of Spokane and Washington Water Power on a waste-to-energy feasibility study. They contracted out the work on that study to Morrison-Knudsen, then contracted with Parametrix, Inc., for a Solid Waste Master Plan (required by the Washington State Department of Ecology). Solid waste activities are now coordinated locally among the county utilities department, SWDP, the city of Spokane's Solid Waste Department, the Spokane County Air Pollution Control Authority, and the Spokane County Health District.

In 1984, as required by state law, the county adopted a Solid Waste Management Plan. It identified four major goals: (1) development of solid waste practices that protected the environment, (2) promotion of an economically responsible approach, (3) reduction of the waste stream and the land required for disposal, and (4) recognition of the importance of materials recovery as a way of reducing the volume of waste to be disposed of.[68] The plan was approved by WDOE in 1986, and later revisions have become the official statements of solid waste management policy in Spokane County.

In 1985, the county, as part of a general revision of its code provisions regulating solid waste disposal, adopted a flow control ordinance, requiring that all solid waste in its jurisdiction be delivered to a "site which is consistent with the Spokane County solid waste management plan and a part of the county's solid waste management disposal system."[69] That ordinance was seen as a crucial part of the solid waste management plan. It was also considered essential for assuring adequate revenue from collection and tipping fees to pay for the waste-to-energy facility. Still, in 1992, to facilitate the development of a local composting company the commissioners amended the flow control ordinance to exempt compostable materials from the requirement that waste be sent to SWDP.[70] (The impact of the Supreme Court's *Carbone* decision that a similar flow control ordinance was a violation of the Commerce Clause of the U.S. Constitution will be discussed in the next chapter.)

In 1988 the county adopted a strict litter control and antidumping ordinance, and amended its zoning code to cover solid waste management–related activities.[71] The litter ordinance provides for fines up to five hundred dollars, community service of up to sixteen hours collecting litter, and a cumulative civil penalty of fifty dollars per day until the person cleans up his/her litter. It also says that when "three or more items [bear] the name of one individual, there shall be a permissible inference that the individual whose name appears on such items committed the unlawful act of littering." If neither the violator nor the landowner clean it up, the county can have it done and bill the landowner.[72] One zoning code change exempted the waste-to-energy facility from height restrictions around the airport; another eliminated the need for a public hearing to grant a permit to build the facility near the airport.[73]

There were also a number of other sections in the zoning code that pertained to solid waste management. Provisions prescribed the conditions under which landfills, composting operations, incinerators, and recycling or transfer sites could be constructed in a rural residential zone. Recycling/transfer sites were also allowed in semirural residential zones, suburban residential zones, and regional business zones. There were various provisions regarding acceptable ways to store refuse in residential and business zones. Finally, a chapter was added to the zoning code "to protect the [Spokane-Rathdrum] Aquifer from further long-term quality degradation due to land use changes" and to "define the responsibilities of several county departments in implementing and enforcing land use controls for the protection of Aquifer water quality."[74]

Over time, Spokane County's government structure has seen only minor alterations, but the duties it performs and the services it provides have changed significantly. By the 1970s, its solid waste management activities looked more like those of a city. As its activities have become more like those of a municipal government, the county has seen more reason to work with the city to coordinate services. It has also relinquished some of its authority to special districts. In 1985 there were 42 special districts in Spokane County.[75] Some of those special districts are involved in solid waste management, and it is to those that we now turn our attention.

Special Districts

Special districts became a significant form of local government as part of the reform movements of the late nineteenth and early twentieth centuries. Washington State has shown a particular penchant for them, ranking eighth in the country in the number of special districts. In 1980 there were 1,130 special districts (not counting school districts) in Washington.[76] It is not surprising, then, that the state legislature has provided for both air pollution control authorities and health districts in the more populous counties. The use of special districts is evidence of a moralistic political culture's belief that government should be proactive in its pursuit of the common good. Given the review of Washington State's political culture in chapter 3, it is not surprising that the state legislature has been generous in granting authority to create special districts. And given the review of Spokane's political culture, it is not surprising that Spokane County opted to create both health and air pollution control districts.

Spokane County Health District (SCHD) Health districts were designed to replace county departments of health and to supersede municipal health departments.[77] In 1970, the city and county of Spokane adopted such an arrangement. The governing body of the district, the Spokane County Health Board, is composed of the three county commissioners, three members of the city council, and the mayors of two of the smaller municipalities.[78] The board appoints a health officer, who must be a physician and hold a master's degree in public health, to administer the agency.

State law authorizes the health district to oversee solid waste management.[79] Once established, a health district is to issue regulations regarding the management, transportation, utilization (including recycling and energy recovery), and final disposal of solid waste. Included in those regulations are minimum functional standards (MFS) for the proper handling of solid waste and a requirement that the best available technology be used in siting, building, operating, and closing solid waste facilities.[80]

MFS regulations of the SCHD include:

- general facility requirements (e.g., plan of operation, record keeping, reporting, inspections, signs, and fencing)

- locational standards (e.g., no landfill sites over a sole source aquifer; no facilities within 10,000 feet of an airport runway being used by jets)[81]
- on-site storage, collection, and transportation standards
- recycling facility standards (e.g., standards for preventing materials from becoming a nuisance to neighbors)
- transfer station standards (e.g., access must be controlled and operations must be screened from the view of neighbors)
- storage and treatment piles standards (e.g., used tire piles)
- energy recovery and incinerator standards (e.g., facilities must maintain continuously recording devices, and must also conform to Spokane County Air Pollution Control Authority air quality standards)
- landfilling standards

In order to facilitate the district's oversight, a permit system was developed.[82] In addition to a number of general permit requirements, the permit for a particular site or facility sets forth requirements specific to that site or facility. The permits must be renewed each year. The original application and each renewal requires that the health district determine whether it meets the requirements of the district's regulations, Spokane County's Comprehensive Solid Waste Management Plan, the Department of Ecology's MFS standards, zoning and land use regulations, and all other "applicable laws and regulations."[83] Each permit must include a general description of the facility, the types of wastes handled, a record of weights or volumes, an inspection schedule and log, and proof that any treatment facility serving the permitted facility is also being reviewed under Washington Department of Ecology guidelines. New or expanded facilities must also document a geohydrological assessment, preliminary engineering reports and plans, an operation plan, a closure plan, and a postclosure plan.

The health district also has regulations providing for variances and appeals. Variances may be granted only when they "do not endanger public health, safety, or the environment . . . [and compliance] would produce hardship without equal or greater benefits to the public." Initially, appeals must be directed to the Board of Health. The board's decisions may be appealed to the Spokane County Superior Court.[84]

Spokane's solid waste management policies were significantly affected by the need to meet all the regulations, standards, and permit requirements of the health district. This would seem to place the health district in a powerful position in determining local solid waste management policy, but for reasons that will be explained more fully in the next chapter, the health district's role is better understood as implementing the policies set by state and federal policy makers. In addition, it is difficult for the health district to use any independent authority it has to question the policies worked out by the city council and the county commission because they hold six of the eight positions on the Health Board.

The health officer's power to affect policy rests mainly on authority delegated by the state and federal governments and on the officer's personal ability to persuade the members of the board. Because SCHD does not have the resources to become much of a player in solid waste (it has no one assigned to solid waste on a full-time basis), the delegated authority provides little power to influence policy. In January 1988, Spokane's health officer urged SWPD to increase recycling,[85] but no significant increase took place until the director of WDOE required it as a condition of the $60 million grant. In 1992 the health officer promoted allowing the Marshall landfill to accept trash in order to generate cleanup funds,[86] but the county commissioners did not agree. The Health District required SWDP to do a human health effects study, but when funding was inadequate had to settle for an environmental monitoring study (collection and analysis of air and soil samples).[87]

On paper SCHD would appear to be a major player in Spokane's solid waste policy making and implementation, but because of its relationship with city and county elected officials and because it has not applied many of its resources to solid waste, it has had a much more limited role. In fact, in July 1995 the county commissioners announced that they were planning to use authority granted by the 1995 state legislature to dissolve the Health District and take over its operations, but as of June 1996 that had not taken place.

Spokane County Air Pollution Control Authority (SCAPCA) Under the Washington State Clean Air Act of 1967, counties were given the option of creating their own air pollution control authorities or being part of a regional air pollution control authority.[88] Created to implement the state Clean Air Act, to comply with the federal Clean Air Act, and "to control the emissions of air contaminants from all sources"[89] in Spokane County, SCAPCA is governed by a five-member board composed of two county commissioners, one representative of the city, one representative for the other municipalities in the county, and one member at large chosen by the other four.[90] The board's formal authority includes the ability to "take such action as may be necessary to prevent air pollution including control and measurement of the emission of air contaminant from a source" and to appoint a competent professional as control officer to enforce SCAPCA's regulations, rules, ordinances, orders, and resolutions. SCAPCA is authorized to issue both criminal and civil penalties; depending on the nature of the offense, persons may face time in county jail and/or a fine.[91]

Parallel to the health district's permit system, SCAPCA requires "registration" of air contaminant sources.[92] Included among the sources that must register are: any stationary source to which a federal standard applies, any source subject to the federal clean air act, any source with a "significant emission" (as defined by the Washington Administrative Code), boilers, composting operations, active landfills, incinerators designed to handle more than 99 pounds per hour, refuse systems, and utilities. Prior to the construction or installation of a potential air contaminant source, SCAPCA may require "the submission of plans, specifications and such other information as it deems necessary in order to determine whether" the source can operate within SCAPCA regulations.[93] Approval for construction will be withheld unless SCAPCA is convinced that the source can operate without causing an emissions standard violation, that the equipment incorporates the best available control technology (BACT) and will meet U.S. Environmental Protection Agency (EPA) and Washington Department of Ecology (WDOE) standards, and that "operation of the source will not result in an ambient air standard being exceeded."[94]

In its regulations regarding specific emissions,[95] SCAPCA includes several affecting solid waste management. It specifies one kind of incinerator as the standard against which proposed incinerators will be compared, and states that the control officer may require installation of additional control devices if s/he finds that it is required for proper operation. It lists odors and particulate matters as nuisances that must be kept to a reasonable minimum, and restricts visual emissions and water vapor emissions. It also includes in its standards for controlling asbestos standards for waste disposal sites that receive asbestos.[96]

Like the health district, SCAPCA is also authorized to grant variances, but only after public notice and following a finding that the variance does not endanger public health or safety and that compliance "would produce serious hardship without equal or greater benefits to the public."[97] Initial appeals of SCAPCA actions are heard by the Pollution Control Hearings Board of Washington. After that, judicial review begins with the Superior Court.[98]

These regulations appear to place SCAPCA in a powerful position in delimiting local solid waste management policies, but it too is less independent that it appears. SCAPCA's authority is also delegated by the Washington State Department of Ecology (WDOE) and U.S. EPA. Because 60 percent of its governing body positions are held by county and city representatives, SCAPCA's ability to act as an independent check on the environmental effects of solid waste management policies and programs is limited. Though the control officer must be a competent professional, the person holding that position knows that she or he can be removed by the board at any time. Therefore, any power the control officer has beyond that derived from the state and federal delegations is mostly a function of the respect local elected officials have for the individual in that position.

SCAPCA's control officer, Eric Skelton, says the board interferes very infrequently with his running of the authority, calling it a "99 percent hands off" board. But with membership on a number of other committees and boards in addition to their elective positions, some of the board members may in their actions on the SCAPCA Board pursue agendas deriving from their other positions. Relations between the board and the control officer may vary over time with the entry and departure of specific members and the rise and fall of public interest in SCAPCA actions.

An example of what can happen when the board becomes interested in a specific SCAPCA decision point is the controversy surrounding SWDP director Phil Williams's decision to accept a contract to burn containers from Canada that had been used to hold pesticides. Skelton wanted Williams to request permission to burn the containers, but Williams burned them without getting SCAPCA approval. Williams said the containers had been triple-rinsed and were not toxic. The SCAPCA Board requested and received an independent legal opinion on whether SWDP violated their permit. Their legal consultant said there had been a violation, but the city of Spokane presented another legal consultant's opinion stating that there was no violation. Instead of listening to their control officer and their legal counsel, the board decided that the city's consultant's opinion established doubt as to whether there had been a violation and chose not to authorize any sanction against SWDP.

Like the health district, SCAPCA represents a recognition of the value of professional management of local public affairs. Each special district is administered by a qualified professional. They do not, however, constitute an unqualified victory of professional public management over politically influenced public management. Both are overseen by boards composed of local elected officials who have the authority to hire and fire.

Interlocal Agreements

Interlocal agreements have also created local political institutions that become involved in solid waste policy making. In 1967 the Washington State legislature passed the Interlocal Cooperation Act.[99] Amended in 1975 and 1979, it authorizes all local government entities to contract with each other for the delivery of services.[100] Prior to creation of the Solid Waste Disposal Project, the city and county had previously engaged in at least 27 different cooperative agreements, including joint funding, joint operations, and various types of service contracts.[101] In relation to solid waste management, three interlocal agreements or cooperative ventures are significant.

Spokane Aquifer Water Quality Management Plan   In 1978 the Environmental Protection Agency designated the Spokane-Rathdrum aquifer a "sole source" water supply for the area.[102] In 1979, acting under the authority of the federal Water Pollution Control Act (Public Law 92–500, Section 208), and with the assistance of Washington State Referendum 26 funds administered by the Washington State Department of Ecology, Spokane County, the city of Spokane, and the smaller municipalities of the county, working with and through the Spokane Regional Planning Conference, produced a water quality management plan for the Spokane aquifer.[103]

The plan recommended a "no further degradation" policy as a guiding principle for protecting the aquifer and provided specific recommendations regarding solid waste disposal. Detection of groundwater pollution from the Colbert and Northside landfills was received with great alarm. As a consequence it is now extremely difficult to justify placing additional solid waste management facilities over the aquifer.

The 1992 Spokane County Comprehensive Solid Waste Management Plan therefore recommended that future landfill sites be limited "to the West Plains area (southwest of Spokane river, west of Hangman Creek) and to areas of outcrop granite or other pre-tertiary metamorphic basement rocks."[104] SWDP eventually purchased land in the West Plains area (Heyer Point) as an in-county landfill site, but chose to haul its ash to a mega-landfill in Klickitat County. Currently, although it still has the option of locating a landfill at Heyer Point, SWDP does not maintain an active landfill for garbage within the county. Its only remaining landfill activities in the county are operation of a fill for construction debris, and closure and postclosure operations in former landfills.

The lasting impact of the aquifer protection plan is that any solid waste management activity over the aquifer must show that it is extremely unlikely to contribute to a further degradation of the aquifer. As was true with the special districts, the power of the aquifer protection plan to affect solid waste management is a function of state and federal authority and leverage. The dynamics of those influences will be discussed further in the next chapter.

Spokane International Airport Board The West Plains site chosen for the waste-to-energy facility is near the Spokane International Airport. In the public debate over the facility, one of the most contentious issues was whether the site was appropriate. One issue dealt with whether the stack (or its emissions) would constitute a danger to aircraft landing or taking off from the airport. The main issue, however, centered on whether the emissions from the facility would increase the amount of fog at the airport. According to the project opponent most responsible for keeping this issue alive during the debate, "Spokane International ranks among the top ten foggiest airports in the country."[105] Because the worst fog season at the airport spans the Thanksgiving and Christmas travel periods, area residents were quite aware of the problem fog creates at the airport. SWDP had to respond to their concern.

The result of the fog debate was that SWDP reached an agreement that it would, upon receiving a request from the airport, shut down the waste-to-energy facility to avoid any possible contribution to the fog.[106] In addition, SWDP funded the placement of several very sophisticated fog detectors around the airport. As a result, the incinerator has been shut down 10–12 times per winter (most fog episodes occur at the airport in the period from October to March) for an annual downtime total ranging from 200 to 400 hours.

Solid Waste Disposal Project (SWDP) Easily the most significant interlocal agreements for solid waste management in Spokane are those dealing with SWDP. There have been several iterations.

The project was created by the city and county in 1985. SWDP was placed formally within the structure of the city bureaucracy (see figure 4.2); its director reports to the city's director of planning and engineering services, but is in practice responsive to both the city council and county commission (see figure 4.1, above). Along with the project, the agreement called for a Project Policy Committee (PPC) comprising the county administrator, the city manager, a county commissioner, a city council member, a "citizen at large," and a nonvoting representative of the Washington Department of Ecology. The committee was to oversee the first phase of the project—including recommending to the council and commission (1) methods for waste disposal, (2) ways of acquiring and constructing the project, (3) ways of dealing with issues identified in the Spokane County Solid Waste Management Plan, and (4) public information and participation policies. The project coordinator also made recommendations to the committee, which considered them and made recommendations to the council and commission.

The agreement also allowed for the creation of a Technical Advisory Committee (TAC). Its members and duties were not initially delineated, but it became a significant player in the early stages of the decision-making process, advising on technical reports like the feasibility studies and the EIS documents. One indication of its status was the fact that the first executive director of SWDP attended the TAC meetings, but sent his assistant to the SWAC meetings (SWAC will be discussed next). Another indication of the higher status of the TAC was its membership; it was made up of individuals selected for their expertise in technical fields related to solid waste management. Creation of TAC was not required by state law, and it initially was not sensitive to its role as a public body. Seeing its mission as providing technical

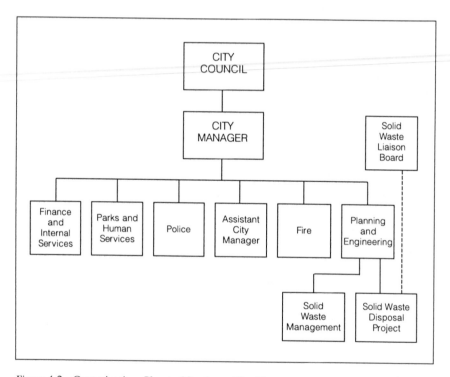

Figure 4.2   Organization Chart of Spokane City Government

advice, it met in closed sessions until the local paper challenged the legality of that practice. TAC is no longer meeting, its function as advisor on technical reports having been completed when it advised on Requests for Proposals for different portions of the project's facilities.

In order to comply with the requirements of RCW 70.95.165, the commission and council appointed a Solid Waste Advisory Committee (SWAC). Failure to create such a committee would have resulted in the city and county losing eligibility for state funds to assist in preparing or updating the state-required comprehensive solid waste management plan. Differences in language between the RCW and the interlocal agreement appear to indicate a reluctance on the part of Spokane's local officials to give the SWAC the role intended by the legislature. The RCW said that SWAC members were to be appointed by the county legislative authority (the commission), but the interlocal agreement described the SWAC as "appointed by the Board [i.e., county commissioners] with the consent of the [City] Council," and serving at the discretion of the Project Policy Committee as an advisor to that committee. According to the RCW, the SWAC was to be an active participant in "the development of programs and policies concerning solid waste handling and disposal."[107] In the interlocal agreement the SWAC's role includes commenting on project proposals, informing the Project Policy Committee of public concerns, and assisting in educating the public about the project — but only as requested by the Project Policy Committee.

Spokane's SWAC has both advised SWDP and served as a vehicle for disseminating information to the general public through presentations at high schools and community groups. As an advisor to the project, however, it has been overpowered by the TAC, the Project Policy Committee, and the Project Liaison Board (see below). Other than that contributed by the individual citizens on the committee, Spokane's SWAC has not been a very effective channel for input from citizens to the SWDP. When citizens were most interested in the project the SWAC was overshadowed by opposition groups. As a consequence, SWAC members have been forced to defend their committee against charges that it is merely a rubber stamp for SWDP.[108]

In 1987 the interlocal cooperation agreement was reaffirmed and updated in a waste-to-energy facility agreement.[109] Noting that the county had adopted a "flow control" ordinance, the agreement committed the county to naming the waste-to-energy facility as its sole disposal site and to enforcing the ordinance. It also provided that if the flow control ordinance were declared invalid by a court, the county would have to either provide sufficient solid waste to meet its obligations or pay for the difference between what it delivered and what it promised.

The 1987 version of the interlocal agreement also created a Project Liaison Board (PLB). Replacing the PPC, this board was designed to "create a forum for discussion among the City, the County and the Regional Cities concerning the [waste-to-energy] Facility and to create a body to whom information concerning the Facility can be provided."[110] The PLB was composed of two representatives from the city and two from the county—in effect, the PPC without a citizen or WDOE representative. Though the PLB was given no independent decision-making authority, it provides recommendations to the commission and council, and those recommendations have seldom been rejected.

In 1988 the city and county entered into another interlocal agreement, the "Rate Stabilization Fee Agreement." It set up a plan to impose increased tipping fees in city and county disposal sites. The additional revenue from these fees would be used to offset the increased cost of waste disposal in the new incinerator, allowing the city and county to spread the necessary increase in tipping fees at the incinerator over several years. Without such a fund, tipping fees would have increased sharply when the waste-to-energy plant began operation. Local government officials realized that area residents would not be happy with the increased fees, so they wanted to increase the fees gradually to avoid a citizen rebellion.

The solid waste agreement was also revised and updated, and combined with the rate stabilization agreement in 1988.[111] The first significant revision in this document was that it now referred to a solid waste management system, rather than just the waste-to-energy facility. In this version, the county was to designate as its sole disposal site the system (all property used by the city in collecting and disposing of solid waste), not just the waste-to-energy facility.

In 1989, the rate stabilization fee and solid waste management system agreements were amended again. In response to county residents' complaints that they were without representation in solid waste policy making when the city officials made decisions, included in the amendments were several provisions designed to enhance the role of the county in making solid waste decisions. The most important of these gave the county authority to veto the siting of a landfill. Since any landfill for the ash of the waste-to-energy facility inside the county would be located in the unincorporated area, and much local opposition to the prospective sites had been generated, it was important to the commissioners that they have a clear voice in the siting decision. The only concession the county had to make to gain this power was an agreement that if the county did not consent to a landfill siting and that action resulted in "a material adverse effect on the Revenues, the County [would]. . . pay to the City an amount of money equal to the economic value of increased disposal costs due to such a refusal."[112]

Another addition in the 1989 agreement was the reformation of the PLB as a five-member board. In addition to the city and county representatives it now included one nonvoting representative of the smaller municipalities. The new member was not given a vote because the smaller cities generated only 6 to 8 percent of the county's solid waste.[113] This amendment was required in recognition of an interlocal agreement including the other Spokane County municipalities in the solid waste system.

In addition to the waste-to-energy facility, the Spokane Regional Solid Waste System includes three recycling/transfer station operations, a composting operation, and a landfill for construction debris. It is involved in various programs to promote better solid waste management — including a recycling awareness program, curbside collection in urban unincorporated areas, a program to help businesses improve their recycling practices, school education programs, and a recycling hotline. Finally, the system is involved — almost exclusively as the generator of funds — in the closure of city and county landfills that no longer meet standards.

Formation of SWDP was a creative utilization of authority given by the state to local governments. Through the interlocal agreements regarding SWDP, Spokane County, the city of Spokane, and the other municipalities in the county were able to benefit from each other's strengths and authorities in addressing the problems of solid waste management in the late twentieth century.

Summary and Conclusion

Under the banner of Progressivism, municipal reform and sanitation reform marched hand in hand, promising to clean up the cities of America. Sanitation reform at first appeared to have the less complicated task; cleaning the streets and disposing of the refuse promised to be relatively straight-forward assignments. Municipal reform, since it had to be accomplished through the same political structures that created the need for the reforms, could not be expected to be smooth going. Both tasks, as it turned out, entailed greater challenges than the reformers could have known.

The late nineteenth- and twentieth-century lessons in municipal solid waste management were not lost on Spokane. The local community began the twentieth century allowing private collectors to gather the urban refuse for further utilization in a variety of ways or for dumping in sites outside the city limits. The city was like others in the nation in its early twentieth-century dependence on incinerators and land dumping and in the trend away from private garbage service toward municipal service. In the mid-twentieth century the area used landfills exclusively, and for most of the century's second half it used sanitary landfills. As the century moved to a close, the city and county jointly adopted a solid waste management system that included recycling and composting, but depended heavily on a waste-to-energy incinerator built and operated by a national company specializing in waste management technology and a privately owned and operated mega-landfill approximately 200 miles away.

Special districts such as health districts and air pollution control authorities provide the advantages and disadvantages of government reforms seeking politically neutral expertise. Their ability to be more businesslike and technically expert in their operations sometimes comes at the expense of responsiveness and accountability to the public. In addition, they fragment local government.[114] But that fragmentation is countered by the ability of elected officials to control the governing bodies of the special districts. Interlocal agreements also help to overcome potential fragmentation of local governance.

Through SWDP Spokane has attempted to address one of the major scientific, technical, environmental, economic, and political problems of our times. The limits of SWDP's ability to affect the problems of late twentieth-century solid waste management are a function of the limited ability of any local government to address those problems adequately. The structure of SWDP allowed Spokane to benefit from the improvements in local government associated with urban reforms enhancing technical and professional competence. With elected officials on key boards and committees, it also retained elements of local government that help keep it responsive to the public.

Federal and
State Policies

S olid waste management in the United States has historically
been the responsibility of local governments. In the late
1960s and 1970s, with about 75 percent of the nation's population living in urban areas[1] and with increasing numbers of them
becoming aware of environmental issues, that began to change.
Increased demands were placed on the federal government to deal
with environmental issues. Air, water, and land pollution became
problems the federal government could not ignore. Having no direct legal relationship with local governments, the federal government operated through its relationship with the states. Federal and
state laws, regulations, and court decisions now create pressures,
guidelines, and requirements local governments must heed as they
decide and act (see fig. 5.1).

Many factors have contributed to the movement away from local autonomy in solid waste management. In the latter half of the
twentieth century the federal government has been the primary
authority in almost any area of policy in which it decided to act.
State and local governments, while maintaining some autonomy in
their traditional areas of responsibility, have as likely as not had to
act within limits set by the federal government. Both environmentalists and business interests have had reason to encourage further
centralization of solid waste policy making. Environmentalists are
aware of the many ways environmental problems refuse to honor
the jurisdictional lines drawn by governments. The larger the jurisdiction, the greater the likelihood that a government will be able to
adopt effective policies. Some people also associate greater profes-
sionalism and more technically rational policies with the larger political units. In addition, business interests often find themselves
preferring national solutions—when the federal government sets

policy it does not have to attempt to comply with fifty different sets of state regulations and/or thousands of local rules.

The relationship between the federal government and municipalities has also changed. Many problems the cities would formerly have been left to handle alone (e.g., housing, crime, social welfare) are now seen as national problems requiring national solutions. In the 1960s and 1970s, solid waste joined that list. The volume of solid waste increased — the National League of Cities estimated the rate of increase after World War I at five times the rate of population growth[2] — and the nature of that waste changed. Eventually it became clear that municipalities were not up to the task. They had attempted to deal with the problem by dumping it in the surrounding countryside. In addition, the solid waste problems of the postindustrial "throw-

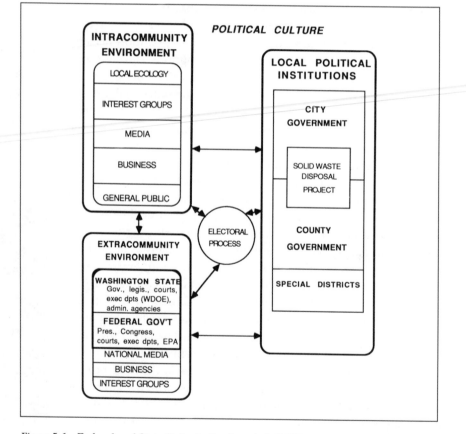

Figure 5.1   Federal and State Roles in Spokane's Solid Waste Policy System

away" consumer culture of the United States were simply not tractable at the local level. The sources of waste could not be controlled by local governments. The costs of managing the collection, handling, and disposal of those wastes exceeded the fiscal capacities of the cities and counties. Further, the generation and disposal of those wastes entailed environmental consequences that exceeded both the jurisdiction and the expertise of local governments. The state and federal governments had to get involved.

ENVIRONMENTAL INTERGOVERNMENTAL RELATIONS

Federal and state involvement in solid waste policy was born in an era of increasing attention to environmental issues. The nation had already begun to recognize air and water pollution problems. By entering into solid waste problems, they were recognizing what William Small called "the third pollution."[3]

Federal environmental laws most often have called for national, state, and local government action. The character of the federal call for action varies, however. Ruhl suggests that there are three types of intergovernmental approaches to environmental policy making: cooperative interstate agreements, federal coordination of interstate cooperation, and federal coercion of the states.[4] Others, however, have discerned two levels of federal coercion: true coercion or preemption, and partial preemption.[5] In solid waste policy making, partial preemption best describes the general pattern.

In the partial preemption approach, federal laws establish guidelines that serve as minimum criteria for state action. States may pass more stringent statutes, but not less stringent ones. In addition, federal statutes encourage states to establish their own policies and programs (which must meet with federal approval), but the statutes retain regulatory authority in a federal agency that may act if any given state does not act (or does not act in a manner that satisfies the federal regulators). A more gentle approach is for the federal government to encourage action by offering financial and technical assistance to those states meeting federal guidelines. When states have adopted national goals and guidelines, the federal government allows them more responsibility in policy implementation.

Since the Johnson administration's Great Society, each administration has tried to top the last in reconfiguring intergovernmental relations to devolve more responsibility to the state and local governments. The Reagan and Bush administrations made highly touted efforts to return power and authority to the states.[6] Whether those efforts were effective, however, is subject to dispute. Scicchitano and Hedge are optimistic about the new partnership between federal and state agencies, but Tobin reports that—at least in the eyes of state environmental program directors—not much changed during the 1980s and early 1990s.[7] According to Tobin, the Environmental Protection Agency (EPA) continues to show little confidence in the states. It exerts much control over state priorities, does not allow much increase in state discretion, and shows little sensitivity to the problems state directors faced. One example of that insensitivity involves the way the federal government imposes mandates on state and local governments without providing funds to cover compliance costs. For example, environmental mandates are expected to cost Columbus, Ohio, $1.3 billion in the 1990s, and to account for 27 percent of the city's budget by the year 2000.[8]

As Peretz points out, "The loss of state autonomy can foster hostility between the states and EPA."[9] Indeed, state and local governments often resent the federal requirements they must meet, the ways those requirements preclude actions that meet their own view of the proper priorities, and the additional resource and time costs associated with addressing federal priorities. Following the Republican victories in November 1994, Congress responded to these concerns by passing the Unfunded Mandates Reform Act in 1995.

Even when the federal government has delegated to them considerable authority, however, states still tend to complain about federal regulations and control.[10] The delays and uncertainty that state officials experience when waiting to finalize rules and regulations until federal regulators issue their own rules and regulations are serious irritants. On the other hand, state officials admit that the impact of the federal presence in environmental regulatory policy has positive aspects too. For one thing, it adds a "good cop, bad cop" dynamic to their conversations with members of the private sector. With the EPA behind them (the "gorilla in the closet"), it is sometimes easier for states to enforce their regulations.[11]

Though its threat value may help state regulators, the EPA's power to withhold technical and financial assistance means that it is also a threat to state regulators. The portion of a state regulatory agency's budget that comes from the federal government has declined in recent years, but the need for each federal dollar available remains strong. State agencies are not likely willingly to forgo federal assistance.

There are also significant variations within the general patterns of federal-state relations. For example, Gormley reports that Wisconsin and Ohio regulators differed significantly in their attitudes toward federal environmental policies.[12] Federal regulators were likely to gain compliance from Wisconsin officials through simple verbal persuasion, but even administrative edicts, refusals to release funds, and lawsuits did not always obtain compliance from Ohio regulators. We must also keep in mind that each federal statute leads to specific arrangements unique to the administration of laws and regulations under its authority.

Given this general understanding of environmental federalism, I will now focus in on solid waste policy. First I will discuss federal solid waste policy; then state policy, using Washington State as the specific example; finally, I will examine the impact of intergovernmental solid waste policy making on Spokane's experience in the late 1980s and early 1990s.

FEDERAL SOLID WASTE POLICY

Prior to the latter half of the twentieth century, the federal government was not much involved in solid waste policy making. Its main role in that area had been a function of its interest in public health. The Rivers and Harbors Act of 1899 included provisions giving the federal government jurisdiction over discharge of wastes into navigable waters; the Refuse Act of 1899 also limited its concern to water pollution issues.[13] In the 1950s, the Public Health Service Act gave the surgeon general authority to research and develop regulations relating to potential communicable diseases, including those associated with the open land dumping of garbage.[14] In the 1970s the Resource Conservation and Recovery Act prohibited open dumping and established requirements for sanitary landfill design in order to promote public health. Even today concerns regarding air, water, and land pollution are based on considerations of public health impact; but now those concerns involve health problems related to exposure to environmental hazards at least as often as to communicable diseases.

According to Melosi, "Solid waste disposal emerged as a significant national problem when it was linked with other forms of pollution."[15] The federal government has now established its presence in solid waste policy making both directly and indirectly (in related areas such as water and air quality management). The executive branch has provided leadership in making initiatives, Congress has passed laws, the EPA has promulgated regulations, and the federal courts have made decisions that set the parameters for state and local laws and regulations.

The federal government began its direct entry into solid waste policy making when in 1965 President Johnson, in a special environmental message, recognized the need for "better solutions to the disposal of solid waste" and proposed federal aid to state governments for research, development, and planning.[16] On the advice of his Scientific Advisory Committee, Johnson also ordered a study of the problem. As a result, the White House, Public Health Service, Department of Agriculture, Department of Defense, Department of the Interior, and other groups produced in 1968 the first modern study of the solid waste problem at a national level: the National Survey of Community Solid Waste Practices.

Responding to President Johnson's initiative, in 1965 Congress passed, as an amendment to the Clean Air Act, the Solid Waste Disposal Act. The act recognized the traditional role of state and local government in solid waste management, but asserted that the problem was national in scope and required federal action. Initially that federal action came in the form of technical and financial assistance designed to encourage local governments to develop alternatives to open burning of garbage in dumps.

There have been many amendments to the Solid Waste Disposal Act and its successors. In 1970 Congress passed the Resource Recovery Act; it amended the Solid Waste Disposal Act and began a new federal emphasis on recycling, resource recovery, and waste-to-energy. The Resource Conservation and Recovery Act (RCRA) of 1976 amended the Resource Recovery Act; it in turn has been amended by the Solid Waste Disposal Act Amendments of 1980 and the Hazardous and Solid Waste Amendments (HSWA) of 1984.

Focusing on (nonhazardous) solid waste, RCRA's Subtitle D was the foundation for the first "national waste management program."[17] It encouraged states to develop and implement comprehensive solid waste management plans and told EPA to provide them with technical and financial assistance. The state plans were to identify or establish the organizational structures responsible for the act's implementation, to prohibit new open dumps, to close or upgrade existing open dumps, to allow local governments to contract with private companies for resource recovery facilities, and to provide for environmentally sound disposal of solid waste. The 1976 act also mandated EPA to develop criteria for classifying solid waste disposal facilities and practices. With the criteria came mandatory minimum technical requirements for facilities.

The 1984 HSWA amendments to Subtitle D focused on steps solid waste management facilities should take to ensure environmentally sound handling of the small quantities of hazardous waste they would inevitably receive from households and other "small quantity generators." They required EPA to establish criteria and said that state plans must include a permit program to ensure that facilities meet the criteria.[18]

The 1980 Comprehensive Environmental Response, Compensation, and Liability Act (CERCLA) and the 1986 Superfund Amendments and Reauthorization Act (SARA), now commonly together referred to as Superfund, though directed at hazardous waste management, have also become involved in solid waste management issues because hazardous wastes are often found in landfills. Superfund set up a foundation from which the federal government might respond to environmental pollution around such sites. Acting under the authority given it by CERCLA, EPA has designated over 200 municipal landfills as Superfund sites.[19]

In the area of water quality Congress has passed several laws with significant impacts on solid waste management: RCRA, the Federal Water Pollution Control Act (FWPCA), the Clean Water Act, the Water Quality Act, and the Federal Safe Drinking Water Act. The FWPCA's National Pollutant Discharge Elimination System[20] (NPDES) is the federal government's main enforcement mechanism for point source discharges into navigable surface waters. Waste materials may be discharged directly or indirectly (i.e., after treatment) into the nation's waterways, but only as regulated by the NPDES permit system, which is designed to limit the concentration of toxics or pollutants discharged. When the body of water into which waste is to be discharged is a sea or ocean, discharge is regulated by the Marine Protection, Research and Sanctuaries Act.

Drinking water quality is covered by the Safe Drinking Water Act (SDWA) and RCRA.[21] SDWA sets drinking water standards and regulates underground injection wells. EPA's RCRA program uses SDWA standards as guidelines for corrective actions. The two statutes also interact in prohibiting underground injection of hazardous wastes. The FWPCA's Section 208 provisions promote state development of plans to protect groundwater (for instance, the Spokane-Rathdrum aquifer protection program discussed in the previous chapter).

Air pollution laws also impact solid waste management. As noted earlier, the Solid Waste Act was initially passed as an amendment to the Clean Air Act (CAA).[22] The Clean Air Act effectively prohibited open-air burning, which was at that time a common practice at municipal landfills. Because burning solid waste significantly reduces its volume, this prohibition contributed to the problem of landfill space. According to EPA, RCRA and CAA interact primarily in regulation of air emissions from incinerators and other solid waste facilities, and of the management and disposal of the by-products of air pollution control technologies.[23] Section 111 of the CAA established performance standards for existing solid waste incineration units. Section 129(a) of the 1990 CAA Amendments directed EPA to establish new source performance standards for solid waste combustion. Title 5 of the 1990 CAA Amendments required states to create operating permit regulations for air pollution sources, providing for renewal of the permits every five years. The overall impact of the 1990 amendments on municipal solid waste management was to discourage incineration, a technology that had been promoted by EPA in the 1980s as an alternative to landfills.

Congress has also acted in more sweeping manner with regard to environmental policy. The National Environmental Policy Act (NEPA),[24] with its Environmental Impact Statement (EIS) provisions, created a new set of requirements and procedures that significantly affect the planning and construction of facilities for handling solid waste. NEPA declared that it is the responsibility of the federal government to act as trustee of the environment, to assure for all Americans safe, healthful, productive, and pleasing surroundings, to attain benefits from the environment without degrading it, to preserve historic, cultural, and natural aspects of the national heritage, to achieve a balanced use of resources, and to enhance recycling and use of renewable resources. The main mechanism for assuring that the federal government meets its responsibility is the EIS, a detailed statement analyzing the environmental impact, long- and short-term effects, local and general implications, and irreversible and irretrievable commitments involved in any major federal action, and describing alternatives to the proposed action. The EIS procedure (or some variation of it) has become a requirement for all "major actions" by federal, state, and/or local governments.

The Environmental Protection Agency

When it comes to administering the myriad environmental hygiene statutes, EPA is the primary federal administrative agency. It administers federal water and air pollution programs, and its Office of Solid Waste (now the Office of Solid Waste and Emergency Response — OSWER) handles federal solid waste programs. When the federal government first stepped into solid waste policy making, "responsibility [for it] was passed from agency to agency like an orphan."[25] First it was split between the Public Health Service and the Bureau of Mines, with the former overseeing municipal waste and the latter overseeing mining and fossil fuel waste from power and steam plants. The EPA was created in 1970 to consolidate federal environmental regulatory activities in one agency. Much environmental legislation has been passed since then; in 1994 the EPA administered no fewer than ten comprehensive environmental protection laws.[26]

EPA was initially more interested in hazardous waste issues, and proposed to limit its activities to that area; but opposition from Congress, the Council of State Governments, the National Association of Counties, the National League of Cities, and the United States Conference of Mayors squelched that proposal.[27] Nonetheless, the federal role in solid waste policy making, as embodied in the EPA, remained ambiguous well into the 1970s.[28] EPA was reluctant to recommend federal intervention, and it generally limited its reports to descriptions of ongoing activities and future options. EPA Administrator William Ruckelshaus emphasized in 1972 that the federal government would not be able to solve the solid waste problem, and suggested that the states, local governments, and industry held the keys.[29] According to Blumberg and Gottlieb, "During the Nixon and Ford administrations, EPA consistently spent less on solid waste programs than the level of appropriations made available through Congress."[30] When it passed in 1976, RCRA was the most aggressive federal solid waste legislation to date, and it authorized EPA to administer its provisions. But that still did not mean EPA was ready to make final decisions regarding solid waste management. The main thrust of its activity involved technical and financial assistance to state and local governments.

Gradually, however, EPA's solid waste version of partial preemption began to gain teeth. In 1979 EPA published guidelines for state solid waste management plans.[31] These included requirements that states close or upgrade (to meet EPA criteria) open dumps, develop a strategy for encouraging waste reduction and recycling, ensure that states have adequate capacity for environmentally sound disposal of waste, involve the public in developing and implementing solid waste policy, and establish a means of coordinating the division of authority for various aspects of solid waste policy among institutions in their jurisdictions. States were also required to coordinate their plans and implementation with other federal, state, Indian reservation, and "substate" environmental laws, regulations, and programs. In addition to the comprehensive plan, the states were required to submit an annual work program for EPA approval. Failure to gain approval would cost a state its eligibility for federal financial and technical assistance.

In 1979 the EPA also promulgated criteria for solid waste disposal facilities and practices.[32] Those guidelines included avoiding interference with flood plains, disturbance of endangered or threatened species, and contamination of groundwater. They also restricted facilities' air and water pollution and set safety standards. (Revised contaminant levels took effect October 9, 1993.)

The 1984 HSWA amendments to RCRA increased federal involvement. They authorized EPA to become involved in the regulation of solid waste facilities through the permitting process. EPA was to set standards for landfills and the states were pressured to meet federal expectations and guidelines. (In most states, however, the state permitting process has met or exceeded federal expectations. In Washington State local permitting processes have predominated, the single exception being related to Superfund cleanups.) EPA regulations included guidelines for classification of solid waste facilities and practices and eight criteria regarding the location, design, operation, cleanup, closure, and monitoring of new and existing landfills.[33] If EPA determined that a landfill posed a threat to public health and safety, it could require closure, which entailed submission to EPA of a detailed plan and a program for monitoring and management of the landfill for at least thirty years.

As required by the HSWA amendments, the EPA in 1988 submitted a report to Congress on the adequacy of their solid waste guidelines and criteria for protecting human health and the environment.[34] This comprehensive review of policy concluded that municipal solid waste landfills were harming the environment and that current federal, state, and local regulations were not adequately addressing the problem. The report signaled a new willingness on EPA's part to become an active leader in dealing with the national solid waste problem. On September 22, 1988, EPA established what has come to be known as the waste management hierarchy, a favored rank order of how waste should be managed: (1) source reduction, (2) recycling, (3) waste-to-energy incineration, and (4) landfilling.[35] At the same time, EPA set some goals for 1992: a 25 percent reduction in the amount of waste created, a target recycling rate of 25 percent, and incineration of 20 percent of the remaining waste in waste-to-energy facilities.

On September 9, 1991, EPA announced new regulations governing landfilling. They required landfill operators to monitor nearby groundwater for the presence of 70 pollutants, to use double liners of flexible materials, and to have a leachate collection system.[36]

Under the authority of HSWA, EPA has also suggested revisions to Subtitle D setting new criteria for municipal solid waste landfills. The revisions, adopted in October 1991 and put into effect in October 1993,[37] addressed location restrictions, design requirements, operation requirements, avoidance of groundwater pollution, and closure and postclosure requirements.

Rules regarding financial assurance for closure and postclosure care were adopted at the same time but did not become effective until April 1994.

EPA also regulates municipal incinerators. In December 1989 it proposed New Source Performance Standards (NSPS) for municipal incinerators and guidelines for existing facilities. On February 11, 1991, the adopted NSPS and guidelines for existing facilities were published in the Federal Register.[38] The standards for existing facilities essentially provided time to bring the old facilities up to standard or to phase them out of operation. The NSPS included numeric limits on air emissions, combustion operating standards, and materials separation requirements. Air pollutants included were organics (e.g., dioxins and furans), metals, acid gases (hydrogen chloride and sulfur dioxide), and nitrogen oxides. Emission standards were based on best demonstrated technology (BDT), meaning the best technological system, taking into consideration cost and health and environmental side effects. Operating standards specified requirements for various aspects of the hardware; they also required that the chief facility operator be certified by the American Society of Mechanical Engineers, and that the site maintain an annually updated, site-specific training manual. In 1994 EPA planned to propose new standards for existing municipal solid waste incinerators and new NSPS. They expected to publish the final rule early in 1995.

RCRA and its amendments have changed the practice of solid waste policy making in the United States. Though state and local governments remain the leaders in implementing solid waste policy, under RCRA EPA has become the federal leader in solid waste policy making. It has forced the closure of existing landfills, placed significant new requirements on the construction of new landfills, and (temporarily) instigated a rebirth of incineration technology. The new standards for landfills made them much more expensive. The standards for municipal incinerators also entailed huge investments. Both the distribution of powers in the regulatory regime and the regime's attendant costs have taken local government out of the driver's seat in solid waste policy making.

Federal Courts

Federal courts have also become involved in solid waste policy making through rulings in cases involving interpretations of the Commerce Clause of the U.S. Constitution and in cases involving the scope of EPA's authority in interpreting and implementing laws passed by Congress. The impacts of their decisions have further diminished local governments' power in solid waste policy making.

In *Philadelphia v. New Jersey* (1978)[39] the U.S. Supreme Court decided that garbage was to be treated like any other commercial commodity under the Commerce Clause, which gives Congress authority to regulate interstate commerce. In the majority opinion (7–2) of the court, New Jersey had tried to impose on out-of-state commercial interests the burden of conserving its remaining landfill space. The court said that a state may not try to isolate itself from a common problem by prohibiting importation of items of commerce simply because those items originate outside its borders. In his dissent, Justice Rehnquist said that the court had previously allowed discrimination against out-of-state commerce that posed health dangers, and that "New Jersey should be free under our past precedents to prohibit the importation of solid waste because of the health and safety problems that such waste poses to its citizens."[40]

Fort Gratiot Landfill v. Michigan Department of Natural Resources[41] turned on very similar arguments. As a matter of fact, the majority opinion (again 7–2) said that this case could not be distinguished from *Philadelphia v. New Jersey*. The importance of the case for current solid waste management policy making is that Michigan had included a provision allowing each county to prohibit garbage from out-of-county as one element in a comprehensive solid waste management act designed to fit federal guidelines. Though the act as a whole might be fairly characterized as a health and safety measure, the court found that this provision unambiguously discriminated against interstate commerce and that Michigan provided no legitimate health or safety reason why a facility should be able to accept waste from inside the county but not from outside the county. The court further argued that the goals of the solid waste management plan could be attained without discriminating against interstate commerce. Dissenting again, Rehnquist continued to be more cognizant of the environmental health and safety risks.

In a case presenting a slightly different twist,[42] the Oregon Supreme Court ruled that a statute authorizing higher fees for disposal of out-of-state waste did not on its face violate the Commerce Clause. The surcharge in question was authorized as a means for covering specific costs incurred in regulating the out-of-state waste. The U.S. Supreme Court granted certiorari and in April 1994 reversed the Oregon Supreme Court's decision.[43] Writing for a 7–2 majority, Justice Thomas found Oregon's surcharge for disposing out-of-state waste "discriminatory on its face." Since it was discriminatory, the surcharge could only be allowed if it advanced a legitimate state purpose that could not be served through an approach less discriminatory. Oregon's attempt to portray the surcharge as a compensatory tax and its argument that "Oregon citizens should not be required to bear the costs of disposing of out-of-state waste" were not convincing. Justice Thomas said that the effect of the surcharge was to have out-of-state shippers pay the full costs while in-state shippers paid less than the full cost. Oregon's argument that they were engaging not in economic but in resource protectionism (the resource being landfill space) was rebuffed as an attempt to isolate itself from a problem common to all states.

The Supreme Court also ruled in 1994 on a New York case involving flow control ordinances.[44] The ordinances direct where garbage in a local government jurisdiction is to be delivered. They do not restrict importing; they do exporting. Twenty-six states have statutes that allow local governments to pass such ordinances. Often the need for such an ordinance is economic. The local government has signed a "put or pay" contract with a private solid waste management company. The contract guarantees a minimum flow of garbage through the privately operated facility. If the minimum flow is not reached, then the local government must pay the private company a sum equal to the revenue it would have generated if it had processed the promised minimum amount of garbage. Garbage hauling companies have argued that the flow control statutes and ordinances violate the Commerce Clause of the U.S. Constitution because they restrict the free flow of commerce across state lines.

Courts were generally accepting of flow control ordinances and regulations in the 1980s, but seem to have swung the other way in the 1990s. In Rhode Island a district court found that restricting the disposal of solid waste to facilities within the state in order to secure revenues for the Rhode Island Solid Waste Management Corporation was an impermissible interference with interstate commerce. Flow control ordinances in two counties supporting a jointly built facility in Minnesota were found unacceptable, as was a single county's flow control ordinance in North Carolina.[45] In May 1994 the U.S. Supreme Court struck what appeared to be a fatal blow to flow control ordinances with its *Carbone* decision. (Whether it will in fact be a fatal blow rests in the hands of Congress, which since *Carbone* has considered a number of bills to allow local governments to enforce flow control ordinances.) Justice Kennedy, writing for five members of a 6–3 majority decision, held:

> The avowed purpose of the [Clarkstown, New York, flow control] ordinance is to retain the processing fees charged at the transfer station to amortize the cost of the facility. Because it attains this goal

by depriving competitors, including out-of-state firms, of access to a local market, we hold that the flow control ordinance violates the Commerce Clause.[46]

Kennedy also said that revenue generation was not a government interest that could justify discrimination against interstate commerce. Justice O'Connor concurred, but felt that the ordinance, because it treated in-town competition the same as out-of-town competition in not allowing any alternative to the favored processor, did not discriminate against interstate commerce. In her opinion, the unconstitutionality of the ordinance derived from the burden it placed on interstate commerce in restricting the flow of goods.

The U.S. Supreme Court has made it clear that states and municipalities cannot, under their own authority, regulate the flow of solid waste into or out of their jurisdictions. Nonetheless, the courts may not have had the last word on whether state and local governments may be authorized to engage in regulating the commercial flow of solid waste across their jurisdictional lines. In the summer of 1995 the U.S. Senate voted 94–6 in favor of a bill that would allow them to regulate the transportation of municipal solid waste across their jurisdictional lines.[47] Should such a bill become law, state and local governments would be able to act under the authority given to Congress in the Commerce Clause.

Federal courts also hear cases involving interpretation of statutes and the regulations promulgated under their authority. In 1989 two U.S. District Courts heard cases[48] in which the central issue was whether the ash generated by a municipal incinerator that burns household waste along with other municipal waste is to be regulated as solid waste under RCRA Subtitle D or as hazardous waste under RCRA Subtitle C. Noting that EPA regulations first identified such ash as solid waste and that Congress, when it later amended RCRA, did not attempt to override that interpretation, the courts ruled that it was proper to treat the ash as solid waste. But the Court of Appeals reversed the decision and the Supreme Court in *City of Chicago v. EDF*[49] agreed that EPA had no authority to interpret RCRA in that fashion. The ash from municipal incinerators that do not restrict their fuel source strictly to household waste must be managed as hazardous waste if it tests as hazardous waste. Writing for a 7–2 majority, Justice Scalia said that the RCRA exemption from management as hazardous waste given to household waste did not apply to municipal combustion waste if the incinerator accepted anything in addition to household waste. EPA's interpretation, the court said, went against the plain language of the statute and its "express declaration of national policy that '[w]aste that is . . . generated should be treated, stored, or disposed of so as to minimize the present and future threat to human health and the environment.' "

The courts may not have the last word on this policy issue either. In January 1995 EPA announced new rules regulating the management of municipal incinerators and the ash they generate.[50] New testing procedures were to be established for determining whether the ash is hazardous. Using those procedures municipal ash would not be as likely to be classified as hazardous. Having been told by the Supreme Court that they did not have the authority to interpret RCRA in a manner that exempted municipal ash from management as hazardous waste, EPA planned to use its authority to determine the procedures for testing the ash as a means of avoiding the "hazardous" classification.

Federal court decisions have tended to restrict state and local government control over solid waste when their actions have interfered with interstate commerce. The executive and legislative branches of the federal government have given the responsibility for developing and implementing solid waste management plans to state and local governments, but those same governments have been told by the judicial branch that they do not have the authority to control elements they consider essential to effective implementation of those plans. They must bear the costs of implementation, but are allowed neither to enforce revenue generation mechanisms to pay for those costs nor to enforce measures designed to avoid increases in costs generated by activities outside their jurisdictions. Further, if municipal ash were classified as hazardous waste the cost of disposal would be higher. (Depending on the approach taken — whether the fly ash is separated so that a lesser volume requires treatment as a hazardous substance, for example — Phil Williams, executive director of the Spokane Regional Solid Waste Disposal Project, estimates the cost at two to four times the pre–*Chicago v. EDF* level.) Because of local governments' limited financial capacity, such a cost increase could further restrict their ability to manage solid waste.

Aggressive actions by the federal government could mean the end of local governments' management role in solid waste policy making. To date, however, the federal presence has loomed over solid waste management, but has not taken it over completely. Recently the rhetoric from Washington, D.C., has indicated that the short-term trend would probably be toward devolving more authority to state and local governments, and toward expecting those levels of government to carry more of the financial load. The

ɔunties, special districts, and cities desire more autonomy, but they
be sufficiently strong fiscally to cope with new responsibilities.

WASHINGTON STATE SOLID WASTE POLICY

Solid waste policy making in Washington State has been affected by the
nature of American intergovernmental relations, by the state's political culture, by the provisions of its constitution, by the nature of its legislature, and
by its regulatory regime. Partial preemption has meant that the state needed
to have an administrative agency adequate to the tasks the federal government handed it. The state's populist tradition has left it with a constitution
that authorizes a legislature of part-time lawmakers and allows for initiatives
and referenda. The need for a viable professional agency and the relatively
weak position of the legislature meant that the Washington State Department of Ecology (WDOE) became the predominant force in solid waste
policy making. The individualist elements of the state's political culture
supported a belief that legislator should be a part-time job; its moralist
political culture aspects were behind the professionalization of state government and the empowerment of agencies such as WDOE.

Even though legislators are part-time and the legislature holds a full
session (set by the constitution at a maximum of 105 days) every other year,
the state of Washington has been a leader in passing progressive solid waste
legislation. When the federal government passed the Solid Waste Disposal
Act (SWDA) in 1965 there were only two state-level solid waste programs in
the country, and only twelve states reported activities in any aspect of solid
waste management.[51] SWDA made federal funds available to states contingent on their creating a solid waste management plan and designating a
state agency responsible for all aspects of solid waste services. As a result,
"The decade since [its passage saw] a virtual explosion of state legislation
relating to solid waste management."[52] In Washington State, that explosion
continued beyond the early 1970s into the late 1980s; in 1972 there were 54
provisions in the state code related to solid waste, and by 1990 that number
had increased to at least 205.[53]

As at the federal level, all three branches of the state government are
involved in solid waste policy making. The legislature leads in policy making
by considering and passing legislation; the governor initiates some legislation and issues executive orders; executive departments and administrative
agencies adopt regulations and administer programs; and the judiciary
hears cases and makes decisions that affect policies and programs.

State governments have also passed legislation, promulgated rules, and run programs both directly related to solid waste and indirectly affecting solid waste management through such environmental activities as protection of water and air quality specifically, and the environment generally, and through other governance activities — for example, regulation of intrastate commerce. Most states require a permit for disposal of solid waste, either from the designated state agency or from an authorized local agency. They also have passed statutes relating to inspection of solid waste facilities and enforcement of regulations. According to EPA, "Typical [state] regulations cover information and other requirements for obtaining a permit, site selection, specifications concerning proximity of water resources, prohibited types of disposal, and construction, equipment, operation, reporting, monitoring, and closing requirements."[54]

The state of Washington's role in formulating solid waste policy has in several ways been typical of state governments: (1) it has acted to implement federal policies, guidelines, and standards; (2) it has set its own policies, guidelines, and standards; and (3) it has seen that the local governments and private solid waste companies meet state requirements. In other ways Washington State has not been typical. It led the nation in passing the first state solid waste act in 1969, and by 1989 it led the nation in the percent of waste recycled, reporting a rate of 28 percent.[55]

The 1969 Washington State Solid Waste Management Act anticipated the direction the federal government would take in RCRA (1976). Washington State's Solid Waste Management Act "established a comprehensive statewide solid waste management program."[56] It also explicitly recognized that the primary responsibility for solid waste policy belonged to local governments. It gave the state approval rights on disposal permits and required each county to prepare a comprehensive solid waste management plan in coordination with the cities and/or health department within its jurisdiction. Spokane County first met this requirement with its 1973 plan.

The state legislature has amended the Solid Waste Management Act several times. The 1976 amendments dealt separately with hazardous wastes, codifying their management under the Hazardous Waste Disposal Act.[57] Those amendments also modified the solid waste policy priorities to recognize resource conservation and recycling as better ways of managing waste than disposal. In 1984, the amendments mandated each county to form a Solid Waste Advisory Committee (SWAC) to assist in solid waste planning and policy making. They also redefined the state's solid waste management priorities (in rank order) as: reduction, recycling, energy recovery or incineration, and landfilling.[58]

Another amendment of the Solid Waste Disposal Act, the 1989 Waste Not Washington Act put a new emphasis on waste reduction and recycling. It directed the Washington State Department of Ecology (WDOE) to prepare a new comprehensive state solid waste management plan,[59] and required it and the county comprehensive plans to include strategies for waste reduction, source separation, and recycling. The source separation strategies were to include urban and rural programs, yard waste collection programs, and educational and promotional programs encouraging waste reduction and recycling. Waste Not set a recycling goal of 50 percent by 1995 and again set new priorities for solid waste management: (1) waste reduction, (2) recycling and source separation, (3) energy recovery, incineration, or landfilling of separated waste, and (4) energy recovery, incineration, or landfilling of mixed waste.

The recycling goal and the priority list were not mere posturing; the act required the city and county solid waste management plans to meet WDOE approval. And there were other provisions of Waste Not that promoted waste reduction and recycling. It placed a $1 per tire tax on the replacement of tires. It prohibited improper disposal of vehicle batteries and encouraged proper disposal by charging $5 extra for the purchase of a new battery when no used one was turned in to the dealer. The tire tax money was placed in a fund to aid in eliminating scrap tire piles through public education and by assisting in establishing recycling markets. The act also authorized funds for local government composting demonstration programs. Still, because of the absence of markets and plant capability in the United States, much of Washington State's recycled goods found their way to Asia.[60]

There have, of course, been other state statutes regulating solid waste. Washington State joined the "beautify America" movement in 1971, passing a Model Litter Control Act.[61] The act (which has been amended six times, most recently in 1992) grants authority to WDOE and other state and local agencies to enforce litter control regulations. Some of the specific programs established under this act include WDOE's Ecology Youth Corps, the Department of Corrections' nonviolent drug offenders litter control program, and the Department of Transportation's Adopt A Highway program, which encourages private groups to take responsibility for clearing the litter from specific sections of the state highways. In 1983 the legislature passed another bill related to litter; it prohibited beverage containers with detachable pull tabs.[62]

Washington State has also joined the federal government in protecting municipal governments from the financial burden of classifying ash from municipal incinerators as hazardous. In 1987 the state legislature passed the Special Incinerator Ash Disposal Act (SIAD).[63] Asserting that "incinerator ash residues from the incineration of municipal solid waste that would otherwise be regulated as hazardous wastes need a separate regulatory scheme," the legislature sought to ease permitting and reporting regulations for ash handling. Legislators favored incineration over landfilling because they said it reduced waste volume and environmental health risks. SIAD, therefore, legislatively defined municipal incinerator ash as "special" in an attempt to prevent its designation as hazardous, and so avoid significant increases in the cost of ash management and disposal.

The state legislature has also mirrored Congress's mixed stance in regard to the proper role of local government in the solid waste management regulatory regime. In an action that appeared contrary to the general direction of Washington State solid waste policy, the 1989 Waste Not Washington Act restricted local government authority by passing a "ban on bans."[64] It prohibited local government bans on packaging, which could be used to encourage businesses to reduce packaging and to make packaging easier to recycle. The ban on bans was intended to give a state Product Packaging Task Force time to develop statewide strategies for encouraging less wasteful packaging. Many local governments passing different kinds of packaging restrictions was thought to be an unproductive way to address the problem. The ban was allowed to "sunset" on July 1, 1993, but local governments have not been eager to take advantage of this freedom.

Other state environmental legislation that affects solid waste management includes water and air quality legislation. Washington State's Water Pollution Control Act asserts the role of the state in insuring water quality, while recognizing that the federal government also has an "interest in the quality of navigable waters of the United States."[65] It also designates WDOE as the state agency with authority to implement federal clean water laws, and it deals with three kinds of intergovernmental cooperation — state-federal, state-state, and state-provincial (Canada). This act translates into state policy the impact of federal water quality laws on solid waste management. Several of its provisions also affect solid waste management directly. For example, it specifically regulates the disposal of leachates (formed in landfills as water seeps through the waste dissolving some of the materials and carrying the resulting pollution with it). Both sanitary and ash landfills must have leachate collection systems, and the leachates must be disposed of properly.

Washington State laws and regulations also interrelate with federal rules in protecting groundwater and air quality. RCW 35.88, "Water Pollution — Protection From," gives local governments authority to protect public water supplies by enjoining any threatening activity. Washington Administrative Code (WAC) 248–54 sets the maximum contaminant levels for drinking water supplies, and WAC 173–200 establishes quality standards for groundwater. The Water Resources Act declares that protection of sole source aquifers is an "uppermost priority" and says that waste management programs "shall explore all possible measures for the protection of the aquifer."[66]

The Washington Clean Air Act (1971, extensively amended in 1991) was intended to preserve levels of air quality that protect human, animal, and plant health and safety and to comply with the federal Clean Air Act through a coordinated statewide program encouraging regional air pollution control programs.[67] The state program had to meet with federal approval and adopted many of the same basic approaches as federal pollution programs. It provided for technical and financial assistance from WDOE, but put regional or county air pollution control authorities on the front line (unless none were established, in which case authority reverted to WDOE). It called for the adoption of a permitting system that established new source performance standards (NSPS) and required the use of best available control technology (BACT), to be determined on a case-by-case basis. Permit requirements were to be the most stringent of the federal, state, or local standards. Continuous monitoring was required. Criminal and civil penalties were established. Finally, if any regional or county authority was found to be inadequately protecting air quality, the state reserved the right to take over local enforcement.

Washington State's attempt to protect the environment in a more general way is embodied within the State Environmental Policy Act (SEPA).[68] Its general purposes and declarations echo NEPA. Like NEPA, it requires that state and local agencies take environmental issues into consideration on major actions through preparation of an EIS. The Waste Not Washington Act required an EIS prior to the construction and operation of new solid waste incinerators. Landfills also require an EIS prior to their operation.[69]

The Washington State Department of Ecology (WDOE)

In Washington State, the primary executor of environmental hygiene laws and regulations is WDOE. The federal Clean Water Act gave EPA authority to delegate powers to state agencies; in Washington State the agency was WDOE. WDOE is the enforcer of standards set by the federal Clean Air

Act and of state air and water quality statutes; it also acts as the state's primary agency in areas related to solid waste management.

But WDOE is not the only state agency that administers policies related to solid waste. The 1991 Washington State Solid Waste Management Plan listed no fewer than eight departments and agencies with regulations concerning solid waste.[70] The Utilities and Transportation Commission supervises and regulates solid waste collection companies. The State Board of Education and the State Superintendent of Instruction require environmental education in grades K–12. The Department of Trade and Economic Development is the lead agency in developing markets for recycled materials and assists in educating businesses and consumers about the advantages of using recycled materials and products. The Department of Revenue administers solid waste–related taxes and fees like the $1 per tire fee for new automobile tires. The Department of Wildlife prohibits disposal of litter on its lands. The Department of Agriculture in its regulation of meat inspection establishes requirements for disposal of carcasses and parts. The Pollution Control Hearings Board hears appeals regarding WDOE and/or local government environmental actions like granting air and water pollution permits.

Still, the main actor in matters relating to solid waste is WDOE. In that role it administers a waste reduction research and development program, assists local governments in developing cooperative agreements related to implementing solid waste policy, promotes waste reduction and recycling in state agencies, promulgates regulations for state agencies, and sets minimum requirements for local authorities. It also ensures that state regulations effectively interrelate with federal regulations.

In 1972 WDOE published the first Washington State Solid Waste Management Plan and adopted the first Minimal Functional Standards (MFS) for Solid Waste Handling.[71] These state standards predated RCRA and EPA criteria, but they have been updated periodically to meet changes in federal standards. The MFS describe the division of functions between the state and local governments and the responsibilities of persons and government agencies under state law and regulations. Requiring that the best available technology be used, they allow local governments to adopt more stringent, but not less stringent standards. The standards deal with such matters as facility location and operation. Closure and postclosure requirements are also detailed. Transfer stations, incinerators, and landfills are regulated, and a permit system is established.

WDOE has also adopted regulations governing incineration of solid waste. It adopted certification programs based on programs developed by national associations and the federal government for incinerator operators in 1991.[72] The facilities must comply with WDOE general air quality regulations as well as those specified for solid waste incinerators. If more than one regulation applies, the more stringent one takes precedence. Incinerators must use the "best available control technology (BACT) which is determined on a case-by-case basis . . . [and the emission limits] may be more stringent" than those specified in the regulations.[73] In addition, the Washington State Air Toxics Regulation[74] applies to new or modified permits for municipal solid waste incinerators.

The incinerator regulations address emission of particulates, hydrogen, chloride, and sulfur dioxide, as well as opacity of emissions. They regulate the minimum temperature at which solid waste is to be burned, the maximum temperature of the particulate control device, and the source of the combustion air. Continuous monitoring and recording of specific air pollution–related indicators is required. If limits are exceeded WDOE or the local air authority may require that the facility be shut down until the problem is corrected.

Under the authority of the Special Incinerator Ash Disposal Act, WDOE has also created management standards specifically for municipal incinerator ash.[75] They prohibit disposing of ash in the same landfill cell with unburned solid wastes. They establish procedures and requirements for ash handling management plans. Permits are required for construction, alteration, expansion, or closing of an ash handling facility, and a detailed permitting system is established. The regulations also include facility siting, operation, closure, and postclosure requirements, as well as ash treatment and utilization standards.

In 1987 WDOE published the Best Management Practices Analysis for Solid Waste. It was the first comprehensive analysis of solid waste policy and management in the state. It also presented recommendations designed to further the state's solid waste objectives, which it described as: (1) cost-effective waste reduction, (2) source-separated recycling, (3) to the degree that source separation is not accomplished, postcollection separation of recyclables, and (4) efficient and environmentally sound disposal.[76]

WDOE also oversees the management of landfills. In 1991, relying on programs developed by national organizations and the federal government, it adopted a certification program for operators of incinerators and landfills.[77] In 1993 WDOE announced new criteria for municipal solid waste landfills (MSWLF) that took effect in April 1994.[78] The criteria were designed to implement rules made by EPA under RCRA Subtitle D and the federal Clean Water Act, Section 405(d). A MSWLF that fails to meet the criteria is considered an open dump and is prohibited by RCRA. The criteria addressed location restrictions similar to those described earlier, but added new groundwater, sole source aquifer, drinking water supply well, and surface water protection. Operating criteria addressed restriction of dangerous waste receipt, cover materials, dust and litter control, disease control, explosive gas control, air quality, control of public access, water run-on and run-off, personnel qualifications, record keeping, and annual reports. They also required MSWLF operators to provide opportunities for recycling. Finally, they included design criteria and established a permitting system that included provision for appeals to the Pollution Control Hearing Board (PCHB).

Though Superfund is aimed at hazardous wastes, not solid wastes, the Washington State legislature and WDOE have recognized that "many of our municipal landfills are current or potential hazardous waste sites and present serious threats to human health and the environment."[79] This program too, then, becomes involved in solid waste policy making. Superfund activities in Washington State are implemented under the oversight of WDOE, but are exempt from state and local permitting requirements. The Model Toxics Control Act[80] was adopted by a vote of the people, not by the legislature (and therefore is discussed further in a later section). It authorized WDOE to establish procedures and programs and to carry out activities in cooperation with and parallel to Superfund and its National Priorities List. An important part of WDOE's activity in this area involves financial assistance to local governments engaged in remedial action — including site hazard assessments, remedial investigations, cleanup actions, and the purchase of long-term monitoring systems.[81] WDOE was also directed by the act to provide public participation grants of up to $50,000 for persons and not-for-profit public interest groups (including federally recognized Indian tribes) interested in "the implementation of the state's solid and hazardous waste management priorities."[82]

WDOE is also responsible for Washington State's implementation of plans and standards, as provided for by the federal Clean Air Act. The Washington Clean Air Act established a statewide program that placed county or regional air pollution control authorities on the front line in the battle against air pollution. WDOE was seen as the state guarantor of a coordinated statewide system. Although it was given some specific administrative duties, such as monitoring acid rain deposition,[83] its main air pollu-

tion tasks involved adopting federal or setting more stringent state standards[84] and ensuring that regional and county air pollution authorities
effectively enforced them. New sources of air pollution may not be constructed without a "notice of construction" from WDOE or the local authority.[85] Sources emitting "criteria" pollutants in areas that meet federal air
quality standards for those pollutants must obtain a PSD (prevention of
significant deterioration) permit in order to operate. WDOE PSD permits
and the procedures surrounding the permitting process incorporate EPA
regulations to a great extent.

WDOE was also given responsibility for statewide administration of water quality laws.[86] As the state water pollution control agency for all purposes
of the Federal Water Pollution Control Act, it established the state permit
program that operates as part of the NPDES system under the authority of
FWPCA and the state Water Pollution Control Act. It is responsible for the
administration of the NPDES system through monitoring, recording, and
reporting authorities and requirements. It has established water quality
standards for the surface waters of the state. The department also has authority to investigate suspected violations and to seek both civil and criminal
sanctions.[87]

With respect to groundwater management, WDOE has established quality standards that are more stringent and broader in scope than those set by
EPA under the Federal Safe Drinking Water Act. In addition it adopted a
policy stating that groundwaters that exceed WDOE standards will be pre-
served at the higher quality level. WDOE has also initiated formation of local
groundwater management programs by encouraging cooperative partnerships among local, state, tribal, and federal interests; WDOE appoints a lead
agency, which is then responsible for implementing the program.[88]

Finally, though all state agencies are required to comply with the State
Environmental Policy Act (SEPA) and to establish their own SEPA procedures, in solid waste policy WDOE has the task of overseeing the administration of SEPA and its EIS process. The two main SEPA goals — involving
the public and including useful and accurate environmental information in
decisions that may significantly affect environmental quality — have made
the EIS process one of the most technically complicated and politically
charged aspects of solid waste policy making. The technical aspects generally require hiring consultants and subcontractors to do the work. As will be
shown in the next chapter, complex and significant political dynamics result
from the contracting aspect of EIS. To further complicate matters, at each
stage of the EIS process, whether it is a Determination of Nonsignificance

(DNS) decision, a scoping hearing, a draft EIS, a final EIS, or a supplemental EIS, public involvement can include emotional and dramatic exchanges, as well as legal challenges.

As the primary enforcer of environmental laws and regulations in Washington State, WDOE has been a key element in the state's leadership in solid waste policy making. From the development of Minimum Functional Standards and Best Management Practices for solid waste management to administration of water and air quality laws, WDOE carries much responsibility for the way solid waste is managed in Washington State.

Washington State Courts

Washington State courts most commonly get involved in solid waste policy issues when they are asked to review the procedures and the reasonableness of government agencies setting solid waste policy. After exhausting administrative appeals, dissatisfied parties may take their complaint to a court for review. For example, when a party is not satisfied with a decision of the PCHB, an appeal may be made to superior court.[89] The dissatisfied party may be a group of active citizens who question a government decision or process, a private company involved in a contract (or denied a contract), or a government agency dissatisfied with the decision of another government agency. For example, in December 1993 the King County (Seattle) Solid Waste Division sued WDOE for failure to comply with SEPA and the Washington State Administrative Procedures Act in promulgating their municipal solid waste landfills MFS.[90] Issues taken to court affecting SWDP included whether Proposition 4 required that the citizens of Spokane vote on the waste-to-energy facility and whether the Spokane County Comprehensive Solid Waste Management Plan was adequate.

Sometimes cases affecting solid waste policy go all the way to the Washington State Supreme Court, as for instance with the question of whether Spokane's Proposition 4 required the city to put the waste-to-energy facility to a public vote. Proposition 4 required "a vote of the people for capital expenditures . . . requiring indebtedness of the taxpayers and property owners for capital projects . . . including the proposed mass burn plant for refuse disposal (Waste to Energy Plant)." The case turned on what kind of indebtedness funding the waste-to-energy facility would incur. Noting a previously recognized distinction between indebtedness paid off with special funds generated through fees and that paid from general taxes, the court found that the waste-to-energy project did not lead to indebtedness of the taxpayers.

In response to the argument that the voters intended Proposition 4 to cover the waste-to-energy plant, the court argued that "intent is not relevant unless there is ambiguity in the language." It found the phrase "requiring indebtedness of the taxpayers and property owners for capital projects" unambiguous and went on to chastise the appellants for implying that the voters might not understand "the difference between revenue and general obligation bonds." The court added, "We believe any such claim of lack of knowledge on the part of the electorate as to this fundamental distinction is unwarranted."[91]

The dissenting opinion expressed astonishment that the majority chose to ignore "the final 13 words of the ordinance: 'including the proposed mass burn plant for refuse disposal (Waste to Energy Plant).' " Noting that the initiative was triggered by the waste-to-energy project and was clearly intended to apply to that project, the minority found it very troublesome that the majority would disregard that intent. The dissenters found the decision a threat to "the right of the citizens of this state to govern themselves."[92]

In another case that had implications for SWDP (because it involved the scope of the state's authority in regulating Wheelabrator's largest stockholder, Waste Management, Inc.), in 1994 the Washington State Supreme Court ruled that Washington State's Utilities and Transportation Commission (WUTC) could not examine the financial records of any Waste Management, Inc., subsidiary company other than the one requesting a garbage-hauling rate increase. WUTC said it needed to examine the records to ensure that Waste Management was not hiding the profit level of the garbage-hauling subsidiary by passing the profits on to another subsidiary.[93]

Through cases such as these Washington State courts have had a distinct and long-lasting impact on solid waste policy making. But more often their impact has been felt in the expense and time involved in obtaining court review of administrative decision-making processes. That impact will be discussed later.

Atypical Aspects of Washington State Solid Waste Policy Making

Washington State stands out nationally for its leadership in environmental policy making. Other unusual aspects of the policy-making milieu in Washington State merit some attention: the impact of direct democracy policy-making techniques (referenda and initiatives) and the impact of tribal relations.

In contrast to the federal government and to many of the nonwestern states, Washington State allows citizens to participate directly in policy making through referenda and initiatives. Almost as soon as Washington State became involved in solid waste policy making, the people were invited to participate. Referendum 26 gained voter approval in 1972. It authorized up to $195 million in general obligation bonds "for the planning, acquisition, construction, and improvement of public waste disposal facilities, [not including] the acquisition of equipment used to collect, carry, and transport garbage."[94]

Another referendum related to solid waste policy — one that had a significant direct impact on Spokane's waste-to-energy project — was Referendum 39, which passed in 1980. It provided for financial assistance to local governments in support of new but reasonably well-tested solid waste technologies. Authorizing over $450 million in financial aid, it specified that at least $150 million "shall be used exclusively for waste management systems capable of producing renewable energy or energy savings as a result of the management of the wastes," including the generation of electricity through incineration of wastes.[95]

Initiative 97, the Model Toxics Control Act, was passed by the voters in November 1988. Declaring that "each person has a fundamental and inalienable right to a healthful environment," the act recognized that municipal landfills posed serious threats to the environment. It established means for raising funds to clean up existing hazardous waste sites and to prevent creation of new ones. Recognizing WDOE as the state agency authorized to implement all the programs under the federal CERCLA, it also established a toxics control account and specified that one percent of the money in that account would be earmarked for public participation grants, "to facilitate the participation by persons and organizations in the investigation and remedying of releases or threatened releases of hazardous substances and to implement the state's solid and hazardous waste management priorities."[96]

Another atypical aspect of Washington State solid waste policy making involves the 26 federally recognized Indian tribes in the state. In 1989 the governor and leaders of those tribes signed an accord in which they pledged to work together on a government-to-government basis.[97] Solid waste facilities on tribal reservations are required to comply with federal standards, but state and local governments do not have direct authority over tribal facilities. Because environmental issues do not respect political jurisdictions, local and tribal authorities have been encouraged by federal authorities to work together in seeking solutions to solid waste problems. Pursuant to that federal policy, EPA's Regional Office in Seattle has run a project to facilitate local and tribal solid waste planning efforts. They recommended that tribal authorities be involved in local SWACs, but most often that has not happened. When it has, the tribal representatives have found that they do not have much effect on policy. Nonetheless, on a case-by-case basis tribes and local officials are beginning to see the need to work together.[98]

Impacts on Solid Waste Policy Implementation

What does this mean for the day-to-day implementation of solid waste policy? These intergovernmental relations impact the implementation of solid waste policy in countless ways. This section will briefly discuss some of the most important: the contents of the laws and regulations, the regulation adoption process, the EIS process, the permit process, legislative deliberations, the influence of individual legislators, state financial assistance, lawsuits, and postclosure operations.

Perhaps the most obvious effect of the partial preemption regulatory system on solid waste policy is in the substance of the policies themselves. A few examples will suffice. When the Washington State Legislature decided to designate ash from municipal incinerators "special waste," they sidestepped a move by WDOE to classify it as hazardous. If the ash were declared hazardous, there would be a stricter and more expensive regime of standards for its handling and disposal. Beyond the obvious limiting factor they placed on the management of ash residues from the waste-to-energy facility, WDOE's standards also affected SWDP because the ash standards were being revised even as the SWDP was attempting to prepare an EIS for a landfill for the ash from their facility. This created an atmosphere of some considerable uncertainty for local administrators, which was exacerbated by EPA's attempt to interpret federal law to allow virtually all municipal ash to be exempted from management as hazardous.

In addition, when EPA and/or WDOE establish maximum emission standards for incinerators, they affect the cost of building and operating those facilities. A change in the standards, a clarification of previously ambiguous standards, or a change in the technique used for measuring compliance with the standards can have significant implications for the operation of municipal incinerators. In Spokane's case, about one year after the waste-to-energy plant began operation SWDP identified an ambiguity in the sulfur dioxide emission regulation. SWDP told SCAPCA that there was no averaging time specified for one of the two ways for demonstrating compliance. SCAPCA agreed and asked WDOE for a clarification, suggesting a

24-hour averaging time. Though WDOE could have adopted a one-hour averaging time, it chose the 24-hour specification, saying that it was consistent with federal standards. If the limit had been based upon hourly readings, two sheets of wallboard could make the plant exceed the standard, and plant records showed that it had been in violation if the averaging time were one hour. With the limit based on a 24-hour average, plant records showed that it would have no difficulty meeting the standard.[99]

Similarly, two decisions by EPA made life easier for SWDP officials. When EPA decided not to include recycling among the practices evaluated in their BACT requirement for the waste-to-energy facility's initial air permit, it saved SWDP a lot of time and energy revising their permit application. Also important to SWDP was EPA's judgment that incinerator ash does not need to be managed as hazardous waste. The Supreme Court decision overruling EPA's authority to interpret the law to expand the congressionally authorized exemption posed a real threat to Spokane's solid waste management system. Classification of its ash as hazardous could increase handling and disposal costs, and thus the overall cost of running the waste-to-energy facility, to the point that it could not compete with the cost of long-hauling the raw garbage to a huge regional landfill.[100] Using its authority to establish testing procedures that make it easier for municipal ash to pass the toxicity test, EPA took a step that could save SWDP millions of dollars.

The regulation adoption procedure also affects solid waste policy making. Both the federal and Washington State governments have adopted administrative procedure acts and environmental policy acts that define the steps an agency must take in order to adopt environmental regulations. The acts require opportunities for public input prior to regulation adoption. Often that requirement is met through public hearings. When the subject under discussion at the hearing has gained the attention of the public, the hearing can be valuable for both the agency and the public. For example, when WDOE held hearings in Spokane on their proposed ash landfill MFS, a number of citizens voiced concern that they might be living in the neighborhood of an ash landfill; as a result, both parties were informed and prepared to grapple with the issue.[101] It is not unusual for EIS hearings to fit this description. If the EIS is on a more general plan or set of rules, the hearing may not draw a large number, but when an EIS is on a specific proposed land use, the nature of the project is likely to energize an interested public. The Spokane solid waste disposal project was significantly affected by the EIS process's requirement for at least three public hearings for each EIS—a scoping hearing, a hearing on the draft EIS, and one on the final EIS. Those hearings are opportunities for opponents to question and challenge the adequacy of the EIS—from the assumptions it makes to the specific work done to verify its conclusions. Although the EIS hearings for Spokane's waste-to-energy facility did not attract a large number of citizens, when the topic moved to where to dispose of the ash, hundreds of citizens attended. More than 200 were at the scoping hearing, and about 300 attended the hearing on the draft EIS.[102]

On the other hand, public hearings have often been subject to one of two problems: either very few people come, or a large number of people come to talk about something other than the policy question or questions that initiated the hearing. When few people come, the hearing has not provided the desired public input. When the people in attendance want to talk about issues beyond the scope of the official agenda, the hearing fails to meet the goals of the agency and frustrates the attendees' attempts to provide input. At a WDOE hearing to discuss nitrogen oxide limits for Spokane's waste-to-energy plant, opponents of the plant were frustrated with the limited scope of WDOE's review. They wanted WDOE, in deciding whether to grant a permit, to consider a larger agenda, including the track record of the company that would build and operate the plant. WDOE, however, said it was not authorized to take that into consideration. The citizens were told that once the plant was operating, WDOE would be able to penalize the company for exceeding the emissions limits, but it could not deny the permit on a presumption that violations would be commonplace.[103] Since many in attendance did not trust the plant to operate safely, this was not a satisfactory response.

Permitting processes are another avenue for potentially meaningful discussion of the policy issues at hand, but they do not always meet the needs of either the citizens or the government officials. Whereas citizens complain about the effectiveness of the hearings, arguing that their views are not given serious consideration, officials complain about the time the process takes. The story of the Spokane waste-to-energy plant's order of approval (for construction of the facility) illustrates the problem. First, the permit had to be approved by the local air pollution control authority, SCAPCA. Then it went to WDOE for approval, and then to EPA for approval. EPA sent the permit back to WDOE once because it lacked a standard for small particulates, then again when it found that procedural rules were not followed.[104] WDOE had to revise its standards and redo its procedural steps to meet EPA guidelines, so the permit was delayed. WDOE issued another approval eight months after its initial approval.

During the same period the Pollution Control Hearings Board (PCHB) was considering an appeal of SCAPCA's granting a "notice of construction." One and a half months after WDOE's air permit approval, PCHB approved the notice of construction, but in its approval the board placed stricter limits on air emissions. The city of Spokane appealed that decision and got a rehearing by PCHB, which one month later relaxed the standards for nitrogen oxide and dioxin emissions.[105]

One week later, reacting to an appeal by plant opponents and taking notice of the PCHB ruling, the Seattle Office of EPA recommended to the national EPA office that the air permit be sent back to WDOE for reconsideration of two issues: whether the limits for nitrogen oxide should be reduced, and whether source separation and recycling should be considered as means of reducing air emissions. This delay in receiving the permit caused local officials serious concern. The city of Spokane in the previous month had dodged daily penalties of $15,000 from Wheelabrator for delaying construction by issuing a "conditional notice to proceed." If the air permit were delayed further while EPA considered these issues, the city would again face the added cost of renegotiating the escalator clause in its contract with Wheelabrator. When the decision had not been made by April 27, 1989, the city had to pay $8,500 per day until Wheelabrator could restart work on the project,[106] which was contingent on receipt of the air permit.

In early June EPA approved the air permit contingent on reduced nitrogen oxide limits but did not require a study of the impact of waste reduction and recycling on air emissions. WDOE responded by issuing a preliminary permit incorporating the nitrogen oxide change and scheduling hearings and accepting public comment only on that change. On September 1, 1989, WDOE issued the air permit. Opponents appealed, but on January 3, 1990, thirteen months after issuance of the initial permit, EPA rejected their appeal and issued the final air permit.[107] In that decision, acting EPA administrator F. Henry Habicht said it would not be appropriate to hold Spokane's plant hostage to proposed changes in EPA rules. By that time EPA had proposed rule changes that would require recycling of at least 25 percent of the waste that would otherwise go to an incinerator. The fact that the Spokane plant's initial permit did not include a required recycling rate did not exempt it from EPA's rule. When that EPA rule changed, it applied to existing as well as new incinerators, and permit renewal required meeting the new standards.

Another way intergovernmental relations affect solid waste policy making derives from legislative deliberations. Especially when the legislature

considers statutes that would mandate (or restrict) local government action, local governments lobby for their interests. Local government lobbyists
were quite active in ending the ban on bans,[108] but there has not been a
groundswell of local governments passing packaging bans. Many agreed
with the legislature that it made little sense for jurisdictions that represented
such tiny portions of the economic market to play that card. However, they
did not like being told they could not do it even when they had no interest in
doing it.

Citizens also get involved in lobbying the legislature when they see a
potential for affecting local policy. Both Spokane officials and incinerator
opponents went to Olympia to testify at House Capital Facilities and Financing Committee hearings in an effort to influence an appropriations bill that
contained the $60 million Referendum 39 grant for the waste-to-energy
facility.[109] The groundwork for Spokane's Referendum 39 grant had been
laid in 1982, when Dennis Hein, Director of Solid Waste Management for
the city of Spokane, first applied for it to support the construction of a
waste-to-energy project. The Spokane application was one of the first on the
table and remains the largest grant yet given by WDOE. Even though WDOE
had deliberated on the application four years before approving the grant
funds, as the project became more controversial the wisdom of providing
the funds became an issue at both WDOE and the state legislature.

Hearings held in the local area by legislative committees can also affect
the dynamics of local disputes. In December 1988, when the dispute over
Spokane's waste-to-energy facility had begun to heat up, the legislature's
Joint Select Committee on Solid Waste Management, preparing for legislation that would become the Waste Not Washington Act, held a public hearing in Spokane.[110] Despite the fact that the committee sought input on a
long-term approach to the state of Washington's garbage problem, opponents of the facility made the hearing into an opportunity to voice their
specific opposition to the incinerator.

It is also true that individual legislators, in what Mayhew calls position
taking (emphasizing what they say, not what they do), may affect the political dynamics of a local policy dispute.[111] In the case of Spokane's incinerator, Art Sprenkle, a Democratic state representative from Monroe,
Washington (about 200 miles from Spokane), and chair of the Joint Select
Committee on Solid Waste Management, took several opportunities to become part of the dispute. In October 1988, because he thought sunk costs
were restricting the local governments' ability to evaluate the waste-to-
energy project, Sprenkle called the incinerator "Spokane's Vietnam" and

asked WDOE to reevaluate their commitment to the $60 million Referendum 39 grant. He later offered to support Spokane's incinerator in return for support for the Waste Not Washington Act, which placed more stringent recycling requirements on new incinerators. Seven months after that, in a forum held at Gonzaga University in Spokane, he returned to criticizing the facility.[112]

Local state legislators also became involved in the dispute. Jim West, Republican state senator from Spokane, wrote a letter asking WDOE director Christine Gregoire to reconsider the $60 million grant. Several other local state legislators participated in a meeting in Spokane called by Gregoire to discuss the project. Local legislators also combined efforts in surveying their constituents' support for the project, and the results were used in a newspaper article about citizen opposition to the waste-to-energy facility.[113]

Even a U.S. senator became involved. At a cocktail party, Sen. Slade Gorton pressed an EPA official to speed up the review of the incinerator's air pollution permit.[114] U.S. Rep. Tom Foley, however, took no actions that became public knowledge.

As was evident in the preceding sections on federal and state policy, financial assistance is a deliberately designed technique for influencing solid waste policy and its implementation by lower levels of government. The federal government has used financial assistance to impel the states to adopt statutes and regulations that follow their federal counterparts very closely. Washington State has also used financial assistance to get local governments to move solid waste policy and its implementation in the preferred direction. Though the state has provided grants for such purposes as purchasing equipment needed in curbside recycling programs and assisting in cleanup efforts at closed landfills, perhaps the clearest example of the impact of financial assistance in the Spokane case is the $60 million Referendum 39 grant.

Despite having first been promised the grant in 1986, in 1988 Spokane could not be overly confident that it would actually receive it. Legislators from both parties, both legislative houses, and both sides of the state had urged WDOE to reconsider the grant. With this additional leverage WDOE Director Gregoire decided not to rescind the promise, but did attach significant new strings in her December 22, 1988, letter awarding the grant. In that letter she explained her decision not to rescind the grant, saying that not following through on the department's 1986 commitment "would set a precedent that could have dramatic implications" for all local governments receiving grants from WDOE. The new strings she attached to the grant included: (1) beginning a curbside recycling program by January 30, 1991, "unless a superior alternative approach . . . can be demonstrated"; (2) conducting a human health and environmental toxic substances monitoring study, (3) creating a household hazardous waste collection program, and (4) developing a program for separating out possible sources of heavy metals. Though the Liaison Board to SWDP had voted in November 1988 to see whether a voluntary recycling program depending on schools and non-profit groups could meet the goal of a 26 percent rate by 1991, in anticipation of Gregoire's letter they voted on December 12, 1988, to start a curbside program by early 1991. The city needed assurance it would receive the grant before it could sell bonds to finance the rest of the project. County commissioners and city council members held a special meeting on Friday, December 23, to vote to accept the new conditions. Though the city wanted to try the voluntary approach to recycling, they realized the lead time required to have a curbside program operational by the end of January 1991 meant that they would not be able to prove the voluntary system was superior to curbside collection. Consequently, the council voted in March 1989 to adopt a time line for starting a curbside program.[115]

In addition to the major cases mentioned earlier, courts become involved in solid waste policy making through lawsuits filed over a remarkable array of issues. After the $60 million grant went through the decision-making process described above, two citizens' groups filed a suit challenging WDOE and Spokane's right to take such an action without first filing a supplemental EIS. Once the air permit was finalized by EPA, opponents filed an appeal of that decision in the Ninth U.S. Circuit Court of Appeals. The right of Wheelabrator to conduct business in the state was challenged because they had failed to register properly. There was a suit claiming that radio ads promoting the incinerator were in violation of the state Consumer Protection Act because they were misleading. Opening of the landfill in Klickitat County to which SWDP had decided to send its ash was delayed by suits filed by environmental groups, neighbors, and the Yakama Indian Nation, forcing the development of an EIS for the landfill and challenging the Klickitat County Comprehensive Solid Waste Management Plan.[116]

Opponents of the waste-to-energy project sued, claiming that the "put or pay" clause in the Wheelabrator contract constituted a lending of credit or a gift to Wheelabrator that violated the Washington State Constitution.[117] The suit also claimed that the Solid Waste Management Plan was not legal because so much more money was to be spent on lower-priority waste-to-energy incineration than on waste reduction and recycling, which had higher priority. The same suit challenged the adequacy of the EIS for the waste-to-energy facility, saying that it did not compare the costs and risks of burning trash to those of other alternatives.[118]

Owners of the Marshall landfill, which the Spokane County Comprehensive Solid Waste Management Plan identified as a facility to phase out of operation, filed a lawsuit claiming that the plan was invalid. They said the interlocal agreement between the city and county was an improper delegation of county authority to the city and challenged the flow control ordinance passed by the county in 1985. Their suit also complained that the plan did not properly analyze the contribution of recycling and made unsupported assumptions regarding the sizing of the incinerator.[119]

Local government officials felt the main impact of these lawsuits was the additional costs in time and money. By delaying construction of the waste-to-energy facility, the suits forced the city and county to pay inflation assessments to Wheelabrator as a result of an escalator clause in the contract. The county also had to pay about $200,000 in additional interest costs when they could not wait for the income from the long-term bonds sold in connection with the incinerator and had to sell short-term bonds to cover the costs of landfill cleanup operations.[120] Overall, local government officials said the lawsuits and permit appeals cost the project an additional $12 million.[121] The active citizens, on the other hand, felt their unrelenting use of the administrative and court appeals resulted in an earlier and more ambitious recycling program, a waste-to-energy facility that polluted less, and disposal of the ash outside the county.

Intergovernmental relations affect solid waste policy in yet another way. When a landfill is closed, there remain decades of postclosure operations. Landfills closed by the city and county of Spokane include Colbert, Mica, and Northside. The costs of postclosure management of Colbert (expected to total around $16 million), under the first Superfund cleanup agreement reached in the area, are being shared by Spokane County, WDOE, EPA, Key Tronic Corporation, and the U.S. Air Force.[122] Even though the head of the Seattle office of EPA called the Colbert cleanup plan "a model of how a cooperative effort should work between state and local governments and the private sector," it took eight years to reach that agreement and begin the postclosure cleanup effort — a task expected to take upwards of 30 years.[123]

A similar effort at the city-owned Northside landfill carries a price tag of $25 million. Intergovernmental relations on that project have been less than harmonious. City officials have bridled at WDOE and EPA regulations, complaining about the steps required and the reasonableness of state and federal regulators. Local officials disputed the need for a system to pump contaminated water out of the aquifer, saying that covering the landfill with a plastic liner should be sufficient to make the contamination plume in the aquifer disappear. In the opinion of the city's director of solid waste, "They've gone to cleaning the environment rather than protecting human beings." Another official complained, "Their idea of negotiating is they will tell you what to do and you will pay for it."[124]

The county has also had its share of conflict with WDOE. In the post-closure work on their Mica landfill, they have disputed WDOE's insistence on the need for a synthetic cover to prevent contaminated leachates from reaching the aquifer. At least since 1989, the county has tried to change WDOE's position on the cover,[125] and in 1993 simply stopped work on it, claiming WDOE was behind in funding their half of the project's costs. Complaining about the "one-way dialogue" with WDOE, the county public works director said the action was an attempt to ask WDOE, "Have we gotten your attention yet?"[126] The dispute was cleared up, and the county continued work on the cover. In a dispute similar to the Mica liner argument, because of the county's dire financial situation WDOE agreed to monitor the rate of pollution at the Greenacres landfill through 1996. If at that time the site should not pass its groundwater tests, the county would be required to cap that site also.[127]

CONCLUSION

Beyond the frustration and confusion caused by the frequently changing maze of federal and state rules, regulations, standards, criteria, guidelines, and expectations, state and federal policies and the dynamics of intergovernmental relations have real and significant impacts on how solid waste is managed at the local level. In Spokane, officials blamed the costs associated with permitting processes and appeals of permitting decisions on those who opposed the various operations. However, those processes are an established part of intergovernmental relations in solid waste policy making, so officials should expect the time delays associated with their use.

With the movement of federal and state governments into solid waste policy making, much has changed. Local governments, long the dominant force in solid waste management, may have had their day. Unless the current movement toward devolving responsibilities to state and local governments leads to outright abdication of the federal role, local governments will never again see the degree of autonomy they had throughout most of the twentieth century. And the reasons for federal involvement have not disappeared. The garbage problem is now too large and its management and disposal too expensive for local governments. The business of hauling and disposing solid waste has attracted giant corporations whose activities carry the waste across local and state political boundaries. If for no other reason than the limits of their jurisdictions, local governments are simply too small to continue in their traditional role of deciding how solid waste will be managed. Local landfills have become too small and too difficult to site, so they are being replaced by large regional landfills that are often privately owned and operated. If Congress does not reinstate local governments' authority to pass flow control ordinances, local governments will not be able to guarantee that local wastes will flow through facilities built by or for them. That may mean that incinerators and other expensive facilities have become too costly for local governments. Even with flow control capabilities, local governments often could not continue to make and implement policies without a federal, state, and/or private partner. In Spokane, construction of the waste-to-energy facility was made possible by a $60 million grant from the state, a $105 million bond issue, and a contract with Wheelabrator to construct and operate the plant.

Few state governments have ever been major actors in deciding solid waste policy. Barring abdication by the federal government, states probably never will be. They delayed too long their entrance into the field. By the time they became players, actions by the federal government and by large corporations made their jurisdictional limits inappropriate to the problem. Even leaders among the states, like Washington State, can do little more than tinker at the margins of federally mandated policies. Although those margins can have some significance for solid waste policy implementation, they do not constitute a major role for states.

The timidity of states has also reduced their potential role. William Ruckelshaus, former administrator of EPA and currently chief executive of Browning-Ferris Industries, Inc., has complained that state governments could use their authority to do much more to deal with the garbage problem.[128] Though his complaint related to the state's failure to facilitate waste facility siting, the argument is equally strong in a different area—states have not exercised their authority sufficiently to reduce the creation and increase the recycling of waste products. Some have tried to create demand for recycled goods through their procurement policies, but budgetary problems have often interfered. They could ban products that can be recycled from their landfills, but none has been that bold. They could require publishers and other businesses to increase their use of recycled goods, but they have been reluctant to exercise such authority.

Though it was a latecomer to solid waste policy making, the federal government has developed a gently coercive approach that has dramatically changed the way solid waste is managed. Congress has led the way in recognizing that solid waste is a national problem. The federal priority list of ways to manage solid waste reaches down through the states to affect local government solid waste policies and implementation. If the federal government and Washington State had not been pushing for incineration as a means of reducing the volume of waste landfilled, Spokane probably would not have a waste-to-energy facility. Through its Commerce Clause decisions, the Supreme Court has made it clear that, to a significant degree, the solution to the solid waste problem has to be a national one. Together Congress and the Supreme Court have begun to tell the states what they must do, and what they cannot do. Still, one has to wonder whether they are up to the next challenge — telling the private sector generators of solid waste what they must do to help address this national problem, and what they cannot do because it will make the problem worse.

EPA's initially grudging and lumbering entrance into the arena has evolved into a national program for managing solid waste the parameters of which may well point by implication to what the next generation of solid waste management will look like. If voluntary efforts toward reducing waste, mandatory recycling programs, volume reduction technologies, and variously sized plastic-wrapped caches of the remaining waste (lined and covered "state of the art" landfills) are sufficient only to delay the day of reckoning, then voluntary reduction may have to be replaced by mandatory reduction.

Business Influence

In the mixed capitalist economy of the United States, we should expect business to be a major influence on public policy, and it is. American governments rely on businesses to provide a wide variety of goods and services, from military technology and supplies for our troops to assistance in calculating our income taxes. "Contracting out" is not a new phenomenon — the Pinkerton detective agency contracted to provide the original Secret Service. According to Kettl, "The government's reliance on the private sector, with the blurring of public-private boundaries that accompanies it, has become the dominant administrative pattern of postwar [WW II] policy."[1] It is a trend clearly on the increase as we approach the twenty-first century.

The trend has had impacts on both the economic and the political aspects of American life. According to Bruce Ackerman, the U.S. constitutional regime has undergone three major alterations. The Modern Republic began under the New Deal, and its main distinguishing features are government's increased authority over economic and social development and its "repudiation of laissez-faire economic relationships."[2] Under the Modern Republic, business relations are neither as foundational for nor as independent of the political sphere as they once were. Political affairs no longer depend so much on economics for their legal foundation. The Modern Republic's repudiation of laissez-faire economics entailed an undermining of that foundation, and Ackerman says the foundation that followed was based on public, political freedoms: "If individuals and groups were to protect and further their interests, they would have no choice but to participate actively in the ongoing political life of the state and nation."[3]

This means that while business relationships no longer provide the model for political relationships, businesses have had to partici-

pate more actively in political life. The resulting realignment of business-government relations is still evolving; at the close of the twentieth century it would appear that economic relationships are either making a last gasp effort to reassert the dominance they lost under the Modern Republic, or in fact regaining that dominance. Though the legal foundation of political life is no longer based entirely on economic relationships, the most popular metaphor for political relationships, pluralism, is based on a marketlike dynamic among competing interests. In political culture terms, the Modern Republic rescinded some of the nation's individualistic beliefs, expecting politics to be less subservient to the economic system, but its model of political dynamics began to look more like its model of economic dynamics. As the Progressive moralistic belief in government action as a means of

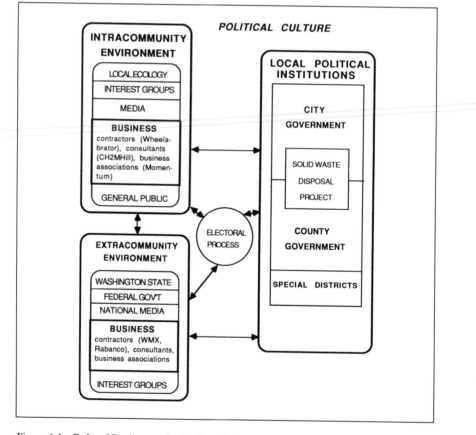

Figure 6.1   Role of Businesses in Spokane's Solid Waste Policy System

promoting the general welfare gained more support, a neotraditionalistic web of relations developed that would assist in maintaining the advantages inherent in the economic hierarchy.

As government-business relations have evolved, the changes have played themselves out in virtually all aspects of American policy making, including solid waste policy making. In this chapter, I will examine a variety of ways in which business-government relations affect solid waste policy making (see fig. 6.1). First, because they will assist in explaining the role of business in solid waste policy making, I review what the major public policy theories say about business-government relations in general. Then I discuss business influence on policy making and policy implementation, including some national examples that involve solid waste policy making. These examples are significant for the Spokane Solid Waste Policy System both because of what they indicate generally about the role of business in solid waste policy making and because business influence in the local dynamics comes in significant ways from national and international businesses. Finally, I describe a variety of ways businesses have influenced, and been influenced by, solid waste policy making in Spokane.

THEORIES OF BUSINESS INFLUENCE

In the second half of the twentieth century three major streams of explanation have guided descriptions of the role of business (and of businesses) in U.S. public policy. (In this chapter, the term *business* is meant to refer to the general institution that includes international corporations and small proprietorships. The term *businesses* refers to discrete enterprises that are part of the institution of business. I will also sometimes distinguish between big businesses and small businesses.) These three streams were introduced in chapter 2 as elitist theory, pluralist theory, and structuralist theory. I discuss the theories not to demonstrate which is best, but to demonstrate how these three approaches help us to better understand the role of businesses in solid waste policy.

The solid waste management industry, providing a vital service to the public while striving to promote the interests of the businesses that collectively constitute it, is an excellent example of the dynamics of business influence in public policy. The number of specific, narrow interests in the solid waste policy area is immense. From the large international corporations like WMX Technologies, Incorporated (formerly Waste Management, Incorporated), to the national consulting firms like CH2M Hill, to the statewide partnerships like Rabanco Companies of Washington State, and to local businesses like Ecocycle, solid waste management issues have serious financial implications for business interests. From its formulation to its implementation, businesses have interests in and significantly affect solid waste policy. Businesses' impact on solid waste policy may be understood in part as a function of the ubiquity of business interests in policy formulation and implementation, in part as a function of the power of elite individuals and circles, and in part as a function of the structure of business-business and business-government relations in the American political economy.

Elitist, pluralist, and structuralist theories all posit a significant role for business in policy making. Pluralists may admit that business is a very influential group in policy making, but they grant it no special place in the dynamics of policy making. Like other interest groups, businesses and business people join in voluntary associations and hire lobbyists to promote their interests in a relatively democratic competition. Pluralists do not ascribe as much power to business as elitists and structuralists do, but they agree that business interests have historically wielded much influence in American policy making.[4] Though business interests are not a monolithic entity, they account for 70 percent of the interest groups in Washington, D.C.[5] Through lobbying, campaign financing, litigation, networking, and even grassroots organizing, business interests command a wealth of resources and are among the most effective interest groups in America.

Business is seen in elitist and structuralist literature as the overwhelming source of power in America.[6] It therefore becomes necessary for elitists and structuralists to explain why business allows government to regulate its activities. Reflecting a recognition of Ackerman's Modern Republic, Koenig gives a concise answer: "Big business frequently does not attempt to keep the state out of the economic sphere; rather, it encourages government regulation (even while sometimes publicly resisting it) because such regulation in fact works to the advantage of industry."[7] In waste management, the symbiotic relationship between government regulations and market potential has occasionally led to a direct request for more regulation.[8]

It is apparent, however, that businesses do oppose specific proposed laws and regulations. Sometimes they prevail and the law or regulation is not adopted, or is significantly modified. Sometimes they do not prevail, and the law or regulation is adopted. In the latter case businesses have two options — fight the law or regulation in other government venues (e.g., courts, the White House, or, in the case of an administratively imposed regulation, Congress) or adapt to it. The literature is full of evidence regarding the first option;[9] the second is less well examined and will be discussed in a later section on implementation.

In the pluralist view, business interests remain dominant, but in the complex dynamics of late twentieth-century American politics their dominance is not unchallenged. The interest group universe has expanded and diversified.[10] Citizens' groups, government-induced groups—groups whose very existence is clearly a function of government action or policy—universities, churches, foundations, government-related groups, and individual corporations have all become significant elements in interest group activity. Some find this expansion encouraging—increasing the representativeness of American politics and opening up the process—but others are discouraged by the enhanced impact of narrow interests on a political process that should aspire to pursuit of the public good.[11]

For several reasons, the depiction of business interest groups as one among many types of interest groups, though enlightening, is not sufficient. First, treating business interests as one kind of interest group implies that they are sufficiently similar to citizens' and public interest groups that their influence can be studied in the same way. But as Mundo demonstrates, the differences among types of interest groups have significant implications for their roles in public policy making and implementation.[12] Second, the models of interest group politics have become too complex to allow business interests to be treated as a monolithic, homogeneous force. Sometimes business interests operate collectively, sometimes competitively. Moreover, interest group politics is no longer accurately described as an iron triangle of mutual accommodation among a few interest groups, an administrative agency, and a House and/or Senate committee. The number of interest groups has grown dramatically since the 1960s, and their interests often touch on more than one or two general topic areas.

The impacts of business in the public affairs of a community are complex and multidirectional. As Thomas Edsall points out, "It is corporate America that produces both pollution and jobs, that creates wealth and the maldistribution of wealth, that generates industrial carcinogens and equips shock-trauma units, that abandons central cities, and that writes the paychecks financing an enlarged middle class."[13] Though the degree of business interests' power over the political agenda of a community or nation certainly fluctuates over time,[14] there can be little doubt that the fluctuations are between great and greater, not between much and little.

The fluctuations in power may also be between segments of business interests, rather than between business and other interests. There is a ten-

dency to identify the high tides in business interest impact with eras dominated by political conservatism; but if Vogel is correct in identifying the era
(the late 1960s and early 1970s) in which the federal government became a
significant force in pollution regulation as a recent high point of the liberal
alliance,[15] then it must also be recognized that a huge industry in pollution
control and waste management has grown out of the policy direction begun
in that era. In 1992 the hazardous waste management industry, for example,
was worth $14.6 billion and was estimated to be growing at a 5–7 percent
annual rate.[16] In the United States, pollution abatement and control has
risen from a $70 billion industry in 1980 to $129 billion in 1991.[17] Given that
this country will continue to have a relatively free market system, it is likely
that businesses will continue to discover ways to benefit from the very regulatory regimes they opposed prior to passage.

William Browne offers an interpretation of recent changes in the dynamics of interest group influence that helps to understand how fluctuations could be misread as changes in the power of business interests.[18] He
says that interest groups generally no longer attempt to influence a wide
range of public policies. Instead, they limit their attempts at influence to
"issue niches" — the set of issues interest groups decide they must address.
As power in Congress has become more fragmented, interest groups have
found more opportunities to develop instrumental relations with specific
members or with the members of a specific subcommittee. As a result, "The
more an organization stakes out narrow policy claims, defines its identity in
terms of expertise over those claims, fixes its political assets within only that
specific range of identifiable problems, and provides a variety of issue-
related services to policy makers, the less its key issue positions will be contested and challenged. This produces a politics of interest group accommodation"[19] — not interest group competition, as the pluralists have described
it. What appear to be fluctuations in power may instead be fluctuations in
the issues being actively considered for policy changes. As the issues affect
different businesses differently, the appearance of influence on policy varies. So for several reasons a description of business's role in politics as a set of
interest groups competing with other interest groups, though accurate to
some degree, is no longer adequate.

Both sophisticated elite and structuralist theories attempt to address
that inadequacy. In elitist literature the impact of businesses on public policy is described as a function of the power of individual elites and of the
influence wielded in networking among small groups of elites. In classic
elite theory, the elite are not expected to become directly involved in policy

making; instead, they are depicted as controlling things from behind the scenes. In later, more sophisticated elite theories, the business elite "either become state officials or use their power to dominate those who are."[20]

As I argued in chapter 2, structuralist theory can be understood as a sophisticated version of elitist theory that in utilizing a kind of institutional process theory avoids being dismissed as conspiracy theory in academic clothing. What it adds to the mix of insights regarding the role of business in American politics is a recognition that in the mixed economy of the United States, "the government is constrained to serve the interests of large corporations by the economic, ideological, and political underpinnings of capitalism (by the 'structure' of American society), regardless of the intentions of government officials or the machinations of business leaders."[21] The structure of government-business relations in the United States, their complex, multidirectional interdependence, means that government cannot afford to do serious harm to business and business cannot afford to undermine government.

BUSINESS INFLUENCE IN POLICY MAKING

Just as important for the role of business in influencing public policy making has been the ability of businesses to recognize, adapt to, and benefit from the reification of pluralism in American politics. As the description of American politics in pluralistic (special interest group) terms has been adopted by an increasing number of analysts, those wanting to participate have turned increasingly to interest group techniques. The description first became a prescription, then evolved into a self-fulfilling prophecy. But government need not be subordinate to business for business to benefit from government action. As the pluralists point out, those interests that organize and work through political channels are likely to benefit. As the structuralist theorists point out, the interdependencies between business and government virtually dictate that government will act in ways that benefit business.

Greider used the story of Superfund legislation to illustrate the ways business has adapted to the reification of pluralism in American politics.[22] Superfund represented a serious loss for business interests. It assigned the costs of site cleanup to the specific companies that contributed hazardous materials to the site. But businesses did not waste time sulking over their loss; they put together strategies for limiting the damage. Businesses are constantly trying to influence government policy making through traditional lobbying and what Greider calls deep lobbying—the sponsoring of research at think tanks or ad hoc research groups established to influence the parameters of public discussion well before any specific legislation is pending. In this case a professional association, the Coalition on Superfund, was created by such companies as Dow and DuPont in collaboration with major insurance companies to analyze the implementation of Superfund and to begin a technical/rational critique aimed at influencing its implementation and amending its provisions when it came up for renewal. The coalition succeeded in having William K. Reilly's Conservation Foundation named by EPA to do a $2.5 million study of the Superfund law. As a result of these and other efforts, business was able to place on the public agenda a critique of Superfund that could be expected to resonate with some general themes of public dissatisfaction with government—it was flawed and a wasteful use of taxpayer money. In order to blunt the attack, instead of telling businesses what they must do to clean up Superfund sites, EPA began to negotiate Superfund compliance measures. But business did not relent in its opposition to Superfund. In preparation for reauthorization in 1994, the Chemical Manufacturers' Association pushed for two major changes in Superfund: (1) replacing the joint and several liability provisions with a "fair share" plan, and (2) replacing the cleanup standards aimed at restoring sites to precontamination conditions with site-specific, risk-based approaches to protecting the public health.[23]

Because many municipal landfills are on the Superfund list, Greider's Superfund story has direct implications for solid waste policy making. The cleanup procedures required by EPA and their attendant costs directly affect the rates local governments must charge for solid waste services. Moreover, the dynamics of that Superfund story are repeated in various ways in solid waste policy making at the federal, state, and local levels. For example, *World Wastes,* the industry's journal, suggests that local waste associations be formed in order to identify common goals, develop strategies, and lobby state and local regulators.[24] The main theme of those stories, whether they are told in pluralist, elitist, or structuralist terms, is that business is very active and effective in influencing solid waste policy making.

The issue of business influence in solid waste policy takes us through the societal generalizations of public policy theories and into the mechanisms of influence. Business influence in policy making can be analytically divided into influence at the policy-making stage and at the implementation stage. In the former, businesses want to affect both the parameters of policy and the specifics in policy statements—statutes, regulations, and administrative rulings. WMX, for example, has twenty-two lobbyists and a political action committee in Washington, D.C.[25] When EPA was considering the appeal of the air pllution permit for Spokane's waste-to-energy facility, WMX officials — and other industry groups, including the National Resource Recovery Association — wrote urging EPA administrator William K. Reilly to deny the appeal.[26]

Examining the policy-making influence of business, Anker, Seybold, and Schwartz delineate four kinds of structural links often found between business and government that directly affect policy making: personnel transfers, policy planning groups, advisory commissions, and boards of directors.[27] By personnel transfers they mean the movement of persons through a metaphorical "revolving door" from business to government employment, or vice versa. William Ruckelshaus's movement from private sector to EPA director, to the Weyerhauser Company, back to EPA director, then to his own environmental consulting firm, Ruckelshaus and Associates, and to CEO of Browning-Ferris Industries (the second largest waste management company in the country) exemplifies the revolving door, but it operates at many levels in the organizations.

Policy planning groups are established by businesses to develop policy proposals they then attempt to persuade government to adopt. As was explained earlier, the Coalition on Superfund is a good example of that kind of group at the national level. In the Spokane case, at the local level the various working committees formed as part of Momentum's structure were intended to fulfill a policy planning function. Occasionally those committees hire consultants to do specific reports aimed at influencing local policy.

Advisory commissions are created by government officials to formulate policies or to advise government officials as they formulate, modify, or implement policies. Washington State law establishes a state-level Solid Waste Advisory Committee (SWAC) and requires that each county create a SWAC. The degree of influence by these county SWACs over policy making varies widely. Some provide a symbolic involvement of citizens but exercise very little influence on policy making; others are given more substantive policy-making roles. In the Spokane case, the advisory bodies that wielded significant policy influence were the Project Liaison Board (PLB) and the Technical Advisory Committee (TAC). The PLB was composed entirely of government officials. The TAC included professionals whose expertise was expected to assist in making substantive policy or policy implementation choices.

Boards of directors may be composed entirely of business representatives, entirely of government officials, or a mixture of the two. Typically this body formally adopts major policies and hires and fires the chief executive officer of the public institution they serve. As noted in the chapter on local government, both the Spokane County Health District and the Spokane County Air Pollution Control Authority have boards of directors. Both boards are peopled by local government officials, some of whom, because of the part-time nature of their government position, are also actively engaged in private business. Questions arise periodically concerning whether their actions and votes reflect an understanding of the public welfare or protection of their business interests.

Structuralists and elitists see these linkages as evidence of the subordination of government to business. Pluralists see them as mechanisms through which interest groups attempt to defend and pursue their interests. From either viewpoint, the linkages and mechanisms are ways businesses proactively attempt to influence policy making.

Businesses also influence solid waste policy making through their responses to the structure and content of regulatory regimes. Environmental regulation in the United States took its present shape as part of an era of social regulation. In that era, governments began to use approaches previously applied only to economic activity in their attempts to regulate social and environmental activity. Economic regulation, obviously, aimed to have an economic impact on an industry. Social and environmental regulation cut across industries, being concerned with specific aspects of their operations (e.g., employment practices, air pollution, or water pollution). Business advocates complain that the restricted focus on specific aspects of industrial activities "can result in a total lack of concern over the effects of its [the regulatory agency's] specific actions on a company or industry."[28] For example, a regulator whose sole charge is to control air emissions may not show much concern for the economic costs associated with a required control technology.

Because solid waste management is regulated through the partial preemption approach, states are left with some flexibility in how their regulations promote compliance with federal standards. This means that companies can take into account the regulatory regimes of the various states in deciding where to conduct their business. Whether such considerations are significant factors in firms' location decisions is not clear. Davis reports that slightly more than half of his respondents said state regulatory climate was an important factor in relocation decisions, but two-thirds said access to markets and raw materials were the key concerns.[29] Furthermore, Feiock and Haley report that states with sufficient fiscal capacity can socialize the costs of stringent regulations, thus reducing the financial burden of compliance.[30] If companies are more concerned with the final fiscal impact of compliance than with the stringency of regulatory regimes, then fiscally healthy states need not weaken their regulations. However, when states generally do not find themselves in excellent fiscal health, business sensitivity to the structure and content of regulatory regimes is a matter of serious concern, and states are less likely to risk displeasing them than they would be in fiscally healthy times.

This dynamic was also part of Spokane's solid waste policy making. Both the probusiness editorial board of the local paper and the business-promoting interest group Momentum frequently expressed concern regarding the impact on economic development of deciding not to build the waste-to-energy facility. They also expressed concern regarding the impact of the polarized public discourse on businesses that were considering moving to Spokane.

In sum, businesses and business associations influence the formulation of public policy by playing the pluralism game, by acting as interest groups. But business influence on public policy making runs deeper than that. Because local government officials and businesses are concerned about them, the reactions (or potential reactions) of businesses to infrastructure capacity and reliability and to the regulatory climate in states and communities also affect policy making.

BUSINESS INFLUENCE AND IMPLEMENTATION

Business influence on public policy does not stop when policies are formulated. Business interests know that there are many decisions to be made in the implementation of policy, decisions that have a substantive impact on what the policy really is and how it will affect them. In addition to the day-to-day lobbying they engage in with respect to the government bodies implementing policy, businesses also involve themselves, in a variety of ways, in the process of turning policy statements into policy actions. When government agencies implement major new policy programs, two types of groups almost automatically develop in response: service recipients and service deliverers.[31] The media devote much attention to recipient groups, but the impact of delivery groups on implementation is where business influence is more likely to be found. "Because many service delivery groups offer their members vitally important selective material incentives (financial advantages and job opportunities), they are usually better organized than most recipient groups."[32] Especially in an era in which it is easier to adopt or maintain public service programs that depend on the private or nonprofit sector to administer services instead of creating new government bureaucracies, the growth of businesses and industries can depend heavily on their role(s) in delivering the services government policy requires.

In the United States, the government depends on the cooperation of businesses in the implementation of the vast majority of its policies. According to Kettl, "every major policy initiative launched by the federal government since World War II . . . has been managed through public-private partnerships."[33] Structural theorists have focused on the overall patterns of government-business relations and have made a good case that the patterns influence the potentials of public policy. Even when direct investment of corporate resources is not needed, "every important government activity requires the continuous and voluntary cooperation of major businesses."[34] For example, of the five major sources of government revenue (loans, income taxes, tariffs, sales taxes, and property taxes), only property taxes are collected directly by the government. Various levels of government contract with businesses to provide a wide variety of services, from the building of roads, bridges, and sewer systems to running jails and providing secretarial support.

In solid waste policy, businesses are involved in delivering waste management services at least as much as are state and local governments. They construct and operate solid waste facilities and the pollution control technologies those facilities use. They collect garbage and deliver it to those facilities. They haul garbage from transfer stations, incinerators, or other intermediate facilities. They recycle and reuse some materials, operate landfills in which much of the remaining waste is disposed, close the landfills when they are full or no longer meet standards, and conduct postclosure monitoring of the landfills.

The ways these kinds of business roles affected Spokane's solid waste policy making will be detailed in a later section. First, it may be helpful to review some of the ways business influences policy implementation in general, and to provide some examples of how those kinds of influence affect substantive policy areas like solid waste.

Privatization

When businesses become involved in policy implementation through contracts, it is called "privatization." It is common practice across the country for a municipality to contract with private firms to run its solid waste facilities and/or to provide other contracted services such as construction or operation of a facility, garbage collection, or promotion of recycling programs. Waste-to-energy facilities, because they involve a sophisticated, relatively new technology (often including proprietary processes licensed to specific companies) and because they are very expensive, are frequently built and operated (and sometimes owned) by private companies. According to *Moody's Municipal Issues*, private companies are eager to enter the waste-to-energy facility operation market because it provides a long-term revenue stream.[35]

Another way U.S. governments depend on businesses in the development and implementation of public policy is through contracts to provide personnel and expertise not found in government bureaucracies. According to Kettl, "Consultants and other contractors have helped the government plan programs, evaluate their results, answer citizens' inquiries, write congressional testimony for cabinet secretaries, organize logistics, make photocopies, and perform virtually every other service one can imagine."[36] Some of the contracted services are needed to implement specific steps required in the formulation of policy options; some are needed to implement actions required by the policy options chosen.

Kettl's description of how EPA and businesses shared governance power under Superfund demonstrates how consultants and contractors have become an integral part of solid waste policy implementation. At the same time it told EPA to address the problem of land pollution, Congress mandated personnel ceilings and capped (and gradually reduced) EPA spending on administrative costs. In an evaluation of contracting at EPA, the General Accounting Office estimated that half of EPA's professional and administrative staff spent some of their time on the contracting process.[37]

EPA also found that it lacked the necessary on-staff expertise. High turnover, especially among hydrologists and environmental engineers, exacerbated the expertise shortage. "The average tenure for Superfund remedial project managers, the officials responsible for supervising the cleanups in the field, was just eighteen months." Clearly EPA could not expect to do the job through its own staff. "EPA therefore came to rely on contractors for nearly every phase of Superfund work."[38] They also contracted for assistance in work related to EPA management and policy making — writing job descriptions, preparing site studies, preparing statements of work for other EPA contractors, responding to congressional inquiries, analyzing legislation, advising citizens, drafting regulations, drafting records of decisions, and even writing the Superfund program's annual report. By 1989 contractors accounted for around 90 percent of the Superfund budget. EPA's dependence on contractors was so complete, Kettl concluded, that "they knew only what the contractors were telling them. They could consider only those options that contractors suggested and could assess only those technologies that the contractors developed."[39]

The impact of business on the Superfund program was further enhanced by the vertical integration of related businesses. "Although hundreds of private contractors worked in the field, most of the business was highly concentrated; just six firms received 70 percent of Superfund's contract dollars."[40] Firms that helped write regulations and statements of work also performed the cleanups. Evaluation of the performance of contractors was compromised by EPA's dependence on contractors to do the evaluating (sometimes of their own work). Even when a contractor was evaluating another contractor's work, two factors could have compromised their objectivity: they might be lenient in order to maintain good intraindustry relations, or competitive relations with the other contractor might lead them to either indulge the competitive spirit or bend over backward to avoid the appearance of prejudice. Moreover, the limited supply of qualified contractors meant that poor evaluations were unlikely to disqualify a contractor for future contracts.

Superfund assured a market niche for businesses that could clean up hazardous waste sites, help manufacturers reduce their creation of hazardous waste, and/or help manufacturers meet EPA's antipollution standards. Because the Superfund program created a multibillion-dollar market of government contracts, businesses eagerly entered the field of cleanup technology and expertise. A regulatory regime initially aimed at exacting the costs of environmental cleanup from the businesses responsible for the pollution actually created a new niche for businesses. This dynamic manifests itself in a variety of ways in solid waste policy making, some of which will be discussed below in the section on Spokane solid waste policy. For the moment, it may suffice to say that *World Wastes*, the waste industry journal, actively promotes the development of public-private partnerships in developing landfill, waste-to-energy, composting, and recycling solutions for solid waste problems.[41]

The issue of private versus public solid waste management is not a new one. Around the turn of the century there was considerable disagreement regarding who should own solid waste facilities.[42] Opposition to contracting for refuse management focused on the inherent disadvantages of the contract system. First, contracts often were awarded for political reasons; charges of favoritism and bribery were common. Second, contracts were most often awarded for only one or two years, which meant that contracting companies had no incentive to engage in long-range planning and were not likely to invest in capital-intensive improvements, the costs of which would need to be amortized over a number of years. Consequently, turn-of-the-century sanitary engineers argued that a permanent public agency was better suited to the job of refuse management.

Debate on the advantages and disadvantages of public and private ownership of solid waste management facilities continues in the last quarter of the twentieth century. Antunes and Halter's list of the advantages of public ownership, however, shows that the terms of the dispute have become more sophisticated: "(1) exemption from federal and state income taxes; (2) tax free bonds; (3) lower interest rates on bonds; (4) sales tax exemption on equipment purchases; (5) fewer zoning problems; and (6) exemptions from some state regulations affecting site location."[43] (The sales tax exemption does not apply in all states; Washington State, for example, does not exempt government purchases from the sales tax.) There has also been considerable progress since this list was compiled. The two disadvantages to private ownership Antunes and Halter discuss — time limitations on contracts and difficulties in developing a solid waste management plan that extends beyond the limits of the contract — generally have been overcome.

Privatization as a means of implementing solid waste policy has been around for at least a century. As we close the twentieth century, it appears to be on the rise. The influence of business on public policy, then, will probably also increase.

Privatism and Market Mechanisms

Even if government implementation of solid waste policy is not contracted out, it is still possible for business principles to override public service principles in the implementation of policy. When government is not contracting with business to implement its policies, it sometimes tries to run its own affairs in a more "businesslike" fashion. One of the more recent trends in environmental regulation is the replacement of command-and-control methods with market-based mechanisms. Under command-and-control methods, the regulatory agency determines a level of allowable pollution at each pollution source and orders the source to reach that level. It then monitors the source's compliance and punishes it for violations. The movement toward market-based mechanisms is premised on (1) a judgment that command-and-control regulatory methods have failed and (2) an assumption that markets are inherently superior regulatory instruments.

Government command-and-control approaches to environmental regulation have been found wanting in several respects. They have been described as inefficient, undemocratic, ineffective, overly complex, and time-consuming. Consequently, another major force in environmental policy in general, and solid waste policy in particular, that has emerged in the last quarter of the twentieth century is an "increasing reliance of government upon the private sector and market mechanisms"[44] — an approach known as privatism. It is based on a belief that attempts to control private interests have generally failed, but private interests can be manipulated to promote the public welfare.[45]

Compared to command-and-control systems using technology-based standards and performance standards, the argument runs, market mechanisms can achieve the same reduction in pollution at the aggregate level at less cost; in addition, they require less government meddling in the affairs of business and provide market incentives for pollution control improvements.[46]

The deposit-refund system is the market-based approach most readily identified with solid waste policy. "Bottle bills" that entail a surcharge on beverage containers are the most well-known example. The surcharge in such a system is refunded when the containers are returned for recycling. Deposit-refund systems could be used for a much wider variety of recyclables, from the glass, plastic, and aluminum containers for soft drinks to milk cartons, plastic dish soap and detergent bottles, individual-serving yogurt containers, catsup and salad dressing squeeze bottles, batteries of all kinds, vehicle tires, and vehicle carcasses.

Other market-based mechanisms have been or could be applied to solid waste policy.[47] Pollution charges or "green fees" can be levied either as a fee or as a tax on the amount of pollution a source generates. "Pay as you throw" systems for collection and disposal of garbage have been used and could be used more widely, to generate new revenues or to reduce the impact of other revenue-generating mechanisms.

But there are problems with pollution charges, too. The greatest difficulty with pollution charges is determining how much to charge. It is not easy to calculate the amount or rate needed to achieve a specific level of pollution reduction. Assuming that such a calculation can be accurately made, there is no guarantee that the political process by which such charges are set will produce the economically correct charge. In addition, the costs of government monitoring may be substantial and difficult to forecast.

Another market-based mechanism is the tradeable permit system. It has been used in air pollution control and could be used in recycling programs in the form of recycling targets with tradeable permits. In this approach, the government sets an overall level of tolerable pollution and allocates emission levels through a permit system. Firms that can reduce their emission level are allowed to sell or lease their surplus. This system's utility depends on the existence of a sufficiently competitive market for the pollution credits without an excessive number of regulated sources. If there are too many sources, the costs of regulation can be high; if there are too few, there may not be sufficient competition for the mechanism to work.

Government officials who do not want to appear unfriendly to business have found that adoption of a regulatory approach that mimics the market is one way of avoiding that appearance. But the market has an inherent tendency to ignore "externalities," and adaptation of a market mechanism so that it addresses environmental impacts that have traditionally been considered externalities must be accomplished through governance mechanisms. Though markets may be better than command-and-control mechanisms at achieving economic efficiency, governance mechanisms must be employed to determine the end toward which efficiency is to be measured. As the environmental justice movement makes clear, efficiency is not the only policy objective sought through regulatory regimes.[48] The distribution of benefits and harms resulting from economic activity is also a concern of the community, the government, and enlightened businesses. For example, one analysis of the costs of air and water pollution control found their distribution among economic classes to be regressive, with those at the lower end of the spectrum spending 12.4 percent and 4.2 percent of their income, and those at the upper end paying only 3.4 percent and 1.6 percent, respectively.[49] One way this aspect of the problem frequently manifests itself in solid waste policy is that the siting of a facility imposes greater costs on one portion of the community (those nearest the site) than on others. Since opposition to solid waste facilities has historically been stronger among liberal, college educated, relatively young, middle- and high-income groups in urban areas, facilities have tended to be placed in minority and low-income communities.[50]

Privatization and the use of market-based mechanisms enhance the involvement of businesses in implementing solid waste policy. Privatization places delivery of services directly in the hands of business. Market-based mechanisms place the choice of specific approach used to reach standards set by government regulators in the hands of private business. Though businesses may be well suited to enhancing efficiency, without government pressure they are not effective in addressing other solid waste policy goals.

WASTE REDUCTION

The United States' difficulty in addressing the goal of waste reduction more effectively demonstrates how dependence on business may hinder government's attainment of its regulatory goals. Businesses are the source of the vast majority of the solid waste generated in this country. Waste reduction is recognized throughout the country as the approach that would have the greatest impact on the solid waste problem. Nonetheless, very little progress has been made in promoting solid waste reduction. In 1992, while 38 states had recycling goals, only 7 had reduction goals.[51] Instead of reporting how much they have reduced the waste stream, states take pride in slowing its growth — or they emphasize how much of the waste stream is diverted from landfills through recycling and composting programs. Compared to other economically adavanced countries, the United States uses more packaging, recycles less, and is willing to consider only relatively weak policy measures.[52] Though the Clinton administration announced a new emphasis on "pollution prevention," what impact it will have remains to be seen.[53] Blumberg and Gottlieb conclude that in the United States "the waste issue ultimately remains a question of disposal and not generation."[54]

Both EPA and many states have adopted waste management priority lists that place waste reduction at the top, but the federal government has not enacted legislation requiring solid waste reduction. Since announcing their "waste management hierarchy," EPA has retreated from the strong waste reduction stance it initially took and has instead emphasized the need to work on all components of the "integrated hierarchy," conceding that "strict adherence to a rigid hierarchy is inappropriate for every community." Instead of taking direct action, EPA has preferred to see itself as an information exchange and a financier of waste reduction studies.[55]

When the Congressional Budget Office studied ways the federal government might reduce waste, it restricted its examination to ways of encouraging households and businesses to reduce their waste-generating activities. Focusing on economic incentives, the 1991 study said the ideal pricing system would charge households and businesses "according to the amount and toxicity of waste they disposed of."[56] However, the study argued that such a system is not feasible, so it proceeded to examine four alternative policies based on a singular assumption — that the proper role of the federal government is to encourage waste reduction through economic incentives. The four policy alternatives were: (1) a disposal tax and reuse subsidy, (2) a virgin material tax, (3) an investment tax credit for recycling, and (4) a recycling credit system. The hegemony of market-based mechanisms in this study speaks volumes about the influence of business on the federal government's approach to reducing waste.

The situation in Washington State is quite similar. In 1988 the Washington State legislature created an Office of Waste Reduction in WDOE and "charged it with encouraging waste reduction through technical assistance to waste generators and other means."[57] As noted in chapter 5, the Washington State legislature also passed a temporary "ban on bans" prohibiting local governments from utilizing a waste reduction tool that would otherwise have been available to them. The legislature argued that banning types of packaging from a local market was not likely to have the desired effect of altering a company's packaging practices; but rather than relying on persuasion to make this point, they directly prohibited local prohibitions of packaging. WDOE has also been reluctant to take an aggressive stance on waste reduction. For example, they provided a grant to the League of Women Voters of Washington to conduct a survey to learn what strategies businesses were already using. The League interviewed 257 businesses, then wrote a report and distributed 500 copies of it.[58]

One provision of the Waste Not Washington Act was the establishment of a Packaging Task Force; the legislation specified that at least 50 percent of the task force should be industry representatives. Its actual membership was 64 percent industry representatives, 11 percent state government, 11 percent local government, 7 percent environmental group representatives, and 7 percent citizen representatives. Objecting to the dominance of the industry perspective, some members representing local government and citizens' and environmental groups requested that the task force report be a consensus document. That request was rebuffed, and minority viewpoints were given a place in Appendix Q. The report itself plainly states: "This is an industry document."[59]

One reason for the lack of government policies that boldly address waste reduction is the importance of the packaging industry in the United States. Though the industry contributed 31.6 percent of municipal solid wastes in 1988,[60] its size and the functions it serves have made it a difficult target for government bodies to attack. It is a $300 billion industry dominated by a small number of multinational corporations including Dow, Monsanto, Du-Pont, Union Carbide, Mobil, and Allied-Signal.[61] The packaging industry's impact on the lives of consumers is, of course, considerable; the Worldwatch Institute estimates that packaging costs U.S. consumers around 10 percent of their total expenditures on food and beverages.[62] Though a major function of packaging in the United States is marketing, it also protects consumers from the potentially life-threatening impacts of product tampering, protects the product from damage in transportation, helps keep some products fresh, and helps keep products clean.

The packaging industry has not been receptive to suggestions that it be subject to government regulation. Lobbying through the Society of the Plastics Industry, the Polystyrene Packaging Coalition, and the Food Service and Packaging Institute, the industry has wrapped itself in the banner of the free market economy, and has blamed the consumer for generating packaging wastes.[63] Packaging corporations have promoted incineration as the best way to reduce the volume of materials destined for landfills, and, recognizing incineration's declining public appeal, have recently camouflaged their support for it by talking about "integrated waste management" as the best approach to the solid waste problem.[64]

But waste reduction policies targeting specific types of packaging have met with some success in the United States. Sixteen states banned non-degradable six-pack loops before Congress required EPA to institute the ban nationwide. States have also passed a variety of "bottle bills," designed to keep beverage bottles out of the waste stream. One antipackaging effort, dubbed the McToxics campaign, targeted the plastic foam containers used in McDonald's franchises across the country.[65] Coordinated by the Citizens' Clearinghouse for Hazardous Wastes, complemented by a Friends of the Earth campaign against all fast food plastic foam packaging, and coinciding with news media interest in the "CFCs deplete the ozone layer" story, the campaign played a part in spurring state and local governments to consider plastic foam fast food container bans. A number of local governments around the country passed ordinances banning the containers. Maine and Vermont banned them, and in 1988 twenty-one other states were considering banning them. In response, McDonald's agreed to phase out its use of plastic foam containers made with CFCs, and DuPont (the largest producer of CFCs in the world) decided to stop producing CFCs. At first, McDonald's used plastic foam containers without CFCs and planned a recycling program that would collect the containers and convert them into other plastic products; but when the amount of plastic foam it could supply was much smaller than estimated (because so little of it remained on site), McDonald's dropped the plastic recycling approach and switched to paper packaging.

One of the greatest impacts of business on solid waste management has been to resist aggressive attempts to reduce waste generation. The largest portion of the nation's waste stream is corrugated cardboard, and although reusable containers are a viable option, over 90 percent of all manufactured goods in the United States are shipped in corrugated cardboard boxes — most of them used only once.[66] When Suffolk County, New York, passed a ban on polystyrene foam containers, the plastics industry filed a lawsuit.[67] Despite the priority of waste reduction in both federal and state solid waste management plans, and despite the clear fact that reducing waste is the most important step that can be taken in dealing with the solid waste problem, business has stubbornly resisted all significant waste reduction measures. In the case of hazardous waste, the rate of increase in generation has declined because of the costs associated with safe management and the potential costs related to liability.[68] If state and federal governments' verbal support of solid waste reduction were accompanied by similar straightforward policies that were effectively enforced, solid waste reduction could have a much greater impact.

Given the nature of business-government interdependence and the national policy milieu favoring market-based mechanisms, such policies — not to mention their effective enforcement — seem unlikely in the 1990s. Business influence in policy making is well positioned to rebuff proposals that would do more than provide incentives. Government dependence on businesses in implementing whatever policies are passed gives business ample opportunity to turn operational policy toward business-friendly approaches.

In the Spokane Solid Waste Policy Making System, this aspect of business influence, though located in the external environment, is crucial to a proper understanding of the role of business in local solid waste policy making. As the last chapter showed, policies adopted at the national and state levels of government have tremendous impacts on the options local governments have to choose from. Just as encouragement from federal and state policy makers pushed Spokane toward building a waste-to-energy facility, the influence of business in restricting national and state policies to those considered more business-friendly limited Spokane's ability to consider waste reduction seriously. Moreover, the character of business-government relations described above also reaches into local communities. The federal government has difficulty resisting business influence, and state and local governments are much less favorably positioned in their relations with business.

Businesses and Spokane's Solid Waste Policies

The impact of business on solid waste policy making in Spokane must be understood as part of the national and state policy milieu. The nature of business dynamics is such that political jurisdiction lines are recognized mostly as an annoyance. Still, businesses do attempt to influence policy at each available venue. Business influence at the national and state levels affects the parameters within which Spokane makes its policy decisions.

As noted in chapter 3, the West has a history of resenting the power of big business in influencing local and regional policy. Western antipathy toward business influence derives in significant part from the days when railroad interests were the dominant force in western state politics. According to Hrebenar, the narrow focus of the economies of many western states explains why business interest groups can wield so much influence in their politics. Today business interests, and the interest groups and lobbyists that represent them, remain among the most powerful in western politics.[69]

Political scientists characterize Washington State as strongly influenced by interest groups, and they list among its more powerful groups Boeing, labor, manufacturers of timber and forest products, banking, and power companies and utilities.[70] Since 1972, when Washington State voters passed Initiative 276 regulating lobbying and campaign financing and opening it to public scrutiny, it has been easier to describe the activities of interest groups with some degree of accuracy. In 1983 the number of registered interest groups was 480, and the number of registered lobbyists was 583 (local government representatives and independently active citizens are not required to register). By 1990 those numbers had almost doubled. More than half of the ten most powerful interest groups in the state are business interests.[71]

If the amount of money they spend is any indicator, interest groups in Washington State have increased their influence in recent years. In Washington State there are no limits on the amounts individuals or groups may give to political campaigns, but campaign finance records are public information. In 1980 PACs provided about 37 percent of the money contributed to legislative election campaigns; in 1990 that figure had risen to 60 percent. In 1984, "Of the twenty PACs with the largest amounts of receipts and expenditures, sixteen had business connections and four were affiliated with unions." Similar amounts have been spent on lobbying efforts, and in 1990 eight of the top ten spenders on lobbying among interest group categories were business-related. Also in 1990, business PACs gave the largest percentage (29.7 percent) of the contributions received by legislators, and individual businesses were fourth on the list with 15.4 percent.[72]

Solid waste policy has, of course, been a target of some of this lobbying. In 1988 and the first two months of 1989, "competitors in Washington's solid waste industry spent at least $250,199 for lobbying and legislative campaign contributions." Because they feared deregulation would put WMX in a position to use its economic resources to "freeze out the smaller companies," the Washington Waste Management Association, representing the private waste companies in the state, spent $62,387 in that same period lobbying against deregulation of the waste management industry.[73]

WMX and its subsidiaries joined in the lobbying in the state capitol when their interests were at stake. At one time, former Washington State Governor John Spellman represented WMX in Olympia. During the fourteen-month period mentioned above, WMX spent $176,812 lobbying and contributing to the campaigns of legislators.[74] In 1987, when ash disposal regulations were under consideration, the company lobbied aggressively to promote treatment of ash as "special waste." In 1989, when others were pressuring the legislature to rescind the $60 million grant for Spokane's waste-to-energy facility, Wheelabrator joined city officials in lobbying intensively to have WDOE honor its earlier commitment. (In 1989 WMX owned about one-quarter of Wheelabrator; in 1990 it purchased a majority share.)[75]

WMX subsidiaries have also lobbied in Spokane. During the 1989 city council election that determined whether Spokane would go forward with its plans for a waste-to-energy facility, Wheelabrator (the company under contract to build the facility) became more aggressive in promoting a favorable corporate image, buying ads in the local newspaper and on commercial radio and television stations, and securing promotional recognition on the local public radio station. They also began contributing more to various charitable causes.[76]

But WMX was not the only business lobbying to influence solid waste policy in Spokane. A few examples may suffice to illustrate the extent of the lobbying efforts.[77] Two companies, Rabanco and Finley Buttes Landfill Company, competed with WMX for the contract to haul and dispose of the ash from Spokane's waste-to-energy facility. The effectiveness of their lobbying (probably accompanied by concern about becoming too dependent on a large company from back east) put the largest waste management company in the country in last place; Rabanco won the contract and Finley Buttes was designated as the backup if Rabanco had difficulty finishing its ash landfill. Riedel Environmental Technologies, Inc., after obtaining its first contract for a commercial-scale composting plant from Portland Metropolitan Service District, came to Spokane to promote its technology as an alternative to the proposed waste-to-energy plant. And during the 1989 primary election campaign, Washington Water Power Company, a local private utility, allowed one of its engineers to publish a guest column in the local newspaper supporting the waste-to-energy project.

Business associations were also involved in the local solid waste policy discourse. After conducting a poll of local Chamber of Commerce members and finding that 85 percent favored construction of a waste-to-energy facility and 52 percent were not opposed to the proposed airport business park location, the Energy and Environmental Committee of the Chamber recommended that it support construction of the facility at the airport site.[78] When the EPA was considering the facility's air pollution permit and the 1989 Spokane city council election was in full swing, the Air Transport Association of North America asked EPA not to grant the permit until it carefully considered the potential dangers to aircraft at Spokane International Airport—not a consideration normally examined when granting or denying an air pollution permit.[79] When the cost of canceling the waste-to-energy plant became an item of heated controversy and widely varying estimates (from $700,000 to $57 million), Momentum, a group formed by local business executives to promote economic development, commissioned a study that eventually estimated the cost at $50–75 million. The study was released in the last ten days of the 1989 election campaign.[80]

Business influence was also felt in the implementation of Spokane's solid waste policies. Spokane's waste-to-energy facility was built and is operated by Wheelabrator. Obtaining that contract was important to Wheelabrator because it was the company's first waste-to-energy facility in the western United States. Though Wheelabrator had historically preferred to own the facilities they operated, under the terms of the contract the city of Spokane retained ownership of this facility. The advantage to Wheelabrator was that it avoided the cost of ownership. Public ownership also made the facility eligible for a WDOE grant for $60 million and for funding through municipal bonds, issued at a lower interest rate than would have been available for a private facility. The terms of the $94 million construction contract were quite favorable to Wheelabrator, providing for penalties the city would owe if it or government processes beyond its control delayed construction and/ or initial operation of the facility.[81] The contract also included a "put or pay" clause in which the city promised to deliver a specific minimum amount of garbage to the facility each year or to pay Wheelabrator an amount equal to the sum it would have paid for the facility's processing of that minimum amount. And if additional pollution control equipment were required by SCAPCA, WDOE, or EPA, the city would have to pay for it.[82]

In addition to building and operating Spokane's waste-to-energy facility, WMX was part of other local solid waste management considerations. WMX subsidiary Waste Management of Spokane contracted to collect garbage and provide curbside recycling in unincorporated areas in the northern part of Spokane County and the southern part of Stevens County, the next county north.[83] WMX subsidiary Washington Waste Systems competed unsuccessfully in Spokane for the contract to haul and dispose of the ash from the waste-to-energy facility.[84] When Spokane was considering how to enter the world of composting, WMX subsidiary Wheelabrator Environmental Systems was the exclusive licensee in North America for the Buehler-Miag process, one of the major names in composting technology.

The political and policy impacts of WMX on the Inland Northwest's solid waste management went beyond those deriving directly from contracts to provide services for the city and county of Spokane. The size and scope of the WMX collection of companies (nearly 500 subsidiaries) makes it a major player wherever it gets involved in waste management. WMX holds the long-haul contracts for both Seattle's and Portland's garbage, and it disposes of those two cities' garbage in a huge regional landfill in eastern Oregon owned by WMX subsidiary Oregon Waste Systems.[85] The Portland contract is "the largest single government services contract in Oregon history."[86]

WMX has also proposed to place a huge regional landfill near Washtucna, Washington, at a site in Adams County about 75 miles southwest of Spokane.[87] The corporation planned to bring garbage from Seattle and Canada to that landfill. County residents were sharply divided over the proposal: some were attracted to the potential of thirty to thirty-five landfill jobs; others, who formed the Organization for the Protection of Agricultural Lands (OPAL), were worried about the impact of having a landfill as a neighbor to their farms. OPAL hired attorneys and consultants and tried to get Congressman Foley to urge EPA to designate their aquifer a "sole source" aquifer. The 1992 Adams County commissioners' election campaign centered on the dispute. Two of the candidates for commissioner accused WMX of trying unfairly to damage their campaigns. The conflict even spread into Washington State's 1992 U.S. Senate campaign, with Senate hopeful Patty Murray reportedly receiving improperly aggressive phone calls from WMX spokesperson Scott Cave. The Adams County Planning

Commission, in an action that constituted a recommendation to the county commissioners, first voted 4–3 against the zoning permit to allow the landfill; but when that vote was voided as a violation of the state's open meetings law, in a second vote they deadlocked at 4–4. In 1994 the Adams County Commissioners approved WMX's land use permit for the landfill, and in 1995 WMX submitted a permit application to build and operate a 560-acre regional landfill.

The arid climate, vast spaces, and good transportation infrastructure of the Inland Northwest have made places like Adams County attractive to WMX and other solid waste management companies as sites for their facilities. Rabanco, ECOS, and WMX subsidiary Chemical Waste Management have scoured the region for host communities for hazardous waste incinerators.[88] In 1989 WMX opened the first huge regional landfill in the area, the Columbia Ridge landfill, in Gilliam County, Oregon. Rabanco, a Seattle-based company, has a large regional landfill in Klickitat County, Washington. Tidewater Barge Company of Vancouver, Washington, has one in Morrow County, near Boardman, Oregon.[89] All three are close to the Columbia River and the highways and railroads that run along it. Residents of the Inland Northwest have come to fear that their region will become a popular location for facilities for waste from places like Los Angeles, Chicago, and even New York City. In fact, in June 1995 it was announced that Napa County, California, would be sending their solid waste to Rabanco's landfill in Klickitat County.[90]

Successful as it has been in establishing a presence in the Pacific Northwest, WMX has not been able to overcome the region's traditional distrust of large private companies. When the city of Seattle was considering three competitors for an out-of-county landfill—Burlington Environmental, Inc., Rabanco Regional Landfill Company, and Washington Waste Systems (a WMX subsidiary)—it contracted with outside legal counsel to examine the companies' recent histories of civil and criminal actions related to "corrupt practices, price fixing, violations of environmental standards at landfills, or similar concerns"[91] filed against them. The investigation found that all three competitors (or their subcontractors) had records of environmental standards violations. Though the report argued against condemning the company, WMX was the only competitor found to have been convicted of offenses involving anticompetitive activity and public corruption.[92] According to *Business Marketing*, "The company [WMX] has received enough bad press over the years to fill several landfills."[93] So when the right of the Washington Utilities and Transportation Commission to examine the books of one WMX subsidiary (Wheelabrator) to determine whether the rates set by another WMX subsidiary (Waste Management of Spokane) led to an unfair profit was at issue, Spokane's newspaper editorialized: "Should Washington lower its defenses while the world's biggest garbage company extends its scandal-stained tentacles around the state's consumers? No way."[94]

There were, of course, many other contractors involved in Spokane's movement into a new generation of solid waste management. Wheelabrator contracted with Clark-Kenith, Inc., as the general contractor for construction of the waste-to-energy facility; Clark-Kenith, in turn, subcontracted with Western Security for fences and security systems, Budinger and Associates for site testing and quality control, and West Wood Corporation for site preparation and earth work. Unions were asked to provide most of the laborers needed to construct the plant.[95] After rather bitter competition with WMX and Finley Buttes Landfill Company, Rabanco received the contract to haul the ash from the incinerator and dump it in a special monofill at its Klickitat landfill. Rabanco subcontracted with Western Refuse, Inc., to haul the ash away from the incinerator.[96]

Privatization has also had an impact on Spokane's solid waste management. With SWDP accepting "clean green" compostables and a variety of other recyclables at its waste-to-energy facility and transfer stations, the local recycling and composting operations are examples of public-private cooperative enterprises. At first, local recyclers challenged the need for government intervention to increase the recycling rate, saying that rising garbage rates would be sufficient incentive.[97] But the city council, at the urging of WDOE, insisted on taking steps to promote recycling and composting. After running its own pilot composting operation, SWDP granted a contract to O. M. Scott & Company to run a permanent facility.[98] Another local company that competed but did not win the contract, Ecocycle, also set up operations — and later complained that the public-private operation was devastating its business. Cooperation between SWDP and local recycling companies helped to avoid that kind of friction in recycling noncompostables. Spokane Recycling Products (a leader among those who had expressed concern about government involvement) and Pacific Hide & Fur received contracts to handle the recyclable materials gathered by the city's curbside collection service.[99]

Development and implementation of Spokane's solid waste management policy also involved contracts with many consultants. One area where consultants had an impact was on the public discourse surrounding the waste-to-energy project. For example, Auble and Associates and Century

West Engineering prepared a report designed to alleviate concerns that those owning land next to an ash landfill would face declining property values. The report said people's fears can instigate a short-term drop in values, but that in the long term, if the landfill does not lead to environmental problems, property values are not affected.[100] Fears that the waste-to-energy facility would exacerbate fog problems at Spokane International Airport (SIA) were addressed, in part, by SWDP's hiring a consultant to study the potential for problems. The consultant concluded that the facility might need to be put on standby as much as 300 hours per year, but that "if appropriate decision processes are developed . . . the Facility can be operated with little, if any impact on the fog at SIA."[101]

Occasionally, consultants were flown in for a brief visit just to buttress the case for the project. For example, SWDP brought in the vice president of Clement and Associates, a consultant to EPA, to participate in a forum sponsored by the Spokane Medical Society addressing the health and environmental risks of the project. He questioned the risk management expertise of the panelists at the forum and effectively reduced the significance of the health issue in the debate.[102] SWDP also brought in a chemist who was a technical advisor to the U.S. Conference of Mayors to hold a press conference and counter opponents' claims about the toxic nature of incinerator ash. He argued that labeling the ash as toxic was not a proper use of the term: ash needed to be handled carefully, but it did not have "an immediate, pending health impact on the workers and the people living around [it]."[103]

Opponents of the project also used consultants. When Sheri Barnard, the only city council member to oppose the waste-to-energy facility, ran for mayor and was pressed for her alternative to the incinerator, she used calculations done by an economic development and consulting firm, Allied Management and Development, to argue for hauling raw garbage to Rabanco's regional landfill in Klickitat County. Those figures showed the city saving $87.5 million over the next 20 years. SWDP's financial analyst, from Seattle Northwest Securities, responded that over 20 years long-hauling raw garbage would cost $50 million more than the waste-to-energy facility.[104] David Bricklin, an attorney in Seattle with the Washington Environmental Council, argued many of the legal challenges made against the facility.[105] Local attorneys who helped included Bill Powell, an established attorney who over the years has taken many cases challenging the authority of government agencies, and Lynn Mounsey, a young attorney fresh out of Gonzaga Law School, who later accepted a position as assistant to Mayor Sheri

Barnard.[106] Finally, one of the consultants flown in by opponents to contribute to the policy discourse was Dr. Paul Connett, a chemistry professor at St. Lawrence University and a consultant affiliated with the Citizens' Clearinghouse for Hazardous Waste who travels the nation helping opponents of waste incinerators.

Much of the work of developing the information base needed for the project was done with the help of numerous consultants.[107] The city of Spokane, Spokane County, and Washington Water Power engaged Morrison-Knudsen to do a feasibility study of a waste-to-energy project for the Spokane area. Parametrix prepared the 1984 solid waste management plan update and the 1992 solid waste management plan and final EIS. Henningson, Durham & Richardson (HDR) contracted with the city and county to conduct Phase I services in developing a waste-to-energy project, prepared the Request for Proposals and the Request for Qualifications, and prepared the EIS for the waste-to-energy facility. Century West Engineering subcontracted with HDR to do the environmental impact analysis for the waste-to-energy project, and looked for and screened potential ash landfill sites. Financial and legal consultants were also involved; the financial advisor for the project was Seattle Northwest Securities. The bond counsel was Preston, Thorgrimson, Ellis, and Holman.[108]

Public information programs also led to contracts with a local business. Alliance Pacific, Inc. (API), received several contracts totaling over $1 million to promote the waste-to-energy facility and the recycling program. From 1985 to 1988, API received over $400,000 in contracts to promote the incinerator. In 1989 API was awarded a $327,000 contract to promote recycling awareness. Much of the recycling awareness program was aimed at elementary school children and included a Star Wars–type robot named R3U2 (representing the idea that you, too, should reduce waste, recycle, and reuse).[109]

Superfund and other landfill cleanup operations also entail contracts. In Spokane County four landfill sites have been placed on the Superfund national priority list: Northside, Mica, Greenacres, and Colbert. Most of the cleanup work is done by private firms under contract with government agencies or with other private firms. For example, CH2M Hill, a nationally renowned firm with offices in Spokane, has done much of the planning and design work on landfill closures in the Spokane area. Landau & Associates of Edmonds, Washington, received a $4.3 million contract to extract and treat polluted ground water from under the Colbert landfill. Delhur Industries received a $10.2 million contract to place a cover over the Northside landfill. Private sites that were put on the Superfund list included a Kaiser Aluminum waste yard and junkyard used by at least five different private owners.[110]

Superfund activities have also involved private businesses as parties liable for cleanup costs. WDOE, EPA, Key Tronic Corporation, and the U.S. Air Force agreed to pay for the estimated $15–20 million Superfund cleanup of the Colbert landfill. Spokane County sued Lloyd's of London, Pacific Indemnity, and seventeen other insurance companies for the expected $35 million cost of cleaning up its three Superfund landfills. The city of Spokane was able to settle out of court with two insurance companies for $13 million for the cost of treating groundwater from the Northside landfill, part of the $25 million cost of the cleanup. Key Tronic also sued its insurance carriers for the $4.2 million it agreed to pay, but it lost in Spokane Superior Court.[111]

Similar impacts resulted from the identification of sites requiring cleanup under the Washington State Model Toxics Control Act. In Spokane County, the Marshall landfill was identified under that act and its owners were named as potentially liable. The owner then searched company records for other potentially liable parties and found quite a few, some of them with relatively deep pockets. Included on their list were Kaiser Aluminum, Fairchild Air Force Base, and United Paint and Coatings.[112]

The revolving door between business and government was also seeing heavy traffic in Spokane during this case study. After directing the SWDP for about three years, David Birks resigned to work as a private consultant. When he left, the city seriously considered hiring HDR's Russ Menke to direct SWDP.[113] Eventually Phil Williams, the city's director of environmental services, was hired as the second director of SWDP. He had previously worked for WDOE, then Kaiser Aluminum, prior to taking the position with the city in environmental services.[114] Jessie Lange, recycling coordinator for SWDP, got her background in recycling by running a nonprofit, largely voluntary effort in Cheney, Washington. Well respected among the local environmental community for her work in Cheney, she brought a significant amount of credibility to a part of SWDP that was in great need of it. In the early stages of the project, the waste-to-energy facility received virtually all the attention, and as that part of the project became the target of considerable criticism, SWDP needed to enhance its public image by developing and emphasizing the more popular recycling aspect of the project. Lange's ability to help in this regard was most clearly demonstrated by her obtaining a biweekly five-minute commentary spot on the local public radio station — a spot in which she regularly promoted SWDP's recycling program.

Other local businesses were affected indirectly by the new direction in solid waste policy, some for better and some for worse. Recycling firms found increasing interest on the part of local businesses to contract for pickup of recyclables the city would not collect.[115] Other firms simply benefited from the spinoffs of the new national (and international) policy direction. For example, a local firm, Recycling Equipment Manufacturing, grew from a six-employee operation to a thirty-employee operation between 1986 and 1990. Because its market—it manufactures equipment for sorting recyclables picked up in curbside programs—expanded to include Europe, Asia, and Central America, it had to expand its facilities to meet the demand.[116]

Even Boeing was indirectly affected by the politics of Spokane's solid waste policy making. Several of the groups that were fighting the incinerator momentarily challenged plans to build a Boeing plant west of Spokane without having a full EIS prepared. When it appeared that they were doing damage to their credibility and support in the community, the groups withdrew their challenge.[117]

Most other local businesses saw themselves as being adversely impacted because their direct costs for waste disposal increased. Local builders, for example, found that construction materials they could dispose of for free 25 years ago cost $75 per ton in 1993. Consequently, they had to develop new, more environmentally sound ways of doing business.[118] The long-term impacts for society may be overwhelmingly beneficial, but the short-term, direct costs to businesses, in tipping fees and in retraining, were significant.

A significant loser directly involved in Spokane's politics of garbage was the owner of the only active private landfill in the county. As early as 1988, Glenn Gillson, owner and operator of the Marshall landfill, sued the city and county for damages he would suffer when his landfill was forced to close as a result of the flow control policy adopted with the 1984 comprehensive solid waste plan.[119] Saying originally that he would challenge the flow control ordinance, Gillson later announced a plan to compress and bale garbage and compete with the incinerator for the area's garbage. Shortly thereafter he filed suit saying that the solid waste plan was invalid.[120] Two and a half years later, the new principal stockholder (Gillson's daughter) was still trying to convince Spokane County to allow the company to operate a landfill, but this time there were plans to construct a new state-of-the-art cell and import garbage from within a 250-mile radius of Spokane County. The idea was not well received by the Spokane Solid Waste Advisory Committee and was eventually formally rejected by the county commissioners.[121]

A final way business influenced solid waste policy in Spokane involved specific contracts SWDP could have or did acquire to burn in the waste-to-energy facility loads of materials for various businesses. An interest in having the incinerator help pay for itself underlay SWDP's considering such contracts, and stemmed from SWDP's desire to have not just an incinerator, but a waste-to-energy facility. As the facility burns garbage, it generates electricity, which SWDP contracted to sell to Puget Sound Power and Light. Though the facility had previously accepted contracts to burn top secret floppy disks from Boeing, carbon dust from Kaiser Aluminum, and ink sludge from Cowles Publishing Company, the practice of accepting such industrial waste did not become part of the public awareness and discourse until SWDP burned used pesticide containers from a Canadian company. At that point, these business ventures by SWPD became part of a public relations and intergovernmental relations nightmare for the project. A union worker at the facility complained to WDOE that he got a headache when the containers were burned. WDOE referred the complaint to the Washington State Department of Labor and Industries, which has jurisdiction over workplace hazards. The editorial board of the local newspaper criticized the decision to accept the containers. SCAPCA, the local air pollution control agency, threatened to fine SWDP director Phil Williams for failing to obtain permission to burn the containers.[122] Though no fine was assessed, six months after the burning of the containers the PLB was still discussing the matter.

The post–World War II pattern of government reliance on business was quite evident in this case study. From lobbying for policies favorable to their interests to contracting with the government to provide needed services, businesses have been an integral part of Spokane's solid waste policy making and implementation.

CONCLUSION

The impact of business on solid waste policy in Spokane was a function of its influence on national, state, and local policy making, and of its role in national, state, and local policy implementation. At the local level, the influence was most obvious in the different public-private contracts involved in researching, promoting, and implementing the policy. SWDP purchased both physical and intellectual work from the private sector; it bought both goods and services. Acting as an entrepreneur, SWDP also sold its services to specific businesses.

Business also had its impact through various lobbying efforts by specific businesses and business associations. Both the local Chamber of Commerce and Momentum supported the waste-to-energy facility and took steps to promote its development. Because they could see that the project was a potential source of revenue, specific businesses were also supportive, but they expressed their support more quietly, hoping to avoid the ill feelings that surrounded the polarized public discourse.

Whether it is viewed through the lenses of pluralist, elitist, or structuralist theories, the role of business in solid waste policy making is a matter of concern for a nation that considers itself a democracy. As Douglas Greer points out, "Ideally and essentially, business pursues its own self interest by providing products and services that best satisfy the preferences of those in society. . . . Profit is the incentive. . . . But profit can also be made in 'antisocial' ways."[123] Government economic regulation is often the answer society relies on to correct the market-driven, antisocial activity. When government depends on business and/or on market mechanisms to pursue its ends, it is not clear where a corrective force might come from if it were needed.

And the need for some corrective force is not terribly unlikely. Greer lists four general kinds of market problems,[124] most of which are more likely to exist in a government-created market than in one that arises from free market forces: (1) market imperfections such as monopolistic power and information inadequacies; (2) market failures such as externalities, public goods, and common property resources; (3) dynamic incapacities such as instability, on both micro and macro levels; and (4) ethical criteria such as equity, the inherent merit/demerit of certain goods, and social or political goals.

This does not mean the impact of business on public policy making necessarily leads to unsavory results. Our development of a mixed economy is based on the belief that the private sector should be allowed to operate as freely as possible so that the economy can benefit from the forces of competition. It does mean, however, that we must look to other components of the policy-making system to provide checks on business influence and to bring into the policy discourse values and ends not likely to find expression through business. To paraphrase Vogel, business may make its own political history, but it does so within a dynamic system where it may find opportunities to lead, but which it cannot control.[125]

Citizen Participation

A s chapter 5 explains, the National Environmental Policy Act (NEPA) and the Washington State Environmental Policy Act (SEPA) require environmental impact statements for projects that will have significant impacts. Both RCRA and Superfund include provisions requiring citizen participation. The Washington State law on solid waste policy, RCW 70.95, also requires counties to develop comprehensive solid waste plans and form solid waste advisory groups with citizen representation. In addition, citizen participation may have a legal basis in constitutional provisions, judicial decisions, or unwritten conventions.[1] Because such legal provisions require public involvement in the policy decision-making process, they have led to the development of administrative procedures that include additional efforts to obtain citizen participation.

Often when people discuss citizen participation in American governance, they refer to modes of participation like voting, working in an electoral campaign, contributing toward the campaign expenses of a candidate, and putting a placard in one's yard. As the Spokane case study demonstrates, solid waste policy making is not cleanly detached from election-related citizen participation, but most of the citizen participation that directly affects it is distinct from electoral campaign participation. The focus of this chapter will be on citizen participation in policy-making processes. Citizen participation takes place at the national, state, and local levels of government. It includes the activities of interest groups and of the general public. Some of the opportunities for citizens to participate in solid waste policy making are found in and related to legislative deliberations — lobbying of legislators, testifying at committee hearings, speaking out at city council and county commission meetings, and so forth. Many of the participation opportunities are related to administrative policy making — testifying at public hearings, participating in public workshops, speaking out at meetings related to the EIS process, submitting written comments on the scope, draft, or proposed final version of an EIS, providing spoken and/or written comments on a request for a pollution permit, and so on. There are additional opportunities at the vortex of executive and administrative policy making, where staff advice and citizen input both reach officials who will make the final decision on a matter.

The citizen participation we will examine most closely here takes place at the local level. As Fiorino points out, "At the national level, most participation takes the form of people acting in their capacities as elected representatives, appointed administrators, interest group professionals, or technical experts."[2] It is easier for citizens to participate in policy-making processes that take place where they live and work. Most citizens cannot take time away from daily obligations to go to the state or national capital. So, participation in policy making by amateurs occurs most regularly at the local level.

This chapter begins with a general look at citizens' contributions to policy making. Because local participation in policy making is most directly influenced by how citizens and public administrators relate to each other, I will quickly review the history of how American public administrators have viewed citizen participation. Next I will narrow the focus to citizen involvement in solid waste policy making, then to citizen participation in Spokane, before concluding with some comments regarding the impact of such participation.

CITIZEN PARTICIPATION AND POLICY MAKING

Because it appears to fit so well with the democratic ideal, citizen participation may be difficult to question openly. As the Advisory Commission on Intergovernmental Relations (ACIR) noted in a 1979 report on citizen participation in the U.S. federal system, "few can object to the goal of involving citizens in governmental decisionmaking."[3] Consequently, there is a wealth of literature that generally supports citizen participation.[4] Sometimes, as in Entman's *Democracy Without Citizens* (1989), support for citizen participation is framed as a warning about the future of democracy if participation is not improved.[5] At other times, it is a straightforward argument in favor of the benefits of more participation. In this vein, Spiegel contends that "probably no other issue is as vital to the success of solving America's urban crisis than the viable participation of urban residents in planning the neighborhoods and cities in which they live and the social programs which directly affect them."[6]

Still, both the practice of and the literature about citizen participation reveals considerable disagreement about the effects, intended purposes, and value of citizen involvement.[7] Perhaps one of the most stinging statements regarding the value of citizen participation is found in Dye and Ziegler in *The Irony of Democracy* (1981):

> Democracy is government "by the people," but the survival of democracy rests on the shoulders of elites. This is the irony of democracy: elites must govern wisely if government "by the people" is to survive. If the survival of the American system depended on the existence of an active, informed, and enlightened citizenry, then democracy in America would have disappeared long ago, for the masses of America are apathetic and ill informed about politics and public policy.[8]

There are also those who voice objections to citizen participation. Smith and Ingram describe three common complaints about citizen participation in the United States: (1) There is too much citizen participation. Because of the high number of access points, citizens (most often through interest group activity) prevent the formulation and/or implementation of effective public policy as they use those access points to prevent damage to their special interests. (2) Citizen participation, except through such rather stable institutions as political parties and interest groups, is too fragmented and sporadic to produce effective resolutions to enduring policy problems. (3) Empowering citizens may lead to increasing the power of "the wrong people" and lead to the adoption of "the wrong policies."[9]

Often citizen involvement in public policy making is justified from a process standpoint. Because participation provides evidence that the process is open, it is deemed desirable regardless of the extent to which it affects the substance of policy.[10] Sherry Arnstein departs from this process orientation in describing a typology of citizen participation based on the degree of power granted to the citizen.[11] Ventriss and Pecorella also transcend the process orientation as they outline two models of citizen participation.[12] The learning organization model emphasizes confrontational communication techniques, educating and mobilizing citizens. In the cooptation model, citizen groups sacrifice their original goal of autonomous citizen participation to achieve political efficacy in a bureaucratic context. Contacts with policy makers tend to be cooperative and congenial, and contacts with citizens consist of passing on information prepared by government officials.

Citizen participation in policy making may take many forms. In 1979 the ACIR listed thirty-one different forms of participation.[13] Those forms determine, in part, the kinds of participation opportunities citizens are given, and the kinds of participation make a difference in the potential contributions of citizens. Surveying five institutional mechanisms for citizen participation (public hearings, initiatives, public surveys, negotiated rule making, and citizen review panels) and evaluating their merits in promoting the democratic process, Fiorino finds that the more common mechanisms for citizen participation (hearings, surveys, and citizen review panels) do not fare well.[14] The other two mechanisms also have problems. Initiatives offer citizens a direct opportunity to share authority with policy elites, but no single individual has a large share of the authority. Negotiated rule making provides for equality, shared authority, and meaningful discussion, but is unlikely to include citizens who are policy-making amateurs.

Differences in citizen participation can also result from the styles of participation citizens bring to the table. Building on the work of Ventriss and Pecorella, I suggest a three-model typology of citizen participation: a coopted participant model, a prudent participant model, and a confrontive participant model.[15] Coopted participants are most concerned with political efficacy: striving to maintain good relations with and tending to support and work for the agenda of governing officials. Prudent participants are most concerned with policy impact, striving to maintain good relations with government officials, but willing to conflict openly with them if circumstances seem to warrant it. They have their own agenda but are willing to compromise. Confrontational participants are most concerned with policy determination; not expecting to maintain good relations with government officials (often seeing them as the enemy), they have a definite substantive agenda and tend to be unwilling to compromise.

The coopted model and the confrontive model are similar to Ventriss and Pecorella's cooptational model and learning model, but the prudent model is new and crucial to an adequate delineation of the basic styles citizens may bring to policy-making forums. Later in this chapter I will use these models to analyze citizen participation in Spokane's solid waste policy making.

Administrative Attitudes Toward
Citizen Participation

Since citizen participation in solid waste policy making is most frequent and most vociferous in relation to administrative decisions, the attitudes of public administrators toward citizen involvement are a crucial part of the dynamics.

Citizens and their participation in governance have been viewed in a number of ways.[16] Jefferson is said to have believed there were no mysteries in public administration and that "the ordinary affairs of a nation offer little difficulty to a person of any experience."[17] In the late twentieth century, however, the notion that public administrators are experts and citizens are qualified for a very different role in a modern democracy is well established.

The field of public administration was built on a clear differentiation between the roles of citizen and public administrator. In an 1887 essay that was belatedly identified as a symbolic beginning of the field, Woodrow Wilson worried that popular sovereignty would delay development of a "much-to-be-desired science of administration" and complained that it could be a "clumsy nuisance" if allowed to interfere with the daily details of administration rather than to superintend "the greater forces of formative policy."[18]

This view of citizen-administrator relations derives from what has come to be known as the politics/administration dichotomy and might be characterized as a mediated model. It says that elected officials set policy, so they are the ones who should hold administrative officials accountable for implementation that is consistent with the policy's intent.[19] In that view, elected officials are the link between administrators and citizens: elected officials hold administrators accountable through their oversight function, and citizens hold elected officials accountable through elections. Administrators are to attend to the daily details of implementation. Elected officials are to set particular policies and to oversee their administration in a manner sufficient to determine that implementation is consistent with their policies, but not in a meddlesome way. Citizens are to elect officials who will support the general policy stances they hold, but they are not to try to influence the administration of policy. In other words, citizen-administrator relationships should be mediated through elected officials.

In the mid-twentieth century, the mediated model of citizen-administrator relations began to unravel. The Administrative Procedures Act (1946) established a national standard for minimal inclusion of citizens in administrative decision making. Its "notice and comment" provision was intended to ensure that all national administrative rule making was done publicly and with an opportunity for interested parties to provide input to the decision-making deliberations. By 1979 the Advisory Commission on Intergovernmental Relations (ACIR) had identified 155 federal programs that had their own specific requirements for citizen participation. State and local governments have similarly increased their expectations that administrators will include citizen participation elements in their decision making. As Cooper notes, "The result of these proliferating requirements is that most public administrators are confronted with the necessity for planning, managing, reviewing or assisting in citizen participation processes at some point in their work."[20]

By the late 1960s, there was evidence of a more positive perspective on citizen participation in the field of public administration. In 1969, for example, Auerbach argued that the usual methods for resolving differences of opinion used by public administrators did not appear adequate.[21] He suggested that administrators needed to be more open to input from citizens.

Continued suspicion and distrust between citizens and administrators, it could be argued, would likely lead to what Sabatier, Hunter, and McLaughlin label "the devil shift." In the devil shift "actors involved in a public discourse tend to perceive opponents to be stronger and more 'evil' than they actually are."[22] Indicators of this shift are found in the degree to which actors impugn their opponents' reasonableness and/or motives, offer excessively harsh evaluations of their opponents' behavior, and see their opponents as more influential than they are.

Though suspicion and distrust are certainly still evident in citizen-administrator relations, by the 1980s some in public administration began to see improving relations as a key to revitalizing the public service. An indicator of that change is found in a 1984 special *Public Administration Review* symposium entitled Citizenship and Public Administration. In summing up the papers and discussions at the symposium, Ralph Chandler concludes that participants were trying to describe a new role for the American public administrator: representative citizen. "There is intentional ambiguity and tension between the ideas of *representative* citizen and representative *citizen*. The former carries with it something of the tradition of the philosopher-king. The latter preserves the public servant commitment of radical egalitarianism."[23]

The role of *representative* citizen might imply that public administrators could substitute for citizens in making policy. The role of representative *citizen* carries the implication that public administrators have a duty to work for citizens in policy making. Both roles signify an important break from the mediated model of citizen-administrator relations that dominated the field during its first century. Both also expect quite a lot from those exercising citizenship. As another contributor to that volume writes, "Popular self-government exists only when citizens are very, very smart about their civics."[24]

John C. Thomas, however, holds a less demanding view of what is required for citizens to contribute to policies and administration in pursuit of the public interest.[25] He acknowledges administrative disadvantages that might accompany citizen participation — unpleasant antagonism, devaluing of professional judgments, increased costs in dollars and time — but says those disadvantages are more likely to result from citizen involvement that was not welcomed and supported by public administrators. In addition, he points out that certain administrative advantages derive from participatory administration — better channels of communication, improved program implementation, more services for the dollar, protection from criticism, and increased clout in the budgetary process. Furthermore, participation in governance makes citizens more attached to the pursuit of the public interest.

Though it has been shaken by changes in the citizen-administrator relationship and changing perspectives on that relationship, the mediated model continues to influence the perspective of many late twentieth-century public administrators — a perspective in which administration serves the values of efficiency and neutral competence and citizens are most often seen as an interference in the pursuit of that mission. For example, MacNair, Caldwell, and Pollane describe federal and state requirements for citizen participation as a "national enigma" and complain that those requirements foster "ineffectiveness and inefficiency." They see citizen participants as "a nuisance and a potential threat to program stability"[26] and suggest that the major reason for encouraging citizen participation is to bolster the position of one's agency: "Public agencies avoid citizens if their position is strong, in order to maintain organizational stability. Relatively powerless agencies, however, are more likely to risk close alliance with their citizen participants in an effort to promote a stronger constituency."[27]

Another way public administrators keep citizens at bay in administrative policy making is to recognize participation as inevitable but to limit its impact. In 1949 Selznick identified formal cooptation as a common strategy used by public administrators to ensure that citizen participation supported administrative goals.[28] Similarly, Cupps in 1977 saw that citizen participation had become "one of the most distinctive features of American administration," but he was concerned that citizen participation was not being properly managed.[29] He said he supported citizen involvement, but he warned that citizens' demands were "no substitute for independent, carefully reasoned, professional judgements regarding the nature of the public interest."[30] Like the founders of public administration, he was concerned that the expertise of the administrators would be overwhelmed by the less-informed opinions of citizens. Unlike the creators of the politics/administration dichotomy, he saw the task of public administrators to be "as much political as administrative in nature."[31]

In the last quarter of the twentieth century, the value of an independently powerful public administration is no longer seen as a function of separating politics from administration. Those who continue to argue for it are described as the "discretion school."[32] They say that autonomous administrative discretion is required by the special role public administrators serve in seeking the public interest.[33] In this view, public administrators protect the governance process from capture by special interests. It is public administrators' professional expertise that allows genuine concern for the public interest, rather than special interest pressures, to drive public policy making.

This description of the special role of public administration in American governance points toward the most powerful remaining argument used by public administrators to exclude citizens from policy making: that the increasing complexity of modern government has led to a decline in the relevance of citizen participation.[34] Charles Levine, for example, explains: "During the late 1960s and throughout the 1970s, the intricately complex political and administrative structure of the public sector became hopelessly beyond the reach of the average citizen through the traditional formal mechanisms of political participation."[35]

Nonetheless, the line of thought that sees good relations between citizens and administrators as crucial to better governance has gained popularity in the 1990s. Developments in public administration theory and in the popular literature regarding public administration have contributed to this growth.[36] Public administration theorists have begun to trace its roots in the discipline. For example, Cooper notes that although the emergence of the Progressive movement in the United States supported a view of public administrators as usurping the role of citizens in governance, rather than "as an instrument of the citizenry to provide access to governance,"[37] this view was not shared by all public administrators in the early twentieth century. He notes that Mary Parker Follett saw "citizenship development at the grass roots as the first and most fundamental task of democratic reform."[38] But her view "did not become a dominant influence on the development of American public administration in the ensuing decades of the twentieth century."[39] Cooper contends, however, that making that view more influential is the fundamental project for American administrative reform in the latter years of the twentieth century: "The public administrator's most fundamental obligation is to encourage citizens in their active pursuit of the common good."[40]

Joining in that project, Stivers describes the Community Health Care Center program of the U.S. Department of Health and Human Services as a real-world example of public administration that includes citizens as equal partners in developing agency policy.[41] She believes that citizens are improved through meaningful participation and that public administrators have an obligation to society to encourage that improvement.

It is not clear that this new vision of citizen-administrator relations has become influential among practicing administrators, but another development, arising from popular management literature, has gained much attention and acceptance among them. Its proselytizing armies, while moving generally in the same direction (toward closer ties with citizens), march under several flags: the search for excellence, total quality, and entrepreneurialism.[42] No matter which flag is flown, a common element emphasizes serving the customer — and, in the context of government, to a significant degree that means serving the citizen. Scholars, however, have identified problems with equating citizen and customer.[43] Citizens also see a problem. When the U.S. Forest Service held a public meeting to learn how they could better serve their customers, they were told by several members of the public, "We are not your customers. . . . We are your owners."[44]

The impact of this new vision on governance in the United States is widespread. President Bush's Executive Order 12637 instigated entrepreneurial quality improvement programs throughout federal executive departments and agencies.[45] In 1987, a law was passed creating the Malcolm Baldridge National Quality Award.[46] In 1988, the President's Council on Management Improvement established the Federal Quality Institute. The Clinton administration has taken this perspective even farther. The report of the National Performance Review prepared under Vice President Al Gore is also clearly inspired by this popular new vision.[47] In a study of the values of federal executives, Posner and Schmidt find that the most notable shift between 1982 and 1992 is the high priority given quality and customer service.[48] State and local governments are also busy adopting entrepreneurial, excellence, and/or quality initiatives.[49]

The perspectives of citizen participation within the public administration profession have expanded in recent years to include acknowledging a direct relationship between citizens and public administrators and a need for administrators to pay more attention to that relationship. It would be difficult to find a profession that has changed more in its view of such a crucial topic.

Citizen Participation and Solid Waste Policy Making

Former mayor of Houston Louis Welch summed up the main public relations problem for late twentieth-century solid waste management: "Everyone wants us to pick up his garbage, but no one wants us to put it down."[50] Though today's solid waste managers might find it difficult to believe, in the early twentieth century city officials did not worry much about citizen protests regarding what disposal method they selected. Collection methods were most often the targets of popular protests. Expedience, expense, and efficiency were solid waste managers' main concerns when it came to selecting disposal methods.

The movement toward local governments taking responsibility for managing solid waste coincided with and was influenced by a rise in local civic involvement that derived from populism but was also part of the Progressive reform movement. Progressives believed the improvement of human beings required improvement of their environment. In 1906 William Mayo Venable summed up the connection between environmental improvement and human improvement:

> The same spirit that leads men to realize the corruption of politics
> and business, and to attempt to remedy those conditions by adopting
> new methods of administration and new laws, also leads to a real-
> ization of the primitiveness of the methods of waste disposal still
> employed by many communities, and to a consequent desire for
> improvement.[51]

Arising from sporadic protests in the late nineteenth century and running parallel to reform efforts by sanitary engineers, citizens' associations began to be concerned about garbage and its attendant problems and to promote municipal sanitation efforts. The melange of citizen groups that arose from the Progressive movement included such names as the City Improvement

Society and the City Government Club; they advocated sanitation reform as part of their civic-minded push for aesthetic and moralistic improvement of urban life. According to Melosi, "the Ladies' Health Protective Association of New York City (LHPA) was possibly the most influential civic group in the country."[52] In the late nineteenth century, LHPA assisted in sanitation reform by putting the problem in terms the general public found easy to understand — cleanliness. In combination with the City Beautiful movement of the 1890s, civic associations promoted a belief that city life need not be overwhelmed by the filth caused by high population density and industrialization. Though much of the City Beautiful movement focused on art in the city, some participants were quick to remind people that the aesthetic pleasures of art were affected by their context. In the words of Caroline Bartlett Crane: "It is well to remember that civic art without civic cleanliness is a diamond ring on dirty hands. The adornments of a dirty city do but emphasize its dirtiness, while cleanliness has not only a virtue but a beauty of its own."[53]

Citizen groups sought both to influence government officials and to educate the public. Because citizen groups were dominated by women, Melosi observes, "the term 'municipal housekeeping' became synonymous with sanitation reform."[54] The groups sponsored investigations of street-cleaning practices, lobbied for sanitation ordinances, pushed for comprehensive refuse plans and modern cleaning methods. The Women's Municipal League of New York City was able to force the resignation of an incompetent street-cleaning commissioner, but "the influence that citizens' groups enjoyed with city officials was inconsistent at best,"[55] so they directed much of their efforts toward influencing the public. They conducted antilittering campaigns, organized traveling exhibits, and held civic rallies. They distributed garbage cans to those who could not afford them and encouraged those who could to buy cans with tight lids. In Louisville, the Women's Civic Association actually produced a motion picture, *The Invisible Peril*, depicting the connection between sanitation and health.[56]

Citizen participation was also encouraged by some government officials. Recognizing the importance of civic involvement, in New York City George Waring (a pioneer in municipal sanitation who was introduced in chapter 4) formed an advisory committee of civic leaders and spoke regularly before civic organizations such as the Good Government Club, the Ladies' Health Protective Association, and the City Improvement Society. Waring's most celebrated civic involvement effort was the Juvenile Street Cleaning League.

Regarding its members, he said, "[They] are being taught that government does not mean merely a policeman to be run away from, but an influence which touches the life of the people at every point."[57]

Civic education was a part of the Progressive reform movement promoted by both government officials and citizen associations. Its main target was the young, because they were readily reached through the established education system and because in reeducating them one might affect the future. It was also hoped that the children's impact on their parents might effect some near-term changes. Educational efforts combined with city cleanup efforts in which children played key roles epitomized the citizen participation aspect of solid waste management in the early twentieth century. They were nonthreatening, often officially sanctioned, and easily co-opted activities.

The story of late twentieth-century citizen participation includes elements that echo the earlier era, but it also includes more threatening, anti–government official, confrontational elements. In the 1960s and early 1970s, most citizen-initiated solid waste participation activities were directed at demonstrating small-scale alternatives such as recycling cooperatives. Public protests in the 1970s were directed mainly at landfills. Because the main problem with landfills was their emission of hazardous pollutants, hazardous and solid waste issues became fused in the minds of many citizens. RCRA, which deals with both hazardous and solid waste, "was passed in part because of the growing strength of community groups."[58] By the late 1980s and early 1990s, with public disaffection widespread and grass-roots activism on the rise, citizen participation in solid waste policy making was certainly not limited to officially instigated or sanctioned activities.

When local groups first began to form around the nation in opposition to solid waste management facilities, most national environmental groups appeared reluctant to become involved (notable exceptions included Greenpeace and the Environmental Defense Fund). Eventually, however, assisted and enabled by the Citizens' Clearinghouse for Hazardous Wastes (CCHW), local active citizens found a national network of similarly situated and activated community groups. CCHW began operations in 1981 and began its Solid Waste Action Project in 1986.[59] Among the many items one may obtain from CCHW are corporate profiles on both WMX and Browning-Ferris Industries, as well as a variety of documents relating to those two companies' histories of environmental and business practices violations.

CCHW has also put together a number of easily read pamphlets designed to assist local grass-roots efforts. In *How to Deal with a Proposed Facility*, CCHW says previous editions have helped over 1,000 grass-roots groups.[60] Taking the position that siting a facility is a political (not a technical) decision, they provide guidance on a number of topics, including terminology, organizational structure, recruitment, research, media relations, strategies, tactics, how to use experts and lawyers, and whether and how to propose alternatives. They further suggest that active citizens refuse to use proponents' terms for waste facilities. For example, instead of "resource recovery facilities" or "waste-to-energy facilities" they recommend "incinerators." Their preferred organizational structure is one that gives each member an important role to play (not a hierarchy with a few leaders doing all the work and the others attending meetings). They emphasize the role of face-to-face contact in recruitment and recommend a set of standard questions to include in any research. Communication with other local groups in similar circumstances (using CCHW to provide the contacts) is also considered a key part of the research. They advise using the news media in ways that are guided by an awareness of what "hooks" reporters. Because "duelling experts" is a losing proposition for citizen groups, they promote sparing use of lawyers and experts. Community meetings, on the other hand, are considered essential. Yard signs, youth auxiliary groups, protests, and demonstrations are highly recommended.

CCHW's *Solid Waste Action Project Guidebook* repeats some of the advice in the aforementioned volume, but is essentially a primer on solid waste management.[61] It tells its target audience of grass-roots activists that it is not a question of whether landfills will leak, but when and how much. The guidebook says that incinerators are not an effective way of dealing with solid waste because they deal with the symptoms rather than the cause. They do not replace landfills; rather, they require their own new kind of landfill. "At best, incinerators can only play a little magic trick on waste. . . . All burning does is disassemble waste and put it back together in a different way, with a different set of problems." Large-scale recycling, combined with a serious toxics reduction effort, on the other hand, the reader is told, could leave only "a small, manageable quantity of waste." Because CCHW believes that it is possible to do without incinerators and landfills, it recommends confrontive modes of citizen participation: "At the next public hearing, stop being so nice."

According to Blumberg and Gottlieb, increasing public opposition to landfills and waste-to-energy facilities was the reason Cerrell Associates was commissioned by the California Waste Management Board to address the problem of facility siting.[62] The Cerrell report took note of the historic differences among different kinds of communities concerning their ability to organize effective opposition, and recommended locating in communities that were least capable of resistance.[63] It said that the easier communities in which to site a facility were rural and had a population that was low-income and elderly with limited education. The report claimed that if in such a community a facility were presented properly by a public affairs coordinator, it would have the best chance of gaining acceptance. Facility proponents often consider this kind of approach to public education the key to their citizen participation program.[64]

There are, however, other aspects to facility proponents' citizen participation programs. Some aspects are designed to buttress their defenses. Even if they are not required by law, most consultants recommend the use of citizen advisory committees. There are also attempts to enlist respected citizen groups such as the League of Women Voters and the Sierra Club in support of "integrated waste management" approaches that include waste reduction incentives, waste-to-energy facilities, landfills, recycling, and composting. Attempts to build bridges between the solid waste industry and national environmental groups have led to such successes as having Dean Buntrock, chief executive officer of WMX, named to the board of directors of the National Wildlife Federation.[65]

Other aspects are designed to sharpen their attacks. Proponents may complain that active citizen opponents misleadingly confuse solid waste issues with hazardous waste issues.[66] They have also been known to attack opponents with the media-reified label *NIMBY*. NIMBYs are criticized for their fear of chemicals and their emotionalism, but they are also credited with the power to kill most projects they oppose.[67] They have been described as "hit-and-run" citizen participants:

> Nimbys are noisy. Nimbys are powerful. Nimbys are everywhere. Nimbys are people who live near enough to corporate or government projects — and are upset enough about them — to work to stop, stall or shrink them. Nimbys organize, march, sue and petition to block the developers they think are threatening them. They twist the arms of politicians and they learn how to influence regulators. They fight fiercely and then, win or lose, they vanish.[68]

In effect, the label NIMBY has come to designate people who resist for selfish, parochial reasons a project that would serve a need for the general community. In using it, one implies that the proposed project serves the general welfare and the only reason the NIMBYs oppose it is that it has been proposed on a site in their "back yard." Since use of the label puts those so labeled on the defensive, and much of their energy and time must then go to justifying their opposition, less attention is paid to whether the project actually serves the general welfare. Having been labeled a NIMBY, a person's arguments against a project are discounted.

Sometimes active citizens have had the courage to embrace the NIMBY label and explain that because the ill effects of a landfill or incinerator would disproportionately affect them, it is their duty to require the general community to explore its conscience and determine whether it is fair to ask them to pay such a price for the rest of the community.[69] The only people who have raised the question of distributional justice with discernible success are racial minorities who have complained about environmental racism.[70] But to characterize their objections as successful may also give too much credit to the public policy response. After all, it is because waste management facilities have been sited more often near racial minorities that the charge of environmental racism became part of the policy discourse.

Polarization is one of the more common elements related to citizen participation in solid waste policy making. Though the solid waste industry and government officials have sought to incorporate citizen participation mechanisms into their policy-making structures and processes, they generally have had to face active citizens who have entered into the policy-making dynamics on their own volition. Attempts to marginalize the self-activated citizen participants by drawing attention to the efforts of coopted participants have met with mixed results. Even when facilities have been successfully sited, the presence of a hostile, active group of citizens has meant that each operational decision became subject to public criticism that might stimulate legislative micromanagement and/or second-guessing.

Though modern solid waste management has always included openness to some kinds of citizen participation, solid waste administrators generally have a hard time welcoming self-activated, hostile citizens into the process. Nonetheless, as public administrators have learned, effective administration of public services increasingly requires recognizing the value of active citizen involvement in decision making. In the last analysis, whether administrators welcome active citizens or not, they are going to be a force with which solid waste administrators must reckon.

Citizen Participation in Spokane

Washington State's history has been influenced by populism and Progressivism. One result of this is that, as in many states in the American West, Washington state laws provide for several mechanisms of direct citizen participation in the formulation of laws: the direct initiative, the indirect initiative, the legislative referendum, and the petitioned referendum. These citizen participation mechanisms have enjoyed varying, but significant use over the years.[71] For example, although the initiative has been used extensively since 1932, its use has practically doubled since 1974. On the thirty petitioned referenda prior to 1985, the voters upheld the legislature only twice. So, Spokane's citizen participation activities arise from a statewide context and tradition supportive of citizen involvement in policy making.

The formulation and implementation of solid waste policy in Spokane proved to be a democratic trial for the community. Citizen participation, in terms of both numbers and intensity, increased rapidly as construction of the waste-to-energy facility drew more near. Siting decisions for the plant and a potential in-county ash landfill led to the formation of a number of new community- or neighborhood-based groups to protest each site.

The solid waste issue evolved into an extremely divisive and hotly contested battle between pro–waste-to-energy and anti-incinerator forces, and was a major factor in Spokane's 1989 local election campaigns. When the proponents gained a close but decisive victory in those elections, the primary remaining contentious issue concerned where the ash from the facility would be landfilled. After officials decided in favor of long-hauling the ash to a large regional landfill in Klickitat County, they faced smaller skirmishes around transfer stations and a compost facility, but generally only a few active citizens continued to monitor implementation of the project. (Some of them were aided in this work by a citizen participation grant from the state.)

Because the impetus for their involvement often was the threat of a waste management facility in their neighborhood, many of the citizen activists were called NIMBYs. But a number of participants who entered the Spokane policy discourse as stereotypic NIMBYs later began to be active in more general efforts to oppose the waste-to-energy emphasis in the solid waste management plan. They became a vital part of the local solid waste policy discourse, helping to improve the air pollution controls on the waste-to-energy plant and pressing SWDP for earlier adoption of effective recycling programs.

There were almost as many avenues for citizen participation in this case study as there were forums for discussion of solid waste policy options. Citizens participated in city council and county commission solid waste policy discussions. They addressed local and state administrators and regulators, state legislators, the governor, and state courts. They appealed decisions they did not like to the EPA and to federal courts. They attended public hearings and contributed at each step of the permit and EIS processes. They addressed the general public through community meetings, political demonstrations, petitions, letters to the editor, guest columns, news conferences, news interviews, and radio and television talk shows.

No fewer than eighteen groups of citizens participated in some portion of Spokane's solid waste policy discourse. When in 1986 the EIS for the waste-to-energy facility was being drafted the local chapter of the Sierra Club was among those testifying at a public hearing. By 1988 two local grass-roots groups, Citizens for Responsible Waste Management and the Greater West Plains Association, constituted the main active citizen opposition to the waste-to-energy facility. They evolved into the Coalition Against Incineration and were eventually replaced as the leading citizen activists by the Council for Land Care and Planning (CfLCaP) and Citizens for Clean Air (CfCA). Spokane Area Watchdogs (SAW) later grew out of CfLCaP and CfCA, and adopted a more aggressive style than its parent organizations. Other groups formed around specific subissues in the solid waste policy dispute. Citizens for the Right to Vote was created to promote a local charter amendment requiring that large capital projects be put to a popular vote for approval. The Lance Hills Coalition for a Clean Environment organized to fend off the possibility of an ash landfill in the Lance Hills area. It later evolved into the Lance Hills–Heyer Point Coalition to combine the efforts of those worried about the threat of an ash landfill at the Lance Hills and Heyer Point sites. (The two sites were in close proximity in southwestern Spokane County. See fig. 1.1.) Grove Road Neighbors Association also formed to resist a potential ash landfill in the Marshall area. The Marshall Community Coalition formed to monitor and influence activities at the Marshall landfill. Working together with the Yakama Indian Nation, Klicktat County Citizens vs. Imported Waste tried to stop development of the regional landfill that eventually became the dump site for Spokane's ash.

There were also citizen participants who favored (or at least were not organized expressly to oppose) the waste-to-energy project. SWDP formed two citizen advisory groups: the Solid Waste Advisory Committee (SWAC) and the Technical Advisory Committee (TAC). From the perspective of

SWDP, SWAC was intended to be the voice of the general citizenry. TAC was a select committee whose members were chosen for their technical expertise in matters related to solid waste management. The League of Women Voters of the Spokane Area held community forums and contracted with SWDP to assist in running public workshops and hearings. There was also a citizens group organized specifically for the purpose of supporting the project, Citizens for Responsible Refuse Disposal (CfRRD). Jim Correll, head of the local CH2M Hill office, led this group of business people, but its members never did much more than provide financial and moral support for Correll's efforts to counter opposition arguments through letters to the editor and the white paper "Waste to Energy Works" (see chapter 1).

Citizens were also involved in less assertive ways. They were polled periodically regarding their attitudes toward solid waste policy options (see chapter 3). They were invited to meetings where officials would present information about the project. They were also the targets of SWDP public relations moves. For example, when SWDP spent $15,000 taking a dozen people, both opponents and proponents, to visit an incinerator in Mulbury, Massachusetts, they made sure reporters and television cameras met them as they got off the plane.[72] SWDP was prepared to take advantage of the opportunity to promote the project and to display themselves as reasonable and fair — they had paid opponents' expenses.

Citizens were involved in various aspects of the implementation of their community's solid waste policy, from taking their garbage cans to the curb for pickup, to delivering their compostables to one of the transfer stations, to voluntary participation in the project's evolving recycling program. Before the city or county introduced its curbside recycling program, residents recycled 28 percent of their wastes.[73] On the first day of the city's curbside program about 40 percent of those with recycling bins participated, and officials hoped eventually to achieve a 70–80 percent participation rate.[74] SWDP's composting program depended both on people bringing their "clean green" to transfer stations and on a group of "Master Composters" who went around teaching people how to establish their own backyard composting operation.[75]

Another form of citizen participation in the implementation of Spokane's solid waste policy was supported financially by WDOE. In 1992 CfCA received a public participation grant to assist it in monitoring SWDP's operations.[76] They used it to hire consultants to review pollution data, rent office space, and put out a newsletter. But prior to receipt of the grant they were already actively monitoring SWDP. In December 1991 they sent letters to

city and WDOE officials contending that the tests of the incinerator conducted in November would have to be repeated.[77] During the test, because
of fog problems at the airport, the plant had not run continuously as specified in the contract. The director of SWDP argued that the shutdowns
actually made it more difficult for the waste-to-energy facility to pass the
tests, and he was not required to redo them.[78]

The WDOE grant helped CfCA maintain its watchdog vigil over SWDP.
The group became a regular counterpoint for journalists covering the incinerator's operations. They argued futilely against switching from hourly to
daily figures to compute the incinerator's compliance with sulfur dioxide
emission limits.[79] When there was too much garbage for the incinerator to
burn and SWDP sent raw garbage to Rabanco's Klickitat County landfill,
CfCA told reporters SWDP should more aggressively promote recycling.[80]
CfCA members also wrote a guest column in the *Spokesman-Review* opposing
the idea of an additional burner for the incinerator and proposing that the
city consider converting the incinerator "into a mechanized recycling and
recovery plant."[81] In response to repeated proposals to burn tires in the
incinerator, CfCA repeatedly promoted recycling as a better alternative.[82]
CfCA's president was questioned by a newspaper reporter seeking a quote
from the other side when SWDP director Williams ordered the burning of
Canadian pesticide containers without SCAPCA's approval. SCAPCA had
been advised by a consultant that Williams had violated the rules, but refused to approve fining him.[83] In response to a report that garbage fees were
going to have to increase, CfCA suggested that SWDP could be combined
with the city Solid Waste Management Department to reduce administrative
overhead.[84] No matter what the issue, CfCA had become the voice of the
opposition.

Citizens have also participated in activities relating to the closing of landfills. Both the Marshall Community Coalition and the Colbert Landfill Citizens Action Committee received public participation grants from WDOE.[85]
The Marshall Community Coalition became deeply involved in the closure
and cleanup of the Marshall landfill. They worked with the landfill operators to monitor groundwater pollution and urged WDOE to place the site
higher on the state toxic cleanup priority list. When work fell behind schedule, the group put pressure on state and local officials to proceed with the
legally required cleanup. When operators of the landfill stopped testing
nearby wells, the coalition complained to the Spokane County Health District, and when the health district did not respond quickly, they threatened
to take their concerns to EPA. The coalition also testified against reopening

the site, extending the site's mining zone, and allowing the site to be used for a composting operation.

Citizen participation was also activated by the decision to long-haul Spokane's ash to Rabanco's regional landfill in Klickitat County.[86] Active citizens included both proponents and opponents of the landfill. Proponents touted the economic benefits the landfill business would bring to an area suffering from agricultural and forestry products industry troubles. Opponents included farmers near the site, some leaders of the Yakama Indian Nation, and residents along the Columbia River Gorge. They cited environmental risks and potential impacts on the area's ability to attract "clean" industries. The Yakamas expressed concern regarding ancient burial grounds. Though opponents gathered 2,000 signatures on a petition, they were not able to get the county commissioners to put the issue to a vote. (Because Klickitat County has no initiative process, an appeal to the commissioners was the only avenue for bringing the question to a vote.) In a joint meeting, the Spokane county commissioners and the city council listened to public testimony on the ash disposal options, and active citizens from Klickitat County came to speak.[87] The Klickitat County public works director and a Rabanco official spoke in favor of the Klickitat landfill. The Chairman of the Yakama Indian Council came to speak against it (though the Yakamas were divided on the issue, and some in fact spoke in favor of the landfill).

Still, most citizen participation efforts surrounding Spokane's solid waste policy discourse were aimed at diverting Spokane from relying on an incinerator as the central component of its new approach to solid waste management. The 1986 public hearing on the waste-to-energy facility's draft EIS was attended by about sixty people.[88] Among those in attendance were officials from Kaiser Aluminum, which was expected to purchase steam power from the facility if it were built on an adjacent site in the Spokane Valley. It was at this hearing that the company openly expressed concern about the reliability of the proposed facility. Kaiser's reservations about becoming involved with the facility played a major role in the decision to locate it near Spokane International Airport. A Sierra Club spokesperson who attended the meeting on the draft EIS expressed concern about air pollution. The Sierra Club virtually disappeared from the ranks of the opposition after this hearing, but some of the first and longest-lasting actively involved participants came from the ranks of those who initially complained about the proposed facility's pollution.

Active citizens lobbied legislators and members of the executive branch, attempted to persuade administrators and judges, and appealed in every way they could think of to the general public. In 1988 members of the Greater West Plains Association were among those who argued against the incinerator at a joint hearing run by WDOE and SCAPCA to consider environmental impacts of the proposed facility.[89] Later that year Citizens for Responsible Waste Management asked the governor and state auditor to order an audit of the project's books to see if it was following proper procedures in awarding contracts. At the same time they pressed the city council to do a comparative study of the costs of an incinerator and a new landfill. They also pressed the county health district to review a Portland study that found unacceptable health risks associated with incineration.[90]

In 1988 there was an attempt to bring the waste-to-energy facility to a public vote. In November 1977, 70 percent of the voters had approved a city charter amendment requiring voter approval of large capital projects requiring tax money, but it was tied up in a court battle over whether it applied to the waste-to-energy facility. (The Washington State Supreme Court eventually ruled that it did not; see chapter 5.) In January, council member Sheri Barnard asked the city council to put the incinerator to a vote, but after more than four hours of public testimony in which better than 80 percent of those testifying spoke against the incinerator and/or asked for a vote, the council decided 6–1 against the motion for a vote.[91] In September active citizens, organized as Citizens for the Right to Vote, again tried to place a charter amendment on the November ballot. This time, the amendment would have required voter approval of major capital projects no matter how they were financed. Confusion regarding the number of signatures required (it varied depending on which ballot it was validated in time for), problems with the legality of the wording, and two more refusals by the city council to place the proposed amendment on the November ballot resulted in this effort failing also.[92]

In the summer of 1988, when a Century West Engineering study identified three potential sites for further consideration as locations for an in-county ash landfill, people living near Lance Hills, Grove Road, and Gelbert Mountain jumped into action. Neighbors who had never met before visited each other and talked about how to keep an ash landfill from being sited near their homes. They held meetings in yards, living rooms, local grange halls, churches, and public schools to organize and plan strategies.

The newly activated citizens began their communication with SWDP with a complaint that they had not been given adequate time to prepare for the scoping hearing for the ash landfill EIS.[93] Nonetheless, thirty days after the initial notice, the scoping hearing took place with more than 200 people attending.[94] At the meeting citizens complained about the way the meeting itself was structured, saying they wanted an opportunity to ask questions and get answers from project officials. The meeting format that night divided participants into 22 small groups for discussions and development of a list of questions and concerns. Each group was coordinated by a member of the Spokane Area Chapter of the League of Women Voters, which had contracted to assist SWDP in that fashion. Toward the end of the evening, each group presented its questions and concerns to the general meeting.

The group discussion format kept citizens talking to each other and consumed considerable time in redundant reports to the general meeting; but some members of the group used the evening to circulate a petition requesting another session where they could put questions to project officials. Project officials said they would be willing to hold such meetings only if they were limited to about twenty participants, because "there needs to be some control."[95]

Shortly thereafter, a farmer in the Latah-Fairfield area bought the potential site at Gelbert Mountain and took it out of consideration. In response, SWDP staff and consultants examined remaining potential sites and added the Heyer Point site to their short list. That move, of course, brought out a new set of concerned citizens. They joined with the nearby Lance Hills group and formed the Lance Hills–Heyer Point Coalition.

Together, Citizens for Clean Air, Grove Road Neighbors, and the Lance Hills–Heyer Point Coalition became leading forces behind citizen attempts to stop construction of the incinerator. Leaders in the Grove Road and Lance Hills–Heyer Point groups argued that the best way to assure that the site nearest them was not selected for ash disposal was to stop the incinerator. They pursued their cases through the public hearings in the EIS process — gathering 300 strong at the hearing for the draft EIS.[96] Though many of them were county residents, group members also became regular attendees at city council meetings, because the city was the lead agency. Several times they kept council members late into the night urging them to seek alternatives to the incinerator.[97]

Separately, these three groups also proceeded to pursue their own agenda priorities. As the central group opposing the incinerator, CfCA acted through a number of avenues — administrative, legislative, and legal. At public hearings and through written comments, they argued against permits for the waste-to-energy facility and appealed to the EPA WDOE's approval of an air pollution permit for the incinerator (see chapter 5). In court, with occasional help from the Washington Environmental Council,

CfCA sued to force the city to put the incinerator to a vote, challenged the facility's EIS, contended that the contract with Wheelabrator constituted a gift and was therefore a violation of the state constitution, and challenged the $60 million grant from WDOE as a violation of the state's Environmental Policy Act.

Situated at the southwestern edge of Spokane County, the Lance Hills–Heyer Point Coalition explored the option of seceding from Spokane County and becoming part of Lincoln County.[98] Such a move, they believed, would protect them from attempts by city residents to dump garbage in their community and better assure the preservation of their rural lifestyle. They also got the Lincoln County commissioners involved in opposing the Heyer Point site because it drained into the main aquifer for Lincoln County.[99] Being closer to town and more densely populated, Grove Road focused on demonstrating community solidarity, doing things like posting "Stop the Ash Dump" signs throughout the area.

Citizen activists also engaged in various activities designed to communicate directly with the general public. They held demonstrations, fund raisers, rallies, workshops, forums, and press conferences. One of the more creative demonstrations was clearly staged as a media event. In it members of CfCA, Lance Hills, and SAW — wearing face masks, black arm bands, and other clothes designed to attract attention — presented bags of ash, dead fish, and a homemade certificate called the Dead Carp Award to the city manager and SWDP director.[100] Another colorful demonstration was conducted outside city hall prior to a city council meeting. People wore gas masks, carried signs, and sang songs. When one of the participants tried to sing her testimony to the council as part of their meeting, she was escorted out of the chambers.[101] Most of their meetings, however, were not colorful or dramatic. CfCA held periodic public informational meetings, and they became a significant source of new members.[102]

March 1989 saw two actions by groups opposing the waste-to-energy facility that at face value were aimed at local officials, but they are probably better understood as ill-conceived attempts to draw the attention of the public. First, SAW launched a bid to recall all city council members except Sheri Barnard, the lone waste-to-energy opponent on the council. The move made headlines but was dismissed by a judge who said it lacked an adequate legal justification. It may also have played into the hands of project proponents, who wanted to portray opponents as overly strident and not representative of the community mainstream.[103]

Second, CfCA, SAW, the Greater West Plains Association, and the Council for Land Care and Planning appealed a decision by SCAPCA not to require Boeing to file an EIS for a plant they planned to build just west of the city of Spokane in Airway Heights.[104] The plant was expected to employ 350 people and would produce floor panels and plastic and fiberglass ducts for airliners. This action by the groups known for their opposition to the incinerator did much to soften their support in the community. It gave officials an excellent platform from which to voice various charges against them: that they did not speak for the community, that they wanted to assert their own agenda over that of the community welfare, that they were antigrowth and would cost the community jobs, that they were irresponsible in their use of government appeal procedures. When group members attempted to answer those charges, their denials were phrased in the terms chosen by their antagonists and further tarnished their image: "We're not a bunch of rabid, no-growth nuts out here."[105] Saying that conversations with Boeing had satisfied them, the groups dropped the challenge a couple of weeks after they had filed it. This series of events also damaged the credibility of citizen activist opponents of the incinerator.

As early as April 1989, people were beginning to anticipate a showdown between project proponents and opponents in the November general election. Sheri Barnard had already announced her candidacy for mayor. With Mayor Vicki McNeill retiring, council member Rob Higgins, a project proponent, said he was "99 percent sure" he would run against Barnard. After the September primary election, the mayoral race was between Barnard and Higgins. Barnard seemed to come out of the primary with a comfortable lead, having garnered 52 percent to Higgins's 27 percent in a four-way race.[106]

The races for city council seats also shaped up as pro- and anti-incinerator confrontations. And again, the anti-incinerator side appeared to have the lead heading into the general election: two of the three biggest vote-getters in the primary were anti-incinerator. Position 1, held by project supporter Jack Hebner, was contested by five candidates in the primary. B. J. Krafft, long a member of CfCA and an active incinerator opponent, won the right to challenge Hebner in the general election, drawing 29 percent to Hebner's 38 percent in the primary. Krafft ran a single-issue campaign, and Hebner was sufficiently concerned about anti-incinerator sentiment that he softened his verbal support for the project in the final months before the election.[107] Position 2 was contested by five newcomers, as the incumbent, Dave Robinson, was retiring. Katie Reikofski, a pro–waste-to-energy business counselor, and Bob Apple, a cofounder of CfCA, survived the primary and faced off in the general election. Reikofski had drawn 31 percent in the primary while Apple received 37 percent. Position 3, also an open seat (Higgins was vacating it to run for mayor), was contested by four candidates, all of whom expressed some degree of opposition to the waste-to-energy facility.[108] The two remaining candidates after the primary, Mike Brewer (28 percent) and Bob Andren (37 percent), differed in the degree of their opposition to the project. Brewer favored burning garbage, but felt that the project should be put to a vote and that a better location than the one near the airport could be found. Andren was more adamant in his opposition to the incinerator.

The morning after election day, citizens opened their newspapers to find that with the exception of Barnard, none of the anti-incinerator candidates had won election.[109] Opponents had wanted a referendum on the project, had gotten one by proxy, and had lost. Had all of the anti-incinerator candidates won their races, they would have had a majority on the council and would have been able to control who was appointed to complete Barnard's term as council member. Before the general election they appeared on the verge of moving from a 6–1 minority on the council to a 5–2 majority. Instead, Barnard remained the sole vote against the project on most issues. From that day forward, despite legal and administrative appeals and continued lengthy and heated arguments against it at public hearings and city council meetings, the project moved toward completion, and in September 1991 the plant began burning Spokane's garbage.

Though they marked significant decreases in the amount of citizen participation in Spokane's solid waste policy making, the 1989 election and the 1991 startup of the waste-to-energy facility did not end the need for solid waste policy making or for citizen participation, or the controversy associated with siting and operating solid waste facilities. In addition to the examples mentioned earlier, nine months after the 1989 election the local League of Women Voters chapter continued to debate whether by assisting in running public workshops for the project it was being used by the SWDP to further its purposes rather than to facilitate meaningful citizen participation. Siting the ash transfer stations generated additional citizen opposition.[110] Building a permanent compost facility also brought several neighboring families into oppositional action. They gathered about 100 names on a petition against the proposed siting of the facility, but the city blunted the opposition by purchasing several of the homes adjacent to the site.[111] SCAPCA continues to receive complaints about odors emanating from the site. At first air pollution control officials were unable to detect any violation firsthand.[112] Eventually, neighborhood opposition became so strident that officials were pressured into vigilant monitoring of the site, and during the spring and summer of 1995 the compost facility was cited three times for air pollution violations. Residents in the area complained daily and were distressed that odors they found intolerable were not violations of any law, so they pressured the city council into voting 4–2 to find a way to end their contract with O. M. Scott, the operator of the facility—a vote that was reversed 4–3 three weeks later. SWDP and SCAPCA officials were not convinced the facility was operating in violation of the contract, and opposed any move that would result in losing a lawsuit for breach of contract.[113]

Predictably, many area residents were less than elated when SWDP announced in 1990 that it had been given a second place award by the National League of Cities for "bringing the citizen's point of view into the planning process."[114] On the other hand, SWDP could feel quite proud that they had weathered the citizen opposition and the trials and tribulations of policy making in a democracy, and had succeeded in bringing to the community what they felt to be a viable approach to dealing with the solid waste problem. Whether the citizens believed in that approach or just accepted it, and whether their preferences or those of SWDP staff would eventually prove the better founded, remained to be decisively determined.

LOCAL ATTITUDES TOWARD CITIZEN PARTICIPATION

Elsewhere I have used the three models mentioned earlier (confrontive, coopted, and prudent participation styles) as the basis for exploring and comparing citizen participant and policy maker perceptions of citizen participation in solid waste policy making in Spokane.[115] In that work I examined the views of citizen group members, city and county administrative staff, and elected officials involved in Spokane's solid waste policy dispute. The purposes they ascribed to citizen participation varied significantly. Citizen group leaders thought of citizen participation in much more active terms than did the local government officials. For example, one citizen group leader said, "Politics is like a stew—if you don't stir in it once in a while all the scum rises to the top. And I guess we are the spoon."

Local government officials saw a difference between the purpose of citizen participation in general and the role of citizen groups. Their descriptions of the general purpose of citizen participation ranged from process-focused statements such as "to get people feeling like they've been part of the process" to substance-focused statements like "to help come up with solutions." They ascribed more active roles to citizen groups. Some saw them in a coopted role — serving "as a real tool for the policy maker [getting] information to the public and get[ting] their reaction to it." Others saw citizen groups playing an important confrontive role, but they also expressed some discomfort with the way local groups had played that role.

Citizen group leaders and local government officials held strikingly different views regarding the openness of the local officials to citizen participation. The citizen group leaders tended to see local government officials as closed: "They have made no bones about the fact that they were elected — once — and at that point we lost our voice"; "We're about as welcome as a skunk at a garden party." I suspect that it was partly because of sentiments expressed in such colorful fashion that local government officials overestimated the negativity of the group leaders' perception. Of the group leaders, 65 percent reported their belief that local government officials were closed to input and 30 percent reported thinking officials were qualifiedly open. Of the local government officials, however, 92 percent believed they were seen as closed, and only 8 percent believed they were seen as qualifiedly open. As Sabatier, Hunter, and McLaughlin's devil-shift thesis would have predicted,[116] each side overestimated the hostility of the other.

Another issue that I examined was whether people thought citizen participation had any impact. When I interviewed participants, it was clear that impact meant different things to different people. Some people saw impact as affecting the substance of the policy; most of the citizens' group leaders would fall in this category, many of them describing their desired impact as "stopping the incinerator." Local government officials, however, most often discussed impact in terms of the decision-making process. Additionally, some of the officials saw impact in terms of their effect on the community: "We may gain the attention of 1 or 2 percent of the population out there, but the other 98 percent is left without any real message."

I was also interested in perceptions of the effectiveness of various approaches to citizen participation. Activities listed by citizen group leaders as most productive included publication of materials and holding community meetings; least effective were lobbying public officials and political demonstrations. But group leaders were not united in these perceptions. Coopted citizen participants were more likely to find being represented on a board, committee, or panel as among the most effective strategies, whereas filing lawsuits was least constructive. Confrontational participants, on the other hand, were more likely to list political demonstrations as among the most effective.

Citizen group leaders also differed in their perceptions of ineffectiveness. Confrontational group leaders were somewhat more likely to include representation on a board, committee, or panel as among the least effective. Their opinion was typified by one individual's statement, "Most of the advisory committees were pretty well hand-picked." Prudent group leaders were more likely to list lobbying among the least effective techniques because "they don't listen." Coopted citizen group leaders appeared slightly more likely to list political demonstrations and lawsuits among the least successful.

Another indication of what citizen group leaders consider effective is what they themselves did: 100 percent reported having engaged in public hearings conducted or sponsored by government officials, and 100 percent said they interacted with the media. Ninety-five percent published materials. Only 35 percent engaged in political demonstrations. There were interesting differences in the activities they engaged in: coopted leaders participated in fewer different kinds of activities than other kinds. Coopted leaders were less likely to participate in lawsuits or lobbying, attend public forums not sponsored by government officials, hold community meetings, or meet with neighbors in their homes; they were most likely to have been chosen for representation on a board, committee, or panel. Confrontational leaders were more likely to engage in political demonstrations. Despite their differences, these citizen group leaders valued highly the potential impact of interaction with the media and publication of materials. They doubted the effectiveness of political demonstrations. Finally, even though they had doubts about the value of public hearings sponsored by government officials, they saw attendance at such meetings as mandatory.

Local government officials were also asked to evaluate the effectiveness of various activities through which citizen groups had contact with administrators. Activities most often regarded as effective were holding conversations and attending public hearings conducted or sponsored by government officials. Among the least effective were political demonstrations and lawsuits. In general, local officials viewed effectiveness as deriving from professionally delivered information. Typical suggestions for improved effectiveness included: "Pick your best spokespersons and organize what you have to say"; "The most effective citizen participation is knowledgeable citizen participation." Those whom local government officials saw as ineffective were generally described as "people who come and give testimony with very little information."

In sum, citizen group leaders and local government officials had significant areas of agreement regarding which activities were not effective, but they appeared to disagree regarding the effectiveness of lobbying public officials. Citizen group leaders listed that activity among the least effective, but local government officials saw various forms of lobbying as quite productive.

For Spokane's local government officials and citizen group leaders alike, the procedural aspects of the citizen participation experience in solid waste policy making brought more satisfaction than did the substantive aspects. Local government officials were asked whether they were satisfied with the amount and the kind of citizen participation they had observed. Some 77 percent were satisfied with the amount, but an equal percentage also said they were unsatisfied with "the kind of citizen participation in solid waste policy making in Spokane." They observed that an impressive number of people participated in the controversy. Typical complaints were: "They oppose things on selfish grounds"; "It's negative; they didn't want to learn, they wanted to discredit [us]"; "They were unwilling to compromise"; "Too emotional, very little serious discussion."

Among citizen group leaders, more were satisfied with the process than the substance of participation. When leaders spoke specifically of their intragroup experience, they were very positive — 87 percent were highly satisfied. When attention focused on the impact of their group, there was a dramatic shift — 58 percent said they were unsatisfied.

Finally, I also examined the relationship between styles of citizen participation and levels of satisfaction. The more confrontational citizen participants tended to be less satisfied with their experience. One reason seemed to be that coopted participants were more focused on the process of participation, while confrontational participants were more focused on the substance of the resulting policy.

CONCLUSION

The impacts of citizen participation on public policy making in general, and on solid waste policy making in particular, are many and varied. It can affect policy making in both procedure and substance. It can affect government officials as individuals, sometimes making them more resistant to altering their policy stances, sometimes helping them to see new alternatives (or to see old ones in a new light), sometimes discouraging the use of public involvement mechanisms, and sometimes encouraging the wider use of citizen involvement. It can also affect citizen participants as individuals — transforming them into either more active citizens or disheartened subjects.

The effectiveness of specific approaches to citizen participation continues to be in dispute. This case study found that citizen group leaders believe they need to reach the community directly, rather than allowing contact with other citizens to be filtered through government officials. Local officials, however, prefer citizens to contact them personally and directly. The common ground in these positions appears to be a belief in the importance of communicating with the public. That seems to imply that both citizen groups and local government officials see the public as a key to affecting solid waste policy making, which is an optimistic note (however minor the key) for democracy in the American administrative state.

This examination of citizen participation in Spokane's solid waste policy making suggests that public officials overestimate the hostility of citizen participants. This may mean that they unnecessarily constrict citizen involvement. If the coopted, prudent, and confrontive models of citizen participation have any relationship to practical reality, then government officials would be wise to identify which participants fit which model and relate to each differently, but to all respectfully. Coopted participants need to be supported and encouraged. Confrontive participants should not be expected to alter their substantive policy differences with the government officials. Their presence should be expected and encouraged, if not enjoyed. Officials' relations with prudent participants can be the key to creating policy problem resolutions that will be acceptable to a majority of the community. Because they are neither unalterably opposed to government officials or their policy preferences, nor reluctant to differ with them, their voices can present to officials problems they missed and alternatives they had not imagined.

Because the procedural aspects of citizen participation can be a source of satisfaction, and because government officials have some control over them, officials might be well advised to assure that procedures do not unnecessarily heighten tensions with citizens. Substantive differences are an inherent part of any significant policy discussion and should be expected, but a set of procedures need not enhance alienation. To maximize the opportunity for increasing satisfaction with the citizen participation experience, procedures should be designed with a constant devotion to inclusion and courtesy.

It is generally agreed that citizen participation is a valued part of a democratic system. There is less consensus, however, on what the purpose of that participation should be, what impact it should have, what the most effective approaches are, when it should take place, and how it should be facilitated.

The dynamics of the dispute in Spokane over solid waste policy followed a pattern that is rather common in solid and hazardous waste policy making. Government officials working with business representatives identified an imminent problem and envisioned a solution to it. Working together, they began to examine the feasibility of their solution and to prospect for the resources needed to make it happen. They dutifully followed the letter of the law in informing the public and inviting them to attend hearings and make written comments, but they initially received little feedback. Not until they had progressed to a point where they had more or less settled on a specific technology at a specific location did the citizenry begin to awaken to the issue. By the time the complex of active citizens interested in the issue included more than the "usual suspects" — active citizens who appear at nearly every hearing to complain about practices and policies (or proposed policies) — the official policy makers had become committed to a course of action. Sensing this, citizens complained that their objections to the proposed policy were not being heard and that their opportunities for input were relatively meaningless.

The mismatch between officials' time lines and citizens' expectations for providing input regarding the most basic issues in the waste management issue necessarily created hostility. It is not necessary for everyone to agree on the purpose of citizen participation as long as the mechanisms for facilitating it allow many purposes to be pursued. This means that government officials must go beyond a minimalist approach, meeting only the legal requirements for citizen participation, and welcome substantive citizen contributions. Communities almost certainly will benefit from the energies and skills citizen participants contribute in informing and advising government officials. In Spokane, active citizens have been credited with making the waste-to-energy plant meet tougher pollution standards, increasing the role of recycling in the new solid waste management system, making the plant mitigate its impact on fog at the airport, and instigating changes in the interlocal agreement to give the county more power. They should also be credited with predicting the impact of new pollution requirements on the project's financial projections, and (given the 1994 Supreme Court decision in *Chicago v. EDF*) should be given some credit for insisting on characterizing incinerator ash as hazardous.

The benefits gained by meaningful citizen participation, however, will most likely come at some cost in efficiency and community cohesiveness. As Yates explains,[117] it is not easy to attain simultaneously the ideals of efficiency and democracy, so we most often find some compromise of the two that fully satisfies no one. Community cohesiveness is also in some jeopardy when democracy is actively exercised. A full discussion of the options available — and of the concerns, interests, and values of community members — entails an authentic discourse of the kind described by Fox and Miller.[118] People will disagree and will divide themselves along the lines upon which the arguments diverge, but democracy presumes that better resolutions of governance problems will be discovered through an authentic discourse on the issues.

"Ordinary people," as Rose calls them,[119] generally do not attend to public affairs unless and until they can see either a significant benefit or a significant harm coming to them as a consequence of specific actions. They see as their primary concerns their daily relations — family, friends, and work — and "do not see the government as the source of their well being."[120] When public affairs have become important to ordinary people, to dismiss these people as NIMBYs, as uninformed, or as too emotional is to miss an important opportunity to expand the pool of participants and perspectives included in the public discourse. More than that, to discourage citizen participation is to pose a serious threat to local democratic governance. As Salisbury notes, "Local political arenas not only have been created but are still very largely maintained and made to work by the devoted actions of republican citizens."[121]

The Impact of
the Media

T he media's presence in late twentieth-century America seems to reach into everything we do. From the most personal aspects of human relationships to the selection of national leaders, whether they are seeking election to legislative or executive positions or are under consideration for judicial or administrative positions, everything becomes part of the media-influenced public dialogue. Because of its omnipresence, the impact of the media on policy making in the United States is more than a function of the editorial positions taken or biases demonstrated by news media organizations. Because we are trying to run a representative democracy in a large and complex society, the nation depends on the mass media for communication between policy makers and the general public. The media are such an important part of our national culture that how they gather, interpret, and present information has a significant impact on public policy making — from setting the public agenda to implementing adopted policies.

Spokane's experience in solid waste policy making was nested within the context of national dynamics. The "media-ization" of public affairs is responsible for an important aspect of the milieu in which policy making occurs. There is no question that the news media affected Spokane's solid waste policy making (see fig. 8.1). The conflict surrounding the waste-to-energy facility and potential in-county ash landfills was, for a time, the hottest ongoing story in the local news. Before discussing the specifics of news media coverage of solid waste policy making in Spokane, we should review briefly the larger question of the impact of the media on U.S. public policy in general. This chapter examines the influence of the news media on three levels: (1) its general impact on political and social activities in postmodern America, (2) the impact of news organizations and media logic on how public policy is discussed, and (3) the specific ways in which the local and national news and information media affected solid waste policy making in Spokane.

THE MEDIA CULTURE OF POSTMODERN AMERICA

Jaques's speech in Shakespeare's *As You Like It* encapsulates the contemporary view of how the news media affects politics and policy making: "All the world's a stage, / And all the men and women merely players." In the postmodern perspective, the media have altered all American social institu-

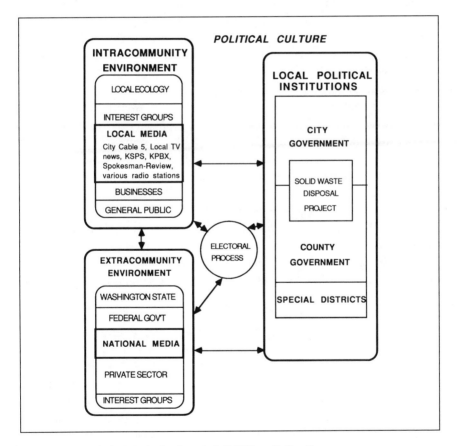

Figure 8.1   Media's Role in Spokane's Solid Waste Policy System

tions, and therefore all American social action. According to Altheide and Snow, ours is a "media world," and all the men and women act and think in media-driven ways.[1]

The postmodern perspective essentially states that "reality is socially constructed through a process of symbolic interaction."[2] One need not subscribe to the extremes to which one could take this position to accept its main implication for this chapter: much of our understanding of our world is affected by how it is presented to us and by our expectations of it. Though we may not believe that reality is totally socially constructed, we may accept that much of what we understand — or think we understand — about our world has been presented to us either by the news and information media or in a format derived from the dominant mass media format. In framing that presentation, the media format significantly influences how we understand what is presented.

We may not live in a media world, but we do live in a "mediated" world.[3] A large part of what we know about public affairs comes to us through various forms of news and information media. That is, "People know what they know about their government primarily from what they read in the newspapers, what they hear on the radio, and what they see on television."[4] Most of what we know about public policy making is not learned firsthand (although some portion of it may be labeled "up close and personal"). It comes to us in a mediated form. Even such uninterpreted reporting as a local cable company's live coverage of city council meetings, C-SPAN's coverage of Congress, or CNN's coverage of hot stories like the Persian Gulf War or the O. J. Simpson murder trial, while less mediated, is still affected by media formatting.

Since we live in such a mediated world, we often expect a media-style format in the information presented to us. Our expectations, to the degree that they have adopted a media format, participate in framing the information and reinforce the focus, style, and limits of the media format. We have adopted a kind of "media logic" that we use to make sense of the world around us. This media logic manifests itself not only as a way of presenting material, but also as a way of interpreting phenomena.[5]

Although there are many kinds of information media in the modern world, each with its own basic format, television has the greatest impact on our lives. "Television news employs the logic of dramatic narrative through verbal and nonverbal symbols, sound, and visual imagery."[6] That logic includes establishing a structure (the beginning, middle, and end of a "story"), a problem, a conflict, and its resolution. Radio remains popular in this television world, but its popularity is based on the way it subordinates itself to the listener's life patterns.[7] Radio does not command the attention of its consumers the way print and television do. People listen to radio while they eat, drive the car, read the newspaper, or do myriad other things. The radio format accommodates to the listener. Print media are more imposing (and more substantive), but they are becoming less important than the electronic media as sources of information and/or entertainment.[8] In addition, the television format has influenced the print media. *USA Today,* with its distribution in boxes that mimic television sets and its very short articles based on the television news approach, is perhaps the most extreme example, but magazines like *People* and other forms of print journalism have also adopted formats that assume the short attention span that television has taught our society.[9]

As Altheide and Snow argue, "American society appears to be adopting a television logic and problem-solving perspective."[10] Television logic has become entrenched not only in our media-provided entertainment, but also in journalism and politics. Journalists have become so captured by the "sound bite" emphasis of television news that they have succumbed to what Ross Perot calls "gotcha journalism." If reporters can successfully pose a "gotcha" question, they are more likely to participate in a major news story. Politicians are not merely wary of this dynamic in their media exchanges; they have adapted to television by becoming competent constructors of sound bite arguments and by making significant efforts to "look good."

Because of the institutions that present information to us and how we make sense of the information we receive, we now live in a "television-style culture." In Postman's words, "Television is our culture's principal mode of knowing about itself."[11] In this media culture, the impact of television on our understanding of public issues is significant. The media affect public policy making in two ways: (1) television viewers—and media consumers generally—expect (or take for granted) some formatting elements that are better suited to entertainment than to politics and public policy; and (2) postmodern media managers have begun to understand that people are more influenced by form than by content. Postman says that the impact of television logic on public discourse can lead us down a path where we amuse ourselves to death. Because television logic places the highest value on entertainment, it therefore demands that our public discourse (in order to qualify for television time) must also be entertaining. This leads to a trivialization of the content in public discourse.

One way the media ensure that the news they present is entertaining is to format it as a story. In the " 'news perspective' " observe Altheide and Snow, "any event can be summarily covered and presented as a narrative account with a beginning, middle, and end."[12] The story format is so entrenched in media news that we take for granted that each item is a story. But stories have structural aspects that are not necessarily appropriate as a frame for electoral contests or public policy discourses. For example, one frame imposed by the news media on election campaigns is the horse race format. Rather than restricting themselves to reporting the campaign event or the speech, commentators are compelled by the horse race story line to tell us what the event or speech means in terms of who is "ahead." This helps turn our national elections into popularity contests and keeps them from being vital elements in assuring representative democracy.[13]

If a reported news item is not given a full-blown story line, the news media may structure it around an easily recognized theme or angle. The use of recognizable themes and angles helps to create order out of complex phenomena by providing familiarity, credible answers, and ready explanations. "News stories . . . do not 'tell it like it is,' but rather, 'tell it like it means.' "[14]

Presenting an item in a familiar way helps the news media to achieve another goal — viewer relevance. Members of the audience want stories about things that are relevant to their own lives. Graber writes, "To make stories attractive, newspeople commonly present them as anecdotes that show their effect on average people. Inflation news becomes the story of the housewife at the supermarket; foreign competition becomes the story of laid-off workers in a local textile plant."[15]

Such framing of the news facilitates the delivery of another aspect of formatting that postmodern American viewers have come to expect — instant gratification. As Altheide and Snow point out, "Television aims for a high degree of clarity that is achieved instantly."[16]

Another aspect of format that takes on overriding importance in television is visual presentation. Convinced that visual support is essential to their presentation, producers of news programs will repeatedly run file footage of a scene, no matter how old the footage is or how recently they used it in connection with another story. In a recent example in Spokane, whenever a local channel ran a story about the court case of two men who had exchanged gunfire with the FBI in northern Idaho, they ran video footage of the two walking in orange jail clothes down a hall — footage filmed on the day they were arraigned. The channel ran that video segment so often that it began to have a "signature effect": whenever that video appeared, people knew the story was about Randy Weaver and Kevin Harris.

The importance of the visual emphasis in public affairs programming is often illustrated by one of two stories. The first is the Nixon-Kennedy television debate before the 1960 presidential election.[17] Those who saw the debate on television tended to think Kennedy had "won"; those who listened to it on the radio tended to favor Nixon. The second is the story of how Lesley Stahl constructed a piece on Ronald Reagan that she thought was a negative story.[18] She learned later that the piece pleased White House officials because they thought the visuals were good for Reagan and that "the public doesn't pay any attention to what you say, they just look at the pictures."

If those officials were correct, how news reporters frame the material they present may be more important than the content of that material. If so, then it is important to become more aware of those frames and how they affect public policy making. The basic elements of the media news format include the following: standard program units; sound-bite brevity; clarity; a story line, theme, or angle; viewer relevance; and visual representations. Let us consider their impact on public policy making in greater detail.

THE MEDIA CULTURE AND PUBLIC POLICY MAKING

In some ways, how public policy is made in the United States is not well suited to presentation within standard media formats. The contemporary news media are not adept at presenting the complexity involved in many public policy issues. Still, it is clear that without the media, public policy issues would be much less public. Despite all their attendant problems, the various formats used by the media in reporting on public affairs do help to engage people in the public discourse.

Programming Units

When one compares the general shape of public policy making with how it is presented in the media, it becomes clear that media presentation changes the appearance of public policy issues. Whereas public policy making comes in a wide variety of shapes and requires various lengths of time to explicate, the mass media tend to package material in standard time units. On the evening news, those units seldom exceed a few minutes. On news magazine shows, the segment is usually 20 or 30 minutes, including commercials. Framing public policy making within homogeneous program units should consistently lead to a "to be continued" tag after each segment. There are many venues in which policy recommendations can be made and many opportunities for reintroducing a proposed policy, even if it was defeated yesterday. So, an issue seldom reaches genuine closure. Recognition of this phenomenon has led many a policy studies professional to speak in terms not of *solving* problems, but of *resolving* them.[19]

Sound Bites

Though the marketing of a policy proposal through mass media channels often depends on encapsulating the thrust of that proposal in a sound-bite slogan, effective implementation requires a thorough understanding of the complexities of the problem. Brief metaphors that capture the spirit of a policy can be helpful in providing general guidance for implementing a policy,[20] but attending to the details of implementation "requires understanding that apparently simple sequences of events depend on complex chains of reciprocal interaction."[21] Sound bites can help to clarify what a policy means, but they can also contribute to a failure to understand what a policy does. The implication of this for public policy making is that for a sufficient understanding of policies, one must commit more time and energy to the task than is involved in even the most painstaking attention to news media accounts and analyses.

Story Lines

The media's use of common story lines, themes, or angles helps the public to make sense of what might otherwise be seen as a chaotic world.[22] Over time, the news-consuming public develops an idea of the normative contours of our society. Public policy making is fundamentally a normative activity,[23] and the role of the public in policy making is weighted toward making the value judgments that underpin policies, so awareness of those contours plays an important part in the public's decisions about public policy problems.

On the other hand, the media's dependence on a story line, theme, or angle can obscure from the public eye the implications of major policy developments. In 1981, instead of examining the implications of the administration's tax legislation, the media imposed a "Republicans are against taxes and Democrats are for them" theme on their treatment of the legislation. In this instance, the media's dependence on familiar story lines, themes, and angles kept them from helping the public understand a policy that has "defined everything that has followed since."[24]

Viewer Relevance

In attempting to assure their share of the audience, media organizations are quite attentive to the relevance of their news for their audience.[25] It can be argued that media help government officials keep in touch with their constituents' priorities. There is some reason to doubt, though, that the priorities that the media express to policy makers are those of the public.[26] Also, the match between politicians' constituents and various media audiences is not terribly precise. The audience for television and radio news is quite different from the audience for newspapers and news magazines. What constitutes relevance varies among the different media audiences.

The electronic news media's emphasis on stories that are relevant to the viewer or listener contributes to the potential for missing the public policy implications of such government actions. Because the electronic news media understand viewer relevance as what it does to or for the average individual, they frequently fail to address the implications of a policy proposal for the general public interest. Print journalism is better at presenting the substance of policy issues, but as it competes with electronic media for a share of the audience, it tends toward less substantive treatment. This does not serve the public interest. As Goodsell points out, an effective public policy-making process requires that policies be examined "in terms broader than naked self-interest."[27]

Visual Supplements

The emphasis placed by television news on visual representation has both positive and negative impacts on the public policy arena. Striking pictures can help increase public awareness of a public policy issue, but the absence of attention-grabbing visuals can keep an important policy issue from obtaining much television coverage. The videotape of the Rodney King beating drew attention to the treatment of African Americans at the hands of the police not only in Los Angeles but across America. The absence of striking visuals, on the other hand, makes it difficult for television reporting to cover adequately problems like the savings and loan crisis.

Though the various forms of news media differ, individually and in combination these standard formatting frameworks reshape public policy making to fit their frames prior to sharing it with their audiences. But the impact of the media on public policy does not end here. There are also effects that derive from the routines of mass media organizations and mediated institutions.

MEDIATED INSTITUTIONAL IMPACTS

Altheide and Snow contend that in our "mediated" culture all institutions are media institutions. I think it is more accurate to describe the media culture's impact as making many of our institutions into mediated institutions — institutions that are affected by the nature of the news media culture. At least four institutions should be examined to better understand the impact of the news media culture on public policy making: media organizations, policy-making organizations, interest groups, and the general public. In combination, these four institutions determine to a significant degree how we define policy problems, and our definitions do much to determine the character of our policies and their implementation.

Media Organizations

The institutional routines of media organizations have a vital impact on how those organizations present policy problems. Since news programs are set within a regular programming schedule and newspaper reporters most often must meet daily deadlines, the timing of events intended to gather news coverage plays a significant role in the amount and kind of "play" they get. Further examples of this phenomenon will be provided later. It is sufficient here to point out that key presidential speeches, such as the State of the Union Address, are now planned so that they air during "prime time" in forty-eight states.

The news media also deliberately (or at least knowingly) take actions that are likely to have an impact on policy making. Graber identifies three general ways in which media organizations and/or media people consciously impact policy making: (1) investigative or advocacy journalism, (2) direct intervention in the government process, and (3) documentary or docudrama production.[28] Investigative reporting has long been a part of journalism, and the industry values it highly. In Graber's words, "Reporters and media institutions whose investigations have led to important social and political reforms frequently win prizes for high journalistic achievement."[29] Media organizations can intervene directly in the governing process in three ways: they can attempt to pressure government officials into action, they can take action one might expect of public officials (for instance, monitoring a contractor's compliance with government regulations and reporting failures to comply), or they can act as communication tools for government officials (through the publication of leaks or exclusive stories).

Perhaps the most controversial way in which media organizations affect policy making is through the production of documentaries and docudramas, which often have obvious political goals. In addition, docudramas in particular compromise the standards of public affairs broadcasting for entertainment purposes. Complaints about the accuracy, fairness, or ideological posture of television dramas are readily deflected by pointing to the entertainment goals behind the program. ABC did this when they were accused of timing their airing of "The Day After," a drama about the effects of a nuclear exchange, for political effect. They claimed that the broadcast was merely planned to air in November because it is a "sweeps" month.[30]

But it is in their role as presenters of news that media organizations have their most profound impact on the policy-making process. In that role, they most consciously mediate the relationship between citizens and government. First, news organizations decide who is able to reach citizens through the media. Second, as the media deliver news and public affairs issues to their audiences, the way they obtain and package the material affects not only the general public's understanding of that material, but also how political leaders and organizations (the sources of the material) package their presentations.

According to policy analysts, defining the problem "is possibly the most critical stage" in policy making.[31] How a policy problem is defined will determine both how a problem is explained and how people attempt to resolve it. As Dunn points out, "There are as many different solutions for a given problem as there are definitions of that problem."[32] Because the electronic media's primary purpose is to attract an audience for its sponsors, radio and television news programs do not tend to discuss the complex technical aspects of a public policy problem. Though the print media do a better job, they also find it difficult to run articles that are long enough to delve into the substance of policy problems. Thus, one of the media's impacts on the defining of public policy problems is to simplify the problem for their audience.

Accurately simplifying a complex policy problem is not easy. Even experts have difficulty in drafting a simple definition. With the possible exception of those who are allowed to specialize in given topic areas, news reporters most often do not have a thorough understanding of complex policy problems. Their simplifying definitions are more a function of the story line, theme, or angle they select for their report than of the nature of the problem. One reporter in Spokane habitually reduced the problem under consideration to a cliche he could bolster with a visual symbol. Once he stood next to a traffic sign used to signify a road intersection to illustrate that the policy being discussed (which had absolutely nothing to do with traffic) placed citizens and decision makers at a crossroads.

Finally, since news organizations are part of the commercial mass media, one of their key goals is to gather news efficiently. Burkowitz and Adams find that journalists' professional values are significantly compromised by the large role played by news sources in setting the agenda.[33] One reason the news media are dependent on their sources is that they are constantly trying to balance the expense of gathering and producing news against the income gained from their sponsors. One way they try to strike a profitable balance is to minimize the cost of gathering news. According to McManus, all but the largest stations depend mostly on their sources to provide convenient, inexpensive news. This passive approach to obtaining the news "tends to surrender control over the public information stream to powerful interests in government and among the wealthy."[34]

Government Organizations

Government agencies and officials deliberately manipulate media formats and expectations. As Altheide and Snow point out, "traditional sources for news organizations, e.g., government agencies and bureaucracies, have adjusted to news formats and now time and frame their messages, intentions, and vocabularies within these guidelines."[35]

Media coverage can often make or break a public policy or program (or the career of a public official), so public officials see the media as both a necessary ally and an irritating menace.[36] This love-hate relationship arises because it is necessary to work through the press to get out the good news about a government program or official; but news reporters have learned to be skeptical of government information (as bureaucratic or political propaganda), and the news industry is fully convinced that bad news attracts a wider audience than good news. It is in this context (in full knowledge that the media coverage they receive not only affects what the public knows about them but also will likely affect the resources available to them) that public officials have recognized the need to manage their relations with the media.

According to Jamieson and Campbell, "The ability to influence news coverage is directly related to an understanding of . . . journalistic norms and routines."[37] One way in which public officials manage those relations is by providing news items in a media-friendly format — brief, simple, with good visuals, dramatic angle, human interest, etc. As part of the marketing effort for his "reinventing government" initiative, Vice President Albert Gore Jr. appeared on *Late Night with David Letterman*. On that program, Gore presented the kinds of government activities that his initiative was aimed at curtailing as "stupid government tricks" (playing off Letterman's standard "stupid pet tricks" routine). Assuming that his initiative would be better received if he could mimic the popular comedian's signature routines, he also participated in the delivery of a list of the top ten benefits of being vice president (playing off another of Letterman's standard routines — humorous top ten lists).

Of course, media-related criteria can be manipulated to reduce the usability of the media as well. For example, instead of providing a good sound bite, an official might deliberately provide a rambling and/or complex technical answer to a question. The news media do not want to lose their audience by presenting information the audience cannot understand, so they are unlikely to carry such an answer. Public managers also pay attention to how the timing of a news release may affect the coverage it gets. According to David Gergen, who has served on the White House staff of both Ronald Reagan and Bill Clinton, "If you've got some news that you don't want to be noticed, put it out Friday afternoon at 4 P.M."[38] Sometimes government officials give live interviews because that approach gives editors less opportunity to "spin" the information into a story angle of their preference, but it also gives less protection against surprise questions.[39] Government officials also select specific reporters and/or programs to suit their needs.

Going "on location" to provide interesting visuals can enhance the coverage of a news story in terms of both audience impact and amount of air time. Disasters such as the flooding along the Mississippi and Missouri Rivers in the summer of 1993 provided excellent opportunities for government officials to take advantage of this media value. It is not necessary for a president to tour a disaster area to announce that he is making disaster relief funds available, but his presence on the scene provides a more relevant visual background. He can also enhance the human interest angle by talking sympathetically with a disaster victim.

In sum, public officials have learned that in order to manage their relations with the media successfully, they have to adopt media logic: "A sensitivity to the media implications of any management decision — internal or external—is essential for the skillful public manager."[40] Rather than attempt to force the media to adapt to their presentation formats (an approach that would probably be futile), public officials have themselves become participating members in the television culture.

Interest Groups and Businesses

Interest groups and businesses have also adapted their strategies for influencing public policy in ways designed to improve their chances for success in the media culture. Interest groups have learned how to use media formats to obtain coverage of events staged specifically for the media. When they are able to entice the media, they can spread their message to the general public much more efficiently than through any other available method. Jamieson and Campbell give an example in which an antiabortion group, after letting the media know of their plans, went to a hospital carrying small white caskets and requested aborted fetuses they hoped to bury. The hospital administrators were not prepared for the request, and their heated exchange with the group was covered by the cameras. The interest group had orchestrated this encounter so that it met several standard media criteria: it was dramatic, visual, personal, out of the ordinary, and addressed an ongoing theme in the news. Set for a convenient location and time, it was also well designed for the practical needs of news organizations.[41]

Interest groups and businesses that can afford public relations firms benefit from additional ways of manipulating the media. "News feeds" are prepared materials sent to media organizations in a ready-to-use format. When they use these feeds, news organizations are saved the time and expense of covering or developing the story themselves. "For example, after a Food and Drug Administration ruling favorable to a client's product, one public relations firm made a videotape for the client in the form of a news report on the FDA ruling, which the firm then distributed to hundreds of television stations—most of whom used it."[42]

In learning to adapt their approach to fit the frames of the media, interest groups have also become active participants in the television culture.

The General Public

When it comes to information about public policy issues, more Americans get their news from television than from any other source. About 40 percent say television is their sole source for news.[43] Because those who are not actively involved in the public discourse obtain much of their information, attitudes, and perceptions from the media, their comprehension of public policy problems tends to be significantly influenced by the media culture's depiction of social reality.[44]

Unfortunately, while the adaptation of policy makers and influencers to the media culture have made public affairs programming more entertaining, they have also made it less informative. As they adapt to the media culture, policy makers and policy influencers have to accept the television frame, and, in Postman's words, "It is in the nature of the medium [television] that it must suppress the content of ideas in order to accommodate the values of show business."[45] Driven by television logic, those who use the media to reach the public must emphasize the dramatic over the accurate.

In their review of studies on how much people learn from television news, Robinson and Levy find no evidence that television viewers gain superior information from their source compared to consumers of other media. Further, those who depend solely on television for their news and public policy information are more likely to be less well informed.[46] Thus, while the general public depends on the mass media for most of their knowledge about public affairs, as television increases its position as the dominant medium for disseminating news and information, the form in which the mediated information is presented (dramatic entertainment) becomes less and less optimal for governance purposes. Ironically, the general public would know even less without the contributions of the mass media.

Because it mediates between politically active organizations and the general public, the entertaining delivery of news and public affairs issues affects not only the content of that information but also its reception. The news media not only influence what people think about, but by affecting what is on people's minds, they also "make a significant contribution to what people think."[47] The impact of media presentations on the ordinary person's attitudes depends on several factors. Most important are the salience of the presentation and the degree to which an individual has established beliefs on the specific issue being presented. The frequency with which stories on a given issue are aired or published and how the stories are presented will also affect the public's receptiveness.[48]

Television's use of a dramatic story format keeps the news interesting, but the format may lead to other results as well. If the story line used by news reporters focuses on the conflict between antagonistic groups, presentation of the story will incline the public to see the issue in that way and will divide their sympathies between the antagonists.[49] In the eyes of the public, opposition between a government agency and an interest group over a public policy proposal becomes a question of loyalty rather than of a policy proposal's effectiveness or how best to serve the public interest. For those who identify with the interest group, or with an individual representing the interest group, loyalty to "their kind" may well override any consideration of facticity or logic. According to Price, this leads the audience not only to exaggerate the differences between group opinions, but also to adopt opinions consistent with those exaggerations. The impact on the body politic is polarization of the two camps.

On the other hand, the recent tendency to blame the media for many of society's ills may be an exercise in scapegoating. For example, many studies have examined the relationship between political alienation and exposure to news media. Most of those studies focused on the national level, and their findings are not consistent. In a study that examines people's exposure to local news reports and their alienation toward local government, Zimmer finds that media exposure and political alienation are largely unrelated.[50] Similarly, a study of adults in San Diego who reported significant exposure to talk radio shows that listening to talk radio is associated more with political activism than with political alienation.[51]

Like media organizations, government agencies, and interest groups, the general public is also part of the media culture.[52] People choose to watch news programs at least as much for drama as for information. The public's role is more passive and amorphous than the roles of news organizations, government agencies, and interest groups, so it is easier to blame the media for certain aspects of public behavior and attitudes. The media are not responsible for creating the behavior and attitudes they feed, but they are responsible for magnifying the degree to which those attitudes and behavior affect public policy making. The choice, however, may be between the ill effects of the media's magnifying those aspects on which it focuses and the ill effects that would follow from a diminution of the role of the media in fostering democratic political discourse.

The Impact of the Media on Solid Waste Policy Making in Spokane

Because making policy about the disposal of solid wastes is often contentious and can lead to dramatic confrontations, it is likely to attract media attention. The clash between a public official and a citizen whose home is near a proposed solid waste facility fits neatly into a Goliath-versus-David story line. The contrast between an emotional display by a citizen who feels threatened and the staid, rational, unfeeling response of the bureaucrat provides a perfect human interest angle. Images of an agricultural or wooded site that may be transformed into a landfill are well suited to the visual emphasis of television news. (Some of the material cited here was supported by borrowed videotapes of the television coverage, on which dates were not noted.)

The national media have affected the public's awareness of solid waste as a public policy problem through their treatment of pollution issues. Through news reports and weekly news magazines (both print and electronic), people in the Spokane area became aware of such waste-related stories as the Islip trash barge, Love Canal, and Times Beach. A poignant regional mediated event, the alar apple scare, also gained Spokane's attention, sensitizing people there to the economic effects of toxins. Through national media, people have become aware of the potential adverse impacts on their lives of hazardous materials such as furans, dioxin, and PCBs. They realize that people like them have had their lives disrupted and damaged by the ignorant or negligent handling of waste by companies and government agencies, and they are ill-disposed toward any action that might increase their chances of being involuntarily exposed to health-threatening agents.

There was a period during which solid waste policy was the talk of Spokane. Private conversations with friends and neighbors — in grocery stores, at high school sports events, on the telephone — often turned to solid waste policy. An editorial in the local paper described it as "the most divisive and acrimonious issue to rend this community in years."[53] During the peak year of the controversy, 1989, the local newspaper carried more than 250 articles related to solid waste, and better than 150 of those were directly related to the solid waste disposal project. The local electronic media were also quite interested in the issue. It was a feature on locally produced talk shows and a regular item on local news programs. A communication studies student at Eastern Washington University, in the final paper for his master's degree, described the situation: "The local pundits, both print and electronic media, watched the issue as closely as a national soap opera."[54] Because local news generally draws a greater audience than national news, the importance of the kind of coverage given by the local media was enhanced. While 49 percent of the nation's adults watch the national news daily, 67 percent watch the local news.[55]

Both for local news in general and for Spokane's local media in particular, the amount and the tone of the issue's media coverage were atypical. Generally local news programs' political stories are as likely to be international or national stories as they are to be local. The main local news features of local news programs are crime, disasters, entertainment, weather, and sports.[56] Generally, local news does not engage in much deliberate negative or controversial treatment of local public affairs. "Critics argue that it [local news] is soft on local politicians because it is not comfortable stirring up conflict among people who know each other personally. It is also soft when it comes to local projects and policies out of a sense of local boosterism."[57]

Spokane media in general, and the news section of the local paper in particular, did not treat the solid waste issue in a soft or boosterish manner. It was not unusual for local television stations to give the story a three- or four-minute spot in their evening news programs, and there were frequent live interviews in the six o'clock programs. The radio stations that gave the most thorough treatment were KXLY (an AM station specializing in news and talk radio) and the local public radio station (KPBX). They presented interviews with various project supporters and opponents, and occasionally broadcast extended discussion of some of the issues involved in solid waste policy making, from economic development impacts to environmental impacts. Reporters from the local paper, though, produced the most in-depth treatment of the issues. The degree of skepticism, and thus the level of independent research and analysis, they brought to their reports varied from reporter to reporter. One in particular continually raised sensitive and difficult issues for project officials. In 1989 the *Spokesman-Review* asked Karen Dorn Steele, a reporter specializing in environmental issues, to bring to the solid waste issue the kind of independent analysis she had previously demonstrated in covering stories about the Hanford Nuclear Reservation. She was not the only reporter who asked difficult questions, but she led the way in raising a skeptical voice within solid waste reporting in Spokane. Including in her reports treatment of problems such as air emissions from the incinerator, the hazardousness of incinerator ash, the impolite treatment of some citizens by some officials at public meetings, and the overly optimistic financial scenarios presented by project officials, Steele brought to the newspaper audience's attention many of the negative aspects related to waste-to-energy facilities.

I do not mean to imply that in covering local solid waste policy making Spokane's newspaper abdicated its role as local booster. Spokane newspapers have honored that role throughout their histories. Since the Cowles family acquired them in the 1890s, the local newspapers have "boosted Spokane as enthusiastically as its chamber of commerce."[58] Throughout the late 1980s and early 1990s, the local newspaper's editorial board steadfastly supported the local governments' proposals for managing solid waste. Only rarely did the paper take an editorial stand against a specific aspect of the solid waste management plan or its implementation. Some of the attention the solid waste issue attracted in 1989 can be explained as a function of the mayoral and city council elections. The waste-to-energy plant was so central to the campaign that people identified candidates as belonging to either the pro- or the anti-incinerator slate. For a while, it appeared that the two mayoral candidates would face off in a debate dedicated to the solid waste topic.[59] With the primary elections taking place in September and the general elections in November, the issue was assured additional coverage from mid-August through early November.

Sometimes the booster role escaped the confines of the editorial pages. The front page of the real estate section displayed one example of the paper's boosterism. Sunday of the Labor Day weekend prior to the start-up of the waste-to-energy facility, the paper ran a story there about how Spokane's infrastructure, including the solid waste disposal system, was capable of handling much greater demands. Spokane, the article said, was "poised for growth."[60]

The booster role was, however, more evident on the editorial page than in other sections of the paper. Near the outset of the 1989 primary election campaign, the paper ran a Sunday editorial reasserting its support of the waste-to-energy project, and calling on people to renew their spirit of "shoulder-to-shoulder civic cooperation."[61] In the middle of the general election campaign, it ran an editorial criticizing Sheri Barnard for opposing the project and not offering an alternative proposal.[62] On the Sunday before the general election, the paper featured an editorial crediting the project's opponents with improving it, but arguing that the sunk costs made canceling it a senseless idea.[63]

Also during the 1989 election season, Wheelabrator, the company contracted to build and operate Spokane's waste-to-energy plant, ran a series of newspaper ads promoting a positive image of the company.[64] After the primary and before the general election, they began to run television ads that used nature scenes (including shots of geese, elk, and a garden area in one of Spokane's major parks) to illustrate a theme of environmental sensitivity. Despite Wheelabrator officials' denial of having a political agenda for the ad campaign, the ads were clearly intended to play into the election dynamics. In addition to the ads, Waste Management, Inc., part owner of Wheelabrator, got at least one timely press release run in the Spokane paper.[65] In it they made — without contradiction — quite positive claims about their huge regional landfill operation in Arlington, Oregon. This contributed to building a positive image of the company.

Electioneering on the solid waste issue did not end after the 1989 election. City council member Joel Crosby postured on the issue in 1990 when he was considering running for county commissioner. The issue also figured in the 1993 mayoral and city council campaigns, but by this time it had only a supporting role in the larger issue of city hall's responsiveness to the citizens.

Throughout the life of the issue, the Spokane media's most common news story line focused on the conflict between proponents and opponents of the project. As Moran describes it, "Media analysis portrayed the overall political issue as a massive struggle of environmentalists against a big, bad government."[66] For example, when construction on the waste-to-energy plant was "finally under way," the paper carried not only that story, but also one that featured the undying optimism of the opponents that the project could "still be halted."[67] In another cleverly self-conscious article on a proposed regional landfill in Klickitat County, one local reporter began:

> Stop me if you've heard this one. A project to handle an entire county's garbage is described by state and local officials as a good project, but comes under fire from a local environmental group.
>
> The environmental group sues the county and the company building the project, saying it needs a better environmental impact statement. Among the group's main complaints is that the citizens never got a chance to vote on the project.
>
> The project becomes a key issue in an election campaign, as opponents of the project file against incumbents who support it. Public officials worry about the issue tearing the community apart.[68]

Television coverage also focused on the conflict. Covering a public hearing regarding the NOx emission limit for the waste-to-energy plant, all three local stations emphasized the hostility in evidence at the meeting. A common feature in their coverage showed one interchange in which the administrator explained to a citizen that his agency was not allowed to consider an applicant's "track record" when deciding whether to permit a facility. Not only did the citizen express outrage at this information, but he also elicited groans from the audience. Two of the three stations carried video coverage of that exchange as part of their story. One anchor characterized the meeting as "combative." Another station's reporter noted the hostility of the questions, and a third station's reporter went out of his way to note the costs associated with the delays in permitting the facility caused by appeals of previous permitting decisions.

Even when there was no conflict directly associated with an event, television coverage included reminders of the potential for conflict. When waste-to-energy staffers held an informal meeting with ash landfill opponents, one reporter noted that the meeting was peaceful, but the "real ruckus" would come at the official meetings. In discussing another nonconflictual story—one featuring the recording of protest songs written by locals specifically for the solid waste issue—an anchor quipped that it was "the first harmony we've seen on that issue."

The environmentalists-versus-the-government story line was significant for the general public because their understanding of the issue was influenced by how the media presented it. As mentioned earlier, when media portray a story in a conflictual frame, their audiences tend to decide where they stand on the issue based on their identification with and/or empathy for people representing one of the two sides. Even at the height of the controversy, the number of citizens actively involved numbered only in the hundreds. For the rest of the citizenry, the media coverage was their perceived reality of the event, not just an interpretation of what occurred.[69]

Local media coverage also affected the behavior and attitudes of project opponents. They regularly used the live coverage of city council meetings to present their view of various aspects of the proposed policy direction to viewers of city cable channel 5. Opponents purchased radio ads in order to explain their interpretation of events.[70] They also staged events with news coverage in mind, consciously using media formatting such as sound bites, story lines, viewer relevance, and visuals. In one example, after giving media advance notice, opponents delivered dead fish and bags of ash to city hall. Some wore surgical masks, some wore black, many carried signs. Along with the dead fish and ash, they presented certificates called "dead carp" awards.[71] The newspaper carried a story accompanied by a 6 × 10½ inch photo, and all three television stations covered this unusual, visually interesting event.

Often local government officials and opponents of the project were consciously vying for favorable media coverage. One particular event helps to illustrate this. Before a meeting at which the city council was expected to approve a study of another potential ash landfill site, opponents obtained a parade permit and marched in a circle and sang protest songs before the entrance to city council chambers.[72] Protesters were interviewed live by two local television stations before the meeting. During the public testimony portion of the meeting, one protester was forced to remove a cloth banner draped over his body before he could testify. Another insisted on singing her testimony even after the mayor warned her that she could not deliver her testimony musically. Two police escorted the singing testifier out of the chambers. All three local stations carried both incidents in their eleven o'clock news shows.

Local government officials also tried to obtain a favorable spin in the news coverage of that incident. Their decision to post police officers in council chambers helped to portray the protesters as dangerous. Television crews were allowed to show both the mayor and the city manager conferring with police about how to respond to the protesters' actions in the meeting. The mayor said the council would adjourn to an executive session somewhere else in the building. The city manager, knowing a camera was on him, told the police that the protesters "might try to tear up the place or something."

It is not clear who got more mileage out of the news coverage of that evening's events. Officials felt that portraying the protesters as dangerous was not only effective but accurate. The protesters felt they gained much sympathy as a result of their treatment at the meeting. Two television reporters appeared to consider the protesters unruly, but another described them as peaceful, and one anchor reported that his station had received calls from people watching the meeting on city cable 5 who thought the council were "running roughshod" over the protesters. The language of the newspaper account was more balanced; characterizations of parties' actions were clearly labeled as specific people's opinions.[73]

There were many other attempts by project opponents, some carefully planned, to use media coverage to some advantage. The Lance Hills Coalition staged a hayride and balloon release for television coverage. Television news stories showed the rural beauty of the area. Children of the coalition's members formed an organization called Kids Against Ruining the Environment (KARE); the active role of the children in the event added a human interest aspect to the story. There was also a political angle, because Sheri Barnard, the opponents' only supporter on the city council, was there. The hayride traveled to the potential ash landfill site at Lance Hills, where the balloon release took place. The balloon release presented a colorful visual supplement for television coverage and was described as a demonstration of where the winds would carry ash if an ash landfill were sited at Lance Hills.

As the winds carried the balloons toward Spokane, participants explained that people in the path of the balloons should be aware that although the site might seem far from them, they could still be directly affected by it.

Project opponents also aggressively sought opportunities to obtain lower-level media access to the general citizenry. Their repeated appearance at city council meetings was motivated in part by the live coverage of those meetings on local cable channel 5. They regularly sent letters to the editors of the local papers — especially the *Spokesman-Review*. They also ran radio ads, appeared on local radio and television news and talk shows, and produced their own public access television shows.

Some attempts to use the media were afterthoughts or secondary aspects of an event. Although it received significant television coverage, the idea of inviting media to the recording session did not even occur to the participants until after it had begun. When Grove Road Neighbors held a forum at a nearby school auditorium, they did not arrange the event specifically for television coverage, but they cooperated with the cameras when they appeared.

Local government officials also worked for advantageous media coverage. They hired public relations firms to assist them in that endeavor. Alliance Pacific, for example, did much to increase awareness of the most popular aspect of the new solid waste management system — recycling. But government officials' efforts went beyond direct advertising approaches. When SWDP invited opponents to join them on a trip to Massachusetts to see a Wheelabrator incinerator in operation, media coverage of the trip was carefully orchestrated. Following close on the heels of the council meeting where police had been posted and the singing testifier had been escorted out of the chambers, the trip was portrayed as a goodwill gesture by SWDP. In the television coverage of their return to Spokane, the travelers were pictured coming off the plane together, and SWDP Assistant Director Damon Taam was shown saying that the purpose of the trip had not been to change minds but to establish better communication and a better information base.

Local officials also approached media representatives directly in attempts to influence their coverage of the issue. A critical story by Karen Dorn Steele on some aspect of the project was often followed by a meeting between local government officials and the *Spokesman-Review* editorial board. By occasionally following such a meeting with an editorial showing their continued support of the project, the board was able to maintain good relations with local government officials (and with local business boosters of the project). At the same time, they continued to support their reporters' critical work, thus retaining a claim to balanced coverage.

The more heated the public discussion became, the more central was the media and the media's framing of it. Moran describes it thus: "As the public debate deepened, the groups . . . reacted again and again to various news reports. The reaction became the news focus, rather than 'the facts' behind the response. The media coverage began to define the rhetorical frame."[74] When SWDP began to run radio ads promoting the safety and economy of the project, the newspaper carried a story on opponents' claims that the ads were misleading.[75] When work was to begin on the waste-to-energy plant site, the newspaper ran a companion story on the "never say die" response of the opposition. Similarly, on the second page of the story about the police-guarded, singing-testimony council meeting, the newspaper ran another article covering a press conference with a consultant who was brought to town by SWDP to assure citizens that the ash from the waste-to-energy incinerator would be safe.[76]

This pattern of a primary story followed by a response was even more evident as the solid waste policy issue merged with election politics. When mayoral candidate Sheri Barnard held a press conference to announce her first specific alternative to the waste-to-energy project, all three local television stations packaged that story with coverage of her opponent's response. The newspaper did not finish the first sentence of its story on her announcement before offering her opponent's description of it as a "politically expedient 11th hour plan."[77] When there was a court hearing on Wheelabrator's failure to register as a contractor in the state of Washington, coverage of it was packaged with coverage of a press conference with Commissioner Randy Franke of Marion County, Oregon, who told how well the waste incinerator in Salem was operating. Later, when the judge ruled that Wheelabrator did need to register, television news packaged that story with one on a consultant's report that it would cost at least $57 million to terminate the waste-to-energy project. In 1990, when council member Joel Crosby was testing the waters for a possible run against county commissioner Pat Mummey, a newspaper story preceding the press conference at which Crosby was to outline his proposal for a yard-waste composting program featured critical responses to the content, style, and timing of his proposal by several officials.[78]

And the story-response pattern remained part of the reporters' approach well after the project's heyday as an important election issue. In 1991 the newspaper concluded a story based on a press conference at which

SWDP director Phil Williams touted the waste-to-energy facility as a "one-stop garbage emporium" with a recap of two arguments by opponents against the facility.[79]

Occasionally, the media used a human interest angle to make a story seem relevant to viewers and readers. Channel 4 featured a story on a family living next to a potential ash landfill site. The camera showed shots portraying the rural lifestyle, including livestock and a creek running through the property. The newspaper carried two articles about a family who had spent three years building their dream house and had only lived in it three months before SWDP announced their intention to build a compost facility bordering on their property. Although they estimated the value of their home at $150,000, the family eventually decided to sell the house and their 4.4 acres to the city for $112,600 plus $8,000 for moving expenses.[80]

As mentioned earlier, this type of human interest angle is a formatting technique commonly used by the media. But their most repeated formatting technique was the battle-between-antagonists story line. It became such a part of the dynamics of the public discussion that government, the public, and even active citizens themselves came to think of themselves as opponents. Certainly, the character of this mediated world of public policy discourse is partly the result of the media's attempt to provide balanced presentations. Covering a SWDP press conference and then asking Citizens for Clean Air for a response creates balance by presenting two opposing views, but it also creates a perception of the dispute as wholly constituted of two opposing views. There are often more than two views on an issue; but a spectrum of opinion is, at best, only infrequently presented by the media. It may be that limiting media presentations to two views is justifiable as a function of the degree of sophistication the media's audience will tolerate. In presenting a more complex view of issues, the media might risk losing their audience. But repetition of the format fosters an unsophisticated "us versus them" view of the world. In trying to keep their audience's attention, the media participate in creating a simplistic understanding of the issues.

PARTICIPANTS' EVALUATIONS OF THE IMPACT OF THE MEDIA

The influence of the media's framing of the story was a source of irritation for SWDP officials. One was disturbed that the media were not objective in their reporting: "I thought their job was to . . . report the news, report it objectively, try to give the reader some sense of events that they would not otherwise get." He felt that the media generally made it more difficult to adopt policies and build a program. Rather than supporting public initiatives, he saw the media as inciting opponents.[81]

The media's need for drama also bothered this official. Realizing that they used drama to make things seem newsworthy, he complained that the drama never favored SWDP's goals. In a related complaint, he noted that in trying to make it tie in with their audience's personal lives, the media often make the news appear frightening.

The impact of this simplification on coverage of the issue also troubled SWDP officials. As another study reported, SWDP Public Information Officer Ann Baylor and Assistant Director Damon Taam felt that the media misconstrued the technical aspects of the project.[82]

SWDP officials were frustrated by the media's frame but knew they had to depend on the media to communicate to the public. They recognized that without the media the public would know nothing about the project. Project officials dealt with this frustrating dependence in several ways. SWDP "attempted to advance the education of the public through additional seminars, hearings, interviews, and most of all, through reliance on the media to spread the word on the project."[83]

They also manipulated media coverage by directly contacting organizations and reporters perceived to be friendly to the project. In addition to addressing their concerns to editors, they identified sympathetic reporters and deliberately gave them an exclusive story, or the first opportunity to report a breaking story. Reporters who were perceived as antagonistic were given information through the slower, formal channels.

SWDP also hired Alliance Pacific, a local public relations firm, to package advertisements and public information presentations.[84] SWDP attempted to put their preferred "spin" on information presented to the public. In one particularly heated period, they ran a series of radio ads and held weekly press briefings.[85]

City officials also recognized that the coverage of city council meetings by city cable channel 5 played a surprisingly large role in influencing public opinion. They scheduled meeting agendas so that presentations by SWDP officials, consultants, or prospective contractors that favored the project consumed most of the prime-time hours. When Sheri Barnard objected to this format, she was told that opponents needed to wait till the proposal had been presented and defended before they could make their objections — protesting a proposal that had not yet been explained would be like putting the cart before the horse. The officials' control of the agenda also often meant that local news crews, in order to meet their deadlines, had departed before much of the opponents' testimony was presented.

But city officials did not perceive these steps as having adequately countered the impact of the opposition. So, in a further response to the way opponents of the project were using city cable channel 5, city officials organized shows of support at the meetings by former city council members and by members of local unions.[86] When opponents tried to respond to the presentation by former council members, the mayor told them they would not be allowed to comment. When one opponent insisted on talking, the mayor called a recess.

Opponents of the project also found themselves in a love-hate relationship with the media. They realized that to obtain media attention they had to fit within the frames used by the media to select stories for coverage. It was also clear that regular attention from the media had a legitimizing effect from which they benefited. When they could no longer command regular attention from the media, they saw that the trendiness of media attention worked to their advantage as long as the solid waste battle was hot news, but not when they were no longer "the flavor of the month."

Like the project officials, opponents found the media's interest in drama rather than "dry facts" disturbing. They also recognized that the media's desire to make their stories relevant to their audience led them to prefer interviews with the "nonpolished, average Joe." That hampered opponents' efforts to inform the public.

Not having as much experience as government officials in dealing with the media, opponents were more intimidated by reporters. Rather than thinking about how to avoid or use sound bites to their advantage, they were more concerned that they not "sound stupid." Opponents were also painfully aware of the power editing can have to color one's statements. They worried about the ability of a reporter to attribute a statement to them without including a direct quotation and thus significantly misrepresenting their statement.

Both sides agreed on three aspects of the media's impact on solid waste policy making. First, both were surprised at the widespread impact of city cable channel 5's live coverage of city council meetings. Neither side expected that so many people would watch the coverage. When they received numerous comments from people who had watched, they gained respect for the potential of that coverage to affect public opinion.

Second, they agreed that there were significant differences among television, radio, and the print media. Local radio coverage was most susceptible to manipulation — both sides found that the local radio stations were much more likely to read a press release precisely as it was sent to them than were either television or the newspaper. The two radio stations that devoted the most time to news, KPBX public radio and KXLY news radio, did not have enough staff to do much firsthand news gathering. Television would respond to convenient, visually interesting activities, but would significantly edit the material prior to airing it. The print media were least likely to use press releases to guide their stories and most determined to control their own story lines.

Finally, both sides described specific reporters as biased. SWDP officials considered Karen Dorn Steele a thorn in their side; project opponents felt she could be trusted to present their story in a favorable light. Conversely, opponents considered channel 6 reporter Hugh Imhoff biased in favor of the project, and SWDP officials thought his stories were fairly presented.

CONCLUSIONS

The ability to control the definition of a situation is an important kind of social and political power, so the significance of our media culture for public understanding of the problems involved in public policy making is difficult to overestimate. It is also virtually impossible to measure with any precision. Because we are all part of the media culture, we cannot attain an objective viewpoint from which to assess the impact of the media.

Nonetheless, it is clear that the impact of the media on our attempts to resolve problems almost guaranteed to attract media and public attention — problems like solid waste management — is substantial. The media's framing of the public discourse has complicated, multidirectional impacts. There are, however, three ways the media impacted solid waste policy making in Spokane that stand out from the rest.

First, without the media there would have been little substantive public discussion of Spokane's solid waste management options. What public discussion there was without media coverage would have been limited to a dialogue among only the most active citizens. The vital role of the news media in our democracy was recognized in the First Amendment to the Constitution, and its singular importance in fostering and sharing public discussion among the general populace is no small matter. This is no less true in solid waste policy making than in other public policy making.

Second, because solid waste policy making involves significant complex, technical elements, the tendency of the media to simplify is particularly problematic. Both proponents and opponents of the project expressed concern about the way the media's drive to simplify the issue for their audience distorted their presentation of information. Still, it must be admitted that the media may know better than others at what level to present policy issues for public consideration. Their livelihood depends on understanding their audience. It is easier to be dissatisfied with the level of discussion found in the news media than to suggest practical ways in which the media might increase the level of complexity without losing a significant portion of the attentive audience.

Third, driven by their need to simplify, to dramatize, and to make their stories relevant to the audience, the media selected an environmentalist — rural dweller versus government — urban interest story line to make sense of developments. Although the media did not create those lines of division, they did much to reify and magnify them. Whether participants in the debate wanted to be portrayed in that light or not, they found the story line nearly impossible to transcend. Thus they became participants in polarizing their community, and most of them were drawn into the us/them dynamic.

An overall effect of the last two impacts of the media was to reduce a complex public policy issue, and the people engaged in the public discourse about it, to a good-versus-evil dichotomy. Consequently, it became more difficult for the community to reach an accord on how to deal with solid waste. Moreover, it created divisions within the community that transcended the solid waste policy issue, and those divisions have since made it more difficult to reach accord on other public policy issues.

Democratic policy making in a large and complex country such as the United States cannot be accomplished without the widespread sharing of information and viewpoints made possible by the electronic and print media. Without a doubt, the media are a vital element in the solid waste policy-making system. They are responsible for carrying the public policy discussion beyond the most active participants and providing a basis upon which members of the general public may make up their minds as to which policy they prefer. It is an important role, and one the various kinds of media play with varying impact. Radio demands very little of its audience, thus making it exceedingly easy for the audience to profit from its broadcasts. Television can be listened to like radio, but to get the full impact of the medium's format, the audience must also watch it. Television differs from radio in its ability to present images that accompany the auditory information, and those images significantly affect its impact on viewers. Newspapers demand more concentrated attention from their audience and therefore are able to provide greater substance and greater detail.

With such a variety of news sources, the information available to the general public is quantitatively high and qualitatively diverse. As I have demonstrated, the dissemination of information via the media nonetheless remains imperfect, and its impact on a governance activity such as solid waste policy making is problematic. It seems that our dependence on the media makes their imperfections more difficult to tolerate. Solid waste policy making seemed messy enough without this further complication.

Conclusion

The systems model described in chapter 2 represents a conception of the more significant elements and dynamics involved in American solid waste policy making. It is difficult to understand such a complex system without some way of organizing one's thinking about it, but the order of the model necessarily exceeds the order found in the phenomena it is used to depict. As I point out in chapter 2, a systems model is an artificial construct, but in that very artificiality lies its ability to help one organize one's thoughts. At the same time, it creates a semblance of order, the model also honors the complex interrelatedness of all its elements.

The Spokane-Rathdrum aquifer provides an example of this interrelatedness. As an ecological factor with which solid waste policy must deal, it is located in the model under "Local Ecology." Recognizing the protection of a sole-source aquifer as an ecological limitation on the placement of solid waste facilities was officially authorized by Congress under Section 208 of the Federal Water Pollution Control Act. Under the partial preemption approach to intergovernmental relations, administration of federal guidelines and standards was delegated to state and local governments. In Washington State, WDOE was identified as the lead agency in implementing the FWPCA. Spokane County revised its zoning code, adding a chapter specifically addressing protection of the Spokane-Rathdrum aquifer. Within Spokane County government, the Engineering Department was authorized to run the Section 208 aquifer protection program. As a result of the aquifer protection program, SWDP's waste-to-energy plant (built and operated by Wheelabrator), its composting operation (run by O. M. Scott), all of the in-county potential ash landfill sites, and the independent composting operation run by the local business, Ecocycle, were all located outside the aquifer protection zone.

The interrelatedness of the elements in the system can also be seen by tracing the connections between the local media and the rest of the system. Local interest groups such as Citizens for Clean Air worried about and consciously worked on how the local media presented their views. They cultivated relationships with individual reporters who appeared sympathetic to their cause. They appeared on radio and television talk shows. They presented testimony before the city council, with attention to the cable television audience. Businesses also utilized the local media. Wheelabrator in particular purchased advertising in the midst of the 1989 election campaign. WMX purchased sponsorships on the local public radio station. Local government's connections with local media ranged from mediated relations resulting from their hiring Alliance Pacific to improve their public relations, to direct relations such as giving specific reporters exclusive stories, holding press conferences, and meeting with the *Spokesman-Review*'s editorial board to complain about reports they considered biased. Most of the connection between the local news media and the state or federal government derived from news coverage of events related to local solid waste policy. Media-covered events included legislative hearings, the passage of legislation, administrative rule making, and judicial decisions. The national media organizations' connection to local media consisted predominantly of information feeds picked up by the local media, but it was also true that some local stories were picked up by national publications such as *USA Today*. Moreover, as I argue in chapter 8, the impact of the media on public policy making goes beyond the impact of specific organizations and into the cultural realm. Because solid waste policy became a topic of interest locally, the local media also monitored and reported relevant stories about national businesses such as WMX and national interest groups such as the Environmental Defense Fund and the Citizens' Clearinghouse for Hazardous Wastes.

Though I treat local government and state and federal relations in separate chapters, the connections among local, state, and federal government actions are numerous and multifaceted. In solid waste policy making, the federal government's entry into the arena has reduced the traditional autonomy of local governments in managing their solid waste and increased the role of state governments. The federal requirement for comprehensive solid waste management plans means that states, counties, cities, and small towns must all participate in their development. In the Spokane area, this has led to a complex set of interlocal agreements and to special districts with boards of directors whose overlapping memberships would be described as interlocking directorates if they were found in studies of private companies.

The entrance of the federal government into the solid waste arena has enhanced the interdependence among governments, both vertically and horizontally.

Including political culture as an enveloping element in the political system symbolizes the more subtle ways in which the elements of the system are interrelated. Though it is an unusual feature to include in a systems model, it is important to explicitly recognize the ubiquitous impact of political culture to understand why elements in the system behave as they do. Including political culture in the model and applying the model to a case study enable us to include temporal and contextual dynamics that are often missing from systems analysis. Inclusion of political culture in this model implies that Spokane's solid waste policy making took place in a context of history and values that is unique to Spokane in its particular manifestations but in general structure and flavor is common to much of the United States. The tensions among the value preferences found in Elazar's individualist, moralist, and traditionalist political cultures are part of the nation's common experience, and the dominance of moralist and individualist cultures found in Spokane also characterizes most of the country. But the ways moralist and individualist values were expressed in Spokane's solid waste policy making were affected by its being part of the American West and were unique to Spokane.

The Proposition 4 story is a good example. Conflict between citizens and government officials over selection and siting of solid waste facilities is commonplace in the United States. In Spokane, that conflict took a particular shape partly as a result of the Progressive and populist elements in the community's history. The individualist strain of Spokane's political culture, with its roots in populism, had already provided for a citizen initiative mechanism in local governance. The moralist strain underlies a belief that local government should take proactive steps to serve the common interest of the community. Drawing on Progressive traditions, local governments cut through partisan and jurisdictional animosities and empowered a professionally staffed government agent (SWDP) to promote and develop a new way of managing solid waste. Opponents of the waste-to-energy project appealed to the individualist element, contending that government should not adopt such a grand scheme without first directly requesting permission from the citizens. In resolving the dispute, the Washington State Supreme Court sided with the late twentieth-century Progressives, but paid homage to the populists in its insistence on assuming that the citizens in drafting and passing Proposition 4 were cognizant of the distinction between taxes and government-imposed fees for services. Only a powerful confidence in the intelligence of the general populace could inspire an authentic belief in that assumption.

The government structures and mechanisms that lay the foundation for the specific manifestations of individualist-moralist tension in Spokane display the many ways in which political culture influenced their character. A review of the special districts will demonstrate this point. Both the Spokane County Health District (SCHD) and the Spokane County Air Pollution Control Authority (SCAPCA) represent attempts to create professionally run, politically insulated government bureaucracies to make and manage policies in technically complex areas. Government organizations of that sort derive from the Progressive Movement. Insulation from political affairs, one of the Progressive themes, was to be accomplished in these special districts by two structural mechanisms: First, each district, though its jurisdiction is coterminous with Spokane County, is separate from county government. The districts' authority comes from the state, not from the county. Second, each district is headed by a person who is educated in a technical field and is appointed to office, not elected. Expertise, not popularity, is the basis on which they hold office.

Still, the insulation is not very thick. Each district has a governing board composed of elected officials from jurisdictions within the boundaries of Spokane County. Since the boards have the power to hire and fire the districts' top officials, those officials cannot make decisions based only on technical grounds; they must also be cognizant of the political implications of their decisions, especially when those decisions have become public because of media coverage. So, for example, air pollution control officer Eric Skelton chose to accept the preference of his board when he did not exercise his authority to send a violation notice to SWDP for burning plastic pesticide containers from Canada. Similarly, SCHD's authority to oversee solid waste management in its jurisdiction has been constrained by staffing decisions that do not give solid waste a high priority and (one must assume) by health officer Dr. John Beare's recognition of the county commissioners' support for the waste-to-energy facility. His political acumen has led him along a course of action in overseeing solid waste management that has occasioned no significant controversies.

The character and dynamics of government-business interdependence in solid waste policy making also reflect the impact of political culture. In an individualistic political culture, government is viewed as a marketplace, so it makes sense that such a culture would depend on the economic marketplace, and/or on deliberately created markets, to implement many of its policies. The use of privatization and privatism in solid waste policy making is only a particular manifestation of that general inclination in the United States. National, state, and local decisions to use government for social and environmental regulation reflect the moralistic political culture, but administering the policies that follow from such a decision demonstrates that the individualistic political culture's influence remains strong. The mixture of the United States' two primary political cultures is evident in solid waste policy making in local government decisions that allow private companies to operate (and sometimes own) waste management facilities. It is also evident in the U.S. Supreme Court's judgment that solid waste services are an item of commerce and may not be structured in a way that interferes with interstate commerce without the express permission of Congress. In Spokane, effective implementation of solid waste policies depends, for better or worse, on the ability of private companies like Rabanco, Wheelabrator, and O. M. Scott to deliver the services they promise. In addition, the American West's traditional mistrust of large eastern corporations surfaced in citizens' reactions to their dependence on Wheelabrator, and their uneasiness was significantly exacerbated by Wheelabrator's relationship with WMX. This same mistrust was also heard in complaints about O. M. Scott's management of the compost facility.

Similarly, the character and dynamics of citizen participation in Spokane's solid waste policy making reflect a unique local mixture of the individualistic and moralistic political cultures. As members of the individualistic culture, people in Spokane believe that those who get involved in politics, particularly office holders, either are (or become in the process) "dirty." But they still believe strongly that it is every citizen's responsibility to become involved. In this mixture of seemingly incompatible beliefs, citizens who participate see themselves as virtuous antagonists battling the evil influences of professional politicians, bureaucratic government, and big business. Though political party coalitions may constitute a subterranean influence on the alliances formed, party cohesiveness is distinctly subordinate to principles and issues. Alliances in solid waste policy making in Spokane during this case study were based on beliefs about the wisdom of adopting a management strategy dependent on a waste-to-energy incinerator, not on party affiliation. In 1989, when national news media were decrying issueless campaigns all across America, Spokane held an election in which party affiliations, personalities, personal histories, and personal character were distinctly subordinate to the candidates' positions on the solid waste issue.

The blending of political culture and media culture have fascinating implications for the study of solid waste policy making. The news media are both a part and a disseminator of the values of our political culture. The individualistic cultural belief that the best government is limited government underlies the First Amendment's guarantee of freedom of the press. As a by-product of their watchdog role, and as a deliberate result of their portrayal of government officials as untrustworthy, the news media regularly promote this belief. In their watchdog role, the media are expected to view officials and their arguments skeptically, and we need an institution such as the press to play that role, but a by-product of that role is exacerbation of the political culture's inherent tendency to distrust government institutions and officials. When the news media portray citizen–government official confrontations as David versus Goliath battles, their framing of the story biases the audience toward identification with the citizen and antagonism toward the official.

Because the individualistic culture is mixed with the moralistic culture in most of the United States, we tend to believe both that politics is a dirty business and that politicians should remain clean. We tend both to expect people involved in political affairs to have moral failings, and to be shocked when we find that a particular politician or government official has succumbed to temptation. In their portrayal of politicians and government officials, the media participate in this cultural cognitive dissonance. And in broadcasting their corrupt politician story line, they extend the reach of that dissonance among members of our society. One way this dynamic plays out in solid waste policy making is demonstrated in our expectation that government officials do what they can to reduce the increased costs related to tougher standards for the management and disposal of solid waste, but when an official proposes to sell a municipal incinerator's services to companies attempting to dispose of tires, medical waste, plastic jugs, ink sludge, and so on, the media portray that official as seeking revenues without adequate regard for health and safety concerns — and the portrayal typically does not simply question the wisdom of the proposal, but also impugns the integrity of the official involved.

Because of the complex interplay among elements of the solid waste policy-making system, it would be intellectually lazy to suggest that any single element is to blame for the overall result. The media's role in this cultural dynamic is not that of creator or instigator, but that of participant and magnifier. The media did not create the tensions among our political culture values. They do, however, extend and enhance those tensions; and they do precious little toward resolving or even confronting them. Similarly, citizen activists can be faulted for so readily rejecting proposals without adequately participating in the creation of options that effectively address all facets of the problem. Popular components of solid waste policy like recycling, composting, and long-hauling delay the day of reckoning, but they do little to address the fundamental problem — the volume of waste that our way of life generates. Businesses may be charged with a kind of argumentative sleight-of-hand when they contend that the volume of waste *they* generate can best be addressed by convincing *consumers* to prefer less packaging, more environmentally benign products, and products using recycled materials. Government officials can be criticized for their unwillingness to listen to testimony about the negative consequences of an approach they favor. When officials are not open to contrary thought as they engage in public discussion of policy choices, they reduce the likelihood of making good decisions. Moving forward on a policy strategy should not require foreclosing discussion. In the American democracy, as a matter of practice, it cannot require such foreclosure. Policy-making systems in the United States include so many loci of authoritative decision making that it is virtually impossible to end the discussion — even after irreversible decisions have been made. The role of each element in the system includes both positive and negative aspects. Rather than trying to blame the problems in solid waste management on a single part of the system, we would be better served by recognizing the applicability of the view espoused by Walt Kelly's Pogo: "We have met the enemy, and he is us."

William Ruckelshaus has argued that solid waste management is "a fundamental ecological issue. It illustrates, perhaps more clearly than any other environmental problem, that we must change many of our traditional attitudes and habits."[1] As true as that statement was in 1972 (and still is today), such warnings have been sounded for almost a century. In 1907, Austin Bierbower, in an article entitled "American Wastefulness," warned: "Nowhere in the world is there such a waste of material as in this country. . . . Americans have not learned to save; and their wastefulness imperils their future. Our resources are fast giving out, and the next problem will be to make them last."[2] His statement remains an appropriate warning today. But if his words represent more than a nostalgic look back at a time when we could have done something to address the solid waste problem, one might reasonably conclude that with all its imperfections, the solid waste policy-making system, as it has evolved over the years, appears so far to have served us fairly well. Nonetheless, as Melosi concluded in 1981, "The knotty problem of how to curb the creation of waste still requires a mechanism of its own."[3]

Until that problem is effectively addressed, solid waste management will continue to deal mostly with volume reduction and disposal. In the early 1980s, much hope was placed on incineration as a technological fix to the volume problem. Incinerating garbage significantly reduces the volume that needs to be landfilled; but the incineration fix has run into practical and political problems. When Wheelabrator came to Spokane with their waste-to-energy technology, they spoke of the Spokane facility as their "beachhead" in the West. Though incineration was commonly used in New England and in the South, it had not been adopted by many western communities. Four years after establishing that beachhead, the Spokane facility remained the only Wheelabrator waste-to-energy plant in the West. Not only has there been a decline in interest in solid waste incineration in the West, but also the national resurgence of waste incineration technology has faltered. The number of operating incinerators in the United States was on the rise in the 1980s. In 1985 American municipalities contracted for 60 new plants, and in 1986 William Montrone, vice president at Paine Webber, Inc., predicted that "virtually every major city" would have a waste-to-energy facility within fifteen years.[4] But the resurgence peaked in 1991 at 171 plants. By 1993 the number had dropped to 162.[5]

The number of landfills operating in the United States has been declining since 1988, when there were around 8,000. In 1993, that number had dropped to 4,482, with another 978 potential closures by the spring of 1994.[6] Despite the decline in the number of landfills, solid waste management in the United States still depends largely on depositing waste on land sacrificed to that purpose. The old landfills are being replaced by larger, more technologically sophisticated landfills, but we have not discovered a way of ending, or even significantly reducing, our dependence on landfills.

Charles Lindblom describes the process of public policy making as "the science of muddling through."[7] In contrast to those who say the best way to make decisions is to prioritize our values, goals, and objectives, and then make decisions that fit with those priorities, Lindblom argues that as we make decisions, we incorporate our values and priorities within them. In solid waste policy, we have established priority lists that generally place waste reduction at the top, but in our decisions regarding what to do, and even more so in our implementation steps, waste reduction has not been given the emphasis that our priority lists imply. I think Lindblom would say that our decisions and our implementation steps are a better indication of our priorities than are our priority lists.

Our solid waste policy-making system is a complex web of interconnected elements. In the results of their interplay we discover what the priorities of our communities and our society really are. Though a particular community's priorities may be overwhelmed by greater forces within our society, notable variations remain among the solid waste management approaches of local communities. Our system places a high value on the freedom of communities to try different ways of approaching the same problem. Still, as the Supreme Court has noted in its Commerce Clause decisions, the basic economic unit in this country is the nation. With the entrance of the federal government into policy areas such as solid waste policy — Tip O'Neill's claim that "All politics is local" notwithstanding — the basic political unit now is also the nation. From the local perspective, solid waste policy making includes many political, social, and economic forces that are beyond the control of local agents — but not entirely beyond their influence. The interconnectedness of the system means that no element can escape the impact of the values, priorities, and actions of other elements within the system — and vice versa.

If we return to the basic political questions asked by public policy theorists and apply them to solid waste policy making, we may conclude that the answer to the question "Who rules?" is "No one does." In this system, no one element has sufficient power to control the system's overall response to a given problem. To the question "Who governs?" the answer is "Everyone does." In this system, everyone is interconnected, so even those who think they are choosing not to participate are, by that decision, affecting the manner in which we govern ourselves and the solutions our governance develops for the problems it faces. To the question "Who benefits?" one might answer, "Almost everyone, and no one." In order to answer the question properly, one must include a time dimension. If we consider the short run, then "Almost everyone" is a defensible answer. In putting off dealing with the true costs of the environmental degradation that solid waste represents, businesses show quarterly profits, governments evade the need to increase taxes (or other revenue enhancing mechanisms), and the general public delays paying the lower market prices, tipping fees, taxes, and time and energy expenditures, and so on, that would result from generating a sustainable level of solid waste. If the answer considers the long run, then it is clear that when the bill on our solid waste credit card comes due, none of us will feel like beneficiaries of the American twentieth-century solid waste policy-making system. To my question, "How well does the system serve the community?" the answer to the "Who benefits?" question serves as an initial response, but there is more to be said. Looking at the brighter side, one can argue that the system served the community well enough to allow the people of Spokane to continue to struggle with problems that were identified long ago, but not so well as to allow Spokanites the luxury of a real solution to the solid waste problem. No matter how well the system serves a community, it will not be able to overcome the need to struggle with problems that are fundamental aspects of our living on planet earth. Solid waste is certainly one of those problems, and I hope we shall be fortunate enough to continue struggling with it for a very long time.

I said in my introduction that this book would not be an attempt to evaluate the available policy options, so in answering the question of how well the system served the community in this case, I have not treated the related question, "Did the system result in Spokane selecting the best policy option?" Even if I wanted to, I could not answer that question with much certainty. Solid waste is a messy problem that appears to have no workable, clean, and safe solution. Building an approach to solid waste management that depends on a waste-to-energy facility means obtaining the advantages *and* disadvantages inherent in such an approach. The volume of waste that requires landfilling is reduced, but the volume of air pollution in the area is increased. Some of the energy value of the waste is captured and "recycled," but many other potential values are lost forever. Long-hauling the ash (and overflow raw garbage) to a distant landfill reduces the impact of disposal on one local ecology, but displaces it to another local ecology. Overall, given the context of its decisions, I think the system enabled Spokane to select a defensible approach to solid waste management. It could have been better; it could have been worse. It will surely continue to be adjusted, and I hope the people of Spokane will at least continue to muddle through.

Spokane's ability to do so, however, depends on many factors beyond its control. Federal and state involvement in solid waste policy making have significantly changed the relations and the dynamics among the elements of the solid waste policy-making system. Federal pressure to reduce the volume of solid waste deposited in landfills and state financial assistance played key roles in Spokane's decision to build a waste-to-energy facility. The Supreme Court's declaration that solid waste management and disposal is commerce and thus accorded the protection of the Commerce Clause increases the power of business to influence solid waste policy. Even without that decision, given the interdependence of public and private sector organizations in implementing solid waste policy, Spokane (indeed, any community in the nation) cannot autonomously decide what it will do about its solid waste problem. Compared to the system of the first half of the twentieth century, the current solid waste policy-making system has enhanced and increased our interdependence. The foreseeable future appears likely to continue that trend, and that means we are all in this together.

Muddling through may no longer be good enough. It is quite likely that the existing dynamics in the system cannot be sustained in the long run. Citizens need to play a more creative role in addressing solid waste problems. Businesses need to discontinue practices that create unnecessary waste. The media need to focus more on communicating the news so as to advance understanding and contribute to a search for common ground. Local, state, and federal governments need to recall that when it's time for a decision, they are expected to listen to all who wish to be heard and are authorized to make decisions that promote the public interest. The solid waste policy-making system will never operate in an ideal fashion, but if those who are part of the system recognize both their interdependence with all the other parts of the system and their role in making the system work for the communities it serves, we will have a much better chance of dealing with solid waste problems in a democratic and sustainable fashion.

NOTES

INTRODUCTION
1. Debra Wishik Englander, "What You Want a City to Offer," *Money*, September 1990, 93.

1. THE SPOKANE STORY
1. League of Women Voters of Spokane, *Solid Waste Study: Spokane and Spokane County* (Spokane, Wash.: League of Women Voters of Spokane, 1978), 9.

2. Glen Yake, Director Public Works and Utilities, and Dr. Hampton Trayner, Health Officer for the City of Spokane, "Presentation to the Washington State Pollution Control Commission," November 17, 1966, 2; copy in author's possession.

3. Spokane County "208" Program, *Spokane Aquifer Water Quality Management Plan* (Spokane: County Engineer's Office, 1979).

4. Spokane County Engineer's Office, *Spokane Aquifer Cause and Effect Report* (1978, with 1983 update) and *Spokane Aquifer Water Quality Management Plan* (1979).

5. James D. Kerstetter and Eric Schlorff, *Municipal Solid Waste To Energy: Analysis of a National Survey* (Olympia: Washington State Energy Office, June 1987).

6. Morrison-Knudsen, *Spokane Municipal Waste To Energy Project. Phase One: Preliminary Analysis of Scenarios* (1984), 1; report prepared for the city of Spokane and in the files of the Spokane Regional Solid Waste Disposal Project Office, 808 W. Spokane Falls Blvd., Spokane, WA, 99201.

7. See Revised Code of Washington, sec. 43.99F.

8. Parametrix, Inc., *Spokane County Comprehensive Solid Waste Management Plan Update, 1984* (Spokane: Spokane County Utilities Department, July 1984).

9. Glen Yake says that he had advised project officials prior to his retirement from city service in April 1985 that Kaiser was not interested in cooperating with the project.

10. Jim Camden, "Garbage Plant Site, Pollution Worry Citizens," *Spokesman-Review*, 17 April 1986, A6.

11. *City of Spokane v. Citizens for Clean Air*, 54765–3 Washington State Supreme Court 7 (1988).

12. Ibid., 8. The referendum explicitly mentioned the waste-to-energy facility, but the court found that it did not apply to that facility. See chapter 5.

13. This list of actions is compiled from the chronology in Curt Messex, *Fallout from the Spokane Incinerator*, 3rd rev. ed. (Spokane: Marciel Publications, 1989).

14. Ted Pankowski, "Incineration Ignites Controversy in Spokane," *Washington Environmental Council Alert!* March–April 1989, 1.

15. Letter from Christine Gregoire, Director of WDOE, to Spokane Mayor Vicki McNeill and Spokane County Commissioner John McBride, 22 December 1988.

16. Century West Engineering, "Residue Facility Siting Analysis," June 1988; report prepared for the city of Spokane and in the files of the Spokane Regional Solid Waste Disposal Project Office.

17. The development of emission standards for the incinerator was detailed in several stories in the *Spokesman-Review*: Karen Dorn Steele, "Burner Permit Approved, Emissions Limit Reduced," 31 January 1989, and "Emissions Standards Relaxed," 1 March 1989; Mike Prager, "Incinerator Issue Far from Settled," 28 June 1989. The information from the second Steele article was clarified and supplemented by personal communication with Eric Skelton, Control Officer at SCAPCA, 17 June 1994. As of this writing, the dioxin limit had not been revised, but SCAPCA was beginning the process. EPA was prepared to propose on 1 September 1994 a 0.5-nanogram limit for dioxin. The limit should have been set by September 1995, to be effective September 1996.

18. Kelle R. Vigeland (environmental engineer at SCAPCA), letter to Phil Williams, 27 August 1993.

19. Karen Dorn Steele, "City Gets Smelly Messages," *Spokesman-Review*, 14 February 1989, B1.

20. Rick Bonino, "Trash Burner Foes March on City Hall," *Spokesman-Review*, 7 March 1989, B1.

21. Rick Bonino, "Group Seeks Council Recall," *Spokane Chronicle*, 15 March 1989, A1; "Challenge to Boeing Plant Criticized," *Spokesman-Review*, 23 March 1989, A1; Mike Prager, "Incinerator Foes Fighting $60 Million Grant," *Spokesman-Review*, 17 March 1989, B1.

22. Jim Camden, "A City Divided: 'Bloody' Election Matches in Store," *Spokesman-Review*, 2 April 1989, A15.

23. Karen Dorn Steele, "Incinerator Issue 'Like a Cancer,' " *Spokesman-Review*, 20 August 1989, A1.

24. Karen Dorn Steele, "Independent Burner Report Touches Nerve," *Spokesman-Review*, 26 June 1989, A1, A5.

25. Larry Shook, "Risking Spokane" (Spokane: Sunshine Publishing, 1989), 6.

26. Jim Correll, "Waste-to-Energy Works," July 1989, 2, 4; copy in author's possession.

27. "Burner's Cancellation Would Make No Sense," *Spokesman-Review*, 5 November 1989, A18.

28. Karen Dorn Steele, "Heyer Point Site Is Recommended for Ash Landfill," *Spokesman-Review*, 9 January 1990, B1, B3; Seattle-Northwest Securities Corporation, "Economic Evaluation of Ash and Bypass Waste Landfill Alternatives," January 1990; report prepared for the city of Spokane and in the files of the Spokane Regional Solid Waste Disposal Project Office.

29. Karen Dorn Steele, "Garbage Firms Bring Rivalry to Spokane," *Spokesman-Review*, 25 June 1990, A1, A4.

30. Karen Dorn Steele, "City Staff Recommends Firm to Haul Ash, Trash," *Spokesman-Review*, 2 June 1990, A1, A5; "Rabanco Chosen to Haul Incinerator Ash," *Spokesman-Review*, 26 June 1990, A1, A5.

31. Julie Sullivan, "Site for Spokane Ash Disposal Runs Into Environmental Snag," *Spokesman-Review*, 18 July 1990, B1–2; Karen Dorn Steele, "Judge Halts Rabanco's Regional Landfill Work," *Spokesman-Review*, 12 September 1990, B1; "Oregon Landfill Site Next in Line for Ash," *Spokesman-Review*, 13 September 1990, B1–2; "Landfill Lawsuit Dismissed," *Spokesman-Review*, 8 June 1991, A8.

32. Resource Conservation Consultants, "What Is Recycling's Role in Managing the Spokane Region's Solid Waste?" Portland, Ore., report prepared for the city of Spokane and in the files of the Spokane Regional Solid Waste Disposal Project Office, June 1987. Opponents of the project were later to argue that the 31 percent goal was too low and that the project underemphasized the potential for waste reduction and recycling. In 1989 the state of Washington set a goal of 50 percent recycling by 1995.

33. Karen Dorn Steele, "Advisory Board Favors Voluntary Recycling," *Spokesman-Review*, 22 November 1988, B1.

34. Mike Prager, "City's Recycling Program Will Start Next Month," *Spokesman-Review*, 18 September 1990, B1.

35. "County Moving Toward Recycling," *Spokesman-Review*, 23 April 1991, B2.

36. Mike Prager, "City Recycling Picks Up Acceptance," *Spokesman-Review*, 18 November 1990, B1–2; Karen Dorn Steele, "Incinerator Can't Keep Up with Trash," *Spokesman-Review*, 6 May 1993, A1, A5.

37. Steele, "Incinerator Can't Keep Up with Trash."

38. Beverly Vorpahl, "Program Generates Flood of Questions," *Spokesman-Review*, 9 October 1990, B1, B3.

39. Prager, "City Recycling Picks Up Acceptance."

40. Kristina Johnson, 1992, "Composting Facility Opposed," *Spokesman-Review*, 3 December 1992, D13; Kara Briggs, "City to Buy Composting Area Homes," *Spokesman-Review*, 23 September 1993, D11.

41. Jim Lynch, "Officials Back Competition in Composting," *Spokesman-Review*, 3 September 1992, A1; Bruce Krasnow, "County Backs Composting Site," *Spokesman-Review*, 23 June 1993, B1; Kristina Johnson, "Compost Battle Continues," *Spokesman-Review*, 16 February 1993, A6; Karen Dorn Steele, "Compost's Stink Upsets Residents," *Spokesman-Review*, 2 August 1994, B1.

42. Kristina Johnson, "Heap of Controversy," *Spokesman-Review*, 25 May 1995, D9; "Compost Plant Gets Ultimatum," *Spokesman-Review*, 20 June 1995, B1; "City Council Votes to Shut Compost Plant," *Spokesman-Review*, 8 August 1995, B1; "City Council May Reverse Vote to Close Compost Plant," *Spokesman-Review*, 12 August 1995, B1, B6; "Council Reopens Composting Plant," *Spokesman-Review*, 29 August 1995, B1, B6; Karen Dorn Steele, "Officials Knee-Deep in Compost Trouble," *Spokesman-Review*, 6 June 1995, A1, A7; Tom Sowa, "For Some Compost Plant Will Never Wash," *Spokesman-Review*, 12 August 1995, B1, B6.

43. John Craig, "Siting of Ash Facility by Wells Has Airway People Worried," *Spokesman-Review*, 18 October 1990, S6.

44. Karen Dorn Steele, "Burner Fines Could Boost Garbage Bills," *Spokesman-Review*, 29 August 1991, A1.

45. Karen Dorn Steele, "Trash Incinerator Gets Final Tests," *Spokesman-Review*, 8 September 1991, A1, A10.

46. Karen Dorn Steele, "Burn Without Permits, Two Councilmen Urge," *Spokesman-Review*, 31 August 1991, A1; Editorial, "In a Hurry to Burn," *Spokesman-Review*, 1 September 1991, A18; Rick Bonino, "Incinerator Fires Up 1st Load of Garbage," *Spokesman-Review*, 7 September 1991, A1.

47. Karen Dorn Steele, "Trash Incinerator Gets Final Tests," *Spokesman-Review*, 8 September 1991, A1.

48. Rick Bonino, "Wheelabrator May Hold Off on Penalties," *Spokesman-Review*, 4 September 1991, A1.

49. Mike Prager, "Incinerator Tests Violated Contract, Critics Say," *Spokesman-Review*, 4 December 1991, B1, B3.

50. Tom Sowa, "Incinerator Receives Go-Ahead to Seek Medical Waste Contract," *Spokesman-Review*, 12 May 1992, B2.

51. Mike Prager, "Council Not Ready to OK Tire Burning," *Spokesman-Review*, 6 October 1992, B1; Karen Dorn Steele, "Plan to Burn Old Tires Rolls into Council's Lap," *Spokesman-Review*, 20 June 1993, B1–2; "Council Set to Reconsider Vote on Tire Incineration," *Spokesman-Review*, 19 December 1993, B1–2; John Craig, "Council Backs Burning Tires at Incinerator," *Spokesman-Review*, 13 July 1993, B1.

52. Jim Lynch, "Incinerator Costs Higher than Expected," *Spokesman-Review*, 27 December 1992, A1, A14.

53. Jim Lynch, "New Limits Could Add to Plant Costs," *Spokesman-Review,* 27 December 1992, A14.

54. "With Incinerator at Limit, Redouble Recycling Effort," editorial, *Spokesman-Review,* 4 January 1993, A10.

55. Karen Dorn Steele, "Incinerator Can't Keep Up with Trash," *Spokesman-Review,* 6 May 1993, A1, A5, "Trash Continues to Outstrip Waste Burner," *Spokesman-Review,* 6 June 1993, B1–2.

56. Curt Messex, personal communication, 9 June 1994.

57. Karen Dorn Steele, "Plant Turns Sludge, Dust into Energy," *Spokesman-Review,* 26 February 1994, B1, B4; John Webster, "Decision to Burn Chemical Jugs Reeks," *Spokesman-Review,* 13 February 1994, A14.

58. The controversy surrounding the chemical jugs was covered in four *Spokesman-Review* articles by Karen Dorn Steele: "Pesticide Containers Incinerated," 8 February 1994, A1, A10, "Toxicity Test Data Requested," 17 February 1994, B1–2, "Lawyer: Incinerator Broke Rules," 14 April 1994, B1, B4; "Workshop on Waste Proposed," 8 March 1994, B2.

59. Mike Prager, "Garbage Rates to Continue to Rise, City Council Told," *Spokesman-Review,* 5 October 1993, B1–2.

60. *City of Chicago et al. v. Environmental Defense Fund et al.,* 92 US 1639 (1994).

61. *C & A Carbone, Inc. v. Town of Clarkstown, New York,* 92 US 1402 (1994).

62. Implications for Spokane of the two Supreme Court rulings were explored in Karen Dorn Steele, "Ash Ruling Likely to Raise Trash Rates," *Spokesman-Review,* 3 May 1994, A1, A4.

63. Bruce Krasnow, "Ash Treated to Cut Cost of Dumping," *Spokesman-Review,* 7 June 1994, B1, B2; Karen Dorn Steele, "Ash Treatment Process to Cost $12,000 a Month," *Spokesman-Review,* 2 August 1994, B2.

64. "EPA Tells Mayors: Smoke 'Em if You Got 'Em," *Spokesman-Review,* 26 January 1995, B3.

65. Jeanette White, "Trash Won't Be Diverted, Lawyer Says," *Spokesman-Review,* 18 May 1994, B1.

66. "Senate Passes Flow Control Bill on to the House," *P.A. [Public Administration] Times,* 1 June 1995, 3.

67. Mike Prager, "Landfill Cleanup Tops List," *Spokesman-Review,* 6 October 1991, A1.

68. Paul Read, "Northside Landfill Remediation Nearly Done," *Journal of Business Special Report: Environment and Ecology,* 22 October 1992, B9, B17.

69. Mike Prager, "Landfill Lid Bid $7 Million Below Estimate," *Spokesman-Review,* 17 March 1992, B2.

70. Ibid.

71. Bill Morlin, "County Stops Work on Cover for Old Landfill," *Spokesman-Review,* 9 September 1993, A1.

72. Dan Hansen, "Landfill Cap Put on Hold," *Spokesman-Review,* 29 July 1993, D12; Kevin Taylor, "County Considers Suing DOE Rather Than Cleaning Up Dump," *Spokesman-Review,* 22 March 1994, B1; "County Defies State Over Plan to Cover Dump," *Spokesman-Review,* 19 April 1994, B1–2.

73. Karen Dorn Steele, "Marshall Dump Looks Beyond County for Garbage," *Spokesman-Review,* 17 July 1991, B1–2; "Landfill Had Loads of Trouble," *Spokesman-Review,* 11 August 1991, A1, A10; Bruce Krasnow, "Marshall Landfill to Close," *Spokesman-Review,* 8 December 1991, B1–2.

74. Bruce Krasnow, "Panel Tells Marshall Landfill to Drop Plan for New Operation," *Spokesman-Review,* 24 April 1993, B1, B5; "County Rejects Plan to Open New Landfill at Closed Marshall Site," *Spokesman-Review,* 21 July 1993, B2.

75. Karen Dorn Steele, "Landfill Owners Want County Aid," *Spokesman-Review,* 22 June 1993, B2.

2. PUBLIC POLICY THEORY

1. David Ricci, *Community Power and Democratic Theory: The Logic of Political Analysis* (New York: Random House, 1971); Thomas R. Dye, *Understanding Public Policy*, 7th ed. (Englewood Cliffs, N.J.: Prentice-Hall, 1992); James E. Anderson, *Public Policy-Making*, 3rd ed. (New York: Holt, Rinehart and Winston, 1984); Christopher J. Bosso, *Pesticides and Politics: The Life Cycle of a Public Issue* (Pittsburgh, Pa.: University of Pittsburgh Press, 1987).

2. Ricci, *Community Power*, 206.

3. Ibid., 221, 219.

4. See for example Anselm Strauss and Juliet Corbin, *Basics of Qualitative Research: Grounded Theory Procedures and Techniques* (Newbury Park, Calif.: Sage Publications, 1990); Barney Glaser and Anselm Strauss, *The Discovery of Grounded Theory* (Chicago: Aldine, 1967); Barney Glaser, *Theoretical Sensitivity* (Mill Valley, Calif.: Sociology Press, 1978); Anselm Strauss, *Qualitative Analysis for Social Scientists* (New York: Cambridge University Press, 1987).

5. Jay White, "On the Growth of Knowledge in Public Administration," *Public Administration Review* 46 (1986), 16.

6. Robert K. Yin, *Case Study Research: Design and Methods*, rev. ed. (Newbury Park, Calif.: Sage Publications, 1989), 21.

7. Hugh Heclo, "Review Article: Policy Analysis," *British Journal of Political Science* 2 (1972), 104.

8. I am indebted to "naturalistic" researchers for the distinction between generalization and transferability. When combined with credibility, dependability, and confirmability, transferability provides a sound basis for others to judge the value of a naturalistic researcher's work. See for example David Erlandson et al., *Doing Naturalistic Inquiry: A Guide to Methods* (Newbury Park, Calif.: Sage Publications, 1993); Yvonna Lincoln and Egon Guba, *Naturalistic Inquiry* (Newbury Park: Sage Publications, 1985).

9. Ricci, *Community Power*, 206.

10. For a classic comparison of these two theories, see Charles Lindblom, "The Science of Muddling Through," *Public Administration Review* 19 (1959), 79–88. It has spawned a number of responses and follow-ups: Amitai Etzioni, "Mixed Scanning: A Third Approach to Decision-making," *Public Administration Review* 27 (1967), 385–92; Lindblom, "Still Muddling, Not Yet Through," *Public Administration Review* 39 (1979), 517–25; Michael Hayes, *Incrementalism and Public Policy* (New York: Longman, 1992).

11. See for example Mark E. Rushefsky, *Public Policy in the United States: Toward the Twenty-first Century* (Pacific Grove, Calif.: Brooks/Cole Publishing Co., 1990), 3.

12. Ricci, *Community Power*, 63.

13. Floyd Hunter, *Community Power Structure* (New York: Anchor Books, 1963).

14. C. Wright Mills, *The Power Elite* (New York: Galaxy, 1959), 11.

15. Jan G. Deutsch, "Neutrality, Legitimacy, and the Supreme Court: Some Intersections Between Law and Political Science," *Stanford Law Review* 20 (1968), 253–54, nn. 281, 283. Others have appropriated this metaphor without giving it quite the same meaning: Daniel Guttman and Barry Willner, *The Shadow Government* (New York: Pantheon Books, 1976).

16. Robert N. Bellah et al., *Habits of the Heart: Individualism and Commitment in American Life* (New York: Harper and Row, 1985).

17. Mills, *Power Elite*, 276, 294.

18. Bosso, *Pesticides*, 19, 256, 258–59.

19. Tom Koenig, "Business Support for Disclosure of Corporate Campaign Contributions: An Instructive Paradox," in *The Structure of Power in America: The Corporate Elite as a Ruling Class*, edited by Michael Schwartz (New York: Holmes and Meier, 1987), 84, 95. See also Yale Magrass, *Thus Spake the Moguls* (Boston: Shenkman, 1981).

20. Everett Carll Ladd, *The American Polity: The People and Their Government*, 5th ed. (New

York: Norton, 1993), B12; David B. Truman, *The Governmental Process: Political Interests and Public Opinion* (New York: Knopf, 1971).

21. Robert A. Dahl, *Who Governs? Democracy and Power in an American City* (New Haven, Conn.: Yale University Press, 1961); Robert A. Dahl, "Reply to Thomas Anton's 'Power, Pluralism and Local Politics,' " *Administrative Science Quarterly* (March 1963), 250–56.

22. Ricci, *Community Power,* 66.

23. Truman, *Governmental Process,* xx, 47.

24. Dahl, "Response to Anton," 254; emphasis in original.

25. Bosso, *Pesticides,* 4–5.

26. Robert A. Dahl, *A Preface to Democratic Theory* (Chicago: University of Chicago Press, 1956), 137.

27. Truman, *Governmental Process,* 448–51.

28. See for example Robert A. Dahl, *Democracy in the United States: Promise and Performance,* 4th ed. (Boston: Houghton Mifflin, 1981), chap. 26.

29. Truman, *Governmental Process,* 448–49.

30. Ibid., xxxvii.

31. E.E. Schattschneider, *The Semi-Sovereign People: A Realist's View of Democracy in America* (Hinsdale, Ill.: Dryden Press, 1960), 104; on political participation, see Sidney Verba and Norman Pie, *Participation in America* (New York: Harper and Row, 1972).

32. Bosso, *Pesticides,* 6.

33. Robert H. Salisbury, *Interests and Institutions: Substance and Structure in American Politics* (Pittsburgh, Pa.: University of Pittsburgh Press, 1992), xvii; for an excellent example of this dynamic, see R. McGreggor Cawley, *Federal Land, Western Anger: The Sagebrush Rebellion and Environmental Politics* (Lawrence, Kan.: University Press of Kansas, 1993), esp. chap. 3.

34. This description of intergroup relations as an exchange relationship should not be confused with the description of group-to-member relations as an exchange relationship. See for example Mancur Olson, *The Logic of Collective Action* (Cambridge: Harvard University Press, 1965); Robert Salisbury, "An Exchange Theory of Interest Groups," *Interests and Institutions,* 34. Salisbury's view of relations among interest groups describes them as part of a system.

35. Dennis Mueller, "Public Choice: A Survey," in *The Theory of Public Choice II,* edited by J. Buchanan and R. Tollison (Ann Arbor: University of Michigan Press, 1984), 23; Robert D. Tollison, "Involved Social Analysis," in *Theory of Public Choice: Political Applications of Economics,* edited by J. Buchanan and R. Tollison (Ann Arbor: University of Michigan Press, 1972), 4.

36. Tollison, "Social Analysis," 5.

37. See for example Buchanan and Tollison, eds., *Theory of Public Choice,* part 4: "Groups as Public Choosers."

38. Buchanan and Tollison, *Public Choice II,* 14.

39. Terry Moe, *The Organization of Interests: Incentive and the Internal Political Dynamics of Interest Groups* (Chicago: University of Chicago Press, 1980); "Toward a Broader View of Interest Groups," *Journal of Politics* 43 (1981), 531–43.

40. Truman, *Governmental Process,* 65.

41. Dahl, *Who Governs?,* 228.

42. Theodore Lowi, "American Business, Public Policy, Case Studies, and Political Theory," *World Politics* 16 (1964), 677–725; "Four Systems of Policy, Politics, and Choice," *Public Administration Review* 32 (1972), 298–310.

43. Hugh Heclo, "Issue Networks and the Executive Establishment," in *The New American Political System,* edited by A. King (Washington, D.C.: American Enterprise Institute, 1978), 87–124.

44. Ibid., 103–04.

45. Ibid., 105, 118.

NOTES TO PAGES 46-60

46. See for example Truman, *Governmental Process,* 52.

47. Ludwig von Bertalanffy, "General System Theory," *Main Currents in Modern Thought* 1 (1955): 1–10.

48. Ibid., 8.

49. David Easton, *The Political System: An Inquiry into the State of Political Science,* 2nd ed. (Chicago: University of Chicago Press, 1971), 129, 132.

50. David Easton, *A Framework for Political Analysis* (Englewood Cliffs, N.J.: Prentice-Hall, 1965), 110.

51. Donella H. Meadows et al., *The Limits to Growth,* 2nd rev. ed. (New York: Signet Books, 1974); H. S. D. Cole et al., *Models of Doom: A Critique of the Limits to Growth* (New York: Universe Books, 1973).

52. Easton, *A Framework for Political Analysis,* 27, 30.

53. Ibid., 50–56.

54. Robert J. Waste, *The Ecology of City Policymaking* (New York: Oxford University Press, 1989).

55. Anthony Downs, *Inside Bureaucracy* (Boston: Little, Brown, 1959).

56. Paul Schulman, *Large-Scale Policymaking* (New York: Elsevier, 1980).

57. Interview with Dennis Hein, director of solid waste management, City of Spokane, 9 November 1990.

58. Randall Ripley and Grade Franklin, *Congress, the Bureaucracy, and Public Policy,* rev. ed. (Homewood, Ill.: Dorsey Press, 1980).

59. Bob Dellwo says he did not even know that his son Dennis represented WMX. They never discussed such policy-related topics in their family gatherings. Commissioner Mummey was fighting ovarian cancer at the time and was accused of "wanting us all to die of cancer." This incident became a common element of city and county officials' explanations regarding why they thought their opponents were behaving irrationally.

60. Larry Luton, "Citizen Participation in Solid Waste Policymaking: The Spokane Experience," *International Journal of Public Administration* 18 (1995), 613–37.

61. Waste, *Ecology,* 108–12.

62. Easton, *Framework,* 65.

63. Ibid., 25.

64. Easton, *Political System,* xiv.

65. Ibid., 353.

66. Ibid., 369–72.

67. Bosso, *Pesticides,* 7.

3. POLITICAL CULTURE

1. Walter Rosenbaum, *Political Culture* (New York: Praeger Publishers, 1975), 4. See also Samuel Patterson, "The Political Cultures of the American States," *Journal of Politics* 30 (1968), 187–209.

2. John Kincaid, "Introduction," in *Political Culture, Public Policy and the American States,* edited by J. Kincaid (Philadelphia, Pa.: Institute for the Study of Human Issues, 1982), 2.

3. Gabriel Almond, "Comparative Political Systems," *Journal of Politics* 18 (1956), 396.

4. For example, Ruth Lane, "Political Culture: Residual Category or General Theory?" *Comparative Political Studies* 25 (1992), 362–87.

5. Lucian Pye, "Political Culture," in *International Encyclopedia of the Social Sciences* (New York: Crowell, Collier and MacMillan, 1968), 12:218; Gabriel Almond and Sidney Verba, *The Civic Culture: Political Attitudes and Democracy in Five Nations* (Newbury Park, Calif.: Sage Publications, 1989), 12.

6. Lane, "Political Culture," 381.

7. Rosenbaum, *Political Culture,* 4.

8. Wallace Stegner, *Where the Bluebird Sings to the Lemonade Springs: Living and Writing in the West* (New York: Penguin Books, 1992), 59.

9. Richard Rose, "England: The Traditionally Modern Political Culture," in *Political Culture and Political Development,* edited by Lucian Pye and Sidney Verba (Princeton, N.J.: Princeton University Press, 1965), 83–129.

10. Daniel Elazar, *American Federalism: A View from the States* (New York: Harper and Row, 1972).

11. Ibid., 95.

12. David Miller, "The Impact of Political Cultures on Patterns of State and Local Government Expenditures," *Publius* 21 (1992), 83–100.

13. Elazar, *American Federalism,* 99.

14. Ibid., 102.

15. Henry N. Smith, *Virgin Land: The American West as Symbol and Myth* (Cambridge, Mass.: Harvard University Press, 1971). Much of this section is based on Robert V. Bartlett, "Political Culture and the Environmental Problematique in the American West," in *Environmental Politics and Policy in the West,* edited by Z. A. Smith (Dubuque, Iowa: Kendall/Hunt, 1993), 101–15.

16. Stegner, *Where the Bluebird Sings,* 60–61.

17. Michael P. Malone and Richard W. Etulain, *The American West: A Twentieth-Century History* (Lincoln: University of Nebraska Press, 1989), 218.

18. John G. Francis and Clive S. Thomas, "Influences on Western Political Culture," in *Politics and Public Policy in the Contemporary American West,* edited by C. Thomas (Albuquerque: University of New Mexico Press, 1991), 50, 24.

19. Bartlett, "Environmental Problematique," 105.

20. Stegner, *Where the Bluebird Sings,* 61.

21. Malone and Etulain, *The American West,* 221.

22. Ibid., 227.

23. Earl Pomeroy, *The Pacific Slope: A History of California, Oregon, Washington, Idaho, Utah, and Nevada* (Lincoln: University of Nebraska Press, 1965), 188.

24. John Fahey, "When the Dutch Owned Spokane," in *Spokane and the Inland Empire,* edited by D. Stratton (Pullman: Washington State University Press, 1991), 179–94.

25. Jay Gitlin, "On the Boundaries of Empire: Connecting the West to Its Imperial Past," in *Under an Open Sky: Rethinking America's Western Past,* edited by W. Cronon, G. Miles, and J. Gitlin (New York: Norton, 1992), 71.

26. Pomeroy, *Pacific Slope,* 187.

27. Malone and Etulain, *The American West,* 219–63.

28. William Least Heat Moon, *Blue Highways* (New York: Ballantine Books, 1982), 136.

29. Ibid., 140.

30. Sara Deutsch, "Landscape of Enclaves," in *Under an Open Sky: Rethinking America's Western Past,* edited by W. Cronon, G. Miles, and J. Gitlin (New York: Norton, 1992), 113.

31. Malone and Etulain, *The American West,* 121.

32. Frederick Jackson Turner, *The Frontier in American History* (Tucson: University of Arizona Press, 1986).

33. Ibid., 32.

34. Ibid., 175; Gordon Ridgeway, "Populism in Washington," *Pacific Northwest Quarterly* (October 1948), 288.

35. Quoted in Malone and Etulain, *The American West,* 57.

36. Malone and Etulain, *The American West,* 62–63.

37. Ibid., 61.

38. Pomeroy, *Pacific Slope,* 232; Malone and Etulain, *The American West,* 270.

39. Malone and Etulain, *The American West,* 272.

40. Donald W. Meinig, "Spokane and the Inland Empire: Historical Systems and a Sense of Place," in Stratton, *Inland Empire*, 12.

41. Ibid., 3.

42. David Stratton, "Introduction," in Stratton, *Inland Empire*, xiv.

43. Philip Jackson and Jon Kimmerling, *Atlas of the Pacific Northwest*, 8th ed. (Corvallis: Oregon State University Press, 1993), 57.

44. *Hammond Discovery World Atlas* (Maplewood, N.J.: Hammond Incorporated, 1991), 127.

45. Timothy Egan, *Breaking Blue* (New York: Berkley Books, 1992), 16.

46. Stratton, *Inland Empire*, xiv.

47. John Fahey, *The Inland Empire: Unfolding Years, 1879–1929* (Seattle: University of Washington Press, 1986), 3, 32; Bill London, *Umbrella Guide to the Inland Empire* (Friday Harbor, Wash.: Umbrella Books, 1990), 80; Meinig, "Spokane," 18–19.

48. Stratton, *Inland Empire*, xiii–xiv.

49. Sid White and S. E. Solberg, *Peoples of Washington: Perspectives on Cultural Diversity* (Pullman: Washington State University Press, 1989), esp. 195–96.

50. Clifford Trafzer, "The Palouse Indians: Interpreting the Past of a Plateau Tribe," in Stratton, *Inland Empire*, 53–81.

51. Aldore Collier, "The Mayor Few People Know," *Ebony* (August 1984), 122, 124, 126; Neal R. Peirce, *The Pacific States of America: People, Politics and Power in the Five Pacific Basin States* (New York: W. W. Norton, 1972), 227.

52. Elazar, *American Federalism*, 108–09.

53. Ibid., 109.

54. Mike Prager, "Council Votes to Begin Composting Program Next Year," *Spokesman-Review*, 20 March 1990, B3; Julie Sullivan and Mike Prager, "County Wants City to Cool It on Composting," *Spokesman-Review*, 3 April 1990, A1, A6.

55. Jim Lynch, "Composting Competition Squelched," *Spokesman-Review*, 26 August 1992, B1; "Officials Back Competition in Composting," *Spokesman-Review*, 3 September 1992, A1, A14.

56. "Commissioners Turn Down Yard Waste–Compost Pact," *Spokesman-Review*, 4 November 1992, C3.

57. Bruce Krasnow, "County Backs Composting Site," *Spokesman-Review*, 23 June 1993, B1.

58. "Spokane Keeps Pace with Growing Demands on Waste Management," *Spokesman-Review*, 1 September 1991, G1.

59. Mike Prager, "Neighborhood Activists Claim Election Victory," *Spokesman-Review*, 5 November 1993, B2.

60. Victoria Plummer, "Politics and Change in Spokane Municipal and School District Governance, 1928–1988" (Ph.D. diss., Washington State University, 1988), 64.

61. Fahey, *Inland Empire*, 217.

62. Ibid., 218.

63. Richard Ripley, "Behind the Scenes in Spokane: Cadre of Top Execs Carefully Wields Influence Here," *Journal of Business*, 15–28 February 1990, 1, 21–24.

64. Plummer, "Change in Spokane," 90.

65. Fahey, "Dutch Owned Spokane," 179–94.

66. Egan, *Breaking Blue*, 8, 23.

67. Meinig, "Spokane," 20.

68. Peirce, *Pacific States*, 256; Jack Olsen, *Son: A Psychopath and His Victims* (New York: Dell Publishing, 1983), 14.

69. William Dietrich, *Northwest Passage: The Great Columbia River* (New York: Simon and Schuster, 1995), 291–92.

70. Meinig, "Spokane," 23; Wayne D. Rasmussen, "A Century of Farming in the Inland Empire," in Stratton, *Inland Empire*, 36, 48.

71. "The Business Year in Review," *Journal of Business*, 21 December 1992, B8.

72. Meinig, "Spokane," 23.

73. Dietrich, *Northwest Passage,* 284.

74. Washington State Department of Trade and Economic Development, "County and Community Profiles" (Olympia, Wash.: General Administration, 30 August 1989).

75. "Nothing New: Housing Sales Continue Onward and Upward," *Spokesman-Review,* 26 August 1990, G2; Vincent J. Schodolski, "Hordes Ride Migrational Tide North," *Spokesman-Review,* 7 September 1993, A1, A10; Jeanette White, "California Newcomers Well-Schooled on NW," *Spokesman-Review,* 20 October 1993, A1, A6; Rick Bonino, "State's Population Increases," *Spokesman-Review,* 6 November 1993, B1–2; U.S. Department of Commerce, Bureau of the Census, "Advance Estimates of Social, Economic and Housing Characteristics" (Washington, D.C.: GPO, 1990), table P-5; Alliance Pacific, Inc., "Waste-to-Energy Facility: Voter Opinion Survey," report prepared for the city of Spokane and in the files of the Spokane Regional Solid Waste Disposal Project Office, July–August 1985.

76. Bureau of the Census, "Advance Estimates," table P-5; *Spokane Facts 1990–91* (Spokane: Spokane Area Economic Development Council), 76.

77. Lane, "Political Culture," 381.

78. Rosenbaum, *Political Culture,* 10.

79. Alliance Pacific, "Voter Opinion Survey."

80. Decision Science Associates, "Waste-to-Energy Pre-EIS Community Attitude Survey," report prepared for the city of Spokane and in the files of the Spokane Regional Solid Waste Disposal Project Office, March 1986.

81. Decision Science Associates, "Survey of Spokane County Registered Voters Regarding a Waste-to-Energy Facility," report prepared for the city of Spokane and in the files of the Spokane Regional Solid Waste Disposal Project Office, May 1987.

82. Karen Dorn Steele, "Poll: Public Vote Sought on Incinerator," *Spokesman-Review,* 30 April 1989, A1.

83. Jim Camden, "Poll: Public Sharply Divided on Incinerator," *Spokesman-Review,* 29 October 1989, A1, A6.

84. Robert Steuteville, "The State of Garbage in America: 1994 Nationwide Survey," *Biocycle* 35 (1994), 51.

4. LOCAL POLITICAL INSTITUTIONS

1. Aaron Wildavsky, "Choosing Preferences by Constructing Institutions: A Theory of Preference Formation," *American Political Science Review* 81 (1987): 3–21.

2. Melvin Holli, "Urban Reform in the Progressive Era," in *The Progressive Era,* edited by L. Gould (Syracuse, N.Y.: Syracuse University Press, 1974), 133–51; Constance McLaughlin Green, *The Rise of Urban America* (New York: Harper and Row, 1965), 128.

3. Theodore Roosevelt, "Practical Work in Politics," in *Proceedings of the National Conference for Good City Government, 1894* (Philadelphia, Pa.: National Municipal League, 1894), 298.

4. Holli, "Urban Reform," 145–46.

5. Samuel Hays, "The Politics of Reform in Municipal Government in the Progressive Era," in *Progressivism: The Critical Issues,* edited by D. Kennedy (Boston: Little, Brown, 1971), 87–108.

6. James Banovetz, "The Nature of Local Government," in *Managing Local Government: Cases in Decision Making,* edited by J. Banovetz (Washington, D.C.: International City Management Association, 1990), 11.

7. Lewis Mumford, *The City in History: Its Origins, Its Transformation, and Its Prospects* (New York: Harcourt, Brace and World, 1961), 75. Much of this section is based on Martin V. Melosi, *Garbage in the Cities: Refuse, Reform, and the Environment, 1880–1980* (Chicago: Dorsey Press, 1981).

8. Melosi, *Garbage,* 13.

9. Ibid., 16.

10. Ibid., 18, 23.

11. Ibid., 33; G.W. Hosmer, "The Garbage Problem," *Harper's Weekly* 38 (1894), 750.

12. Melosi, *Garbage,* 26.

13. Ibid., 36.

14. Ibid., 31.

15. Ibid., 53.

16. Ibid., 63.

17. Ibid., 72.

18. Quoted in ibid., 79.

19. Stanley Schultz and Clay McShane, "To Engineer the Metropolis: Sewers, Sanitation, and City Planning in Late-Nineteenth-Century America," *Journal of American History* 65 (1978), 399.

20. Quoted in Melosi, *Garbage,* 89–90.

21. Rudolph Hering and Samuel Greeley, *Collection and Disposal of Municipal Refuse* (New York: McGraw-Hill, 1921), 4.

22. Melosi, *Garbage,* 100.

23. Ibid., 165, 216.

24. Ibid., 167–68.

25. Ibid., 103.

26. Ibid., 171.

27. William Morse, *The Collection and Disposal of Municipal Waste* (New York: Municipal Journal and Engineer, 1908), 98.

28. Louis Blumberg and Robert Gottlieb, *War on Waste: Can America Win Its Battle with Garbage?* (Washington, D.C.: Island Press, 1989), 8.

29. Ibid., 9.

30. George E. Dyck, *The Treatment of Garbage* (Chicago: n.p., 1916), 4, cited in Melosi, *Garbage,* 182.

31. Blumberg and Gottlieb, *War on Waste,* 10.

32. Melosi, *Garbage,* 183.

33. Blumberg and Gottlieb, *War on Waste,* 6.

34. Lawrence Herson and John Bolland, *The Urban Web: Politics, Policy and Theory* (Chicago: Nelson-Hall, 1990), 354.

35. Blumberg and Gottlieb, *War on Waste,* 16, 20.

36. Melosi, *Garbage,* 192.

37. Quoted in Blumberg and Gottlieb, *War on Waste,* 17.

38. Alan Adelson, "The Garbage Glut: Desperate Cities Seek New Methods to Solve Growing Waste Problems," *Wall Street Journal,* 16 February 1968.

39. Blumberg and Gottlieb, *War on Waste,* 11.

40. William E. Small, *The Third Pollution: The National Problem of Solid Waste Disposal* (New York: Praeger Publishers, 1970); Melosi, *Garbage,* 197.

41. Solid Waste Disposal Act of 1965, 42 USCA, #3251 (1965).

42. Washington State Local Governance Study Commission, *A History of Washington's Local Governments* (Olympia, Wash.: Evergreen State College, Institute for Public Policy, 1988), 1:1.

43. *Amended Charter of Spokane Falls* (1883), 258, 261.

44. *Amended Charter and Municipal Code of the City of Spokane Falls* (revised August 1, 1890, and amended 1891), 261, 272.

45. *Municipal Code of the City of Spokane* (1896), 422, 424.

46. *Municipal Code of the City of Spokane* (1903), 142, 235–36, 298–99.

47. Washington State Local Governance Study Commission, *History,* 1:20.

48. Victoria Plummer, *Politics and Change in Spokane Municipal and School District Governance, 1928–1988* (Ann Arbor, Mich.: University Microfilms, 1988), 64–65.

49. *Charter and General Ordinances of the City of Spokane, Washington* (1928), 266–70.

50. Washington State Local Governance Study Commission, *History,* 1:27.

51. Plummer, *Politics and Change,* 96.

52. *Revised Code of Washington (RCW)* 35.18.010.

53. Plummer, *Politics and Change,* 99.

54. Ibid., 103.

55. Terry Novak, "A Case History: Spokane, Washington's Solid Waste System" (paper presented at the Third Annual Symposium on Municipal Solid Waste Disposal and Energy Production, Orlando, Fla., January 1989), 2.

56. Ibid., 5.

57. Mary W. Avery, *Government of Washington State* (Seattle: University of Washington, 1973), 254.

58. *Constitution of the State of Washington* (1989), art. 11, sec. 11.

59. League of Women Voters of the Spokane Area (LOWV), *Government in Spokane County* (Spokane: League of Women Voters of the Spokane Area, 1985), 10.

60. Marion B. Hess, *The Growth and Development of Spokane County, Washington, 1860–1969* (Spokane: Eastern Washington University, 1969), 4–5.

61. Washington State Local Governance Study Commission, *History,* 1:11.

62. *RCW* 36.58.20; 36.70.; 36.67.510.

63. Greg Adranovich and Nicholas Lovrich, "Local Government Then and Now: The Growth Management Challenge in the 1990s," in *Government and Politics in the Evergreen State,* ed. D. Nice, J. Pierce, and C. Sheldon (Pullman: Washington State University Press, 1992), 165.

64. *Constitution of the State of Washington,* art. 11, secs. 4, 16.

65. LOWV, *Government,* 22; *RCW* 36.58.

66. *Spokane County Code,* sec. 8.40.120, 150, 200; chap. 8.24.

67. Parametrix, Inc., *Spokane County Comprehensive Solid Waste Management Plan and Final Environmental Impact Statement,* report prepared for the city of Spokane and in the files of the Spokane Regional Solid Waste Disposal Project Office, July 1992, 3, 7.

68. Ibid., 7.

69. *Spokane County Code,* sec. 8.56.160.

70. Bruce Krasnow, "Solid Waste Laws Amended by Split Vote of Board," *Spokesman-Review,* 21 October 1992, B1.

71. Parametrix, *Solid Waste Plan,* 8.

72. *Spokane County Code,* chap. 8.26.; Jeff Shea, "Commissioners Approve Anti-Litter Ordinance," *Spokesman-Review,* 31 August 1988, B4.

73. *Zoning Code of Spokane County,* 14.702.080 (3); "County OKs Zoning for New Waste Plant," *Spokesman-Review,* 17 February 1988, A8.

74. *Zoning Code of Spokane County,* 14.606.240 (11–15), 14.608.210 (B. 8), 14.610.210 (B. 7), 14.610.240 (5), 14.612.240 (5 and 6), 14.614.20 (5–6), 14.620.360, 14.622.360, 14.624.360, 14.626.360, 14.628.210 (5), 14.628.360, 14.681.360, and 14.706.

75. Washington State Local Governance Study Commission, *History,* 1:57.

76. Ibid., 1:3, 18, 57.

77. Avery, *Government of Washington State,* 277.

78. LOWV, *Government,* 52.

79. *RCW* 70.05.160.

80. Spokane County Health District, Rules and Regulations for Solid Waste Management and Handling, 18 August 1988, 2–3.

81. Ibid., 16–18.

82. *RCW* 70.95.170 and 70.95.180; *Washington Administrative Code (WAC)* 248–96–170.

83. Spokane County Health District, Rules, 80.

84. Ibid., 97, 99.

85. Jim Camden, "'88 Last Chance for Trash Plant," *Spokesman-Review,* 3 January 1988, 1, 3.

86. Bruce Krasnow, "County Wants Closed Landfill to Open Again," *Spokesman-Review,* 14 March 1992, B1, B6.

87. Jim Camden, "Health Study for Burner, but By Whom?" *Spokesman-Review,* 21 April 1988, C6; interoffice memo from Dennis Kroll of SCHD to Commissioner Mummey, 29 March 1989.

88. Avery, *Government of Washington State,* 280; *RCW* 70.94.

89. SCAPCA, *Regulation 1,* October 1993, art. 1, sec. 1.01, 1.

90. LOWV, *Government,* 52; personal communication with Eric Skelton, 17 June 1994.

91. SCAPCA, *Regulation 1,* art. 2, sec. 2.01, 1, 2.11, 4–5.

92. Ibid., art. 4.

93. Ibid., art. 5 (revised 2 May 1991), sec. 5.02, 1.

94. Ibid., art. 5 (revised 2 May 1991), sec. 5.04, 2.

95. Ibid., art. 6 (revised October 1993).

96. Ibid., art. 9 (adopted October 1991), sec. 9.06, 13.

97. Ibid., art. 3, 1; *Regulation 2* (September 1971), art. 3, 1.

98. SCAPCA, *Regulation 1,* art. 2, sec. 2.06, 2–3.

99. *RCW* 39.34.

100. Washington State Local Governance Study Commission, *History,* 1:63.

101. Novak, "Case History," 5.

102. B. W. Drost and H. R. Seitz, *Spokane Valley-Rathdrum Prairie, Washington and Idaho,* U.S. Geological Survey, Open File Report 77–829 (Tacoma, Washington: USGS, 1978).

103. Spokane Planning Conference, *Spokane Aquifer Water Quality Management Plan: Final Report and Water Quality Management Framework Recommendations for Policies and Actions to Preserve the Quality of the Spokane-Rathdrum Aquifer* (Spokane: Spokane County Engineering Department, April 1979).

104. Parametrix, *Solid Waste Plan,* 13.

105. Curt Messex, *Fallout from the Spokane Incinerator,* 3rd rev. ed. (Spokane: Curt Messex, 1989), 3.

106. Rick Bonino, "Garbage-Burning Plant Gets Airport Board OK," *Spokesman-Review,* 19 February 1988, A1, A15; Russell Carollo, "Airport Approves Incinerator Lease," *Spokesman-Review,* 19 May 1988, B1.

107. *RCW* 70.95.165, paragraph 3.

108. Bob Bocksh and Brenda Bodenstein, 1993, "Panel Serves As Watchdog," *Spokesman-Review,* 1 February 1993, A13. Similar advisory bodies have not acted in ways that would lead to such a charge. See for example Marjorie J. Clarke, "Integrated Municipal Solid Waste Planning and Decision-Making in New York City: The Citizens' Alternative Plan," *Air and Waste* 43 (1993), 453–62.

109. *Interlocal Cooperation Agreement Between the City of Spokane and Spokane County, Washington: Spokane Regional Waste-to-Energy Facility,* 3 November 1987.

110. Ibid., 14.

111. *Interlocal Cooperation Agreement Between the City of Spokane and Spokane County, Washington: Spokane Regional Solid Waste Management System,* 11 October 1988.

112. *Amended and Restated Interlocal Cooperation Agreement Between the City of Spokane and Spokane County, Washington: Spokane Regional Solid Waste Management System,* 10 April 1989, 19–20.

113. Rick Bonino, "County Will Get More Say Over Trash Burner Project," *Spokesman-Review,* 11 April 1989, B1, B6.

114. Washington State Local Governance Study Commission, *History,* 1:34.

5. FEDERAL AND STATE POLICIES

1. Martin Melosi, *Garbage in the Cities: Refuse, Reform, and the Environment, 1880–1980* (Chicago: Dorsey Press, 1981), 190.

2. National League of Cities and United States Conference of Mayors, Solid Waste Management Task Force, *Cities and the Nation's Disposal Crisis* (Washington, D.C.: National League of Cities and United States Conference of Mayors, 1973), 1.

3. William Small, *Third Pollution: The National Problem of Solid Waste Disposal* (New York: Praeger Publishers, 1970).

4. J. B. Ruhl, "Interstate Pollution Control and Resource Development Planning: Outmoded Approaches or Outmoded Politics?" *Natural Resources Journal* 28 (1988): 293–314.

5. See for example Richard J. Tobin, "Environmental Protection and the New Federalism: A Longitudinal Analysis of State Perceptions," *Publius: The Journal of Federalism* 22 (1992): 93–107; Michael J. Scicchitano and David M. Hedge, "From Coercion to Partnership in Federal Partial Preemption: SMCRA, RCRA, and OSH Act," *Publius: The Journal of Federalism* 23 (1993): 107–21.

6. See for example Richard P. Nathan et al., *Reagan and the States* (Princeton, N.J.: Princeton University Press, 1986).

7. Scicchitano and Hedge, "Coercion to Partnership"; Tobin, "Environmental Protection."

8. Michael Pagano and Ann Bowman, "The State of American Federalism, 1992–1993," *Publius: The Journal of Federalism* 23 (1993): 5.

9. Jean Peretz, "Equity Under and State Responses to the Superfund Amendments and Reauthorization Act of 1986," *Policy Sciences* 25 (1992): 191–202.

10. William T. Gormley Jr., "Intergovernmental Conflict on Environmental Policy: The Attitudinal Connection," *Western Political Quarterly* 40 (1987): 285.

11. Scicchitano and Hedge, "Coercion to Partnership"; Tobin, "Environmental Protection," 105–06.

12. Gormley, "Intergovernmental Conflict," 300.

13. *Rivers and Harbors Act, U.S. Code,* vol. 33, sec. 407 (1899); Diane D. Eames, "The Refuse Act of 1899: Its Scope and Role in Water Pollution," *California Law Review,* 1920, 1444–73.

14. Louis Blumberg and Robert Gottlieb, *War on Waste: Can America Win Its Battle with Garbage?* (Washington, D.C.: Island Press, 1989), 61.

15. Melosi, *Garbage,* 199.

16. Ibid., 199.

17. EPA, *RCRA Orientation Manual, 1990 Edition* (Washington, D.C.: EPA, 1990), I-9.

18. *Hazardous and Solid Waste Amendments, U.S. Code,* vol. 42, sec. 6945 (1984).

19. Rodman D. Griffin, "Garbage Crisis," *CQ Research Reports* 2 (20 March 1992): 246.

20. U.S.C., Title 33 — Navigation and Navigable Waters, sec. 1342.

21. EPA, *RCRA Manual,* VI-5.

22. *Clean Air Act, U.S. Code,* vol. 42, sec. 7401 (1970).

23. EPA, *RCRA Manual,* VI-4.

24. *National Environmental Policy Act, U.S. Code,* vol. 83, secs. 852–56.

25. Melosi, *Garbage,* 201.

26. U.S. EPA, *Access EPA* (Washington, D.C.: U.S. EPA, 1992), 5.

27. Melosi, *Garbage,* 202.

28. Blumberg and Gottlieb, *War on Waste,* 63.

29. William Ruckelshaus, "Solid Waste Management: An Overview," *Public Management,* October 1972, 4.

30. Blumberg and Gottlieb, *War on Waste,* 64.

31. Code of Federal Regulations (CFR), vol. 40, sec. 256.

32. CFR, vol. 40, sec. 257.3.

33. Ibid., secs. 240–57.

34. EPA, *RCRA Manual*, II-7.

35. Griffin, "Garbage Crisis," 252.

36. Ibid., 247.

37. CFR, vol. 40, sec. 258.

38. "New Source Performance Standards," *Federal Register,* 11 February 1991, 5488–5527. CFR, vol. 40, parts 51, 52, and 60.

39. *Philadelphia v. New Jersey,* 437 U.S. 617 (1978).

40. Ibid., at 632.

41. *Fort Gratiot Landfill v. Michigan Department of Natural Resources,* 112 Sup. Ct. 2019 (1992).

42. *Gilliam County v. Department of Environmental Quality,* 849 Pacific Reporter. 2nd 500 (1993).

43. *Oregon Waste Systems, Inc. v. Department of Environmental Quality of the State of Oregon,* 114 Sup. Ct. 38 (certiorari granted); combined with *Columbia Resource Company v. Environmental Quality Commission of the State of Oregon,* cases no. 93–70 and 93–108.

44. *Town of Clarkstown v. C. & A. Carbone, Inc.,* 114 Sup. Ct. 1677 (1994); David Tannenbaum, "Whose Trash Is This? Flow-Control War May Get Costly," *City and State,* January 1994, 30–31.

45. Martin E. Gold, "Solid Waste Management and the Constitution's Commerce Clause," *Urban Lawyer* 25 (1993): 21–48.

46. *Town of Clarkstown v. C. & A. Carbone, Inc.,* 1680.

47. "Senate Passes Flow Control Bill On to the House," *P.A. Times,* 1 June 1995, 3.

48. *EDF v. City of Chicago,* 727 F. Su. 419 (N.D. Ill., 1989); *EDF v. Wheelabrator Technologies, Inc.,* 725 F. Su. 758 (1989).

49. 113 Sup. Ct. 2992, certiorari granted; decision reached on case no. 92–1639, 2 May 1994.

50. "EPA Tells Mayors: Smoke 'Em if You Got 'Em," *Spokesman-Review,* 26 January 1995, B3.

51. Blumberg and Gottlieb, *War on Waste,* 62.

52. Alfred J. Van Tassel, ed., *Our Environment: The Outlook of 1980* (Lexington, Mass.: Lexington Books, 1973), 468.

53. EPA, *Solid Waste Laws in the U.S. Territories and States* (Washington, D.C.: EPA, 1972), 381–83; WDOE, *Washington State Solid Waste Management Plan* (Olympia, Wash.: WDOE, 1991), Appendix C, table C-1, Washington State Statutes.

54. EPA, *A Manual of Laws, Regulations, and Institutions for Control of Groundwater Pollution* (Washington, D.C.: EPA, 1976), II-18; EPA-440/9–76–006.

55. *RCW* 70.95; WDOE, *Solid Waste Plan,* 14.

56. WDOE, *Solid Waste Plan,* 5.

57. *RCW* 70.105.

58. WDOE, *Solid Waste Plan,* 6.

59. Ibid., 7.

60. Steve Coll, "Dumping on the Third World," *Washington Post National Weekly Edition,* 18–24 April 1994, 9 and 10; Paul Freeman, "Many Washington Recyclables End Up in Asia," *Journal of Business,* 18 August 1994, B5, B12.

61. *RCW* 70.93, now titled "Waste Reduction, Recycling, and Model Litter Control Act."

62. *RCW* 70.132

63. *RCW* 70.138.

64. *RCW* 70.95C.100.

65. *RCW* 90.48.010.

66. *RCW* 90.54.140.

67. *RCW* 70.94.

68. *RCW* 43.21C.

69. *RCW* 70.95.700; *WAC* 197–11.

70. WDOE, *Solid Waste Plan*, Appendix D, table D-1, Washington State Regulations.

71. Ibid., 5; *WAC* 173–304, 173–351.

72. *WAC* 173–300, 173–400, 173–434, 173–490.

73. *WAC* 173–434–100 (1).

74. *WAC* 173–460.

75. *WAC* 173–306.

76. WDOE, *Solid Waste Plan*, 7.

77. *WAC* 173–300.

78. *Washington State Register,* vol. 93, no. 22, 37–67. Codified as *WAC* 173–351.

79. *WAC* 173–322–010.

80. *RCW* 70.105D.

81. *WAC* 173–322–060.

82. *WAC* 173–321–010.

83. *RCW* 70.94.820.

84. *WAC* 173–400–040, 173–400–050, 173–400–060, 173–400–070, 173–400–075.

85. *WAC* 173–400–110; *WAC* 173–403–050.

86. *RCW* 90.48.30.

87. *WAC* 173–225–010, 173–220, 173–201.

88. *WAC* 173–200–040, 173–200–030, 173–100.

89. *RCW* 43.21B.

90. *King County Solid Waste Division v. Washington State Department of Ecology*, December 23, 1993, Superior Court of Washington for Thurston County; copy in author's possession, also available at Thurston County Courthouse.

91. Ibid.

92. Ibid., dissenting opinion, 1, 2.

93. Karen Dorn Steele, "Trash Company May Have to Return Rate Hike: High Court to Rule on Suit by State," *Spokesman-Review*, 4 January 1994, B1; "Garbage Rate Will Be Decided Without Look at Firm's Profits," *Spokesman-Review*, 31 March 1994, B4.

94. *RCW* 43.83A.

95. *RCW* 43.99.

96. *RCW* 70.105D, esp. 105D.070(5).

97. WDOE, *Solid Waste Plan*, 31.

98. Telephone interview with Fran Stephen, Seattle Office of EPA.

99. Interview with SCAPCA Control Officer Eric Skelton, 17 June 1994; November 1992 "Focus" report by WDOE.

100. Jim Lynch, "New Limits Could Add to Plant Costs," *Spokesman-Review*, 27 December 1992, A14.

101. Karen Dorn Steele, "Ash Landfill Rules Target of Criticism," *Spokesman-Review*, 25 October 1989, B1.

102. Anne Windishar, "Officials Urged to Study Dump's Health Effects," *Spokesman-Review*, 12 August 1988, 21; Karen Dorn Steele, "Crowd Angered by Landfill Plans, Absent Officials," *Spokesman-Review*, 17 November 1989, B1–2.

103. Karen Dorn Steele, "Trash Incinerator Would Harm City, Officials Told," *Spokesman-Review*, 20 July 1989, B1–2.

104. Jim Camden, "Incinerator Changes May Not Get Hearing," *Spokesman-Review*, 25 March 1988, A17; Karen Dorn Steele, "Ecology Department OKs Waste Burner," *Spokesman-Review*, 14 December 1988, A1, A8.

105. Karen Dorn Steele, "Burner Permit Approved, Emissions Limits Reduced," *Spokesman-Review*, 31 January 1989, B1; "Emissions Standards Relaxed," *Spokesman-Review*, 1 March 1989, A1.

106. Karen Dorn Steele, "EPA Urges Review of Incinerator Permit," *Spokesman-Review*, 8

March 1989, A1, A5; "Burner Permit Delay May Be Costly," *Spokesman-Review,* 9 March 1989, 1, 8; "Starting Today, Burner Project Delay to Cost City $8,500 Daily," *Spokesman-Review,* 27 April 1989, A1, A10.

107. From four *Spokesman-Review,* articles : Karen Dorn Steele, "EPA Paves Way for Spokane Trash Burner," 10 June 1989, A1, A5; Mike Prager, "Incinerator Issue Far from Settled," 28 June 1989, A1, A6; Steele, "State OKs Air Permit for Trash Incinerator," 2 September 1989, A1, A5; Rick Bonino, "Go-Ahead Given for Incinerator," 4 January 1990, A1, A5.

108. S. Komarnitsky, "Local Governments Lobby to End 'Ban on Bans,'" *Spokesman-Review,* 16 February 1993, A6, A12.

109. Mike Prager, "Incinerator Foes Fighting $60 Million Grant," *Spokesman-Review,* 17 March 1989, B1–2.

110. Dave Hirschman, "Crowd Threatening at Garbage Hearing," *Spokesman-Review,* 9 December 1988, 1–2.

111. David R. Mayhew, *Congress: The Electoral Connection* (New Haven: Yale University Press, 1974), 61.

112. Jim Camden, "Burner Called 'Spokane's Vietnam,'" *Spokesman-Review,* 18 October 1988, B2; Rick Bonino, "Legislator Will Support Burner if Spokane Backs His Waste Bill," *Spokesman-Review,* 6 March 1989, A8; Karen Dorn Steele, "Legislator: Burner 'Wouldn't Get a Dime' Today," *Spokesman-Review,* 16 October 1989, A6–7.

113. Jim Camden, "State Senator Wants DOE to Withdraw Trash Burner Funding," *Spokesman-Review,* 11 October 1988, B1–2; Karen Dorn Steele, "Lawmakers Split on Trash Burner," *Spokesman-Review,* 13 December 1988, B1–2; Jim Camden, "Surveys Show Public Doubts About Burner," *Spokesman-Review,* 13 April 1989, B1.

114. Karen Dorn Steele, "Gorton's Nudge on Incinerator Permit Stirs Up a Storm," *Spokesman-Review,* 5 April 1989, A1, A5.

115. From five *Spokesman-Review* articles: Karen Dorn Steele, "New Vote on Curbside Recycling," 8 December 1988, B1; "Ecology Department OKs Waste Burner," 14 December 1988, A1, A8; Rick Bonino, "Officials OK New Conditions on Incinerator," 24 December 1988, A6; "Council to Receive Recycling Timeline," 27 March 1989, A6–7; "City Plans Curbside Collection," 28 March 1989, B1–2.

116. From the following *Spokesman-Review* reports: Karen Dorn Steele, "Suit Challenges Trash Burner Grant," 26 January 1989, A12; "Judge Halts Rabanco's Regional Landfill Work," 12 September 1990, B1. Jim Lynch, "Appeals Court Rejects Incinerator Challenge," 31 March 1992, B1; Jim Camden, "Incinerator Pact Legal, Judge Says," 15 November 1989, B3; "Trash Burner Foes Say Advertisements Misleading," 1 September 1988, B3; Julie Sullivan, 1990, "Site for Spokane Ash Disposal Runs Into Environmental Snag," 18 July 1990, B1–2; "Landfill Lawsuit Dismissed," 8 June 1991, A8.

117. Jim Camden, "Incinerator Foes to Get Day in Court," *Spokesman-Review,* 2 March 1988, B1.

118. Jim Camden, "Debate Over Trash Burner Goes to Court," *Spokesman-Review,* 26 February 1988, A17; "Burner Impact Report Labeled Inadequate," *Spokesman-Review,* 17 August 1988, B1.

119. Karen Dorn Steele, "Fill Operators Try to Block Burner Bond Sales," *Spokesman-Review,* 20 December 1988, B1.

120. Rick Bonino, "Legal Battles to Delay Trash Plant Construction," *Spokesman-Review,* 2 February 1988, B1–2; Jim Camden, "Lawsuits Delaying Trash Plant Project," *Spokesman-Review,* 25 February 1988, A1–2; "Trash Burner Project Delays Will Cost County," *Spokesman-Review,* 12 May 1988, B1.

121. Personal communication from former city manager Terry Novak, May 1994.

122. John Craig, "Groundwater Cleanup Begins Near Landfill," *Spokesman-Review,* 9 September 1989, A6.

123. "Waste Cleanup Poses Enormous Challenges," *Spokesman-Review*, 13 January 1989, A4.

124. Karen Dorn Steele, "Officials Celebrate Cleanup of North Side Landfill," *Spokesman-Review*, 24 September 1993, B1; Rick Bonino, "City, EPA Have $4 Million Dispute," *Spokesman-Review*, 4 March 1989, B1; Mike Prager, "Landfill Cleanup Tops List," *Spokesman-Review*, 6 October 1991, A1, A10.

125. Kim Crompton, "County May Be Forced to Close Landfill Sooner than Expected," *Spokesman-Review*, 2 March 1989, B1; "County Wants Waiver on Mica Landfill Liner," *Spokesman-Review*, 24 March 1989, A10.

126. Bill Morlin, "County Stops Work on Cover for Old Landfill," *Spokesman-Review*, 9 September 1993, A1, A9.

127. Personal communication with Roxanne Broadhead of WDOE, 30 June 1994.

128. Frank E. Allen, "As Recycling Surges Market for Materials Is Slow to Develop," *Wall Street Journal*, 17 January 1992, A1, A6.

6. BUSINESS INFLUENCE

1. Donald F. Kettl, *Sharing Power: Public Governance and Private Markets* (Washington, D.C.: Brookings Institution, 1993), 7, 10.

2. Bruce Ackerman, *We the People 1: Foundations* (Cambridge, Mass.: Harvard University Press, 1991), 121.

3. Ibid., 129.

4. John T. Tierney and Kay Lehman Scholzman, "Congress and Organized Interests," in *Congressional Politics*, ed. C. J. Deering (Chicago: Dorsey Press, 1989), 198.

5. See for example Philip A. Mundo, *Interest Groups: Cases and Characteristics* (Chicago: Nelson-Hall Publishers, 1992), 39.

6. See for example Charles Lindblom, *Politics and Markets* (New York: Basic Books, 1977); "The Market as Prison," *Journal of Politics* 44 (1982), 324–36.

7. Tom Koenig, "Business Support for Disclosure of Corporate Campaign Contributions: An Instructive Paradox," in *The Structure of Power in America: The Corporate Elite as a Ruling Class*, edited by M. Schwartz (New York: Holmes and Meier, 1987), 86; see also Frances Fox Piven and Richard A. Cloward, *Regulating the Poor* (New York: Vintage Books, 1971).

8. See for example "Regulate Us, Please," *Economist* 330 (8 January 1994), 69.

9. See for example Frank Shipper and Marianne Jennings, *Business Strategy for the Political Arena* (Westport, Conn.: Quorum Books, 1984); Joseph Frese and Jacob Judd, eds., *Business and Government: Essays in 20th-Century Cooperation and Confrontation* (Tarrytown, N.Y.: Sleepy Hollow Press, 1985); Mike Ryan, Carl Swanson, and Rogene Buchholz, *Corporate Strategy, Public Policy and the Fortune 500* (New York: Basil Blackwell, 1987); Jeffrey Birnbaum, *The Lobbyists: How Influence Peddlers Work Their Way in Washington* (New York: Times Books, 1993); William Greider, *Who Will Tell the People: The Betrayal of American Democracy* (New York: Touchstone Books, 1992), esp. chaps. 6, 15.

10. Burdett A. Loomis and Allan J. Cigler, "Introduction: The Changing Nature of Interest Group Politics," in *Interest Group Politics*, 3rd ed., edited by A. J. Cigler and B. A. Loomis (Washington, D.C.: CQ Press, 1991), 10–11.

11. Ibid.; see also Theodore Lowi, *The End of Liberalism* (New York: Norton, 1979); Mancur Olson, *The Logic of Collective Action* (Cambridge, Mass.: Harvard University Press, 1965); *Public Policy for Democracy*, edited by Helen Ingram and Steven Rathgeb Smith (Washington, D.C.: Brookings Institution, 1993).

12. Mundo, *Interest Groups*.

13. Thomas Byrne Edsall, "Business in American Politics: Its Growing Power, Its Shifting Strategies," *Dissent* 37 (1990): 247.

14. David Vogel, *Fluctuating Fortunes: The Political Power of Business in America* (New York: Basic Books, 1989).

15. Ibid., chap. 4.

16. "Waste Becomes a Big Business: Priorities Shift," *Chemical Marketing Reporter* 245 (10 January 1994): 31.

17. Jayadev Chowdhury, "The Rise of a Dirty Business," *Chemical Engineering* 98 (1991): 44DD.

18. William P. Browne, "Issue Niches and the Limits of Interest Group Influence," in *Interest Group Politics*, 3rd ed., edited by A. J. Cigler and B. A. Loomis (Washington, D.C.: CQ Press, 1991), 345–70.

19. Browne, "Issue Niches," 347.

20. Koenig, "Business Support," 84.

21. Ibid., 84; see also Ralph Miliband, *The State in a Capitalist Society* (New York: Basic Books, 1969).

22. Greider, *Who Will Tell the People,* 42–45.

23. Glenn Hess, "Waste Management '93: Washington — Reform on Hold," *Chemical Marketing Reporter* 244 (29 November 1993): SR13–14.

24. Ellen Allen, "Do You Need a Local Waste Association?" *World Wastes* 36 (1993): 48–49.

25. Jeff Bailey, "Waste Disposal Giant, Often Under Attack, Seems to Gain from It: Waste Management's Jousts with Environmentalists Deter Rivals From Field," *Wall Street Journal,* 1 May 1991, A1, A4.

26. Karen Dorn Steele, "Both Sides Pressing EPA for Incinerator Decision as Deadline Approaches," *Spokesman-Review,* 19 April 1989, B1–2.

27. Laura Anker, Peter Seybold, and Michael Schwartz, "The Ties That Bind Business and Government," in *Power in America*, edited by M. Schwartz (New York: Holmes and Meier, 1987), 104–20.

28. Joint Economic Committee, Subcommittee on Economic Growth and Stabilization, *The Costs of Government Regulation of Business*, report prepared by Murray Weidenbaum, 95th Cong., 2nd sess., 1978, Joint Committee Print, 10.

29. Charles Davis, "State Environmental Regulation and Economic Development: Are They Compatible?" *Policy Studies Review* 11 (1992): 149–57.

30. Richard C. Feiock and M. Margaret Haley, "The Political Economy of State Environmental Regulation: The Distribution of Regulatory Burdens," *Policy Studies Review* 11 (1992): 158–64.

31. Loomis and Cigler, "Introduction," 12.

32. Ibid., 13.

33. Kettl, *Sharing Power,* 4.

34. Anker, Seybold, and Schwartz, "The Ties That Bind," 98.

35. "Resource Recovery: An Overview," *Moody's Municipal Issues* 4 (1987): 5.

36. Kettl, *Sharing Power,* 12.

37. House Committee on Post Office and Civil Service, *Contracting at EPA and Its Effect on Federal Employees: Hearing before the Committee on Post Office and Civil Service,* 101st Cong., 1st sess., 1989, 11–12.

38. Kettl, *Sharing Power,* 109, 105.

39. Ibid., 122.

40. Ibid., 115.

41. Gary Lide, "Public/Private Partnerships Forge New Waste Solutions," *World Wastes* 36 (1993): 44–46.

42. Martin Melosi, *Garbage in the Cities: Refuse, Reform, and the Environment, 1880–1980* (Chicago: Dorsey Press, 1981), 152–55.

43. George Antunes and Gary Halter, "The Politics of Resource Recovery, Energy Conservation, and Solid Waste Management," *Administration and Society* 8 (1976): 69–71.

44. Jerry F. Medler and Alvin Mushkatel, "Environmental Policy, New Federalism and New Privatism: Policy Conflicts in the Coastal Zone," *Policy Studies Review* 11 (1992): 100–01.

45. T. Barnekov and D. Rich, "Privatism and Urban Development: An Analysis of the Organized Influence of Local Business Elites," *Urban Affairs Quarterly* 12 (1977): 432.

46. Douglas F. Greer, *Business, Government, and Society,* 2nd ed. (New York: Macmillan, 1987), 483, 487.

47. Robert N. Stavins, "Harnessing the Marketplace," *EPA Journal* 18 (1992): 21–25.

48. See for example Dick Russell, "Environmental Racism," *Amicus Journal* 11 (1989): 22–32; Anna K. Harding and George R. Holdren Jr., "Environmental Equity and the Environmental Professional," *Environmental Science Technology* 27 (1993): 1990–93.

49. Leonard P. Gianessi and Henry M. Peskin, "The Distribution of the Costs of Federal Water Pollution Policy," *Land Economics,* February 1980, 99–100.

50. Russell, "Environmental Racism," 25; Harding and Holdren, "Environmental Equity"; Julia Flynn Siler, " 'Environmental Racism': It Could Be a Messy Fight: A Planned Incinerator in California Has Led to an Unusual Bias Suit," *Business Week* (20 May 1991): 116; Rachel D. Godsil, "Remedying Environmental Racism," *Michigan Law Review* 90 (1991): 394–427.

51. Bette Fishbein and David Saphire, "Slowing the Waste Behemoth," *EPA Journal* 18 (1992): 47.

52. James McCarthy, "Recycling and Reducing Packaging Waste: How the United States Compares to Other Countries," *Resources, Conservation and Recycling* 8 (1993): 293–360.

53. Carol Browner, "Pollution Prevention Takes Center Stage," *EPA Journal* 19 (1993): 6–8; Matthew Weinstock, "EPA's New Push for Pollution Prevention," *Occupational Hazards* 55 (1993): 33–36.

54. Louis Blumberg and Robert Gottlieb, *War on Waste: Can America Win Its Battle with Garbage?* (Washington, D.C.: Island Press, 1989), 260.

55. Anne Magnuson, "What Has Happened to Waste Reduction?" *American City and County* 106 (1991): 36; Municipal Solid Waste Task Force, *The Solid Waste Dilemma: An Agenda for Action,* Draft Report (Washington, D.C.: EPA, 1988), 18.

56. Congressional Budget Office (CBO), *Federal Options for Reducing Waste Disposal,* October 1991, ix.

57. Environment 2010, *Toward 2010: An Environmental Action Agenda* (Olympia: Washington State Department of Ecology, 1990), 46.

58. League of Women Voters of Washington, *Solid Waste Reduction and Recycling: A Handbook of Strategies Employed by Businesses in Washington State* (Olympia: Washington State Department of Ecology Solid and Hazardous Waste Management Program, 1988).

59. Packaging Task Force, *Action Plan of the Packaging Task Force* (Olympia, Wash.: Department of Ecology Office of Waste Reduction, 1991), v.

60. National Conference of State Legislatures, *Solid Waste Management: 1989–1990 Legislation* (Washington, D.C.: National Conference of State Legislatures, 1990), 8.

61. Blumberg and Gottlieb, *War on Waste,* 265.

62. Cynthia Pollock, "Mining Urban Wastes: The Potential for Recycling," Worldwatch Paper No. 76 (Washington, D.C.: Worldwatch Institute, 1987), 8–10.

63. Blumberg and Gottlieb, *War on Waste,* 263–73.

64. Douglas J. Smith, "Integrated Waste Management Systems Are the Only Solution," *Power Engineering* 94 (1990): 18–25.

65. Blumberg and Gottlieb, *War on Waste,* 259, 270.

66. Fishbein and Saphire, "Waste Behemoth," 48.

67. Pete Grogan and Brad Schwartz, "Strategic Shift to Source Reduction," *Biocycle* 32 (1991): 29.

68. John Rzadzki, "Waste Management '93: In the Dumps," *Chemical Marketing Reporter* 244 (29 November 1993): SR3–SR6.

69. Clive Thomas, "Interest Groups and Lobbying," in *Politics and Public Policy in the Contemporary American West,* edited by C. Thomas (Albuquerque: University of New Mexico Press, 1991), 161, 179; Ronald Hrebrenar, "Interest Group Politics in the American West: A Comparative Perspective," in *Interest Group Politics in the American West,* edited by R. Hrebrenar and C. Thomas (Salt Lake City: University of Utah Press, 1987), 9.

70. Sarah McCally Morehouse, *State Politics, Parties, and Policy* (New York: Holt, Rinehart, and Winston, 1983); Clive Thomas, "Conclusion: The Changing Pattern of Interest Group Politics in the Western States," in *Interest Group Politics,* edited by R. Hrebrenar and C. Thomas (Salt Lake City: University of Utah Press, 1987), 150.

71. Walfred Peterson, "Washington: The Impact of Public Disclosure Laws," in *Interest Group Politics,* edited by R. Hrebrenar and C. Thomas (Salt Lake City: University of Utah Press, 1987), 124, 126; Elizabeth Walker, "Interest Groups in Washington State," in *Government and Politics in the Evergreen State,* edited by D. Nice, J. Pierce, and C. Sheldon (Pullman: Washington State University Press, 1992), 46.

72. Walker, "Interest Groups," 47, 49, 56, 58.

73. "Waste Haulers Do Battle over Deregulation," *Spokesman-Review,* 17 April 1989, A1.

74. Jeffrey Showman, "Solid Waste Planning for a New Urban Environment: A Systems Approach to Developing New Institutions in Seattle, King County, and Washington State" (master's thesis, University of Washington, 1987), 95.

75. Mary Powers and Debra K. Rubin, "Rust Gets a New Shine," *ENR* 230 (14 June 1993), 22.

76. Karen Dorn Steele, "Company Steps Up Lobbying Effort," *Spokesman-Review,* 10 September 1989, A12.

77. Examples are taken from articles in the *Spokesman-Review* by Karen Dorn Steele: "Communities Vie for Spokane Ash, Despite Opposition," 20 June 1990, A1, A5; "Oregon Landfill Site Next in Line for Ash," 13 September 1990, B1–2; "Incinerator Alternative Was Rejected 2 Years Ago," 9 August 1989, B1–2; "Compost-Plant Firm Called Untested, Unethical," 12 August 1989, A8, A11; Douglas Pottratz, "Waste-Disposal Plant: Emission Levels Safe, No Reason for Alarm," 20 August 1989, A19.

78. Memo from the Energy and Environmental Committee to the Board of Trustees of the Spokane Area Chamber of Commerce, on a recommendation adopted 3 February 1988.

79. Karen Dorn Steele, "Airlines Oppose Incinerator Site," *Spokesman-Review,* 30 September 1989, A1, A5.

80. Jim Camden, "Momentum '89 to Commission Burner Study," *Spokesman-Review,* 11 October 1989, B1, B6; "Business Leaders Question Cost of Trashing Burner," *Spokesman-Review,* 20 October 1989, B1, B3; see also "Burner's Cancellation Would Make No Sense," editorial, *Spokesman-Review,* 5 November 1989, A18.

81. Karen Dorn Steele, "Burner Fines Could Boost Garbage Bills," *Spokesman-Review,* 29 August 1991, 1; "Council Will Get Bill for Delays in Trash Burner," *Spokesman-Review,* 26 September 1988, A6.

82. Karen Dorn Steele, "Trash Incinerator Takes Another Big Step," *Spokesman-Review,* 12 February 1989, A1; "City to Renegotiate Wheelabrator Contract," *Spokesman-Review,* 30 July 1989, C1.

83. John Craig, "Curbside Recycling Raises Ire," *Spokesman-Review,* 26 November 1991, B3; "Garbage Rates Going Up for Some," *Spokesman-Review,* 11 November 1993, B5; Karen Dorn Steele, "Trash Company May Have to Return Rate Hike," *Spokesman-Review,* 4 January 1994, B1.

84. Karen Dorn Steele, from *Spokesman-Review:* "3 Firms Bid to Haul Away Burner Ash," 19 May 1990, A8; "Waste-Firm Official Lobbies for Ash Contract," 9 June 1990, A8–9; "Communities Vie for Spokane Ash, Despite Opposition," 20 June 1990, A1, A5; "Garbage Firms Bring Rivalry to Spokane," 25 June 1990, A1, A4.

85. Karen Dorn Steele, "Urban Trash Means Cash for Tiny Town," *Spokesman-Review,* 10 December 1989, C1–2.

86. Culp, Guterson, and Grader, "Report on Charges and Claims of Corrupt Practices, Price Fixing, Violations of Environmental Standards at Landfills, or Similar Concerns, Involving Proposers to City of Seattle's Out-of-County Landfill Request for Proposals," presented to Seattle city council, 16 November 1989, 29.

87. The Adams County landfill issue was covered in the following *Spokesman-Review* articles: by Karen Dorn Steele — "Seattle Looks East to Solve Trash Woes," 13 May 1991, A1, A5; "Canadian Trash May Be Sent to Mega-Landfill," 8 December 1991, B1 and B4; "Landfill Fight Splits Community, Family," 29 September 1993, A1, A10; "Planners Oppose Regional Landfill in Adams County," 1 October 1993, B1–2, "More Hearings Set on Big Landfill," 27 November 1993, B1, B5; "Adams County to Allow Huge Landfill," 25 January 1994, A1, A4, "Mega-Landfill Permit Sought Near Ritzville," 30 June 1995, B1, B4. By Jim Lynch — "Farmers' 'Hired Guns' Fire at Proposed Landfill," 2 June 1992, B1, B3; "Candidates Say Trash Company Playing Dirty," 8 October 1992, A1, A7.

88. Karen Dorn Steele, "Ruckelshaus Is No Stranger to Challenges," *Spokesman-Review,* 10 August 1988, B1–2, and "Foes Challenge Toxic-Incineration Plans," *Spokesman-Review,* 9 December 1991, A1, A8.

89. Karen Dorn Steele, "Northwest Becomes 'Host' to Regional Landfills," *Spokesman-Review,* 8 December 1991, A8.

90. Karen Dorn Steele, "California Garbage Coming by the Trainload," *Spokesman-Review,* 30 June 1995, A1, A8.

91. Culp, Guterson and Grader, "Report," 2.

92. Ibid., 30. Other reports of WMX offenses include: Kim Foltz, "Still Down in the Dumps," *Newsweek* 103 (16 April 1984): 70; Kenneth Dreyfack, "Waste Management's Image Is Still Less Than Pristine," *Business Week,* 9 September 1985, 58; Julia Flynn, "The Ugly Mess at Waste Management," *Business Week,* 13 April 1992, 76–77.

93. "WMX Ad Tries High-Powered Approach to Altering Corporate Image," *Business Marketing,* August 1993, 58.

94. "Titan of Trash Business Deserves Closest Scrutiny," *Spokesman-Review,* 5 January 1994, B4.

95. "3 Subcontractors Picked for Trash Burner Project," *Spokesman-Review,* 31 October 1989, B2; Mike Prager, "Incinerator Project to Use Union Labor," *Spokesman-Review,* 21 July 1989, B1–2.

96. Karen Dorn Steele, "3 Firms Bid to Haul Away Burner Ash," *Spokesman-Review,* 19 May 1990, A8; Jim Lynch, "Company Investigated After Burner Ash Found," *Spokesman-Review,* 24 April 1992, B1.

97. Jim Camden, "Trash Incinerator Controversy Isn't Cooling," *Spokesman-Review,* 13 September 1988, B1–2.

98. Bruce Krasnow, "County Backs Composting Site," *Spokesman-Review,* 23 June 1993, B1.

99. "Firms Named for City Recycling," *Spokesman-Review,* 2 June 1990, A8.

100. Karen Dorn Steele, "Ray of Optimism in Landfill Report," *Spokesman-Review,* 11 January 1989, A1, A4.

101. Rick Bonino, "Study Focuses on Trash Plant, Fog at Airport," *Spokesman-Review,* 2 February 1988, A8; Matrix Management Group, "A Study of the Fogging Analysis Conducted

for the Spokane Regional Waste To Energy Facility Siting Near Spokane International Airport," Spokane Regional Solid Waste Disposal Project Office, 1988, 1.

102. Karen Dorn Steele, "Burner Consultant Discounts Health Risk," *Spokesman-Review*, 31 October 1989, B1 and B3.

103. Karen Dorn Steele, "Incinerator Ash Should Be Safe, Chemist Says," *Spokesman-Review*, 7 March 1989, B2.

104. Jim Camden, "Barnard Offers Long-Haul Option for Garbage," *Spokesman-Review*, 13 October 1989, A1, A6.

105. See for example Jim Camden, "Debate Over Trash Burner Goes to Court," *Spokesman-Review*, 26 February 1988, A17, and "Burner Impact Report Labeled Inadequate," *Spokesman-Review*, 17 August 1988, B1.

106. See for example Lonie Rosenwald, "Energy Plant No Tax Threat, Attorneys Say," *Spokesman-Review*, 26 May 1988, B1; Jim Camden, "Council Blocks Vote Request on Incinerator," *Spokesman-Review*, 4 October 1988, A1, A7.

107. Morrison-Knudsen Company, Inc., *Spokane Municipal Waste to Energy Project: Phase One: Preliminary Analysis of Scenarios* (1982), *Phase Two: Site Selection* (1982), *Phase Three: Final Report* (1983); Parametrix, Inc., *Spokane County Comprehensive Solid Waste Management Plan Update, 1984*, prepared for Spokane County Utilities Department, 1984; *Spokane County Comprehensive Solid Waste Management Plan and Final Environmental Impact Statement* (prepared for the Spokane Regional Solid Waste Disposal Project, 1992); Henningson, Durham and Richardson (HDR), *Spokane Regional Waste to Energy Project: Phase I: Procurement Planning; Step I: Project Definition (1985), Spokane Regional Waste to Energy Project: Request for Proposals* (Spokane: Spokane Regional Solid Waste Disposal Project, 1986); Spokane Regional Waste to Energy Project, *Request for Qualifications* (Spokane: Spokane Regional Solid Waste Disposal Project, 1986), *Final Environmental Impact Statement for Spokane Regional Waste To Energy Project* (Spokane: Spokane Regional Solid Waste Disposal Project, 1986); Century West Engineering Corporation, *Spokane Regional Waste To Energy Project: Environmental Impact Analysis: Technical Report: Project Description* (1986); Century West Engineering Corporation in association with Harper-Owes, Golder Associates and the Transpo Group, *Residue Facility Siting Analysis* (Spokane: Spokane Regional Solid Waste Disposal Project, 1988).

108. HDR, *Phase I, Step I*, 1.

109. From the *Spokesman-Review:* Mike Prager, "Recycling Education in 'Trouble,' " 6 August 1991, B1–2; "Promotional Expertise Is Difficult to Justify," editorial, 13 January 1988, A4; Rick Bonino, "Combined Sewer Plan on Agenda," 13 February 1989, A6; Rebecca Napi, "Kids Love It When Robot Talks Trash," 9 December 1990, F1.

110. From the *Spokesman-Review:* John Craig, "Groundwater Cleanup Begins Near Landfill," 9 September 1989, A6; Mike Prager, "Landfill Lid Bid $7 Million Below Estimate," 17 March 1992, B2; Tom Sowa, "Superfund Status Likely for Hillyard Dump," 14 October 1992, B1, B3.

111. From the *Spokesman-Review:* John Craig, "Groundwater Cleanup Begins Near Landfill," 9 September 1989, A6; Dan Hansen, "County Suing Over Landfill Cleanup Costs," 10 September 1992, D10; Jim DeFede, "County Files Another Suit Over Cleanup," 6 November 1990, B2; Mike Prager, "City May Get $13 Million in Suit," 21 May 1992, B1–2; Karen Dorn Steele, "Officials Celebrate Cleanup of North Side Landfill," 24 September 1993, B1; Jim DeFede, "Landfill Mess No Accident, Judge Rules," 22 June 1991, A6, A8.

112. Karen Dorn Steele, "Landfill Owners Want County Aid," *Spokesman-Review*, 22 June 1993, B2.

113. Jim Camden, "City Looking at Consultant to Run Burner," *Spokesman-Review*, 14 April 1989, B1.

114. "Head of Trash Plant Project Named," *Spokesman-Review*, 1 June 1989, B2.

115. Barb Hill Johnson, "Paper Recycling Becomes Office Protocol Here," *Journal of Business* (11 November 1993), B6–7.

116. Bert Caldwell, "Recycling Boom Benefits City Firm," *Spokesman-Review,* 7 April 1990, A6.

117. Rick Bonino and Kim Crompton, "Challenge to Boeing Plant Criticized," *Spokesman-Review,* 23 March 1989, 1, 7; Rick Bonino, "Environmentalists Halt Boeing Plant Appeal," *Spokesman-Review,* 7 April 1989, A1, A7.

118. Julie Titone, "Disposal Costs Force Builders to Change Ways," *Spokesman-Review,* 5 September 1993, B1–2.

119. Sean Jamieson, "Suit Claims Waste Plan Hurts Dump," *Spokesman-Review,* 18 February 1988, B5.

120. Jim Camden, "Trash Incinerator Controversy Isn't Cooling," *Spokesman-Review,* 13 September 1988, B1–2; Karen Dorn Steele, "Fill Operators Try to Block Burner Bond Sales," *Spokesman-Review,* 20 December 1988, B1.

121. Karen Dorn Steele, "Marshall Dump Looks Beyond County For Garbage," *Spokesman-Review,* 17 July 1991, B1–2; Bruce Krasnow, "County Rejects Plan to Open New Landfill at Closed Marshall Site," *Spokesman-Review,* 21 July 1993, B2.

122. "Decision to Burn Chemical Jugs Reeks," *Spokesman-Review,* 13 February 1994, A14; Karen Dorn Steele, "Toxicity Test Data Requested," *Spokesman-Review,* 17 February 1994, B1–2, and "Plant Turns Sludge, Dust Into Energy," *Spokesman-Review,* 26 February 1994, B1, B4.

123. Douglas F. Greer, *Business, Government, and Society,* 2nd ed. (New York: MacMillan, 1987), 3.

124. Ibid., 23–35.

125. Vogel, *Fluctuating Fortunes,* 292–93.

7. CITIZEN PARTICIPATION

1. Alastair Lucas, "Legal Foundations for Public Participation in Environmental Decision-making," *Natural Resources Journal* 16 (1976): 73–102.

2. Daniel J. Fiorino, "Citizen Participation and Environmental Risk: A Survey of Institutional Mechanisms," *Science, Technology, and Human Values* 15 (1990): 229.

3. ACIR, *Citizen Participation in the American Federal System* (Washington, D.C.: U.S. Government Printing Office, 1979), 2.

4. See for example S. Langton, ed., *Citizen Participation in America* (Indianapolis, Ind.: Lexington Books, 1978); ACIR, *Citizen Participation;* S. Gittell, *Limits to Citizen Participation* (Beverly Hills, Calif.: Sage Publications, 1980); H. George Frederickson, "The Recovery of Civism in Public Administration," *Public Administration Review* 42 (1982), 501–08; Matthew Crenson, *Neighborhood Politics* (Cambridge: Harvard University Press, 1983); Benjamin Barber, *Strong Democracy: Participatory Politics for a New Age* (Berkeley: University of California Press, 1984); Harry C. Boyte, *CommonWealth: A Return to Citizen Politics* (New York: Free Press, 1989); Uday Desai, "Public Participation in Environmental Policy Implementation," *American Review of Public Administration* 19 (1989): 49–65; Camilla Stivers, "The Public Agency as Polis: Active Citizenship in the Administrative State," *Administration and Society* 22 (1990): 86–105; Stivers, "Some Tensions in the Notion of 'The Public as Citizen,'" *Administration and Society* 22 (1991): 418–23.

5. Robert M. Entman, *Democracy Without Citizens: Media and the Decay of American Politics* (New York: Oxford University Press, 1989).

6. Hans B. C. Spiegel, "Introduction," in *Citizen Participation in Urban Development,* edited by H. B. C. Spiegel (Washington, D.C.: NTL Institute for Applied Behavioral Science, 1968), vii.

7. See for example Philip Selznick, *TVA and the Grass Roots* (Berkeley: University of California Press, 1949); James Q. Wilson, "Planning and Politics: Citizen Participation in Urban Renewal," *Journal of the American Institute for Planners* 29 (1963): 242–49; Thomas R. Dye and

Harmon L. Ziegler, *The Irony of Democracy* (Monterey, Calif.: Duxbury Press, 1975); Stephen D. Cupps, "Emerging Problems of Citizen Participation," *Public Administration Review* 37 (1977): 478–87; Douglas Yates, *Bureaucratic Democracy: The Search for Democracy and Efficiency in American Government* (Cambridge: Harvard University Press, 1982); R. H. MacNair, R. Caldwell, and L. Pollane, "Citizen Participation in Public Bureaucracies: Foul Weather Friends," *Administration and Society* 14 (1983): 507–24; H. George Frederickson and Ralph K. Chandler, eds., "Symposium on Citizenship and Public Administration," *Public Administration Review* 44 (1984): 97–209.

8. Thomas Dye and Harmon Ziegler, *The Irony of Democracy*, 5th ed. (Monterey, Calif.: Duxbury Press, 1981), 4.

9. Steven Rathgeb Smith and Helen Ingram, "Public Policy and Democracy," in *Public Policy for Democracy*, edited by S. R. Smith and H. Ingram (Washington, D.C.: Brookings Institution, 1993), 5.

10. See for example Carole Pateman, *Participation and Democratic Theory* (Cambridge: Cambridge University Press, 1984); Curtis Ventriss, "Emerging Perspectives on Citizen Participation," *Public Administration Review* 45 (1985): 433–40.

11. Sherry Arnstein, "A Ladder of Citizen Participation," *Journal of the American Institute of Planners* 35 (1969): 216–24.

12. Curtis Ventriss and Robert Pecorella, "Community Participation and Modernization: A Reexamination of Political Choices," *Public Administration Review* 44 (1984): 224–31.

13. ACIR, *Citizen Participation*, 2.

14. Fiorino, "Citizen Participation and Environmental Risk," 237. For other evaluations of the forms of public involvement, see Thomas Heberlein, "Some Observations on Alternative Mechanisms for Public Involvement: The Hearing, Public Opinion Poll, the Workshop and the Quasi-Experiment," *Natural Resources Journal* 16 (1976): 197–212; William Gormley Jr., "The Representation Revolution: Reforming State Regulation Through Public Representation," *Administration and Society* 18 (1986): 179–96.

15. Larry S. Luton, "Citizen Participation in Solid Waste Policymaking: A Case Study of the Spokane Experience," *International Journal of Public Administration* 18 (1995): 613–37.

16. Larry S. Luton, "In Defense of NIMBYs," in *Public Works Administration*, edited by Lucy Brewer (Newbury Park: Sage Publications, 1995), 316–22.

17. Quoted in Yates, *Bureaucratic Democracy*, 4.

18. Woodrow Wilson, "The Study of Administration," in *Classics of Public Administration*, 3rd ed., edited by J. Shafritz and A. Hyde (Pacific Grove, Calif.: Brooks/Cole Publishing Company, 1992), 16, 21.

19. See for example Herman Finer, "Administrative Responsibility in Democratic Government," *Public Administration Review* 1 (1941): 335–50; Joseph Schumpeter, *Capitalism, Socialism, and Democracy*, 3rd ed. (New York: Harper, 1950); Bernard Berelson, *Voting* (Chicago: University of Chicago Press, 1956); Seymour Martin Lipset, *Political Man* (New York: Doubleday, 1960).

20. Terry Cooper, "Citizen Participation," in *Organization Theory and Management*, edited by T. D. Lynch (New York: Marcel Dekker, 1983), 14.

21. Arnold Auerbach, "Confrontation and Administrative Response," *Public Administration Review* 29 (1969): 639–46.

22. Paul Sabatier, Susan Hunter, and Susan McLaughlin, "The Devil Shift: Perceptions and Misperceptions of Opponents," *Western Political Quarterly* 40 (1987): 450.

23. Ralph Clark Chandler, "Conclusions. The Public Administration as Representative Citizen: A New Role for the New Century," *Public Administration Review* 44 (1984): Special Issue, 197.

24. Eugene B. McGregor Jr., "The Great Paradox of Democratic Citizenship and Public Personnel Administration," *Public Administration Review* 44 (1984): Special Issue, 126.

25. John Clayton Thomas, "Citizen Involvement in Public Management: Lessons from Municipal Administration," in *The Revitalization of the Public Service,* edited by R. Denhardt and E. Jennings (Columbia: University of Missouri-Columbia, 1987), 49.

26. McNair, Caldwell, and Pollane, "Foul Weather Friends," 511.

27. Ibid., 521.

28. Selznick, *TVA.*

29. D. Stephen Cupps, "Emerging Problems of Citizen Participation," *Public Administration Review* 37 (1977): 478.

30. Ibid., 481.

31. Ibid., 485.

32. Charles Fox and Clarke E. Cochran, "Discretion Advocacy in Public Administration Theory: Toward a Platonic Guardian Class?" *Administration and Society* 22 (1990): 249–71.

33. See for example Gary Wamsley et al., "Public Administration and the Governance Process: Shifting the Political Dialogue," in *Refounding Public Administration* (Newbury Park, Calif: Sage, 1990), 31–51.

34. See for example Dye and Ziegler, *Irony of Democracy.*

35. Charles Levine, "Citizenship and Service Delivery: The Promise of Coproduction," *Public Administration Review* 44 (1984): Special Issue, 178.

36. Larry S. Luton, "The Citizen Is Always Right: Teaching Administrators to Value the People They Serve," in *Democracy and the Public Service: Images of Administration for the 21st Century, Proceedings of the Seventh National Symposium on Public Administration Theory* (Hayward: Department of Public Administration, California State University, Hayward, 1994), 167–84.

37. Terry Cooper, *An Ethic of Citizenship for Public Administration* (Englewood Cliffs, N.J.: Prentice-Hall, 1991), 99.

38. Ibid., 122.

39. Ibid., 130.

40. Ibid., x.

41. Camilla Stivers, "Active Citizenship in the Administrative State" (Ph.D. diss., Virginia Polytechnic Institute and State University, 1988); "The Public Agency as Polis: Active Citizenship in the Administrative State," *Administration and Society* 22 (1990): 86–105.

42. See for example Thomas J. Peters and Robert H. Waterman Jr., *In Search of Excellence: Lessons from America's Best-Run Companies* (New York: Warner Books, 1982); David Carr and Ian Littman, *Excellence in Government: Total Quality Management in the 1990s* (New York: Coopers and Lybrand, 1990); Robert M. Krone, "Symposium Introduction, Total Quality Management (TQM): Achievements, Potentials, and Pitfalls," *Journal of Management Science and Policy Analysis* 8 (1991): 195–202; David Osborne and Ted Gaebler, *Reinventing Government: How the Entrepreneurial Spirit Is Transforming the Public Sector* (New York: Penguin Books, 1992); James E. Swiss, "Adapting Total Quality Management (TQM) to Government," *Public Administration Review* 52 (1992): 356–62; Steven Cohen and Ronald Brand, *Total Quality Management in Government: A Practical Guide for the Real World* (San Francisco: Jossey-Bass, 1993).

43. Luton, "The Citizen Is Always Right"; see also Hugh Miller, "A Hummelian View of the Gore Report: Toward a Post-Progressive Public Administration," in *Democracy and the Public Service: Images of Administration for the 21st Century, Proceedings of the Seventh National Symposium on Public Administration Theory* (Hayward: Department of Public Administration, California State University, Hayward, 1994), 184–95.

44. John H. Cushman Jr., "Forest Service Is Rethinking Its Mission," *New York Times,* 24 April 1994, 18.

45. Carr and Littman, *Excellence in Government.*

46. Krone, "Symposium Introduction," 198.

47. Al Gore, *Creating a Government That Works Better and Costs Less: Report of the National Performance Review* (New York: Times Books, 1993).

48. Barry Posner and Warren Schmidt, "An Updated Look at the Values and Expectations of Federal Government Executives," *Public Administration Review* 44 (1994): 20–30.

49. Carr and Littman, *Excellence in Government.* See also National Commission on the State and Local Public Service, *Hard Truths/Tough Choices: An Agenda for State and Local Reform* (New York: Nelson A. Rockefeller Institute of Government, 1993).

50. George Antunes and Gary Halter, "The Politics of Resource Recovery, Energy Conservation, and Solid Waste Management," *Administration and Society* 8 (1976): 55–78.

51. Quoted in Martin Melosi, *Garbage in the Cities* (Chicago: Dorsey Press, 1981), 105.

52. Ibid., 35.

53. Caroline Bartlett Crane, quoted in ibid., 112.

54. Melosi, *Garbage,* 118.

55. Ibid., 117.

56. Ibid., 121–22.

57. George Waring, "The Cleaning of a Great City," quoted in Melosi, *Garbage,* 74.

58. Louis Blumberg and Robert Gottlieb, *War on Waste: Can America Win Its Battle with Garbage?* (Washington, D.C.: Island Press, 1989), 74.

59. CCHW, *How to Deal with a Proposed Facility,* 3rd rev. ed. (Falls Church, Va.: CCHW, 1993), 2; Dick Russell, "The Rise of the Grass-Roots Toxics Movement," *Amicus Journal* 12 (1990): 17–21; CCHW, *Solid Waste Action Project Guidebook* (Falls Church, Va.: CCHW, 1987), 1.

60. CCHW, *How to Deal with a Proposed Facility,* 2.

61. Quotations and information in this paragraph are from CCHW, *Project Guidebook,* 3–4, 7–9, 32. For more on CCHW's evaluation of incineration, see also CCHW, *Solid Waste Incineration: The Rush to Burn* (Falls Church, Va.: CCHW, 1988).

62. Blumberg and Gottlieb, *War on Waste,* 58–59.

63. Cerrell Associates, *Political Difficulties Facing Waste-to-Energy Conversion Plan Siting* (Los Angeles, Calif.: Cerrell Associates, 1984).

64. See for example David McDermitt, "The 10 Commandments of Community Relations," *World Wastes* 36 (1993): 48–51.

65. Blumberg and Gottlieb, *War on Waste,* 75.

66. Ibid., 74.

67. Daniel Mazmanian and David Morell, "The 'NIMBY' Syndrome: Facility Siting and the Failure of Democratic Discourse," in *Environmental Policy in the 1990s: Toward a New Agenda* (Washington, D.C.: CQ Press, 1990), 125–27.

68. William Glaberson, "Coping in the Age of 'Nimby,' " *New York Times,* 19 June 1988, sec. 3, 1.

69. Michael E. Kraft and Bruce B. Clary, "Citizen Participation and the NIMBY Syndrome: Public Response to Radioactive Waste Disposal," *Western Political Quarterly* 44 (1991): 301; Luton, "In Defense of NIMBYs."

70. Dick Russell, "Environmental Racism," *Amicus Journal* 11 (1989): 23–33; Anna Harding and George Holdren Jr., "Environmental Equity and the Environmental Professional," *Environment, Science and Technology* 27 (1993): 1990–93; Sherry Cable and Michael Benson, "Acting Locally: Environmental Injustice and the Emergence of Grass-Roots Environmental Organizations," *Social Problems* 40 (1993): 464–77.

71. Hugh Bone and Herman Lujan, "Direct Democracy in Washington," in *Government and Politics in the Evergreen State,* edited by D. Nice, J. Pierce, and C. Sheldon (Pullman: Washington State University Press, 1992), 104–06.

72. Jim Camden, "Trash Trip," *Spokesman-Review,* 15 March 1989, A3.

73. John K. Wiley, "Officials: Voluntary Recycling Up Sharply," *Spokesman-Review,* 13 March 1990, B1.

74. Beverly Vorpahl, "Crews Find a Few Kinks in Recycling Effort," *Spokesman-Review,* 9

October 1990, B1; Mike Prager, "City Recycling Picks Up Acceptance," *Spokesman-Review,* 18 November 1990, B1–2.

75. Mike Prager, "Council Gives Go-Ahead to '91 Composting Plan," *Spokesman-Review,* 24 April 1990, A1, A4.

76. Jim Camden, "Funding Likely for Incinerator Watchdog Group," *Spokesman-Review,* 7 December 1991, A1, A6; Bruce Krasnow, "State Ecology Grants to Go to 16 Groups," *Spokesman-Review,* 11 December 1991, B6.

77. Mike Prager, "Incinerator Tests Violated Contract, Critics Say," *Spokesman-Review,* 4 December 1991, B1, B3.

78. "Trial by Fire a Success," *Spokesman-Review,* 8 December 1991, A18.

79. "State Revises Incinerator's Sulfur Dioxide Limit," *Spokesman-Review,* 4 December 1992, B2.

80. Karen Dorn Steele, "Trash Continues to Outstrip Waste Burner," *Spokesman-Review,* 6 June 1993, B1–2.

81. Bonnie Mager and B.J. Krafft, "Burning Money: With Costs of Garbage Incineration Going Up and Up, It's Not Too Late to Consider Other Disposal Options," *Spokesman-Review,* 5 September 1993, A15.

82. Mike Prager, "Council Not Ready to OK Tire Burning," *Spokesman-Review,* 6 October 1992, B1; Karen Dorn Steele, "Hebner Moves to Block Plan for Tire Burning," *Spokesman-Review,* 12 July 1993, A6.

83. Karen Dorn Steele, "Lawyer: Incinerator Broke Rules," *Spokesman-Review,* 14 April 1994, B1.

84. Mike Prager, "Garbage Bills to Continue Rise, City Council Told," *Spokesman-Review,* 5 October 1993, B1–2.

85. Information in this paragraph is from the *Spokesman-Review:* Bruce Krasnow, "State Ecology Grants to Go to 16 Groups," 11 December 1991, B6; "Marshall Landfill to Close," 8 December 1991, B1, B5; "County Rejects Plan to Open New Landfill at Closed Marshall Site," 21 July 1993, B2; Karen Dorn Steele, "Wells Near Landfill Contaminated," 10 June 1991, A1, A9; "Residents Will Fight Landfill Leak," 12 July 1991, B1; John Craig, "Marshall Landfill Quit Required Tests of Wells," 23 May 1992, B5; Jim Lynch, "Residents Near Landfill Say Water-Quality Concerns Ignored," 25 June 1992, B3.

86. Karen Dorn Steele, "Giant Landfill Splits Rural Communities," *Spokesman-Review,* 17 June 1990, A1, A12.

87. Karen Dorn Steele, "Communities Vie for Spokane Ash, Despite Opposition," *Spokesman-Review,* 20 June 1990, A1, A5.

88. Jim Camden, "Garbage Plant Site, Pollution Worry Citizens," *Spokesman-Review,* 17 April 1986, A6.

89. David Bond, "Opponents See Nothing but Ill in Waste Plant," *Spokesman-Review,* 8 January 1988, 27.

90. Jim Camden, "Citizens Want Waste Burner Audited, Halted," *Spokesman-Review,* 4 June 1988, A6, A8.

91. Rick Bonino, "Incinerator Vote Rebuffed," *Spokesman-Review,* 19 January 1988, A1, A8.

92. Jim Camden, "Group Seeks Charter Amendment," *Spokesman-Review,* 1 September 1988, B3; "Council Blocks Vote Request on Incinerator," *Spokesman-Review,* 4 October 1988, A1, A7; Rick Bonino, "Council Says No to Vote on Trash Burner," *Spokesman-Review,* 7 September 1988, B1–2.

93. Jim Camden, "Incinerator Ash Burial Concerns Will Get Public Airing," *Spokesman-Review,* 5 August 1988, 1, 17; "Residents to Continue Anti-Landfill Activities," *Cheney* [Wash.] *Free Press,* 4 August 1988, 1, 8.

94. Anne Windishar, "Officials Urged to Study Dump's Health Effects," *Spokesman-Review,* 12 August 1988, 21.

95. "Ash Concern Results in Plenty of Questions," *Cheney Free Press*, 18 August 1988, 1, 10.

96. Karen Dorn Steele, "Crowd Angered by Landfill Plans, Absent Officials," *Spokesman-Review*, 17 November 1989, B1–2.

97. Rick Bonino, "Early Today Burner Foes Kept Talking," *Spokesman-Review*, 11 October 1988, A1, A7; "City Gives Final OK for Burner," *Spokesman-Review*, 4 January 1989, A1, A5.

98. Julie Sullivan, "Lincoln County Unsure About Annexation," *Spokesman-Review*, 19 October 1989, B1.

99. Julie Sullivan, "Anti-Ash Champ Ready for Main Event," *Spokesman-Review*, 6 February 1990, A1, A5.

100. Karen Dorn Steele, "City Gets Smelly Messages," *Spokesman-Review*, 14 February 1989, B1.

101. Rick Bonino, "Trash Burner Foes March on City Hall," *Spokesman-Review*, 7 March 1989, B1–2.

102. Personal communication from Curt Messex, 9 June 1994.

103. Rick Bonino, "Group Seeks Council Recall," *Spokesman-Review*, 15 March 1989, A1, A4; "Judge Rejects Bid to Recall City Council," *Spokesman-Review*, 14 April 1989; Jim Camden, "A City Divided: 'Bloody' Election Matches in Store," *Spokesman-Review*, 2 April 1989, A15.

104. Rick Bonino and Kim Crompton, "Challenge to Boeing Plant Criticized," *Spokesman-Review*, 23 March 1989, 1, 7.

105. Rick Bonino, "Environmentalists Halt Boeing Plant Appeal," *Spokesman-Review*, 7 April 1989, A1, A7.

106. Rick Bonino, "Primary Vote Gives Burner Foes a Boost," *Spokesman-Review*, 16 September 1989, A1.

107. Rick Bonino, "Hebner Stands Behind Trash Burner Project," and "Activist Krafft Wants a Vote on Incinerator," *Spokesman-Review*, 30 October 1989, A1, A7.

108. Jim Camden, "Anti-Incinerator Candidates Vie for Seat," *Spokesman-Review*, 13 September 1989, B1–2.

109. Jim Camden, "City Council Vote Brings New Cast but Same Play," *Spokesman-Review*, 9 November 1989, A1, A4.

110. Kelly McBride, "Resident Voices Concern Over Proposed Ash-Transfer Station," *Spokesman-Review*, 31 May 1991, B2.

111. Kristina Johnson, "Composting Facility Opposed," *Spokesman-Review*, 3 December 1992, D13; "Family Dream Turns to Compost," *Spokesman-Review*, 17 December 1992, A1, A5.

112. Personal communication from Eric Skelton, Air Pollution Control Officer, 17 June 1994.

113. From *Spokesman-Review*: Kristina Johnson: "Heap of Controversy," 25 May 1995, D9; "Compost Plant Gets Ultimatum," 20 June 1995, B1; "City Council Votes to Shut Compost Plant," 8 August 1995, B1; "City Council May Reverse Vote to Close Compost Plant," 12 August 1995, B1, B6; "Council Reopens Composting Plant," 29 August 1995, B1, B6; Karen Dorn Steele, "Officials Knee-Deep in Compost Trouble," 6 June 1995, A1, A7; Tom Sowa, "For Some Compost Plant Will Never Wash," 12 August 1995, B1, B6.

114. "Spokane Wins Waste Disposal Prize," *Spokesman-Review*, 29 July 1990, B2.

115. Luton, "Citizen Participation."

116. Sabatier, Hunter, and McLaughlin, "Devil Shift."

117. Yates, *Bureaucratic Democracy*.

118. Charles Fox and Hugh Miller, *Postmodern Public Administration: Toward Discourse* (Newbury Park, Calif.: Sage Publications, 1994).

119. Richard Rose, *Ordinary People in Public Policy: A Behavioral Analysis* (Newbury Park, Calif.: Sage Publications, 1989).

120. Ibid., 6.

121. Robert Salisbury, *Interests and Institutions: Substance and Structure in American Politics* (Pittsburgh, Pa.: University of Pittsburgh Press, 1992), 229.

8. THE IMPACT OF THE MEDIA

1. David L. Altheide and Robert Snow, *Media Worlds in the Postjournalism Era* (New York: Aldine de Gruyter, 1991).

2. Ibid., xiii.

3. Dan Nimmo and James E. Combs, *Mediated Political Realities*, 2nd ed. (New York: Longman, 1990).

4. Gordon Chase and Elizabeth Reveal, *How to Manage in the Public Sector* (Reading, Mass.: Addison-Wesley, 1983).

5. David L. Altheide and Robert Snow, *Media Logic* (Beverly Hills, Calif.: Sage, 1979), 10.

6. Nimmo and Combs, *Mediated Realities*, 27.

7. Ibid., 23, 25.

8. Neil Postman, *Amusing Ourselves to Death: Public Discourse in the Age of Show Business* (London: Penguin Books, 1985), 28.

9. Nimmo and Combs, *Mediated Realities*, 26.

10. Altheide and Snow, *Media Worlds*, 28.

11. Postman, *Amusing Ourselves*, 92.

12. Altheide and Snow, *Media Worlds*, 64–65.

13. Hugh Miller, "Everyday Politics in Public Administration," *American Review of Public Administration* 23 (1993): 109.

14. Ibid., 71.

15. Doris A. Graber, *Mass Media and American Politics*, 4th ed. (Washington, D.C.: CQ Press, 1993), 118.

16. Altheide and Snow, *Media Worlds*, 33.

17. See for example R. E. Gilbert, *Television and Presidential Politics* (North Quincy, Mass.: Christopher Publishing, 1972), 169–70.

18. Altheide and Snow, *Media Worlds*, 29.

19. See for example R. A. Heineman et al., *The World of the Policy Analyst: Rationality, Values, and Politics* (Chatham, N.J.: Chatham House, 1990).

20. Dvora Yanow, "Supermarkets and Culture Clash: The Epistemological Role of Metaphors in Administrative Practice," *Administration and Society* 22 (1992): 89–109.

21. Jeffrey L. Pressman and Aaron Wildavsky, *Implementation* (Berkeley: University of California Press, 1973), excerpted in Jay M. Shafritz and Albert C. Hyde, *Classics of Public Administration* (Pacific Grove, Calif.: Brooks/Cole, 1992), 409.

22. Elizabeth Bird and Robert Dardenne, "Myth, Chronicle, and Story: Exploring the Narrative Qualities of News," in *Media, Myths, and Narratives: Television and the Press*, edited by J. Carey (Newbury Park, Calif.: Sage Publications, 1988), 70–72.

23. Edward S. Quade, *Analysis for Public Decisions*, 2nd ed. (New York: North-Holland, 1982), 344.

24. William Greider, *Who Will Tell the People: The Betrayal of American Democracy* (New York: Simon and Schuster, 1992), 92.

25. K. H. Jamieson and K. K. Campbell, *The Interplay of Influence: News, Advertising, Politics, and the Mass Media*, 3rd ed. (Belmont, Calif.: Wadsworth Publishing Company, 1992), 125–56.

26. David Pritchard, "The News Media and Public Policy Agendas," in *Public Opinion, the Press, and Public Policy*, edited by J. D. Kennamer (Westport, Conn.: Praeger, 1992), 103–12.

27. Charles Goodsell, "Public Administration and the Public Interest," in *Refounding Public Administration*, edited by Gary Wamsley et al. (Newbury Park, Calif.: Sage, 1990), 104.

28. Graber, *Mass Media*, 170–200.

29. Ibid., 171.

30. Ibid., 191.

31. Quade, *Analysis for Public Decisions*, 68.

32. William N. Dunn, *Public Policy Analysis: An Introduction* (Englewood Cliffs, N.J.: Prentice-Hall, 1981).

33. Dan Berkowitz, "TV News Sources and News Channels: A Study in Agenda-Building," *Journalism Quarterly* 64 (1987): 508–13.

34. John McManus, "How Local Television Learns What Is News," *Journalism Quarterly* 67 (1990): 672–78.

35. Altheide and Snow, *Media Worlds*, 108.

36. Chase and Reveal, *How to Manage in the Public Sector*, 146.

37. Jamieson and Campbell, *Interplay of Influence*, 98.

38. Stephen Engleberg, "The Bad News Hour: 4 P.M. Friday," *New York Times*, 6 April 1984, 10Y.

39. Jamieson and Campbell, *Interplay of Influence*, 108.

40. Chase and Reveal, *How to Manage in the Public Sector*, 150–51.

41. Jamieson and Campbell, *Interplay of Influence*, 109–10.

42. Ibid., 113.

43. Nimmo and Combs, *Mediated Realities*, 25.

44. J. P. Robinson and M. R. Levy, "Interpersonal Communication and News Comprehension," *Public Opinion Quarterly* 50 (1986): 160–75.

45. Postman, *Amusing Ourselves*, 92.

46. John Robinson and Mark Levy, *The Main Source: Learning from Television News* (Beverly Hills, Calif.: Sage, 1986), 232.

47. Robert Entman, "How Media Affect What People Think: An Information Processing Approach," *Journal of Politics* 51 (1989): 347–70. But see David L. Protess et al., "The Impact of Investigative Reporting on Public Opinion and Policymaking: Targeting Toxic Waste," *Public Opinion Quarterly* 51 (1987): 166–85, for a more minimal view of the impact of investigative reporting.

48. Protess et al., "The Impact of Investigative Reporting," 182.

49. Vincent Price, "Social Identification and Public Opinion: Effects of Communication Group Conflict," *Public Opinion Quarterly* 53 (1989): 197–224.

50. Troy A. Zimmer, "Local News Exposure and Local Government Alienation," *Social Science Quarterly* 64 (1983): 634–40.

51. Richard Hofstetter et al., "Political Talk Radio: A Stereotype Reconsidered," *Political Research Quarterly* 47 (1994): 467–79.

52. See for example Roger Silverstone, "Television Myth and Culture," in *Media, Myths, and Narratives: Television and the Press*, edited by J. Carey (Newbury Park, Calif.: Sage Publications, 1988), 40–41.

53. "Challenges Demand Civility, Cooperation," *Spokesman-Review*, 20 August 1989, A18.

54. Michael M. Moran, "The Multivenue Communications Environment: An Application of Kenneth Burker's Pentad to the Communications Environment of the Spokane Waste-To-Energy Project" (unpublished paper, Communications Program, Eastern Washington University, 1993), 3.

55. Graber, *Mass Media*, 347.

56. Ibid., 348.

57. Ibid., 355.

58. John Fahey, *The Inland Empire: Unfolding Years, 1879–1929* (Seattle: University of Washington Press, 1986), 217.

59. Jim Camden, "Barnard Accepts Higgins' Challenge to Debate Merits of Trash Incinerator," *Spokesman-Review*, 27 September 1989, B3; "Idea of Trash-Only Debate Relegated to Back Burner," *Spokesman-Review*, 7 October 1989, A6.

60. "Spokane Keeps Pace with Growing Demands on Waste Management," *Spokesman-Review*, 1 September 1991, G1.

61. "Challenges Demand Civility, Cooperation," *Spokesman-Review*, 20 August 1989, A18.

62. "Too Easy to Say No, Harder to Say What," *Spokesman-Review*, 5 October 1989, B4.

63. "Burner's Cancellation Would Make No Sense," *Spokesman-Review*, 5 November 1989, A18.

64. Karen Dorn Steele, "Company Steps Up Lobbying Effort," *Spokesman-Review*, 10 September 1989, A12.

65. "Huge Regional Dumps Way of the Future, Firm Says," *Spokesman-Review*, 16 October 1989, A10.

66. Moran, "Multivenue Communications," 4.

67. Karen Dorn Steele, "Trash Incinerator Takes Another Big Step," and "Foes: Burner Can Still Be Halted," *Spokesman-Review*, 12 February 1989, A1, A10.

68. Jim Camden, "Klickitat County May Not Be Ready for More Garbage," *Spokesman-Review*, 14 October 1989, A1.

69. Moran, "Multivenue Communications," 4.

70. Jim Lynch, "Tires to Be Burned as Part of Incinerator Tests," *Spokesman-Review*, 28 September 1992, A6.

71. Karen Dorn Steele, "City Gets Smelly Messages," *Spokesman-Review*, 14 February 1989, B1.

72. Rick Bonino, "Trash Burner Foes March on City Hall," *Spokesman-Review*, 7 March 1989, B1–2.

73. Ibid.

74. Moran, "Multivenue Communications," 32.

75. "Trash Burner Foes Say Advertisements Misleading," *Spokesman-Review*, 1 September 1988, B3.

76. Karen Dorn Steele, "Incinerator Ash Should Be Safe," *Spokesman-Review*, 7 March 1989, B2.

77. Jim Camden, "Barnard Offers Long-Haul Option for Garbage," *Spokesman-Review*, 13 October 1989, A1.

78. Mike Prager, "Compost Plan Fueled by Ambition, Officials Say," *Spokesman-Review*, 19 February 1990, A6.

79. Mike Prager, "Burner Includes One-Stop Waste Service," *Spokesman-Review*, 6 June 1991, B1.

80. Kristina Johnson, 1992, "Family Dream Turns to Compost," *Spokesman-Review*, 17 December 1992, A1, A5; Kara Briggs, "City to Buy Composting Area Homes," *Spokesman-Review*, 23 September 1993, D11.

81. Some of the material in this section derives from personal interviews with participants. Interviewees were assured that nothing would be attributed directly to them without their approval.

82. Moran, "Multivenue Communications," 29.

83. Ibid., 34.

84. "Promotional Expense Is Difficult to Justify," *Spokesman-Review*, 13 January 1988, A4.

85. "City Can Sell Incinerator Power," *Spokesman-Review*, 17 March 1988, B1.

86. Mike Prager, "Council Meet a Battleground for Burner Issue," *Spokesman-Review*, 10 October 1989, A1, A5.

CONCLUSION

1. William Ruckelshaus, "Solid Waste Management: An Overview," *Public Management* (October 1972): 3.

2. Austin Bierbower, "American Wastefulness," *Overland Monthly* 49 (April 1907): 358–59.

3. Martin Melosi, *Garbage in the Cities* (Chicago: Dorsey Press, 1981), 239.

4. Bill Paul, "Burning Trash Is Becoming Big Business," *Wall Street Journal,* 13 October 1986, 6.

5. Robert Steuteville, "The State of Garbage in America: 1994 Nationwide Survey," *Biocycle* 35 (1994): 51.

6. Ibid., 46, 50.

7. Charles Lindblom, "The Science of Muddling Through," *Public Administration Review* 19 (1959): 79–88.

INDEX

Abstractness: in process theories, 37–38; in systems theory, 46–48

Ackerman, Bruce, 159–61

Activism, 2, 54–55; against Boeing expansion, 18, 214–15; against composting, 24–25; impact of, 155, 259; against landfills, 11, 20–21; in public policy theories: elitist theories, 39–40; and pluralist theory, 34; in pluralist theory, 42–43; in Spokane's political culture, 59–60, 76, 83. *See also* Ash disposal; Citizens; Waste-to-energy incinerator

Adams County, landfills in, 183–84

Advisory Committee on Intergovernmental Relations, 193, 195, 197

Advisory committees, 167, 208–09, 218–19

Airport, 182. *See also* Fog; Spokane International Airport Authority

Almond, Gabriel, 60

Altheide, David L., 226–28, 232, 234

American Commonwealth (Bryce), 87

American Indians, 66, 72, 147–48

Anderson, James E., 34, 37

Andren, Bob, 216

Anker, Laura, 167

Antunes, George, 173

Appeals, 143, 145–46, 167–68; by incinerator opponents, 145–46, 151, 154–55, 211–13; of special districts' rulings, 110, 112. *See also* Lawsuits

Apple, Bob, 215–16

Aquifers. *See* Spokane-Rathdrum aquifer; Water quality

Aridity, 84; of the West, 63–64, 69–70

Arnstein, Sherry, 194

Ash disposal, 83; competition for contracts for, 181, 183, 185; and hazardous classification of, 29, 134–35, 139, 141, 148–49, 186;

locations of landfill for, 211–14, 253; opposition to landfills for, 15–17, 20–21, 77, 244–45; transfer in, 25, 216

Banovetz, James, 887–88

Barnard, Sheri: in election, 215–16; and media coverage, 246, 248; opposition to incinerator by, 18, 20, 28–29, 186, 212

Bartlett, Robert V., 64

Behavioralism, in political science, 35, 57

Bertalanffy, Ludwig von, 46–47

Best Management Practices Analysis for Solid Waste, 142

Bierbower, Austin, 259

Birks, David, 188

Blumberg, Louis, 129, 176, 204–05

Boards of directors, 167–68, 218–19; of special districts, 109, 111–13, 256

Boeing expansion, activism against, 18, 214–15

Bosso, Christopher, 34, 39–40, 58

Bottle bills, 174, 178

Brewer, Mike, 216

Browne, William, 164

Bryce, James, 87

Burkowitz, Dan, 234

Business: in competition with government, 23–24, 31, 74; influence on public policy, 56, 159–91; and media, 236, 254; mistrust of, 59, 77, 83, 184–85, 257; in political cultures, 61–62, 256–57; in Progressivism, 87, 90–91; in solid waste management, 121–22, 157, 259

Caldwell, R., 198

Campbell, K. K., 234–36

Case study methodology, 3–4, 35, 48–51

Cerrell Associates report, 204–05